The Joan Palevsky   Imprint in Classical Literature

In honor of beloved Virgil—

"O degli altri poeti onore e lume . . ."

—Dante, *Inferno*

Revenge in Attic and Later Tragedy

SATHER CLASSICAL LECTURES

Volume Sixty-Two

Revenge in Attic
and Later Tragedy

Anne Pippin Burnett

UNIVERSITY OF CALIFORNIA PRESS

BERKELEY · LOS ANGELES · LONDON

*The publisher gratefully acknowledges the contribution to this book
provided by the Joan Palevsky Endowment in Classical Literature.*

University of California Press
Berkeley and Los Angeles, California

University of California Press, Ltd.
London, England

Library of Congress Cataloging-in-Publication Data
Burnett, Anne Pippin, 1925–
    Revenge in Attic and later tragedy / Anne Pippin Burnett.
       p.   cm. — (Sather classical lectures ; v. 62)
    Includes bibliographical references and index.
    ISBN 0-520-21096-4 (cloth)
    1. Greek drama (Tragedy)—History and criticism.   2. Revenge in
literature.   I. Title.   II. Series.
PA3136.B79   1997
882'.0109—dc21

                                                      97-22677

Printed in the United States of America
9 8 7 6 5 4 3 2 1

for Ralph and for Michael

"You will see the characters of the true story clearly, as if luminous and on a higher plane, and at the same time they may not look quite human, and you may well be a little afraid of them. . . ."

"O God," said the lady. "What you call the divine art seems to me a hard and cruel game, which maltreats and mocks its human beings."

ISAK DINESEN, "THE CARDINAL'S FIRST TALE," *LAST TALES*

On this visit di Grasso played King Lear, Othello, Civil Death, *Turgenev's* The Parasite, *confirming with every gesture that there is more justice in outbursts of noble passion than in all the joyless rules that run the world.*

ISAAK BABEL, "DI GRASSO," *TALES OF ODESSA*

Contents

Note on Abbreviations

Names of authors and titles of works are abbreviated in accordance with the list in *The Oxford Classical Dictionary,* 3d ed. (1996), pp. xxix–liv.

Preface

Men and women of our century tend to endow the people of ancient Athens with moral concerns almost identical with our own, imposing qualities we like best in ourselves upon Greeks unable to resist. Athenians must have repudiated private violence,[1] we say, must have valued trust and warm pity and close candid relationships, for to think otherwise would be to suppose the people of Athens inferior to ourselves. From which it follows that the tragedians must have worked to enhance these attitudes, and so Greek drama, for all its apparent exoticism, is read as if it were trying to be like ours, a staged presentation of social or moral problems in a mode of instructive realism. Because it was a state theater, the Attic stage is supposed to have offered lessons in the peaceable virtues that the city required,[2] and should a given action seem to praise violence or vindictiveness, we are urged to

1. R. Girard has made "violence" a catchword and has propagated the idea that Greeks, horrified by their own violent tendencies (and especially those leading to vengeance), used sacrifice as a kind of sublimation; see, among other works, *La violence et le sacré* (Paris, 1972), pp. 29–32; *Des choses cachées* (Paris, 1978), p. 20. For criticism of Girard's position, see R. Verdier in *La vengeance,* ed. R. Verdier, vol. 1 (Paris, 1981), p. 14: "il y aurait lieu bien plutôt de se demander si cette conception de la vengeance sans fin et destructrice, loin de se rapporter à la 'fondation du monde,' ne procède pas d'une vision moderne postérieure à l'instauration de l'État, qui en fait une 'affaire privée' quand il s'arroge le monopole de la contrainte et de la sanction. Au plan théorique, Girard nous reporte un siècle en arrière." Criticism from another standpoint comes from Sarah Pierce, "Death, Revelry and Thysia," *Cl. Ant.* 12 (1993) 219–66.

2. See, e.g., J. Winkler, "The Ephebes' Song," in *Nothing to Do with Dionysus?* ed. J. Winkler and F. Zeitlin (Princeton, 1990), pp. 20–62, who speaks of "elaborate symbolic play on themes of proper and improper civic behavior" and "lessons about the trials of manhood" (pp. 20–21). The absurdity of the notion that tragedy is didactic is exploited in the debate at Ar. *Ran.* 1004 ff.: the *Seven* makes a man eager to fight; the *Stheneboea* rouses illicit passions in virtuous women; ragged characters teach rich men how to avoid liturgies, etc.

discover "irony" or, in the most stubborn cases, a work that is unsuccessful, youthful, or enslaved to a primitive tradition.

Meanwhile the plays that survive from ancient Athens steadily resist such moral colonialism. They remain categorically unlike what has been seen in the Western theater for the past five hundred years because their action occurs in a legendary Time/Place distinct both from reality and from the ethics of ordinary life. What is staged are moments in which the discrete realms of gods and men come into contact, then once more separate with their mutual exclusions a little more carefully defined. Outsized and essentially impossible deeds are performed by generalized figures, and human individuality is expressed only as characters at once magnificent and helpless resist or fit themselves into a pattern determined by dominant nonhuman powers. And whether there is conflict or collaboration, the events depicted in these mythic dramas are by definition distorted and extreme because the infinite supernatural cannot break into a finite creation without disturbing whatever order the world has to show. Which means that this theater is in essence a theater of timeless, nonpsychological, extra-moral violence.

The Attic theater, moreover, developed in the ambience of a violent god; its aim was to produce an effect something like that of a Dionysiac epiphany, while its irreducible material was not civic virtue but its opposite, excess and disruption. We who live among tired and demystified political institutions are afraid that individual violence may outrun the restraining violence of the community. Those who gathered into the early Greek cities, however, seem to have felt an opposite fear—that the new and vigorous social units might sap or even suppress those anarchic individual forces that meant survival, freedom, and fertility. That is why, even in the sixth and fifth centuries B.C., fossilized bits of hunter's ritual were preserved in urban cults, and that is why in hundreds of regular celebrations, great and small, emblems of wild nature were carried through the city streets of Greece. In particular, that is why the Athenians, after the establishment of the Greater Dionysia, went every year to the theater to watch costumed figures who (with mixed success) attacked or resisted replicas of the orderly structures and institutions that each citizen valued.[3] This was not a lesson; the theater did not lead the Attic audience, either toward subversion or toward obedience. It did, however, send more vital men back into a more vital city because all had, in unison, vicariously exercised the fullest stretch of isolated human force.[4]

3. Myth, ritual, and festival all allow a man participation in the impossible and the proscribed. It does not matter to this participation whether the fictive outcome is success or failure; the essential is simply that the act be put in motion. See R. Caillois, *Le mythe et l'homme* (Paris, 1938; reprint, 1981), pp. 22–34.

4. A Marxist would say that this theater enforced statist ideology by containing and dispelling what might challenge the city's power, so as to create acquiescence in oppression and

Order, luxury, and culture might be expected to make men submissive, cowardly, and soft (as Pericles suggested in the Funeral Speech), but Athenians maintained their strength because in their city symbolic transgressions, wrought by spectacular figures, annually charged the air with a passionate and healthy extremity of violent action.[5]

Ancient tragedy is thus fundamentally resistant to the imposition of contemporary social ethics or notions of psychology, and this is particularly true of the revenge plays, for their central action—the private deed of violent retaliation—is almost universally condemned by modern moralists and social scientists. As a rule, at the end of an Attic vengeance play a principal whom we would call a criminal has triumphed over a victim whom he or she has attacked by trickery and who is now, if not dead, at least maimed or grotesquely disempowered. The critic in search of modern "goodness" and moral didacticism finds this dramatic achievement radically distasteful and goes to work to show that, though it is represented as success, the central action is somehow dispraised by the poet who staged it.[6] In 1880 Sir Richard Jebb asked himself whether Sophocles intended, in his *Electra,* to "condemn or condone" the murders depicted, and though he was convinced that the dramatist thought much as he himself did, he was hardheaded enough to admit that there was no sign in the play of any condemnation. He therefore somewhat sadly concluded that the drama must have been an experimental return to a more archaic value system which was certainly not the poet's own. Recent scholarship, however, has not been able to allow even this much otherness to a Sophocles so commonly thought of as wise and gentle (like ourselves). Efforts have been made to unearth buried hints of punishment for the avenger, to find depraved neurosis in his sister,[7] and to reverse what the stage shows as a heroic deed into a shameful action.

---

exploitation; see P. W. Rose, "The Case for Not Ignoring Marx," in *Feminist Theory and the Classics,* ed. N. Rabinowitz and A. Richlin (New York, 1993), pp. 211–37. Such theories, however, overlook the extreme youth of the Athenian city-state, overestimate the intentionality of its "dominant group," and fail to notice how often tragedy reaffirms antistatist or extrastatist structures like hero cult, supplication, and sanctuary.

5. In *Praise of Folly,* Erasmus said of carnival that it revitalized fundamental impulses of love and belief by momentarily dissolving the authoritative claims of temporal institutions such as Church and State; see M. D. Bristol, *Carnival and Theater: Plebeian Culture and the Structure of Authority in Renaissance England* (New York and London, 1985), p. 133.

6. So, when the chorus offers a rationale for vengeance at Eur. *Bacch.* 877–81, E. R. Dodds reported (ad loc.) that they are "uneasy" in thus taking a position "against their natural feelings" and added, "It is certainly not the poet's own position."

7. For example, S. Saïd, locating "une attitude moderne" in Sophocles and making reference to Girard, describes an *Electra* debased by her own violence: "La tragédie de la vengeance," in *La vengeance,* ed. R. Verdier, vol. 4, *La vengeance dans la pensée occidentale* (Paris, 1981), pp. 47–90.

The play itself, however, remains an obdurate whole, the imitation of a god-driven, considered, and successful killing that refuses to repudiate even an act of matricide. Apollo has asked a man to do more than any mortal can, to break society's most fundamental law, and the man has done it with no concern for what we want to call "goodness."

In dealing with such plays, critics of our own time tend to ask, like Jebb, how a certain poet has treated the "problem of revenge,"[8] but among early Greeks revenge was not a problem but a solution. It was a form of necessary repayment, the opposite twin to the gracious return of favors that was called *charis*.[9] Repayment, moreover, was an outward expression of the regularity (*dike*) that supported both society and the cosmos.[10] A man offered pleasure or advantage to a fellow and so made a friend from whom would come the eventual return of a similar boon[11] —not merely gratitude but gratitude's objective expression.[12] And in the same way an initial offer of injury created an enemy from whom could be expected an unlovely return, not merely anger but an externalized work of enmity.[13] Making that return, the injured party could be said to repay the harm done him, or he might be described as collecting a reparation that was owed.[14] Either way, the non-mythic model was a money transaction and the general governing principle was equivalence, whether of benefit or harm. And the negative exchange of evil for evil, like the exchange of coin, was a mode of behavior recognized, regulated, and sometimes implemented, by an orderly city. Private vengeance had once been the only form of justice, or so Greeks of the fifth

---

8. E.g., H. D. F. Kitto, *Greek Tragedy* (London, 1966), p. 330.

9. As Mentor/Athena makes clear by promising a single act (ἀποτίνειν) that will serve as a repayment both of Odysseus for benefactions enjoyed and of enemies for evils suffered (*Od.* 22.235).

10. Reciprocity was *themis,* the initial rule fixed by Dike; see D. Saintillan, "Le discours tragique sur la vengeance," in *Anthropologie et théâtre antique: Actes . . . Montpellier,* Cahiers GITA, 3 (Montpellier, 1987), pp. 179–96, where it is argued that the reversibility of *charis* and vengeance is the essential Dionysiac truth.

11. See G. Herman, *Ritualised Friendship and the Greek City* (Cambridge, 1987), p. 41.

12. Moderns tend to think that a benefaction that expects return is somehow corrupt or at least opportunistic; Jesus tells the man who would be good to call others to his table but not to invite equals because they might repay him. In the same way we at least pretend to think that injuries are best left unrepaid: "Turn the other cheek." These attitudes are directly contrary to those of fifth-century Athens.

13. "La vengeance est un dû que l'un des partenaires est tenu d'acquitter, l'autre d'exiger" (Verdier, *La vengeance* 1:17).

14. The active voice of the verb τίνω can be used of the injured party's repayment of evil for evil (as at Soph. *Phil.* 959), though it more often indicates the original offender's payment of a punishment, a *poine* or *dike.* The middle voice is more commonly used for the revenger's act of extracting repayment from an enemy for a misdeed. Another favorite verb for the act of taking vengeance is ἀμύνω (in the middle voice), where the essential meaning is to fight off, or get rid of, something: the avenger puts the original injury/dishonor away from himself.

century believed, and revenge still supplied the pattern for punishments now given out by the state. Meanwhile myths and tales continued to treat this action in its most extreme form, that of blood vengeance, and to recount repayments of exaggerated cruelty, because men wanted to believe that one law at any rate would always prevail: gratuitous outrage would ever be returned in kind, and generously.[15]

Revenge was thus not a problem for Athenian society in the early fifth century, but for precisely that reason it was an action full of difficulties for a dramatist. Stories of achieved retaliation showed that injury and scorn were not without their cures and that men could create a balance among themselves. Their tendency was consoling and also powerfully secular, for the act of repayment was in itself of no interest to the gods: it did not bring its agent to the edge of the fearsome abyss separating men from the divine. Nor did such tales provide serious tension on the secular level; in an act of simple revenge the impulse of raw passion coincided with that of self-definition, so that the avenger could act with his whole being, untroubled by inner conflict. What was worse, a plot of active mortal retaliation was a fictional antidote to the fear induced by examples of divine force in application. When he treated a successful revenge, a dramatic poet might arouse incidental fears along the way, since an avenger ordinarily struck from a position of weakness; but the finished deed was an assertion of mortal self-rule and ingenuity, especially when it was brought about by trickery,[16] and so the emotions stirred up were those proper to what we call comedy.[17]

Revenge was not suited to the purposes of Attic tragedy (though it made good satyr-drama), and yet its characteristic passion—anger—cried out for poet and actor, while its plots and deceptions and disguises invited a kind of metatheater. The Attic dramatists could not resist, and as they

15. Dumas puts the following reflections into the mouth of his Count of Monte Cristo, come to the end of his adventures: "L'humanité malheureuse se soulage, depuis des millénaires par quelques mythes réparateurs. Les plus populaires des personnages mythiques sont l'Enchanteur et le Justicier. Humiliés et offensés attendent avec une espérance que nul échec ne peut affaiblir, tantôt le dieu, tantôt le héros qui viendra redresser les torts, écraser les méchants et mettre enfin les bons à sa droite. Ce justicier fût longtemps l'homme fort au sens physique du mot: Hercule."

16. The inscription on one of Hipparchus' herms was reported as, "Trick not your friend," a rule that supposes the propriety of tricking an enemy ([Pl.] *Hipparch.* 228c–229b). Such trickery could be extremely ugly, as was that of Odysseus when he planted a forged letter in the tent of Palamedes, thus causing him to be stoned to death; see F. Stoessl, "Die Palamedes Tragödien der drei grossen Tragiker," *Wien. Stud.* 79 (1966) 93–101.

17. In Aristotelian terms there was no overturn in such an action since the avenger did not experience a change of fortune but instead wrought for himself a recovery of whatever his condition had been before he suffered injury. However, if the principal is shown as escaping from the alienation of his temporary dishonor, there will be in effect a positive overturn from bad fortune into good; see A. P. Burnett, "Medea and the Tragedy of Revenge," *C Phil.* 68 (1973) 1–24.

applied a tragic sensibility to this essentially reassuring and secular fiction, they contrived certain disruptive dodges that have persisted through the intervening centuries of Western drama. Revenges that failed or were interrupted made their appearance, as did ghosts, commanding divinities, skewed ceremonies, and female agents who took the place of males. In addition, motifs such as kin-killing, madness, incest, cannibalism, and dismemberment were attached to the justice-bringing tale by way of disorderly decoration. These have made the theater of revenge what it is, but this very continuity of superficial generic characteristics has masked an ethical and moral breach between the Attic revenge plays and those more familiar to moderns. In later contexts, Stoic or Christian, these baroque structures and distorted embellishments served to label all revenge as unnatural and morally perverse. In Athens, on the other hand, they had a precisely opposite function, for there they brought the necessary taste of Dionysiac dissolution and terror to a fictional action that was ordinarily considered just and admirable. Or so I shall argue in the chapters that follow, where for reasons of economy the discussion is limited to tragedies in which a principal character performs a deed of vengeance that constitutes his play's major action.

I want to thank the members of the Classics Department of the University of California, Berkeley, for their invitation to join them as Sather Professor in the spring of 1994. And I should also like to thank Canadian writer Bruce Barber, who was companion and guide in explorations of revenge on film.

Anne Pippin Burnett
February 1997

CHAPTER ONE

Huge Frenzy and Quaint Malice

Seneca and the English Renaissance

I

Everyone knows something about revenge.[1] The angry impulse to "rebite him of whom the heart is bitten"[2] is more universal perhaps than aggression itself, which is why Shylock can boast of it as a mark of humanity: "Hath not a Jew eyes? . . . if you prick us, do we not bleed? . . . if you wrong us shall we not revenge?" (*Merchant of Venice* 3.1). The satisfaction of this impulse brings its practitioner a deep pleasure that Seneca's Medea calls *voluptas* (cf. *De Ira* 2.32.1), and Colette speaks of "la tentation la plus poignante, la plus suave, la plus parée de tous les attraits—celle de se venger" (*La vagabonde*).[3] The anger itself is sweet: "Agréable colère! Digne ressentiment, à ma douleur bien doux!" is how Don Diegue salutes the rise of his own passion

1. In 1773 Samuel Johnson wrote, "Revenge is an act of passion; vengeance is justice," but he noted that the distinction was not always observed, nor is it here. In what follows, both terms will be used for a passionate act that returns injury for gratuitous injury, performed by a private individual with what he believes to be justice.

2. P. La Primaudaye, *The French Academie*, Second Part, trans. T. Bowes (London, 1614), p. 325.

3. The joy of revenge is a commonplace. Amphitryon, going to have a look at the body of Lycus, says, "The enemy who dies paying for his crimes is a pleasure to see" (Eur. *HF* 732–33). Congreve gives neat expression to the same notion in the libretto for Handel's *Semele* when, in act 3, Juno sings, "Above measure / is the pleasure which my revenge supplies." As Walter Scott's Ulrica leapt from the flames of Torquilstone, "the inebriating delight of gratified vengeance contended in her eyes with the fire of insanity" (*Ivanhoe*, chap. 32). For the King, in Isak Dinesen's "The Fish" (*Winter's Tales*), the delight of vengeance stands with that of hunting, dancing, tournaments, friends, and women. But compare the revisionist version of Charlotte Brontë: "Something of vengeance I had tasted for the first time; as aromatic wine it seemed on swallowing, warm and racy; its after flavor, metallic and corroding, gave me a sensation as if I had been poisoned" (*Jane Eyre* 1.4).

in Corneille's *Le Cid* (1.6.262–64). Inversely, its frustration leaves a person incomplete, as if he were maimed, and so a whole lifetime may be given over to the recovery of self in a vengeful consummation that will finally, as Shakespeare's Titus says, "ease the gnawing vulture of thy mind" (*Titus Andronicus* 5.2.30–33). One who cannot eventually return evil for evil feels that he has become a slave (Arist. *Eth. Nic.* 1133a), and if he is proud he may run mad.[4]

In the pages that follow, this universal impulse will be considered only as it supplies the central action to certain Western tragedies, and consequently the terms "vengeance" and "revenge" will be used with a restricted sense. By Aristotle's definition, revenge is a self-engaged and retrospective action taken privately against an equal who has injured one's honor. Its purpose is not to get rid of someone who is in the way, or to harm someone who succeeds where the avenger has failed, for it is not a mode of advancement or even of self-defense. Its intention is rather to restore the broken outline of self suffered in an unprovoked attack from a member of one's own class or group.[5] It occurs in cases where an instantaneous and open return of blow for blow is impossible,[6] so that a debt of hatred remains to be covertly repaid to him who has unfairly injured you or someone close to you. Such vengeance is the correction of an imbalance rooted in the past, a calculated harm returned for an intentional, shameful injury or insult gratuitously given by an unrepentant equal.[7] This return is wrought in time, by the disciplined will of an angered individual, and according to its own rules it is good when it is appropriate and timely.[8] It will end as sharply as it began,

4. Like the Messenian Olympic victor Polychares whose son was murdered by his Spartan friend; unable to take vengeance, he began to kill every Spartan that he met (Paus. 4.4.4–8).

5. Response to attack from outside one's group becomes vendetta or war. Injury from an inferior is answered with punishment; from a superior, with assassination, revolt, or curse; see O. Murray, "Solonian Law of Hybris," in *Nomos: Essays in Athenian Law and Society*, ed. P. Cartledge, P. Millett, and S. Todd (Cambridge, 1990), pp. 139–45.

6. Battle retaliation, being an immediate and public response to publicly organized injury, is an action of another sort entirely, though there are points of contact: cf., e.g., *Il.* 14.482–85, where Acamas, whose brother Ajax has killed, goes out to kill Ajax's companion. The aristocratic duel was an alternative to, not a version of, revenge.

7. See the long discussion on the use and misuse of anger (defined as a desire for vengeance) at Arist. *Rh.* 1378a30–1380a. The initial provocation is understood as an act of contempt, ὀλιγωρία or ὕβρις, which publicly blocks a legitimate impulse or action. An answering revenge will be admirable if it is appropriate and timely (*Eth. Nic.* 1125b30) because retaliation, τιμωρία, puts an end to anger, replacing pain with pleasure (1126a20); an angry response to injury is often considered a sign of courage and leadership (1126b1; cf. 1108a, 1116b25). If, however, ignorance, accident, or anger has entered into the initial slight, the agent of that slight is not an unjust man; only when the provocation comes as a cool, insulting choice, while the response is dictated by anger, is retaliation just (*Eth. Nic.* 1135b25–1136a). See G. Courtois, "Le sens et la valeur de la vengeance chez Aristote et Sénèque," in *La vengeance*, ed. R. Verdier, vol. 4, *La vengeance dans la pensée occidentale* (Paris, 1981), pp. 91 ff.

once the debt is paid in full, but it will be ideally complete only when its victim knows by whom and for what he is injured (Arist. *Rh.* 1380b22). At that point the avenger's joy will be equal to that which the enemy felt in performing his initial outrage (*Rh.* 1378b; cf. 1370b9–12), and this satisfactory emotion will be at its highest if he can watch his enemy suffer (*Rh.* 1382a9). "Je ne me vange pas, si je n'en voy l'effet," says the Médée of Corneille, calling the sight "un si doux spectacle" (*Médée* 4.5.1288–89). The present discussion, then, concerns staged representations of this controlled, delayed, individual, honor-imposed, and finally restorative repayment— actions dictated not by petty malice or by a desire to thrust oneself into an advantageous position, but rather by what Stendhal called "la passion italienne . . . la passion qui cherche à se satisfaire" (*La Duchesse de Palliano*).

In its ideal, balancing form, revenge is a disciplined activity that stretches human capacities to their fullest. Stuffed though he is with anger, the revenger is forced not just to scheme but to think; indeed, he faces an intellectual task that is essentially impossible, since he must equate one man's experience with that of another.[9] His is an act that mixes memory with representation because for the most part he cannot return a suffering that is exactly like his own and must be satisfied with something proportionate and similar (cf. Arist. *Eth. Nic.* 1133b, on punishment). Primitive justice assumed that one could take an eye for an eye, but such precision is generally not possible: the man who raped one's sister may not have a sister to be raped in return. A substitute action has to be devised, perhaps one that reconstitutes the original offense only symbolically,[10] and so the avenger necessarily becomes an artist who both imitates and invents.

Inherent in this definition of revenge are characteristics that are already strongly theatrical. Thus when she tells herself, "Il faut faire un chef-d'oeuvre," Corneille's Médée (*Médée* 1.4.249) reminds us that every revenge is an imitation of action with action, and consequently very much like the staging of a play.[11]The avenger needs an audience, if his self-reinstatement is to be complete, and he himself becomes author and director of an improvised

8. So Plutarch praises the revenge killing of Callipus because it was accomplished with the weapon used in the initial murder that was avenged (*Mor.* 553D).

9. Cf. the discussion at Arist. *Eth. Nic.* 1132b21, where the difference between reciprocity and justice is assessed.

10. There is a special category of revenges that are entirely symbolic; for example, when an enemy of the dead athlete Theagenes took to attacking his statue at night, the statue fell upon him and crushed him, after which the dead man's kinsmen threw the statue into the sea, plague came upon Rhodes, and Delphi directed that the statue be fished up and made the focus of a hero cult (Paus. 6.11; Dio Chrys. *Or.* 31; Euseb. *Praep. Evang.* 5.34).

11. The congruence of revenge with drama is a commonplace in Jacobean plays; so, for example, Chettle's Hoffman, speaking of the author of the crime that enrages him, says, "He

episode in which he plays the chief role.[12] In particular, because he has to approach an enemy who is, or should be, on guard against him, the avenger must use deception and in particular must wear some form of disguise.[13] He may literally dress up, like the heroine of Wilkie Collins' *No Name*, who never stops pulling costumes on and off, or he may simply put on false attitudes or emotions, like Euripides' Medea when she does her devastating "take" on the Submissive Little Woman. All of which means that the avenger, like anyone who belongs to the theater, operates on the verge of madness.[14] It is all too easy for him to be taken in by his own illusions, to think that his creative powers have no limits, and to suppose that his revenge plot has been shaped by fate. He will be tempted to create excessive effects, but in the end his "piece" will succeed only if he maintains an exact and accurate memory of the injury done, and a conscious limitation of purpose. The true avenger is to replicate the act of another and by so doing restore his own state to what he once knew as normalcy. If he goes beyond this in doing harm, he is a villain, not a man of vengeance.

In the course of his "plot" the avenger will seize a random moment and transform it into a controlled performance, as if he were a creator of street theater. He thus stands in a peculiarly active relation to accident and time as, like a Pindaric athlete, he toys with *kairos* (cf. Soph. *El.* 22, 75–76) and waits for the signal instant when he can take opportunity as his accomplice—"that bald Madame, Opportunity," in the cynical Jacobean phrase (Tourneur, *Revenger's Tragedy* 1.1.55). When he has seized this moment, however, he parts from the dedicated athlete, because the man of revenge means to challenge a basic rule of the cosmos. Neither mortal nor immor-

---

was the prologue to a Tragedy / That if my destinies deny me not / Shall passe those of Thyestes, Tereus, / Jocasta, or Duke Jason's jealous wife" (*Hoffman* 1.3.18–21). Compare Soph. *El.* 1333, where the Tutor refers to the "performance" they are about to give in the palace as τὰ δρώμενα.

12. Witness Antonio, "Now works the scene; quick observation scud / To cote the plot, or else the path is lost" (Marston, *Antonio's Revenge* 4.3.103–5). The vengeance act is in this sense analogous to its opposite, the Stoic's act of self-containment, which T. G. Rosenmeyer describes as "a planned, a highly contrived and intellectualized activity. It achieves its full meaning only if it draws attention to itself as the central spectacle in a crowded arena" (*Senecan Drama and Stoic Cosmologies* [Berkeley, 1989], p. 48).

13. Avengers, like the tricksters of Renaissance drama, often dramatize the marginality of their action by pretending to be figures from the edge of society—travelers (like Monte Cristo), foreigners (like Orestes the "Thessalian"), madmen (like Hamlet), or people from a lower social caste (like Vindice, who pretends to be a pimp).

14. C. A. and E. S. Hallett attempt an analysis of the Elizabethan/Jacobean avenger, his grief, and his madness in *The Revenger's Madness* (Lincoln, Nebr., 1980), arguing that in defying the social prohibition against killing, the avenger necessarily defies his own superego and enters a fantasy world where he justifies his actions. This, however, is to read a specific and time-bound definition of madness into texts where it does not belong.

tal can make what is done undone, not even Chronos, father of the gods (Pind. *Ol.* 2.15–17),[15] but vengeance, were it perfectly to succeed, would make a past offense as if it had never been. The initial fact does of course remain—the stolen sister or the public scorn[16]—but the psychic balance between the injured man and his enemy returns in principle to what it was before, and so the weight of the past deed is altered. In this sense the avenger acts much as a priest or sorcerer does, and his improvised operation follows their model, for in vengeance as in a religious or magical rite, an ominous past event in which one was powerless is replaced by a replica of itself, a mimed action that is controlled now by the revenger as hierophant. Priestesses burn a pair of snakes on the anniversary of the night when a pair of snakes attacked the infant Heracles,[17] so reversing the dynamism of the past event, and in the same way the avenger imitates the attack once made on himself but takes it into his own control, so that he who was once the passive recipient of an outrage becomes the active author of the replicated deed. Sometimes he may even use a weapon that, like a ritual implement, objectifies the identity of the two situations—as Hofmannsthal's Elektra intended to use Klytämnestra's axe (as Vindice uses the skull of Gloriana). Or in the moment of success he may display a memento from the inaugural crime as if it were a sacred object, as Orestes does the web that caught his father when he reveals the corpses of his own victims.

The revenger is thus impresario, philosopher, trickster, and magician. He is also peculiarly whole and human, as he "keeps his wounds green" but retards his response, tests his will, and risks his sanity in an active definition of himself:[18] animals do not take revenge, Hamlet's "croaking raven" notwithstanding (3.2.248). No wonder then that revenge has been a favorite subject of Western literature, and especially of dramatic literature, for as long as stories have been told. The traditions of literary revenge stretch back from the present day to an unrecorded time before Homer, while certain tricks of plot, like the mock ceremony, and certain themes such as madness or mutilation, seem to link movie westerns, Mafia thrillers, Verdi operas, Jacobean melodramas, Senecan horror plays, and classical tragedy in one long chain. And yet, in spite of this apparent sameness, con-

15. Cf. Pl. *Leg.* 11.934 a.

16. Senecan avengers forget this; so Medea claims that she has regained her "stolen virginity" (*Med.* 984), and Atreus that he has restored chastity to his marriage (*Thyestes* 1099).

17. Theoc. *Id.* 24.89; cf. Phrynichus, *Praeparatio Sophistica*, ed. I. de Borries [Leipzig, 1911], p. 15.12 AB 10.26; Philochorus fr. 177 *FHG* 1.413.

18. In the time of romanticism revenge was admired as one of the accomplishments of the dandy; so Balzac's Baron de Maulincour reminds himself that "se taire à l'avance . . . pour assurer une vengeance meditée pendant trente ans, est une belle étude en un pays où il y a peu d'hommes qui sachent dissimuler pendant trente jours" (*Ferragus*).

temporary audiences, readers, and scholars who in their different ways appreciate *High Plains Drifter, Rigoletto,* or *Hamlet* are usually unsettled by the revenges shown on the Attic stage. If he must watch a *Medea* or an *Electra,* the twentieth-century spectator may admire the actress and the excesses of her role, but as a rule he finds the tragedy itself distasteful, and this is because he comes to it with mistaken expectations.

Attic tragedy remembers vengeance as an honorable imperative essential to the preservation of order, whereas most moderns at least pretend to view revenge as an evil. In our crowded and deculturized societies violence has become mysteriously positive in its organized political forms, and consequently absolutely forbidden in private expression, and we think of revenge in particular as a threat to the humane community. It seems to be an impulse toward regression, and (unconsciously following Nietzsche in the *Genealogy of Morals*) we explain it as an aberration typical only of the weak, the debased, or the deprived, "a perverse form of normal defensive aggression," in the cool phrase of Erich Fromm.[19] All of which means that, as a repudiated act which he nevertheless may in secret long to perform, revenge is for the man of the twentieth century a "dirty" subject suited only to lesser art and acceptable only under fixed conditions. We like to watch *The Abominable Dr. Phibes,* whose crimes are an ingenious imitation of the Seven Plagues of Egypt, or Diana Rigg as she elegantly removes each enemy because of her distorted *Mother Love,* but we cannot allow a fictional avenger to be truly splendid or admirable, nor will we let him succeed and live, except in very special circumstances.[20] He may be sympathetic, even attractive, but we expect that in the end his crime will fail or turn upon him in a way that proves its innate monstrousness. Rigoletto must find that it is Gilda's corpse, not that of the Duke, that he is about to dispose of, and Hamlet, after a final thrust that kills only by chance, must himself die if he is to finish his play as a "sweet prince."[21] Naturally, then, when we take expectations such as these into a theater that shows an Orestes enthroned or a Medea borne up in triumph, we come away baffled.

19. *The Anatomy of Human Destructiveness* (New York, 1973), pp. 271–75.

20. As an example of such circumstances, note Holmes' announcement, in the case of a woman who has killed her blackmailer, that his sympathies are entirely with the killer because certain crimes justify private revenge ("Charles Augustus Milverton," in A. C. Doyle, *The Return of Sherlock Holmes* [London, 1904]).

21. The Count of Monte Cristo, sailing off to the east with Haydee, is a rare example of an avenger who gains his ends and departs, like certain heroes of Western films who are moved by private revenge to do the work of public law and order. Another exception to the rule that punishes the avenger may be in the course of appearing in the contemporary subgenre of rape-revenge, though Thelma and Louise do still go over the cliff; on films of this type, see Carol J. Clover, *Men, Women, and Chainsaws* (Princeton, 1992), pp. 114–65.

Only with a mind cleansed of Platonic, Stoic, Christian, and statist attitudes and only with appreciative faculties freed from the spell of Senecan
and Jacobean drama can one respond honestly to the vengeance dramas
that were produced and enjoyed in the theater of Dionysus during the fifth
century B.C. Consequently what follows here is a rapid review of Western
evaluations of the act of revenge, and a few brief studies of some of its most
influential representations in European drama. It is offered as preface and
control, a slight sketch of what must be forgotten before any attempt can be
made to recover the true flavor of Attic revenge.

II

Vengeance is the work of anger, an emotion which Greeks enshrined in
many of the myths that gave tragedy its subjects. The innate rage of the
Homeric heroes had protected their honor-outlined selves against incur-
sion, as it protected their various homelands, but this aristocratic passion
was too often indistinguishable from arrogance when translated to democratic Athens. When Socrates questioned the archaic rule by which a man
did good to friends and harm to enemies (Pl. *Cri.* 49b–d), he deprived the
old anger of much of its function, as had also the new distinction that was
being made between punishment, which was the work of the city, and
vengeance, as it might be wrought by individual or tribe. At first these were
differentiated as public and private, each with its own appropriate sphere,
but Plato gave them a positive and a negative value. His Protagoras explains
that punishment, *kolasis,* is a reasonable response to an act of wrongdoing,
because it concentrates on the recipient, looks to the future, and tries to
teach virtue,[22] whereas vengeance, which attempts to satisfy him who inflicts
it, is senseless and bestial because it looks backward to strike at a past deed
(*Prt.* 324a–b; cf. Arist. *Rh.* 1369b12). What is more, as the work of passion,
revenge was necessarily reprehensible because passion always brings injustice into the soul (*Leg.* 9.863e–864; *Resp.* 10.609b). The anger of the
wronged individual was to be eliminated, not satisfied, by a lawgiver who
would try to reconcile the family of a murder victim to his killer (*Leg.* 862b–
c). Punishment, meanwhile, would become positive and utilitarian, a dis-
couragement of crime in a just community that had no use for archaic passions. Indeed, since rage of any kind was a turning away from truth, the old
noble anger was now seen to be a contradiction in terms.[23]

---

22. Cf. *Leg.* 11.934a; *Grg.* 525b.
23. Nevertheless anger could still, in the fourth century, be a plea in defense of a violent
action (Dem. 21.41). Even for Plato, anger might attenuate responsibility for a crime: an angry
murder is less serious than one done in cold blood (*Leg.* 868c; 869c–d; 873a–b).

Aristotle tried to qualify. Anger, he said, is a special passion, more reasonable than desire, less unjust than craftiness (*Eth. Nic.* 1149b), and it can feed courage or a just indignation. He was not prepared to call vengeance an act of injustice (*Rh.* 1373a10–16, 18); instead he concluded that the spirit of revenge—typical of free men but not of slaves—was valuable to a city. Hatred of course was dangerous because it was simply aggressive, its essential need being to destroy another man (*Rh.* 1380b12–24). The vengeance emotion, on the other hand, was self-referential, aiming only to restore a personal honor that had been shamefully diminished; if the cause of anger was of a certain sort—that is, gratuitous, public injury to a man's honor (as summarized at *Rh.* 1379a30–b)—and if the response was timely and appropriate, then the passion was praiseworthy (*Eth. Nic.* 1125b).[24] Indeed an angry man was judged to be a manly man and one fit to command (ibid. 1126b), nor could any enemy be defeated unless anger filled the mind and armed the soul, according to a lost Aristotelian text that Seneca cites (*De Ira* 1.9.2; cf. 1.17.1, 3.3.1–2). This subtle and sympathetic analysis of a carefully restricted form of anger suggests a certain nostalgia for the haughty ways of an imagined past (it probably in part reflects the author's reading of tragedy), but it did not suit the subsequent schools of philosophy.

Aristotle had held that anger might provide the energy needed for the punishment of wrongs, but Seneca answered that reasonable punishment could have nothing to do with a passion that is "incapable of distinction and ignorant of truth" (*De Ira* 1.7.2). All passion was error because it drove the soul out of its right relations with actuality and the present. The anger that wants to punish what a man misdescribes as injury was especially erroneous precisely because of the qualities that Aristotle recognized: its amalgam of pleasure and pain, its narcissistic concentration on the outer aspect of the self, and its refusal to be contained in the present (Stob. *Ecl.* 2.176.10c). Instead of submitting to the natural vengeance of time, the angry man tried to control the future so as to alter the past, and nothing could be more absurd. Wrath was defective energy; it was like a weed, according to Seneca (*De Ira* 2.15.2), and as ugly and ferocious as "the hellish monsters of the poet's fantasy, belted with snakes and breathing fire" (ibid. 2.35.3). Anger was moreover ineffective, like a weapon that sticks in the hand and turns upon its user (ibid. 2.35.1). And finally, as the opposite of reason, it was a form of madness (ibid. 1.1.4),[25] a mental crime that tended to become a

---

24. Cf. the observation of Pythagoras that anger might be timely or untimely (DK 1:470, 14–17). Aristotle also cites Apollo at *Il.* 24.33–54 as proof that there were bounds within which wrath was proper (*Eth. Nic.* 1126a34). For a recent discussion of Aristotle on anger, see J. Casey, *Pagan Virtue* (Oxford, 1990), pp. 10–14.

25. This is demonstrated in the case of Ajax: "Furious madness drove Ajax to his death, and anger drove him to that madness" (*De Ira* 2.36.5).

vice because the angry man not only strays into evil but loves such straying (ibid. 2.10.1).

According to Seneca, punishment must be the work of the good man, and the good man, even at the sight of injustice, cannot feel anger, for if he did, his state of mind would be dictated by the actions of others and, what is worse, he would be angry all of the time (ibid. 2.7.1). Even if he sees an outrage wrought upon someone close to him, he will be undisturbed and will avenge that person only as reason dictates, because it is his duty (ibid. 1.12.1–2). Aristotle was wrong, and anger could never have a proper punitive use because, being a passion, it is open to the influence of other passions, of pity for example, so that an angry punishment might wrongly relax into mercy where a dispassionate one would continue always to its reasonable end, destroying whole households if they were harmful to the state (ibid. 1.19.1). Anger thus might be paradoxically not cruel enough for true justice, and in any case it could never be broad enough because the sheer mass of chaotic human wrongdoing defies any wrath to match it (ibid. 2.10.4). And finally, since wrongdoing among the untrained is as natural as the ripening of fruit, even just indignation is a form of insanity, since "no sane man is angry with Nature itself" (ibid. 2.10.6).

On another plane, Seneca saw anger also as an enemy of art (ibid. 2.14.3) while, conversely, he seems to have thought that art—in particular, the art of the theater—might return the compliment by working for anger's defeat. The general rule for keeping anger away is to refuse to define anyone else's action as insult or injury (ibid. 2.29.1), and yet there are events, the rape of one's mother for example (ibid. 1.12.1), that even a wise man can hardly witness without perturbation. In such cases an emotive response will insinuate itself into the mind in spite of reason's patrol (somewhat as a sneeze might, after a dose of pepper), and the wise man will have to deal with this reflex emotion at once, before it becomes a full-blown passion. His reason must quickly partition his soul, isolating the preliminary emotive response and refusing to give it access to the centers of decision and movement. And this is where drama may be useful, for practice in this walling off of emotion is precisely what one gets at the theater. There the spectator's mind is perturbed by shocking scenes (ibid. 2.2.5), and a movement that forebodes passion "steals upon us from the sight of the players on the stage" (ibid. 2.2.3), though without suggesting any action on our part, since we are conscious that the whole experience is artificial (ibid. 2.2.5).[26] Sitting at a play,

26. My understanding of this section of De Ira has been greatly improved by reading B. Inwood, "Seneca and Psychological Dualism," in Passions and Perceptions: Studies in Hellenistic Philosophy of Mind, ed. J. Brunschwig and M. Nussbaum (Cambridge and New York, 1993), pp. 150–83, esp. 176–78. For a different report of Stoic views on the theatrical experience, see M. Nussbaum, "Poetry and the Passions," ibid., pp. 97–149, esp. 143. According to Nussbaum, the

a man may thus usefully exercise the psychic muscles that render emotion inactive (ibid. 2.17.1); he can rehearse himself in not surrendering, and learn to view horror and injustice with no more than an agreeable thrill because his mind has chosen not to be affected (ibid. 2.2.5–6).[27] And finally—though Seneca doesn't say this in so many words—the man who takes this accomplishment out into the world where all men are actors (*Ep.* 80.6–8) will be able to look on actual suffering in the same way. Like Democritus or the modern television addict, he will view even extremes of actual outrage with a wise smile for the insignificance of the illusion.[28] It was with a nicety that more than one movie house of the '40s was named "The Seneca."

III

Revenge-anger in particular needed to be disempowered, according to Seneca. It was especially dangerous because it might seem to be righteous (*De Ira* 1.12.3), and also because it was by definition a thrust toward action. Consequently he himself put revenge into the animal house that he thought the theater might be. His *Medea* is the better known example, but the *Thyestes* is more essentially Senecan, and it is a play that did much to fix the flavor of all subsequent tragic revenge. In it the admonitions of the *De Ira* are restated in the breach, defied by agents of unwisdom who are fleshly embodiments of the senseless madness that the essay describes in flat prose. At the very beginning the prologue's Fury calls out, "Let no work of anger here be found excessive!" (*Thyestes* 39) as she demands a return of crime for

---

spectator was to feel no emotion at all, and to interest himself in the characters on stage only as a concerned doctor might in a patient whose health he hoped to improve. Cf. Rosenmeyer, *Senecan Drama,* p. 32, who supposes that Seneca peopled his tragedies with living, speaking maxims contained in an educational paradigm. It would seem, however, that since teaching could best be done by exempla and exhortation (*De Ira* 3.3.2), Seneca must have had some modified intention when he licensed actors who did not instruct the watching mind but to some extent directly set it in motion (cf. *De Ira* 2.17.1; *Dial.* 4.17.1).

27. Two more mentions of theatrical experience evidently refer to comic nonpassionate mime. This is explicit at *Ep.* 108.8–9, where an audience is drawn together in common enjoyment of depravity by an actor who labels his own vices in sounding verse. The statement at *Ep.* 7.2 seems to belong to this same context, for there it is said that a crowded theater can be a dangerous place for a good man because of the multiple vicious pleasures being experienced all around him (though this might also refer to an ill-conditioned tragic audience). When, however, Seneca refers to the *humanae vitae mimus* (in which we play our assigned parts so badly, *Ep.* 80.6–8), he seems to be thinking of a tragic performance, as also at *Ep.* 76.31, for in both cases the imaginary actor plays the role of a prince. Finally, the performance mentioned at *Ad Marciam de consolatione* 10.1 would appear to be an amateur affair of some sort, since props must be returned to their owners.

28. "Erotic torrents flash on screens instead / Of drenching us" (James Merrill, "Self-portrait in a TYVER Windbreaker," in *A Scattering of Salts* [New York, 1995], p. 94).

crime, and no one in the action that follows could be accused of any restraint. Here, in the *turba peccantium* that proves all anger inadequate, a preeminent outrage has occurred—not the rape of a mother, but the seduction of a wife by a brother. And here a man who is not wise strives to match this erroneous act, which he misperceives as an injury, with a commensurate wrath. Cannibalism, a form of "alimentary incest," is the correct return as fixed by the Atreid myth, and Seneca takes full advantage of this fictional detail because it lets him show revenge as a deed unnatural beyond any other, tantamount to serving human meat for food. The process of ingestion is never forgotten: the motif is established in the prologue with thirsty Tantalus (2, 70, 137; cf. the feast to be offered, 59–67) and continued in Thyestes' emphasized greed (277–78, 450–52, 460, 778, etc.). Consequently, when the impulse toward retaliation "hungers" like a tiger (707–13; cf. the "weary tooth" at 736) for a satisfaction that will be someone else's abominable meal, it is plain that a Euclidean statement is being made: Angry revenge is to wise vindication as the swallowing of human flesh and blood is to a healthy meal. Vengeance is thus error in its extremest form, but Seneca does not initially ask for its categorical repudiation. Instead, he brings the spectator into a partial engagement with it, stretching language and imagery to match the vicious passions of the Tantalids, so that his audience is forced to admire even what it loathes. Only after undergoing this form of "temptation" are we allowed to use the muscles that will suppress our excitement.

The stage situation has been created by Thyestes, a man whose depraved error made him look at his brother's wife, misdescribe her as a sexual object, license his lust, act against Nature, and in this way destroy all fraternal feeling.[29] Atreus can no more love him now than ocean can reach stars or wheat be harvested from the sea (*Thyestes* 476–82; cf. his expression of guilt, 995–97).[30] This was Thyestes' initial error, and he repeats it as soon as he appears, standing outside his brother's palace and once more greedily misdescribing what he sees. He thinks he is being offered the produce of the whole world to eat (463–67), the worship due to a god, and a perpetual orgy (these illusions revealed in a pompous *recusatio*, 463–67), and so in direct opposition to the counsels of reason (407–9 ff.) he hands his sons over to the man who means to kill them. He, the father, follows his boy into the place of horror, not reasonably persuaded but seduced by corrupt

29. See A. C. Lloyd, "Emotion and Decision," in *The Stoics*, ed. J. M. Rist (Berkeley, 1978), pp. 233–46, esp. 242.

30. See the discussion of this passage in Rosenmeyer, *Senecan Drama*, pp. 199–200, where it is convincingly argued that the impossibility trope is phrased so as to suggest that Thyestes maintains a perverse hope.

hopes of pleasure and power (295, 302). This man possesses understanding, as Seneca proves by making him babble bits of Stoic cant (e.g., his fantasy of the simple life, 446 ff.), but he wills not to use it. Instead he chooses to continue in his own pattern of error: soon he will misdescribe the food and drink that is offered to him, and think himself engaged in a proper satisfaction of his appetites while in fact he feasts on his sons' flesh.

Such is Thyestes, the author of the original crime.[31] He is a good example of the delinquent who succumbs to passion, but he nevertheless presents a difficulty to the Stoic dramatist because, however plain his errors may be, his intensely ugly suffering (not to mention the slaughter of his innocent sons) might elicit pity and a sense of outrage from a watching audience. To block such sympathetic response Seneca employs two characteristic maneuvers, one that is direct and one that is not. First and directly, he makes his erroneous Thyestes grossly physical; once inside the palace, this man is all gullet and belly, and his subhuman appetite repels our pity and extinguishes our concern for justice far more effectively than any emphasis on his moral failings might have done. Seneca's second, indirect move is more significant for the inner tension of his drama, however, for with it he brings the spectator into a positive involvement in the intrigue that destroys this man. The audience is not allowed to feel Atreus' anger, but it is nonetheless drawn into a kind of aesthetic collaboration in a vengeance that labels Thyestes as its inevitable, contemptible victim.[32]

The avenger who stands opposite to Thyestes has a name that is almost an anagram for "angry": *iratus Atreus* (*Thyestes* 180). He is a heightened embodiment of the banal wrath that the *De Ira* would have a man banish; he moves with madness, ferocity, and cruelty, as that essay would lead one to

---

31. It has been customary to see Thyestes as "truly humble" (B. Marti, "Seneca's Tragedies," *TAPA* 76 [1945] 240); as "a comparatively innocent, even a good man," "a passive, even virtuous victim" (J. P. Poe, "An Analysis of Seneca's *Thyestes*," *TAPA* 100 [1969] 360, 374); as a "noble character" (C. J. Herington, "Senecan Tragedy," *Arion* 5 [1966] 458); as one who is presented so as to claim audience sympathy (D. Henry and E. Henry, *The Mask of Power* [Warminster, 1985], p. 139). None of these assessments, however, takes account of the consistent identification of Thyestes with physical appetite, nor can any of these critics explain why such a man accepts the power and luxury that he thinks is being offered, or why he, a father, gives way to his son, insisting on being a follower where he ought to lead (*Thyestes* 489). For a more accurate report, see R. J. Tarrant, *Seneca's Thyestes* (Atlanta, 1985) ad 446–70: "The gusto with which Thyestes enumerates the trappings of wealth seems a clear sign that he does not find this existence as distasteful as he claims." Cf. A. J. Boyle, "Hic epulis locus," *Ramus* 12 (1983) 199–228; and also P. Davis, "The Chorus in Seneca's *Thyestes*," *C Phil.* 39 (1989) 421–35, who rightly sees Thyestes' apparent adherence to Stoic values as "superficial" (p. 429).

32. This is the same effect as that described by A. Harbage, "Intrigue in Elizabethan Tragedy," in *Essays . . . Hardin Craig* (Columbia, Mo., 1962), p. 38: "moral judgment stands partly in abeyance as we check the villain's calculations."

expect (cf. *Tranq.* 2.14), and in the end his tragic passion is as the essayist supposed—ugly, fruitless, and inadequate. This anger, however, has been made more formidable in its adaptation for the stage, for here it comprehends both a defiance of the simplest laws of humanity (as shown in the parody of hospitality, 508–11) and also a desire to break the largest bounds of human nature (267–69). It has a political aspect, too, since Atreus hopes to make his power absolute by inspiring absolute hatred and fear (205 ff.). And above all, Atreus' anger has daimonic connections, for it is blessed by an underworld fiend (cf. esp. 54–59), and is a passion that monstrously invades its agent (260, 496), even as that agent invokes and welcomes it (244–53; cf. 237). Consequently, this angry tragic principal is seen to act "against Nature," not simply because he is provoked by wrongdoing that is itself natural (cf. *De Ira* 2.10.6) but also because he would usurp the functions of an incomprehensible extrahuman Order (cf. 867, where the true *monstra* are the stars). Taking this swollen form, Atreus' vengeance-fury attempts an appropriate response to Thyestes' erroneous criminality, but huge though it is, it cannot bring satisfaction. It remains a form of frenzy that betrays the enraged man even as it destroys his enemy, one that leads to actions that even he must finally recognize as senseless and inadequate.

In this dramatic demonstration of the inability of vengeance to satisfy, Seneca gives his revenger two salient features: an aesthetic sense and a monumental impiety. These interact, within the play, to produce a success that is a failure, while they also work directly upon the spectator, so as to keep him at a distance from the scheme he passively seconds. Atreus, it seems, is not moved exclusively by simple anger; he wants to make a masterpiece of his revenge. He uses his reason not to combat his passion but instead to endow it with a marvelous form, and his moment of inspiration is like that of a poet—"something enormous shudders in my mind" (268–70). As he considers each added touch of cruelty, he feels the delight of the creator (*saevum scelus iuvat ordinare,* 715), and it is exactly this pride in his work that first inflates his impiety, then punctures the fullness of his satisfaction, for his desire for fame leads him to play to an audience that will not applaud.

As a conscious stylist with a sense of the genre in which he works (he finds a revenge model in Procne, 272–73, 275–76), Atreus is determined to outdo his predecessors (274–75, cf. 20) so as to win eternal reputation. And for this he must be seen in his triumph not just by the dulled eye of his victim but by all mankind. "Come my soul, let's do a thing that future times will hate but never will forget!" (192). That is his original ambition, but soon even a gathering of all worldly populations to come is not a big enough house, and Atreus decides to force an audience of gods to tremble and admire (265–66, 893–95). Of course he will display his victory to his enemy and to the world that witnessed his own injury, but these are paltry aims. His finished revenge must terrorize the powers who allowed his diminishment; it must disturb the cosmos that surrounds the immortals, for according to

Atreus' bloated sense of injury, every member of this largest audience is an enemy.

Atreus plays overtly to his audience of superhuman spectators when he is in the act of murder. For the eyes of the world, it would be revenge enough to kill his brother's sons, feed them to their father, and then reveal the menu to his guest. Atreus, however, intends as well to force this act of kin-slaughter and cannibal hospitality upon the attention of the gods, as an offensive joke about worship and sacrifice, and so he invents a rite of impiety that becomes the central action of this tragedy. There is, at the core of his palace, a contained bit of unnatural nature, a mysterious sunken wilderness within the structure of political power (641–47).[33] It is decorated with spoils of war, though tools and cultivation are unknown in this place of poisonous growth (654). Above, there are rooms full of light (645), but in this dark place are sources of fate (657–58, 679–82) and remnants of chaos, for a sluggish stream akin to Styx rises here (665–67). One can make contact with the gibbering dead in this lightless grove, but also with the upper gods, and this is where Atreus comes in his rage (*furens*, 682), leading his brother's sons. With finicky attention to detail (686–90), he begins a subverted rite of sacrifice, causing gods and universal powers to give signs of displeased attention with wine that turns to blood, a crown that falls, and ivory that weeps (700–702). Nature itself gives a shake to the earth and sends a sinister comet (696–99), causing terror in the outer world, but Atreus is not afraid. He knows he has the ear of the audience he wants, and he answers these prodigies with menacing threats. Then, in appeasement of his own tigerish hunger for vengeance, he decapitates his human victims at an altar where blood extinguishes the flame, after which he tears out their entrails for a vatic glimpse of what is to come.

Rhetoric causes the Messenger to say that, compared with the feast that followed, this was an act of piety (744), but it is clearly the scene of hellish sacrifice that Seneca would emphasize. Each ritual operation in the abysmal grove is described with care, and the whole account (641–758) is extended by showy similes, whereas the banquet is sketched in a few hazy lines (the cooking gets sixteen, 759–75, the serving and eating just five, 778–82). In particular, the scene of sacrifice is placed in an exact though inconceivable architectural position, and it is evident that with this vast hole so strangely contained in a man-made edifice, Seneca means to describe vengeance itself. It might be a metaphor for the perverse depths of the psyche where unreason lives and whence acts of madness come. Or, with its perfect con-

---

33. This is not an ordinary "palace yard" (Herington, "Senecan Tragedy," p. 460) nor a simple "valley" (Henry and Henry, *Mask*, p. 146); indeed, its crowd of ghosts and its ghoulish illuminations mark it as more sinister even than Tarrant's "perverted counterpart of a courtyard."

tradictions to the topography of Delphi, it might be meant to correct Hellenic tales in which revenge was sanctified by Apollo. Its sense in the immediate action is at any rate perfectly clear, for this locus that has no location serves as a place where initiations occur—an initiation into error for Atreus, but into truth for the mortal Roman audience. Atreus undergoes an explicit change of status in this dark hole, as he first becomes a priest in the cult of his own ferocity, and then, by means of a rite of self-worship, emerges as the equal of the stars (885). Meanwhile in his own view he passes from the condition of ordinary avenger to a higher grade, becoming a cosmic hero who will avenge the limitations of the human condition upon Nature and the gods. He puts aside his mortal definition while he is underground, and comes forth ready to dismiss divinities as if they were nobodies (888). The very Sun he treats as a dispensable accomplice (891), wishing it had stayed to admire his next move, but ready in its absence to play "god of daylight" himself. He will bring illumination to his victim's pollution with no help from the heavens (893–95). It is manifest that Atreus' initiation has readied him to break the boundaries of mere humanity, and this is the substance of the spectator's parallel instruction. He learns, from what is reported to him from this unearthly place, that revenge is not only an impious crime against mankind and the gods but also a metaphysical attack upon the entire order of nature.

Once he is above ground again, Atreus executes his design with a conscious artistry that involves the spectator even as it holds him at a distance. The king plans his brother's unspeakable orgy so that it will have two parts, first the eating of flesh, then the drinking of blood in the presence of the boys' remains. This of course doubles the horror of the meal, but there is another far more important effect inherent in the two-course scheme, for it allows postponement, anticipation, and suspense (782–83). Above all, it shifts the emphasis of the event, so that Thyestes is finally punished not so much in the act of cannibalism as in the recognition of that act. The vengeance, in other words, becomes intellectual, not physical, its agony concentrated in the bloody cup of truth and the final revelation.

Within this scheme the actual butchery and consumption represent the early phase of a continuing process which the audience, however repelled, inevitably longs to see crowned by Thyestes' understanding of what he has done. Though the killing is finished and the flesh tasted, every spectator still feels, with Atreus, that the event is incomplete; all join with him in anticipation of the moment when the victim shall learn the facts that they already understand. There is, in other words, a kind of dispassionate connivance between audience and avenger that effectively erases any possible sympathy for Thyestes. Consequently, when Atreus at last steps directly into the banquet he has catered, each spectator is beside him, an unwilling straight man ready to appreciate a series of nauseous double entendres. To the belching, overfed Thyestes grown sentimental about his sons, his host and brother says, "Think of the lads as right here with you, forever" (976), and, "On the score of those beloved heads I can fill you with satisfaction" (978–79), and even, "They are at this moment mingled with my family and giving themselves to a joyous meal" (980–81). The brute mockery of these speeches resembles the holiday humiliation of a buffoon, and the knowing members of the audience are irresistibly delighted as they catch the sense that is hidden.[34] Like it or not, they stand with Atreus in a common superiority to this glutton who is ignorant even of what his own stomach contains.

The artistry of the Atreus-avenger thus works out from the stage so as to numb any emotional response that the Senecan audience might have felt for the victim. At the same time, however, it has worked within the drama to increase Atreus' appetite for contrived perfection, and he is like an evil master of revels when, for his finale, he calls for a miniature masque. Three slaves enter with three severed heads to serve as recognition tokens, and using these props the king, with exquisite timing, leads his brother to the necessary knowledge. First Thyestes is made to know his sons in these heads; then by the heads to know their death; and finally by their death to know their murderer. This, however, is only the prologue, the paced preliminary to the moment when Thyestes will know himself and learn the full excess of this fraternal vengeance (1052). The climax of both masque and play comes when the banqueter is at last brought to ask about what he does not see, the bodies that once belonged to these heads. Have they met the worst fate of all, been cast out to be eaten by beasts (1033)? The question lets Atreus give pithy proof of how far he surpasses other men in his knowledge of cruelty. "No," he answers with a gesture at the sordid table, "it is you who have eaten them—at this ungodly meal!" (1034). He has invented a fate for the boys that is worse than exposure, he has changed his brother into something beyond beastliness, and he will make him suffer as no animal ever could. According to his own inner revenge script, this should have been Atreus' final speech, but Seneca's larger play will end on a different note.

The revenge is complete. The enemy will be tortured for the rest of his life, and he knows who has caused this agony that comes as repayment for his own initial crime. The witnessing avenger is thus content, or rather, he tries to be. He hails his own triumph and even attempts a boast about the renewed chastity of his infected marriage (1096–99), but chastity, like virginity (like the blood of the murdered), can never be recalled, and Atreus' satisfaction is incomplete. He wanted to commit a limitless crime, and the

---

34. G. L. Evans, "Shakespeare, Seneca and the Kingdom of Violence," in *Roman Drama*, ed. T. A. Dorey and D. R. Dudley (London, 1965), p. 136, reports that Seneca here "falls into that comic trap which always awaits the writer who tries to dignify and shock at the same time." I should say rather that he knowingly uses wit (of a sort) to check the potential pity of his audience.

moment he has finished he sees the paltry limitations of his work (1052–68). His fevered artist's imagination discovers refinements that he failed to bring off—the boys were killed too rapidly, without enough suffering, Thyestes should have been made to suck their blood while they were still breathing, should have been forced to chop and cook them himself, and he should have known what he ate as he chewed! In a fit of self-criticism Atreus discovers that he has not after all created the superlative act of cruelty (1065), and now it is too late, for there is no way to begin again.

The revenge is imperfect, and what is worse, it has made no mark upon the supernatural audience that Atreus meant to impress. There are, in the world of this play, errant evil energies like the prologue's Fury; there is also an outmoded troupe of gods; and beyond these there is a Nature ruled by force or forces unknown. All of these, when the colossal vengeance is done, are seen to be unmoved. The Fury has had and will have her way (25–44); the gods are unworried, and the heavenly bodies refuse any further notice: they will signal neither condemnation of Atreus nor sympathy for his victim (1068–90). True, the eclipse did seem to comment on Atreus' act of sacrilege, but it can also be read as a general premonition of inevitable cosmic decline (so the chorus, 827–84). The Pelopids will continue on their accursed way, and Nature will proceed in its slow relapse into chaos (with the chorus just cited compare 40–46 and 214). Atreus has expended the fullness of his anger, the whole force of his misdirected reason and will, and to these he has added the genius of his artistry, yet for all its style and scale his successful crime is insignificant, and it leaves him with a bitter aesthetic remorse.

Seneca's *Thyestes* left a formal inheritance to a long line of revenge plays, as we learn from the later ghosts and furies who so often pay direct homage to the Roman play. Subsequent vengeance heroes will imitate Atreus' increasing appetite for cruelty, and also his cool wit in the moment of its achievement; their work, like his, will be hideously artful,[35] sometimes a parody of piety reminiscent of his intolerable sacrifice. And meanwhile repulsive victims of the Thyestes type will continue to lend a kind of balance to the ugly central act, making it one which, at least for a time, the audience viciously admires. More important, later avengers will, like Atreus, experience a final defeat in a reverse that does not so much condemn the revenge as show it to have been a grotesque assault upon an order that is impervious. Wholesale mayhem is another striking legacy left by Senecan tragedy,

---

35. Atreus' lines at *Thyestes* 192 ff. become a commonplace: e.g., Francisco, in Massinger's *Duke of Milan* (1.3.316–18), "Or if we be remembered it shall be / To fright posterity by our example / That have outgone all precedents of villainies"; cf. Lodovico, in Webster's *White Devil* (5.1.75–77), "I would have our plot be ingenious, / And have it hereafter recorded for example, / Rather than borrow example."

but there will be radical differences between the earlier and the later uses of stage atrocity. In the Jacobean theater, with its all too human avengers, bodily mutilation will reflect a disordered society and will work directly upon the spectator to create an ecstasy of horror that heightens his other emotions. In the *Thyestes,* by contrast, where the avenger is not just inhuman (268) but a monster opposed to Nature, violations of the human form illustrate a metaphysical truth, and consequently they work to distance the spectator from the fiction. The hacked bodies and skewered heads of the final spectacle are used much as its drunken, belching victim is—to bring about a stunned divorce between audience and every sort of emotion. At first the optical shock may evoke vicious little thrills, but once Thyestes' knowledge is complete, the detached heads inspire only a kind of intellectual satisfaction, along with that disenchanted repugnance which is the essence of the Senecan tragic effect. Rising paradoxically from the gorgeous language, Disgust is the poetic cure, as it inspires a healthy repudiation not just of the witnessed event but also of any premonitions of outrage or distress that may have suggested themselves to the audience. The Senecan spectator sits apart, enjoying induced intimations of horror but knowing that his shudders are mere psychic curiosities. And so he learns to keep passion like a pet, the theater its decorated cage.

IV

Though they inherited certain structures, called themselves Senecan, and reveled in vernacular versions of the cosmic style,[36] the Renaissance revenge plays seem almost to belong to another genre because revenge itself had become in their time an altered and more ambivalent act.[37] In the sacred realm it was labeled by Christianity not as an error into which no wise man would fall but as a sin, a sacrilege to be punished by eternal damnation.[38]

---

36. Fortunately there is no need to broach here the question of actual influences that continues to exercise Renaissance scholars; for a quick summary of opinion, see the review of G. Braden, *Renaissance Tragedy and the Senecan Tradition* (New Haven, 1985) by M. Trousdale in *Medieval and Renaissance Drama in England* 4 (1989) 223–27; also G. K. Hunter, "Seneca and the Elizabethans," *Shakespeare Survey* 20 (1967) 17–26. And for a list of elements often considered "undeniably Senecan," see Evans, "Shakespeare, Seneca," pp. 123–59. In the vengeance plays themselves the debt to Seneca is happily admitted: Kyd has Hieronimo return from a bout of madness carrying a volume of Seneca's tragedies and saying, "*Vindicta mihi*" (*Spanish Tragedy* 3.13.161); Marston makes fun of his rivals' Senecan pretensions by knocking the stoicism out of Pandolpho in *Antonio's Revenge.*

37. Thus Braden, *Renaissance Tragedy*, p. 113, finds in Jacobean revenge plays "an unclassically dense texture of alternative claims."

38. "Whosoever doth revenge himselfe, committeth sacrilege," according to John Eliot, *Discourses of Warre and Single Combat* (1591), cited by F. T. Bowers, *Elizabethan Revenge Tragedy* (Gloucester, Mass., 1959), p. 44 n. 31; "No man may seek revenge; it is permitted for no reason; can be sought upon no man," according to Nicholas Stratford, *A Dissuasive from Revenge*

And meanwhile in the secular world, where feudal ideals of honor persisted even in the new states,[39] this single act carried two definitions that were
contrary each to the other. As Montaigne observed, "Par le devoir des
armes, celuy-la soit degradé d'honneur et de noblesse, qui souffre une
injure, et, par le devoir civil, celuy qui s'en venge encoure une peine capi-
tale" (*Essais* 1.23: "By the law and right of armes, he that putteth up with an
injurie shall be degraded of honor and nobilities, but he that revengeth
himself of such shall by the Civil Law incurre a capital punishment," in the
translation of John Florio published in London in 1603).[40] Furthermore,
Christian thinkers did not reject all emotion but encouraged a set of pious
passions which included pity and indignant wrath.[41] Indeed Luther had
said that Christians should "on behalf of others . . . seek vengeance . . . [and]
protection," though he did not refer to private violence (*Temporal Authority,*
in Luther, *Works,* vol. 45 [Philadelphia, 1962], p. 101). In sum, the Stoic's
hypothetical act of angry unwisdom, easily repudiated by a reasonable man,
no longer existed. In its place there was a current deed, abhorrent and
damnable, but one to which a good man might be prompted "by Heaven
and Hell" (*Hamlet* 2.2.580).[42] Revenge in the Renaissance was thus intimately dreadful and attractive, as error could never be to a pagan sage, and

---

(1684), cited by L. B. Campbell, *Collected Papers* (New York, 1968), p. 160. On this view, revenge
was simply anti-Christian and so was properly figured by Shylock and Marlowe's Barabas.

39. Florentine humanists distinguished noble rage from common vicious anger; so Pico,
"We should feel anger but within measure; revenge is often a work of justice for each must protect his own dignity" (*Heptaplus* 4.5; see E. Wind, *Pagan Mysteries in the Renaissance* [New York,
1968], pp. 68–69 and 1nn. 56–57). Classical scholars in sixteenth-century France recognized an
"Apolline" vengeance which, unlike vendetta, killed only the guilty and left a miasma that
could be purified; see E. Forsyth, *La tragédie française de Jodelle à Corneille* (Paris, 1962), p. 25.
Members of the seventeenth-century Accademia dei Percossi, founded by Salvator Rosa, discussed questions such as: Is it better to pardon or to take vengeance?

40. Compare the summation of Braden, *Renaissance Tragedy,* p. 114: "Revenge is the aristocratic right of private justice, contested and socially stigmatised by the new monarchies but
neither decisively suppressed nor purged from the general social imagination: both sanctioned
and interdicted, a recurrent point of crisis in the indeterminate character of the aristocratic
identity." This statement limits the ambivalence of revenge to the secular area, but it is a
healthy corrective to the frequent assumption of univalence, according to which any act of
vengeance was simply "the execrable Sinne of Murder"; see, e.g., Campbell, *Collected Papers,* pp.
155–70.

41. E.g., August. *De Civ. Dei* 9.5; both St. Gregory and St. Bernard valued a deliberate anger
which did not "burst forth" but came when called.

42. It is often said that any vengeance killing was unequivocally abhorrent to an Elizabethan or Jacobean audience; so Bowers, *Elizabethan Revenge Tragedy,* p. 82, who claims that as
soon as Hieronimo says "Vindicta mihi" the audience will identify him as a murderous sinner.
Compare A. P. Rossiter, *English Drama from Early Times to the Elizabethans* (London, 1950), p.
169: "By English standards revenge was murder." In fact, however, the popular attitude cannot
have been so simplistic, for the so-called Bond Association of 1584 joined together men who
swore to kill not only anyone who might conspire against Elizabeth but also anyone who would

consequently it was a highly desirable "tenant to tragedy" (Tourneur, *Revenger's Tragedy* 1.1.39–40).

The Old Testament seemed to teach that "whosoever pardoneth murder offendeth against the word of God," and Moses had recognized a "revenger of blood" whose duty it was to kill a murderer who had acted from hatred (Num. 35.19). Instructing such revengers, he had said, "Thine eye shall not pity him" (Deut. 19.13), and the Bible gave splendid examples of obedience to this rule in tales like that of Dinah and Tamar, bloodily avenged by their angry brothers (Gen. 34.27–28). Nevertheless the God of Moses had also plainly announced, "Vengeance is mine," and this was later heard as a divine engrossment of all retaliation. Human revenge was prohibited and Paul even developed its unlooked-for reversal, "Bless them which persecute you," etc. (Rom. 12.19–20; cf. Heb. 10.30). When the blood of a murdered soul "cried loude in the eares of the Lord," as Thomas Cooper put it,[43] the Lord would in principle answer—eventually—with disasters, wars, or miracles, and many popular tales expounded this notion.[44] Meanwhile, magistrates who were God's instruments[45] had exclusive control of all punishment imposed by man (Rom. 13.4). They were "the common revengers," doing "public vengeance," in the phraseology of Cranmer and Latimer.[46] Only through such public officials might Christians continue to take "life for life, eye for eye" as the Old Testament had recommended (Exod. 21.23–24, 25). Which of course meant that, in actuality, though the psalmist had sung of how a righteous man would "wash his feet in the blood of the wicked" (Ps. 58.10), an offended party might have to wait a long time for such refreshment.

John Calvin himself had remarked that God "doth oftentimes so beare with the wicked that, as one asleepe, he doth not only suffer them to take

---

profit by such conspiracy, and his heirs. This retribution, to be dealt out even to people innocent of any plot, was to be achieved "by force of armes" and "by all other means of revenge"— in other words by deceit, if necessary. The Association was very popular, and often the oaths by which one entered it were administered in churches; see R. Broude, "Revenge and Revenge Tragedy in Renaissance England," *Renaissance Quarterly* 28 (1975) 38–58, esp. 50 n. 34; also K. Robertson, "*Antonio's Revenge:* the Tyrant, the Stoic and the Passionate Man," in *Medieval and Renaissance Drama in England,* vol. 4 (New York, 1989), pp. 91–106.

43. *The Cry and Revenge of Blood* (1620), cited by Campbell, *Collected Papers,* p. 158.

44. See Broude, "Revenge," p. 54.

45. "We must referre all judgment to GOD, to Kings, and Rulers, and Judges under them which be god's officers to execute justice. . . . And the same St. Paul threateneth no lesse paine than everlasting damnation to all disobedient persons" (*An Exhortation concerning Good Order and Obedience to Rulers and Magistrates* 1.10.1 [1547], cited by M. Scott, *Renaissance Drama and a Modern Audience* [London, 1982], p. 33).

46. Thomas Cranmer, "A Sermon concerning the Time of Rebellion," in *Miscellaneous Writings* (Cambridge, 1846), p. 193; cf. Hugh Latimer, "Epistle for the Twenty-First Sunday after Trinity," in *Sermons* (Cambridge, 1864), p. 495.

many wicked things in hand; but he also maketh them rejoyce at the success of their wicked enterprises."[47] God's justice could be slow, his earthly representatives corrupt, the machinery of state out of order, so that flagrant wrongs went unpunished, and this is the usual premise of the English revenge play.[48] "O world no world but mass of public wrongs / Confused and filled with murder and misdeeds!" is the cry of Hieronimo in Kyd's *Spanish Tragedy* (3.3.3). Of course the Christian should wait, knowing that patience was the honest man's revenge (Tourneur, *Atheist's Tragedy* 5.2.303), but in these plays "Wrongs unspeakable, past patience" (Shakespeare, *Titus Andronicus* 5.3.120)[49] are committed with impunity, often by the magistrates themselves. And so, when he or someone close to him is wronged, one indignant man responds.[50] His anger is personal—he has a view of himself, his

47. *Commentaries on Genesis,* trans. Thomas Timme (1578), p. 251.

48. By "revenge play" I mean one in which the principal would recover injured honor by return of injury, not advance himself by villainy, and one in which the playing out of his intrigue against his enemy provides the central action. Marlowe's *Jew of Malta* is a special case because Barabas in a sense means to take revenge upon all Christians ("Sometimes I go about and poison wells," 3.3.177), yet has in this particular case been injured not in his honor but in his wealth, so that his intrigue is not given an appearance of justice. Marlowe may mean to suggest that all revenge is anti-Christian, and that what men call honor is only a form of greed, but at any rate this is not a typical "revenge play." Plays like Middleton's *Changeling,* Webster's *Duchess of Malfi,* and even *White Devil,* I leave out because their retaliations, which belong to compound actions, are dictated by villainous self-advancement, not by a need to recover honor after injury.

49. Note Jonson, *Sejanus* 4.1.2, "You must have Patience, royall Agrippina.—I must have vengeance first!" reused by Webster, *White Devil* 3.2.270. Cf. Titus's quotation from Seneca ("tam lentus . . .") at *Titus Andronicus* 4.1.81–82.

50. Revenge was the deed of a masculine principal because women were held to have neither honor nor strength: "Oh woman's poor revenge which dwells but in the tongue" (Webster, *White Devil* 3.2.283–84). Injury to a woman mattered only if it were sexual, and in that case it was to be resented by her male protector, a Titus or a Vindice. Bel Imperia tests the limits of female revenge in *Spanish Tragedy;* she would like to be Andrea's avenger but takes it for granted that she can only harm his killer by refusing him sexual favors which she grants elsewhere (1.4.65–66); she does in fact stab Balthazar in the end, but only as a player in Hieronimo's masque, following the plot that he has authored and produced. The more vocally aggressive Charlotte of Chapman's *Revenge of Bussy D'Ambois* disguises herself as a man and wants to prosecute the action that her brother postpones, but she is ordered away by the ghost (5.3.45). The Evadne of Beaumont and Fletcher's *Maid's Tragedy* functions as killer in the revenge intrigue, but she serves more as instrument than as true female avenger. All the noble male characters of the piece are paralyzed by vows of loyalty to the malefactor, who is King, and all the other women are incapacitated by weakness and modesty. As a noble woman dishonored by the ruler, as a "whore," Evadne is outside all regulation and can do what her brother, the great warrior, cannot, and this is demonstrated by the design of her crime. She persuades the royal victim to be bound by what he thinks a "prettie new device" for some novel and perverse pleasure (5.1.47). When he pronounces the words that ought to disempower any attacker—"I am thy King" (5.1.96)—she answers, "Thou art my shame," and gives him repeated "love tricks" with her sword (5.1.103).

name, his house, that will not allow him to submit to injury—but his action is also necessarily political because it defies authority. Furthermore, it is internally contradictory because such a man's "wilde justice," while it resists the total collapse of civil society, nevertheless threatens all Christian order with its defiance of the state. The revenger attacks a power that is rotten, but he is nevertheless a guilty "traitor," as well as a "damned bloody murderer" (Kyd, *Spanish Tragedy* 4.3.194) who will be tortured in hell. A drama centering on such a principal was necessarily seditious in its tendencies, for, as a Presbyterian opponent insisted, "any description of sin on stage causeth magistrates, ministers and statesmen to lose their reputation."[51] And yet, at a time when production could be forbidden, companies "inhibited," and offensive playwrights jailed, vengeance plays were licensed for performance by the Church, the City, and the Court (or just by the Court, after the accession of James).[52] This was because the poets of revenge had put together a package of conventions by which they might pass, in their dramas, from a rebellious premise to a loyal conclusion. Justice, which appeared to dwell with the hero in the beginning, was made to pass back to the state in the end, and in support of this shift the central action was given a double ethical coloring. At the opening, revenge was an honorable deed done in a context of degenerate public power; but at the end, in the presence of a revived authority now laudable, godly, and pure, it was shown as a dark and punishable crime.

The English revenge play thus consists of a kind of extended Antimasque, capped by the briefest of performances in praise of order and power.[53] Somewhere in a decaying foreign state such as Venice, Spain, or antique Rome, right authority has collapsed and there is "abuse, carnall liberty, enormitie, sinne and Babylonicall confusion."[54] Tyrants destroy order rather than upholding it, and hands, noses, and ears are lopped off right and left, in proof of the community's loss of wholeness. Law courts don't

---

51. William Prynne, *Histrio-Mastix: The Player's Scourge,* ed. A. Freeman (New York, 1974), p. 491; cited by J. Dollimore, *Radical Tragedy* (Chicago, 1984), p. 23. Prynne was objecting not just to revenge plays but to theater in every form.

52. See G. Wickham, *Early English Stages,* vol. 2.1 (London and New York, 1963), pp. 84–94. A preliminary informal censorship was exercised by the companies themselves, since they would accept only plays they judged could pass the ecclesiastical or royal licensing process.

53. On the courtly combination of Antimasque of Vice, followed by Main Masque of Princely Power, see Stephen Orgel, *The Illusion of Power* (Berkeley, 1975), p. 40.

54. *An Exhortation concerning Good Order* (1547), p. 69, cited by Scott, *Renaissance Drama,* p. 33. Compare Robert Bolton: "Take Soveraignty from the face of the earth and you turne it into a Cockpit. Men would become cut-throats and cannibals one unto the other. Murders, adulteries, incests, rapes, robberies, perjuries, witchcraft, blasphemies, all kinds of villainies, outrages and savage cruelty would overflow all Countries. We should have a very hell upon earth, and the face of it covered with blood, as it was once with water" (1621); cited by W. Lamont, *Godly Rule* (London, 1969), p. 49.

function,[55] and no man's word is good: "Faiths are bought and sold, / Oaths are but the skin of gold" (Tourneur, *Revenger's Tragedy* 3.1.6–7).[56] In these conditions the same "tigreish rage" that Seneca's Atreus knew becomes a commonplace, so that Shakespeare's Titus can say, "Dost not perceive that Rome is but a wilderness of tigers? Tigers must prey" (*Titus Andronicus* 3.1.53–54). In demonstration, he begins his play with a human sacrifice and the murder of his own son, in a scene that also shows an armed rebellion and an act of imperial treachery. This filthy world wherein revenge seems clean is also marked by sexual excess. Hamlet is increasingly obsessed not just by the lechery of Claudius but by what he sees as a general lewdness that threatens to prevail even in himself. Aaron and Tamora, united by lust, encourage the psychopathic tendencies of her sons, and Lavinia's stumps and bleeding mouth proclaim the Gothic sexuality that has invaded the Rome of *Titus Andronicus*. The final emblem of sexual chaos is traditionally incest, and Tourneur's Vindice sees a whole city given over to this activity. "Dutch lust! Fulsome lust! / Drunken procreation which begets so many drunkards; / Some father dreads not, gone to bed in wine, / To slide from the mother and cling to the daughter in law . . . Oh hour of incest!" (*Revenger's Tragedy* 1.3.57–66).[57]

Under such circumstances the avenger's indignant individual revolt can appear to be not merely necessary but virtuous. In an Elsinore full of fratricide and lust,[58] Hamlet can momentarily claim to be "heaven's scourge and minister" (3.4.177),[59] and in an Italian city that has become the playground

---

55. "It well becomes that judge to nod at crimes / That does commit greater himself and lives" (Tourneur, *Revenger's Tragedy* 2.3.125–26); cf. the perverted judicial process in the same play (1.2) and also that at Shakespeare, *Titus Andronicus* 3.1. Tourneur gives Vindice an almost Dickensian statement of the interminable ineffectiveness of going to law: "What, three and twenty years in law?—I have known those that have been five and fifty, and all about pullen and pigs" (*Revenger's Tragedy* 4.2.54–55).

56. So Hamlet believes that all good faith is gone; Gertrude's is "such a deed as from the body of contraction plucks / the very soul" (3.4.40).

57. In his revenge trick Vindice actualizes his perception of sexuality as hideous and destructive, using what seems to be a woman's mouth/vagina as a container for poison. The poisoned vagina appears in literal form in the Alexander romance and various Italian revenge tales; see R. Caillois, *Le mythe et l'homme* (Paris, 1981), pp. 66–67.

58. For lust as a figure for general disorder, cf. *Gorboduc* 2.2.89–91: "When growing pride doth fell the swelling breast / And greedy lust doth raise the climbing mind, / O, hardly may the peril be repressed." Beaumont and Fletcher's *Maid's Tragedy* begins with a special form of sexual irregularity, the unconsummated marriage, cruelly emphasized with a great marriage masque. The sense of disorder may be intensified with Senecan suggestions of cosmic disturbance; so Tourneur shows the degenerate ducal court as it makes "an artificial noon" of midnight for its revels (*Revenger's Tragedy* 1.4.27), while it puts "the day out of socket" by performing sex acts in the sunlight (3.5.18–19).

59. Compare Hieronimo: "Heaven applies our drift / And all the saints do sit soliciting / For vengeance on the cursed murderers" (Kyd, *Spanish Tragedy* 4.1.32–34); cf. Titus: "We will

of a dirty old duke, Vindice can argue that his mistress' tarted and poisoned skull kills because "Heaven is just" (*Revenger's Tragedy* 3.5.188).[60] Specific details usually enhance this initial air of justification. The Renaissance avenger, unlike Atreus, is weaker than his enemies,[61] sometimes too young, like Hamlet, sometimes too old, like Hieronimo, and he is usually isolated. Also unlike Atreus, he may not know, to start with, who it is who has done him injury, and so, waiting and dissembling like Hieronimo, he can embody the need for an abstract retaliation before a particular hatred invades him. These avengers are further softened by dramatists who allow them emotions other than rage. Driven to the appointed deed by a feudal honor and something like a Senecan sense of self, the Renaissance revenger may nevertheless feel love and grief along the way, as do Titus and Lavinia, who might "of a fresh fountain make a brine-pit" with their bitter tears for one another (*Titus Andronicus* 3.1.130).[62] Senecan anger made a man ugly while it drove him mad, but loving grief can make the later avenger, if not beautiful, at least humane.

Sometimes in these later plays the audience was asked, in un-Senecan fashion, to share directly in the hero's pain and outrage while a representation or replica of the initial injury was actually staged.[63] So young Horatio, surprised at his tryst, is hanged and stabbed before one's eyes in *Spanish Tragedy,* and in Antonio's Venice the torn body of Feliche is hung out of Mellida's window as a "gory ensign" (much like the corpse of Ned in *Unforgiven*).

---

sollicite heaven and move the Gods / To send downe Justice for to wreake our wrongs" (Shakespeare, *Titus Andronicus* 4.3.52–53).

60. Many critics deny that the hero of an English revenge play could be proposed as sympathetic (see above, n. 42), but this prejudice leads to strained interpretations. So Scott, *Renaissance Drama*, p. 33, insists that Tourneur's Vindice is meant to be repellent from the start, the proof being his praise of Gloriana for her power to rouse lust, and his "prostitution" of her in his intrigue. The poet, however, gives us no reason to suppose that the dead woman would not have rejoiced in the nicety of a scheme by which "the very ragged bone has been sufficiently avenged" (3.5.154–55). For another wholly negative view of Vindice, see N. Brooke, *Horrid Laughter in Jacobean Tragedy* (London, 1979), p. 17, and for an opposite report in which he is fully justified, see S. P. Sutherland, *Masques in Jacobean Tragedy* (New York, 1983), p. 60.

61. This is not true of villain-avengers like Francisco in *White Devil*, nor are such nonprincipals necessarily punished: Francisco himself will go on to rule in Florence, though his bravo, Lodovico, is killed. Nor does the rule of relative weakness apply in the Italian plays of villainous persecution, where tyrants similar to the Piero of *Antonio's Revenge* with impunity work tortures upon the relatives of girls who resist them, the most sensational example being the King in Cinthio's *Orbecche*.

62. Antonio, in Marston's parody of revenge, cries, "Mine's Herculean woe!" and "Pigmy cares can shelter under Patience's shield but giant griefs / Will burst all covert . . . my pined heart shall eat on naught but woe" (*Antonio's Revenge* 2.3.133; 2.3.4–8). On this "pathology of grief," see Hardin Craig, *The Enchanted Glass* (Oxford, 1950), p. 177.

63. In *Hamlet* this is achieved by means of the play within the play; in *Revenger's Tragedy*, through the rape and death of Antonio's wife, though this outrage is not actually played.

We look directly at Lavinia—doubly raped, hands chopped, tongue cut—and listen as one of her attackers snarls, "An twere my case I should go hang myself," while the other sniggers, "If thou hadst hands to help thee knit the cord" (*Titus Andronicus* 2.4.9–12), lines that make the mildest spectator want to kill. In an extension of this device the intended victim of the revenge, the Thyestes figure, may be placed at the center of a circus of villainy. Guilty of many past crimes, he continues on this stage to kidnap, slay, maim, and sequester, not sparing even members of his own family.[64] "Will I not blast my own blood for revenge?" asks Piero, the villain-victim of *Antonio's Revenge* (1.1.85). The victim may also be openly blasphemous, like the same Piero, who would "pop out the lights of bright religion" (4.3.142–43).[65] What is more, the villainous enemies bring with them a multitude of malcontents, hangers-on, and lesser thugs, and these creatures, who have been bought, infect the victims' world with a sordid and treacherous greed. "Where words prevail not, violence prevails; but gold doth more than either of them both," says Lorenzo as he bribes one accomplice to murder another (*Spanish Tragedy* 2.1.108–9).[66] In such a welter of abominations the particular outrage that angers the avenger swells to become criminality itself, and so, in the beginning, the hero can appear as a kind of vigilante whose task it is to purify the corruption of an entire society.

Conventions such as these make victims hateful, along with all their supporters, while the avenger is invested with a general and woeful indignation that affects the audience favorably. Nevertheless the plays of Christian vengeance will impose an opposite set of responses when the disorderly "antimasque" is finally capped by a show of legitimate power. At the very end a good authority will step in, whether he be an alien Fortinbras, a new emperor, or a grieving king of Spain. Burials will signal a return to regularity, public justice will revive, and the new ruler will now "order well the state / That like events may ne'er it ruinate" (*Titus Andronicus* 5.3.203–4). Above all, the hero's attack upon the civil and religious order will be punished, either by his own hand or by another's, showing that "Revenge proves its own executioner" (Ford, *Broken Heart* 5.2.147). Often, indeed, the punishment and the achievement of revenge are simultaneous. Hieronimo bites out his tongue, then stabs himself with the penknife that has just

---

64. The evil brothers of *Revenger's Tragedy* do away with each other so effectively that only Lussurioso is left for Vindice to kill; Piero makes use of Mellida in *Antonio's Revenge;* Aaron of Tamora's sons in *Titus Andronicus;* Lorenzo of Bel Imperia in *Spanish Tragedy.*

65. Compare Claudius's distortions of Christian doctrine at *Hamlet* 3.3.43.

66. Compare Lussurioso: "Discontent and want is the best clay to mould a villain of" (*Revenger's Tragedy* 4.1.46–47). In *Spanish Tragedy* Viluppo has slandered a brave man, "not for Alexandro's injuries / But for reward and hope to be preferred" (3.1.94–95). Greed is universal; as Castiza says, "Were not sin rich, there would be fewer sinners" (*Revenger's Tragedy* 2.1.6).

stabbed the Duke, while Bel Imperia has already killed herself within the death-dealing entertainment that closes the *Spanish Tragedy* (4.4.193). Hamlet takes a fatal wound just before giving one (5.2.279, 305); Clermont masters Montsurry in their duel, then turns his sword on himself in grief over Guise (Chapman, *Revenge of Bussy D'Ambois* 5.5.193); Titus is slain by Saturninus the instant the substance of Tamora's dinner is revealed (*Titus Andronicus* 5.3.72); Hoffman dies tortured by the burning crown (Chettle, *Hoffman* 6.3.136); and Vindice and his brother are hauled off for execution because of their victorious boasts (*Revenger's Tragedy* 5.3.104–5).[67] The one exception[68] is Antonio, hero of Marston's mock tragedy.[69] Having completed his revenge, he is hailed as a savior but refuses honors and retires repenting to a monastery with his accomplices (*Antonio's Revenge* 5.6.29). These final assertions of regular justice are sudden but acceptable because a second set of conventions has worked to debase the same man and the same action that have initially been so cleverly enhanced.

First of all, vengeance and the avenger are polluted by the sordidness of their context. The hero may feel genuine love or grief, but his opponents' displays of lechery and feigned emotion cheapen even true passions. Aaron's ferocious love for his son finally has a damaging effect on our response to Titus' attachment to his children; Piero's unregulated desire for Maria devalues Antonio's love for Mellida, and a general villainous manipulation of tears makes even genuine grief suspect.[70] Meanwhile despicable characters stand about mouthing the word "revenge" and turning it into a common crime.[71] So Piero, who killed a man for marrying the woman he

---

67. Francisco is marched away for execution, Eugenia sent to a convent, at the close of Massinger's *Duke of Milan;* Barabas falls through his own trapdoor, sprung by the Governor, in the last scene of Marlowe's *Jew of Malta;* Charlotte, Tamyra, and the Countess, mere sympathizers, all consider suicide but instead "to cloisters flie / in penance pine" because "too easie tis to die" (Chapman, *Revenge of Bussy D'Ambois* 5.5.208–9).

68. This holds only for the English plays; in Spanish honor plays, the protagonist generally punishes sexual transgression, killing his wife/daughter and her seducer, after which he may be pardoned and rewarded by the ruler.

69. Many critics try to take *Antonio's Revenge* seriously, either as a failed Senecan lesson in the dangers of excess (so Bowers, the Halletts, and G. D. Aggeler, "Stoics and Revenge," *Elizabethan Studies* 51 [1970] 512), or else as a drama in which a Herculean hero cleanses society, "a serious examination of resistance to tyranny" (Robertson, "*Antonio's Revenge,*" pp. 91–106). I find support for my own conviction that the piece is meant as parody in R. A. Foakes, "John Marston's Fantastical Plays," *Philological Quarterly* 41 (1962) 235 ff. It may be worth noting that another burlesque of vengeance was current in 1605, the *Jeronimo* that is sometimes attributed to Kyd.

70. Piero exhorts his subvillain, Strotzo: "Fut, weep, act, feign" (*Antonio's Revenge* 1.5.7), and Ambitioso says almost the same to his brother: "Canst weep, thinkst thou? twould grace our flattery much" (*Revenger's Tragedy* 3.5.35–36).

71. In *Spanish Tragedy* Lorenzo and Balthazar term the removal of a love-rival "revenge" (2.1.134); the fratricidal brothers of *Revenger's Tragedy* have the word constantly on their lips—

himself wanted, says "I burned in my breast / Till I might belk revenge upon his eyes" (*Antonio's Revenge* 1.1.27–30). This counterfeit vengeance is powered by greed or lust, and where it is current, even its honorable doublet loses value. What is worse, the hero is forced to imitate such acts and "equall be with villaines" (*Revenge of Bussy D'Ambois* 3.2.100), since he can only repay degenerate crimes with others that are like them—deaths cruelly prolonged or celebrated by some gory revel. So Vindice literally borrows the intrigue of the villainous traitors when he decides to replicate their masque (*Revenger's Tragedy* 5.2). In his need for blood the revenger himself becomes a kind of cannibal. "I'll suck red vengeance out of Piero's wounds," says Antonio (*Antonio's Revenge* 3.2.78–79), and Hamlet in Senecan mood mutters, "Now could I drink hot blood and do such bitter business as the day would quake to look upon" (3.2.408–10). Usually the revenger adds at least one extra crime, and he tends to take a repellent delight in the "quaintness" of his work: "Twas somewhat witty carried / Though we say it" (*Revenger's Tragedy* 5.3.96–97). He tells unnecessary lies, and the emotions that redeemed him at the start are often feigned, once he is launched. Titus pretends to the madness his grief might well have caused (*Titus Andronicus* 4.3, cf. 3.2.26);[72] Hamlet exaggerates his distraction; Vindice apes melancholy (*Revenger's Tragedy* 4.2.27); Bel Imperia protests false love, and even old

---

e.g., Ambitioso, "O death and vengeance!" (3.5.66); Spurio, "I'll be revenged for all; now hate begin. / I'll call foul incest but a venial sin . . . My revenge is just" (1.2.168–69, 189). Tamora calls her sons to avenge an insult which she has invented as a spur for them (*Titus Andronicus* 3.3.113), and toward the end of the same play Aaron curses the company (perhaps the audience as well): "Vengeance rot you all!" (5.1.58). As in so many points, *Hamlet* is here atypical because its secondary avenger, Laertes, is engaged in a justifiable action against his father's murderer.

72. In case any of the audience might have been taken in by the excesses of the arrow-shooting scene (*Titus Andronicus* 4.3), Titus' shamming is made explicit at 5.2.147: "I know them all, though they suppose me mad." Hallett and Hallett, *Revenger's Madness*, p. 61, treat madness as inseparable from revenge and say that it was "obligatory" in the English plays, but this is inaccurate. These dramas do not equate revenge with madness, nor do they cause the two to overlap, for madness is spoken of and shown to be the effect not of anger, as Seneca would have had it, but of grief: "Is't not wondrous strange / I am not mad," says Antonio, as a measure of his woe (*Antonio's Revenge* 2.4.12–13). The axiom "extremitie of griefes would make men mad" (*Titus Andronicus* 4.1.23) is given fullest demonstration in the nonavenging suicidal Isabella of *Spanish Tragedy*. Through her and figures like her (Ophelia, Lucibella in *Hoffman*, Cornelia in *White Devil*), anger and grief—i.e., revenge and madness—are presented as *alternative* responses to an unjust outrage. The revenge act is not committed in a state defined as madness; the only avenger identified as (briefly) genuinely mad is Hieronimo, in the Don Bazulto scene (*Spanish Tragedy* 3.13.68–174), and he returns to a right perception of reality before the revenge is even planned. We might diagnose Antonio as mad at the time of the murder of little Julio, but the play proposes his state as one of grotesque exaltation but not insanity. It is interesting to note further that feigned madness does not make a character look like an avenger to others; rather it labels him as harmless (e.g., Hamlet; cf. Flamineo at *White Devil* 3.2.305).

Hieronimo mimes loyalty (*Spanish Tragedy* 3.14.139–69).[73] Originally moved in part by love, the revenger may in the onrush of his wrath do harm to his loved ones, as Hamlet does to Ophelia, or Vindice, who saw incest everywhere and lent himself to a plot to debauch his sister. Finally, the justified avenger may, once in motion, swell to an almost Senecan defiance of the cosmos as he substitutes his own "wilde lightning" (*Revenge of Bussy D'Ambois* 4.1.16) for the effects of a slower divinity. So Marston, in his parody of revenge, makes a scene that is reminiscent of Atreus in the ghastly grove, putting Antonio in the Basilica San Marco and causing him to stab a boy he is fond of, not for any cause of justice but as a dedication to Vengeance (*Antonio's Revenge* 3.3.62). He has the illusion of becoming a superman; "Methinks I pace upon the front of Jove," he says, "And kick corruption with a scornful heel, / Griping this flesh, disdain mortality" (3.3.17–19).[74]

As an emblem for the equivocal evaluation of revenge, the later dramatists often employed a spectre like Seneca's Tantalus, "A filthie whining ghost," Comedie calls it, attacking Tragedie in the Induction to *A Warning for Fair Women*.[75] Simply by being Senecan and pagan, such an apparition demonstrated the marginal and exotic locale of the hero's ambivalent crimes, for in the plays' own time the ghost belonged to popular superstition, not to Christian orthodoxy.[76] It might be a shape sent by a good spirit, but it might also be a trick of the devil, as Hamlet at first supposes. In the form of a murdered kinsman, the stage spectre seemed to present dematerialized evidence that the avenger acted according to the command of duty, but such a phenomenon could also suggest a hellish inspiration, especially if accompanied by a Fury. Angelic or the opposite, the ghostly figures staged

73. So also Maria feigns love (*Antonio's Revenge* 5.4.18), Hamlet feigns obedience (4.3.50). Castiza provides a curious case (and one that is not quite relevant since she is no avenger) when she feigns a willingness to become a bawd, to test her mother (*Revenger's Tragedy* 4.4).

74. Cf. 5.3.138, where he likens himself to Christ, "standing triumphant over Belzebub."

75. This scorn may have been inspired by the three ghosts of Peele's *Battle of Alcazar* (1594), for they appeared with "shrikes and clamors" crying "Vindicta." The ghost of Andrea opens *Spanish Tragedy* but never directly influences the action; instead he sits quietly with the more powerful Fury, both as spectators. The ghost of Bussy, by contrast, urges revenge on Clermont (*Revenge of Bussy D'Ambois* 5.1.91 ff.), stops Charlotte when she would usurp the avenger's function (5.3.45), orders doors locked in preparation for the showdown at the end of 5.4, and when the revenge is done leads out more ghosts in a dance of triumph (5.5.119). Marston arranges four appearances for the ghost of Andrugio in *Antonio's Revenge*, causing him to offer information about his own death and to urge revenge (most sensationally during the murder of little Julio, 3.3.30). A ghost may, however, dissuade, like that of Montferrers in Tourneur's *Atheist's Tragedy* (2.6.20–23), who urges Claremont to "leave revenge to the King of Kings." The ghost of Isabella (*White Devil* 4.1.115) is an oddity since it has no effect at all and is dismissed by Francisco as the product of his own melancholy and a distraction from revenge!

76. For popular and orthodox beliefs about ghosts and spirits in sixteenth- and seventeenth-century England, see Campbell, *Collected Papers*, pp. 168–70.

the idea that revenge emanated from an ambivalent corner of creation neither good nor bad, and from powers that love carnage for its own sake.
Andrea's ghost, at the end of *Spanish Tragedy,* counts up the play's nine
corpses and exults, "Aye, these were spectacles to please my soul!"
(4.3.310).

So much doubleness leaves the spectator at a Renaissance revenge drama
pleasurably confused.[77] He is asked to applaud and also to condemn both
the indignant criminal and the flawed order that the criminal attacks. And
this bifurcated emotional response is extorted from him even as he is
deprived of his ordinary identity by the sheer gory excess of the show.[78]
What is worse, self-reference and illusion-breaking wit frequently interrupt
his response to remind him that what he sees and is excited by is sham.[79] So
Vindice, dressed as a reveler, stabs the old Duke's corrupt heir, calling out,
"Mark Thunder! Dost know thy cue, thou big voic'd cryer?" after which,
when the machinery rumbles, he notes, "Where Thunder claps, heaven
likes the tragedy!" (*Revenger's Tragedy* 5.3.42–47; cf. 4.2.196).[80] With these
words, the moment of triumph becomes a hollow boom, the baleful star
that just appeared goes out like a match, and the spectator is left admiring
not the event represented but the manner of its representation. After which
he admires himself for liking something so stylish, and begins to regard the
play as his own plaything.[81]

77. Critics tend to resent this teasing and to assume that the spectator is meant to have a
clean and simple reaction, either condemning or giving approbation to the revenger and his
deed. Thus Bowers, *Elizabethan Revenge Tragedy,* p. 82, reports that Hieronimo is "a villain to the
English audience at the end," whereas J. D. Ratliff believes that the same principal was seen
throughout as "an honorable, justified revenger" ("Hieronimo Explains Himself," *Studies in
Philology* 34 [1957] 118).

78. Gore, like obscenity, makes equals of those who are excited by it; so L. G. Salingar can
say that these plays, in their satiric gruesomeness, incorporate "the harsh levelling tendencies
of the Dance of Death" ("Tourneur and the Tragedy of Revenge," in *The Age of Shakespeare,* ed.
B. Ford [London, 1991], p. 337).

79. As when the ghost in *Revenge of Bussy D'Ambois* says, "Clermont must auchthor be of this
just tragedy" (5.3.45). Because it is parody, *Antonio's Revenge* is peculiarly rich in self-reference:
Piero, in the opening scene, calls for "lowde applause" (1.1.19–20); Antonio, at 2.3.103–4,
says, "Madam, I will not swell like a tragedian in forced passion of affected straines"; Balurdo,
at 2.1.21, enters complaining that he hasn't got his beard stuck on yet, and Piero asks, "Why,
what dost thou with a beard?"—a double joke, since the boys of St. Paul's didn't use stage
beards; Pandullfo, at 4.5.47–51, rejecting his past stoicism, says, "Why all this while I ha' but
played a part / Like to some boy that acts a tragedy, / Speaks burly words and raves out passion."

80. Conceits like this, in which the piece pretended to a power over a pretended nature,
are parallel to the Court conceit of the King's power over the seasons; see Orgel, *Illusion of
Power,* p. 43.

81. A similar return of the spectator to consciousness of his own intellectual position outside the play can be effected by literary allusions such as Hieronimo's volume of Seneca, or the

This conscious spectator is encouraged to view himself as a connoisseur, but he is not allowed to become complacent, for these treacherous plays teach him to doubt his own perceptions, his judgment, even himself. He is confronted with his own image, in the form of onstage audiences made up of villains and dupes, and forced to wonder whether he, any better than they, can take the right sense from a representation. Frequent dumb shows[82] suggest that pomps can render a citizen powerless (e.g., *Titus Andronicus* 3.1) and deceive even rulers (*Revenger's Tragedy* 5.3), and this notion of deceptive illusion is borne out within the action. Characters spy on one another and interpret what they see sometimes rightly, sometimes not;[83] they dress up to trick one another, and the ubiquitous play-within-the-play almost always brings disaster to its watchers.[84] Sometimes the silly inner audience takes a mere illusion to be real, as does Lussurioso, when he is humbugged by Vindice's "drunk scene" with the dressed-up Ducal corpse; there is utter confusion here because the dupe is looking directly at his enemy while he mistakes his own father for that same man (*Revenger's Tragedy* 5.1). Sometimes, as in *Spanish Tragedy*, the stage audience on the contrary misbelieves a visible fact, an actual murder, just because it is offered as illusion, taking a real corpse to be no more than a prop (4.4.52, 66, 88; cf. the actual suicide at 67, and the comment at 69). And yet there is no consistency even in these errors, for the onstage spectator is not always deceived. One of the most tortuous examples of inner theater is provided by the brief masque organized by Tamora (*Titus Andronicus* 5.2), when she

---

references to Ovid's tale of Procne and Philomela in *Titus Andronicus* (2.4.25–27; 4.1.47–48, 52).

82. *Revenger's Tragedy* opens as Vindice watches the pageant of the court which he recognizes as illusion. Three of the five acts of *Antonio's Revenge* begin with some form of dumb show (acts 2, 3, 5), of which the funeral that opens act 2 is especially notable because some members of the internal audience see what makes them weep, others see what lets them anticipate more such killings. In general, see D. Mehl, *Elizabethan Dumb Show* (Cambridge, Mass., 1966).

83. The villains Lorenzo and Balthazar spy on the tryst of Horatio and Bel Imperia and learn a truth (*Spanish Tragedy* 2.4); Lussurioso thinks to find advantage by spying on Spurio and the Duchess but is shown a coupling that puts him in danger (*Revenger's Tragedy* 2.3); Claudius and Polonius spy on Hamlet and Ophelia but are deceived by Hamlet's "turn" (*Hamlet* 3.1); with more success, Piero and Strotzo spy on Antonio to enjoy his suffering, themselves increasing his woe, and so their own pleasure, with musical effects (*Antonio's Revenge* 2.3.125).

84. The use of masques as "murder's best face" and "treason's license" (*Revenger's Tragedy* 5.1.176–77) perfectly expresses the revenge tragedy's premise of radical disorder, since a masque was properly the celebration of established authority, a "mystification of power," in the words of D. Grantley, "Masques and Murderers," in *Jacobean Poetry and Prose*, ed. C. Bloom (New York, 1988), p. 209; see also his "Forms and Functions of the Play within a Play," *Renaissance Drama* 8 (1965) 41–61. The wedding masque of *Maid's Tragedy* is a special case because it comes early and is not part of an intrigue but is instead the poet's ironic comment on the sexual disorder at this imaginary court; see Sutherland, *Masques*, pp. 62–73.

disguises herself and her sons as their own infernal counterparts. She comes to Titus' door as Revenge (with reference, surely, to the Revenge of *Spanish Tragedy*), and she brings along her ministers, Murder and Rape, intending to dazzle an audience she believes to be mad. Titus, however, is sane, and this daring truth-telling masquerade in effect puts Tamora into his power; with her performance she gives him the substance of what she thought to offer only as shadow, the chance to take his own revenge.

This sort of thing leaves the external, uncostumed, and unrehearsed spectator self-conscious and confused. He has been made to wish passionately for an act that will bring both triumph and damnation to a figure he both admires and abhors. He has felt satisfaction and repulsion when that act found its bloody accomplishment, and then he has found righteous relief in its final punishment. These contradictory emotions have invited him to think, but the spectacle has made him doubt the possibility of accurate perception, for as part of an audience he has been defined as a consumer of illusion and one who can be deceived. Order is restored, so order must be an ultimate value, and yet the new emperor may give the revenger's corpse a kiss (*Titus Andronicus* 5.3.162), suggesting that a criminal whose disorderly anger reflects a world of vice can nevertheless be an agent of regeneration! In sum, then, where the Senecan spectator goes back to his practice of virtue fitter than ever and ready to keep emotion penned up, the man who watches the later plays gains no such instructed security. He too has been asked to use his mind, but he has been given no cause to celebrate the power of reason. Rather, he has been made to doubt his own observations, to arrive at contradictory judgments, and to question whether an action can ever be clearly wise and good. Within the play's fiction the times are set right in the end, but out in the hall the audience is left seriously out of joint.[85]

Under the spell of this compound tradition, a modern critic, viewer, or reader turns to the revenge plays of fifth-century Athens with a set of inappropriate expectations. He takes it for granted that vindictive violence is forbidden by reason, Nature, religion, and all civilized communities, so that a revenger is necessarily one who defies both god and the public good. He understands such defiance as an aberration, the product of extreme disorder both of mind and society, and he reads the avenging agent as one who responds to a more or less common injury with a mixture of indignation

---

85. This is why Artaud wrote of *Revenger's Tragedy:* "Nous sommes des hommes qui cherchons à vibrer et à faire vibrer. . . . *La Tragédie de la Vengeance* répond entièrement à notre sens, à notre volonté. . . . [La pièce] est très près de nos affres, de nos révoltes, de nos aspirations" ("Théâtre Alfred Jarry," in *Œuvres complètes*, vol. 2 [Paris, 1976], p. 28).

and unbalanced self-concern[86]—an individual who threatens the very idea of political structure simply because a particular state or institution happens to malfunction. He expects such revenges to be revealed as finally despicable, likened by the company they keep to sordid acts of spite and self-advancement. If he finds himself admiring an Attic revenge principal, the modern scholar or spectator hopes for signs of early reluctance or late remorse, and with or without these he assumes that he will watch the deterioration of a potentially heroic soul, poisoned by passion and the spreading infection of villainy.[87] He promises himself an equivocal pleasure as he admires foulness and frenzy in an increasingly loathsome but gloriously spoken production, and he feels safe in doing so because he is sure that there will be punishment of some sort at the end, when the play finally repudiates its errant, mad, or vicious central character. Generations of scholars have tried to bring Attic revenge tragedy into line with these expectations, tried to find a Hamlet in Orestes, a Vindice in Medea, or an Atreus in Hecuba, but no amount of ingenuity can make the older plays conform. They have another tradition, another ethos, another purpose, and also different and deeper pleasures to offer to an audience.

86. The avenger is an "anxious, hoarding, or extremely narcissistic character, for whom even a slight damage will arouse an intense craving for revenge" (Fromm, *Human Destructiveness*, p. 274).

87. "When indignation against wickedness becomes a passion we all know what a wicked passion it can be," said Gilbert Murray, who wondrously transformed the *Oresteia* into a drama of divine forgiveness (*Aeschylus* [Oxford, 1940], p. 198).

CHAPTER TWO

Odysseus, Pindar's Heracles, and the Tyrannicides

I

When, from the murky complexities of Renaissance revenge, one turns back to the Attic plays, the air can seem painfully clear. Some find the earlier avengers dull by comparison with their later fellows, while others look for elements like neurosis or barbarism as compensations for the cosmic arrogance, feverish elaboration, and self-examining wit that gave the later revenge agents their ambiguous charm. The problem goes deeper than mere characterization, however, because what is missing in the Greek plays is the sense of criminal error. Vengeance had been a positive social act in the imagined past, and even in the fifth century it persisted as a practice which, however limited by legislation, was still regarded as an expense of spirit essential to the survival of the group.[1] It was not opposed to communal institutions but was instead the foundation on which the city's law was raised. This meant that the anger of the Greek revenger, though it might be excessive, was a passion neither unwise nor forbidden, while his deed, instead of being innately evil, was in its simple form admirable. Consequently, where later revenge poets would make criminality partially palatable, the earlier dramatists had to take a case of right resolve and render it somehow troubling and questionable.

A number of Greek myths and legends expressed the idea that all order was founded on vengeance. In the cosmos, the first move toward Olympian government was made, according to Hesiod, when Ge enacted a kind of rape-revenge. Suffering because of Ouranus' outrageous refusal to let her

---

1. There was no general Hellenic prohibition against killing. Empedocles' μὴ κτείνειν τὸ ἔμψυχον was peculiar to his sect (Arist. *Rh.* 1373b).

children be born, she first denounced him as the initial offender before a council of the injured (*Theog.* 166, 172), then made a tricky evil plan (160), and took her eldest son as her kin champion. She hid him in ambush and provided him with a secret weapon (174–75), so that they two might have their vengeance (κακὴν τεισαίμεθα λώβην, 165) upon the unsuspecting god. The attack was a success, the injurious enemy was injured in return, and the result was a new era ruled by gods so closely associated with violent vengeance that, according to ancient commentators, they bore its mark in their name, being called "Titans" (209).[2] When Zeus came back from exile to duplicate this action by tricking Kronos, he appeared more as liberator than as avenger, but the war that followed prepared for the ultimate organization of Olympian rule, so that there is a direct Hesiodic sequence from anarchy to order, the first step being secret, individual vengeance, the second the open punishment of battle.

On earth, the prime example of this ordering Hellenic revenge occurred in Homer's Ithaca, where the first fully recounted act of Greek revenge gave the city peace and permanence. The *Odyssey* is not usually cited in discussions of literary revenge because Odysseus is so far from being a Hamlet or even an Orestes. He does not doubt, he is not reluctant, he has no fear for the health of his soul, nor does he injure himself, go mad, or die as he accomplishes his aim. His revenge does not "bitter . . . back on itself recoil," as Milton thought all vengeance should. Instead, Odysseus moves with easy confidence through experiences essentially comic, and his violence puts him finally where he belongs—in his wife's bed and his father's palace. He is a kind of serial avenger,[3] but his mass killings are not punished, nor do they leave him in need of purification.[4] Rather, they are approved by two communities, one mortal and the other immortal, and they leave peace in their wake. He is certainly an angry man, this inaugural and preeminent practitioner of Greek revenge,[5] but his anger is not inimical to nature or

2. The dubious link between Τιτᾶνες and τίνω proves the strength of the ancient scholars' desire to define Titans as avengers who will themselves be punished.

3. M. Davies, "*Odyssey* 22.274–7: Murder or Mutilation," *CQ* 44 (1994) 534–36, observes a sequence of increasing humiliation, from the killing of the suitors, through the beheading of Leodes, the hanging of the maids, and the mutilation of Melanthion.

4. Odysseus purifies his house (*Od.* 22.481–94) but not his own hands.

5. G. Mylonas discusses battlefield "revenge" in A. J. B. Wace, *A Companion to Homer* (London, 1962), p. 480, and concludes: "To avenge the death of a friend or kinsman by killing his slayer or an opponent of equal or even of lower rank was a common Homeric practice." Such actions, however, are not revenge in the tragic or Aristotelian sense because the provocation was not a gratuitous injury to honor, and because the response is overt and immediate. Battlefield retaliations (e.g., *Il.* 13.414 ff.; 17.34–35, 538–39; 14.470, 482–85) are simply ordinary warfare given a special focus, and Achilles' mistreatment of Hector's corpse is an extended and perverse example of the same. There is however a strong flavor of true vendetta in Nestor's

piety or the secular order; instead it is very like the indignant passion that Aristotle could not but admire. And meanwhile, Odysseus' destruction of the suitors shows all the major structural elements—disguise[6] and recognition, discovery of allies, trick to gain access, public claim to the violent deed, display of victim(s)—as well as many of the favorite elaborations—divine aid, rescue of a female relative, exploitation of a ceremony[7] —that were to mark vengeance tragedy as it developed at Athens. What is more important, the narrative that stretches from book 13 through book 24 of the *Odyssey* fixes the ethical flavor of a Greek act of revenge as fundamentally positive and promising.

The outrage that moves Odysseus is unprovoked, dishonoring, and public, so that crude justice demands that he should return it upon his enemies (*Od.* 13.376). They, however, are many, and indoors in a place of strength, while he is alone and outside. Worse, since he is expected to retaliate, should he appear, they will be on their guard against him. The situation is seemingly impossible, but Odysseus is not really alone. He has a constant divine companion who relieves both him and the poem's audience from any harrowing concern. At the very beginning Athena promises aid and predicts success: "The brains and blood of the suitors will spatter the ground," she says (13.393–95). And she continues to be closely involved in every succeeding move. She sends Odysseus to his first ally but insists on deceit, postponing the recognition so that he can test his friends. She then implements his entry into the palace with the magical disguise that turns him into a shabby old beggar; she supervises the timely removal of arms from the hall (19.252), and it is she, at the crisis, who organizes the presentation of the murder weapon to the avenger (21.1–4). Odysseus' confidence fails just once, immediately before the killings, when he remembers the number of his enemies, but Athena is beside him in a trice. There is noise and lewd laughter in the background, but her voice is perfectly clear: "I am a god,"

---

exhortation at 2.355: "Let no man wish for home until he has slept beside some Trojan's wife and so repaired Helen's capture and its griefs."

6. Odysseus' disguise is of an exceptional sort, being a miraculous transformation (*Od.* 13.430) instead of a mere covering mask or costume, and so it emphasizes the presence of Athena as accomplice. In her admirable discussion, S. Murnaghan may slightly exaggerate Odysseus' control: "Odysseus' disguise is an artificial device that allows him to structure the plot of his return by controlling the timing of his self-revelations so that he can at the proper moment disclose himself like a disguised god" (*Disguise and Recognition in the Odyssey* [Princeton, 1987], p. 53).

7. The exploited ceremony has a threefold expression here: the weapon is introduced as part of a pretended Bride Contest (19.576); the suitors are killed on a day sacred to Apollo (20.156; 23.130); a fictive wedding ceremony is announced to cover the confusion after the killings (23.117–73).

she says, "and I protect you through and through, in every difficulty" (20.47).

With this comfortable assurance Odysseus proceeds to perform his revenge. He has no real fear or doubt because the outcome of his *agon* is happily fixed from above, which means that, with a kind of self-discovery, he can relish his own strength and his talent for deception. When he takes the bow into his hands and tests the string, he recognizes himself as one who uses a vengeance weapon the way a singer does a lyre, in the creation of vital events (21.404–15). He draws a sound from this, his instrument, and his enemies are stricken with a strange melancholy, as if enchanted by a song, while Zeus contributes an intensifying chord (412–13). Odysseus, in other words, is shown to be an artist of revenge like Seneca's Atreus or Corneille's Médée, but Homer makes it plain that Olympus joins in the composition of this angry epic *chef-d'oeuvre* of revenge.

Athena's close presence allows Odysseus to enjoy himself and to decorate his scheme, while the resulting certainty of his audience also lets the poet indulge in a rich multiplication of episodes. The suitors' initial crime is restated in a second, seemingly more sinister form when the intruders plan to murder Telemachus, but instead of producing blood, as it would have done in a Jacobean play, this extra piece of villainy is abandoned because of a sign from heaven and the plotters go back to their banquet (20.240–46). The original outrage is also replicated in forms that are comic and crude, like the flying footstool (17.462; cf. 18.394) and the ox-hoof that is thrown at Odysseus' head (20.299).[8] And meanwhile, the ultimate revenge is likewise given various secondary representations which work to lighten its tone. Odysseus' serious intention is to return an outrage for an outrage (ὑπερβασίην ἀποτῖσαι, 13.193; 22.64, etc.), but success in this project can be promised by something as frivolous as Telemachus' sneeze when his mother wishes that Odysseus were at this moment putting paid to the suitors' insults (17.539–40). Effects of this sort reassure the listener, much as Athena reassures the hero, but the poet is ready to go much further. In book 18 he goes very far indeed, for there he stages a gratuitous fight between Odysseus and Iros and develops from it an essentially comic promise that the suitors are about to suffer.[9]

8. The ox-hoof becomes the basis for a grim joke during the actual vengeance when death is given back to Ktesippos as a return "guest-gift" (22.290–91). These comic outrages were exploited in at least two satyr plays, the *Ostologoi* of Aeschylus (*TrGF* 179–80), and Sophocles' *Sundeipnoi* (*TrGF* 562–71). B. Fenik, in his *Studies in the Odyssey, Hermes* Einzelschriften, 30 (Wiesbaden, 1974), pp. 180–84, plots a curve of diminished success in these attacks, prefiguring the suitors' defeat.

9. A. Lord, *Singer of Tales* (Cambridge, Mass., 1950), p. 175, rightly called this "a frustrated, a vestigial recognition scene"; note *Od.* 18.74, where his splendid leg almost gives Odysseus away. On the scene as a whole, see D. B. Levine, "*Odyssey* 18: Iros as a Paradeigm for the Suit-

At the beginning of this book Odysseus is in the worst position possible. He is in the palace, enclosed and outnumbered by his enemies, and with no knowledge that the bow will soon be put into his hands. It is a life-and-death moment, but just here the singer produces a long and unseemly distraction, a buffoonish event that gains emphasis because it interrupts. The Iros episode is no mere postponement, however, for it is designed as a portent, and it conveys both the shape and the flavor of the violence to come. Homer uses it, in fact, as a kind of play-within-the-play, for his listeners get the pleasure of watching an inner audience of suitors as they applaud a representation of their own imminent destruction. The little drama begins, just as the whole revenge action has begun, when the self-appointed resident beggar, a blustering caricature of the suitors, claims the palace as his own turf and orders Odysseus away (18.10–13). Odysseus responds with a threat, and the suitors at once give a special character to this rowdy quarrel. They want to watch a fight, but there is only one way to move the coward Iros and that is through his stomach. He is known as a greedy-gut (18.2–3), and so the well-fed Antinoos, having threatened him with being eaten by dogs if he loses (18.87),[10] sets a goat's paunch as the winner's prize (44). This in turn attracts Odysseus, who pretends to be reluctant but says that his stomach, his γαστήρ (53), commands him to suffer "for the sake of the tripe." The event is thus frankly defined as a Belly War, an impromptu version of the country rite of Driving Out Want,[11] to be fought between one bald old derelict and another.[12]

---

ors," *CJ* 77 (1982) 200–204, where verbal echoes between this and the slaying of the suitors are noted. R. Merkelbach, *Untersuchungen zur Odyssee*, Zetemata, 2 (Munich, 1951), pp. 86–90, discusses this scene at some length as characteristic of his "Revenge Poem"; he notes as typical the grim humor, the paunch prize, the flabbiness of Iros, and the beggar's bag as mark of victory.

10. Antinoos also threatens to send Iros to the bogey-monster Echetos (18.85, 116; cf. 21.308 and Ap. Rhod. 4.1092), where his ears and nose will be chopped off, a detail that enhances the satyresque tone of the episode.

11. According to the Aristotelian analysis of comedy (*Tractatus Coislianus* 6), Iros would be the impostor who is displaced and stripped of his false attributes by a buffoon. The idea that poverty, sickness, or bad luck might be driven out of house or city, as wealth, health, and good fortune were brought in, took many ritual forms; e.g., the ordering out of the Keres during Anthesteria; the driving away of Boulimia at Chaeroneia (Plut. *Mor.* 693E–F), which is associated with Ar. *Plut.* 873 by O. Kern, "βουλίμου ἐξέλασις," *ARW* 15 (1912) 642; the inscribing of doors with invitations to Heracles to enter, as at Thasos (*BCH* 86 [1962], 608–9). For an early poetic version of such a ritual, see Thgn. 351–54, where Penury is ordered out of the singer's door and into someone else's house. In general, see W. Burkert, *Structure and History in Greek Myth and Ritual* (Berkeley, 1979), pp. 64–67; J. N. Bremmer, "Scapegoat Rituals," *Harv. Stud.* 87 (1983) 299–320.

12. For Odysseus' present baldness, note 13.430–37, 18.355, and for the baldness of the satyrs, Aesch. *Dictyoulkoi* 474 *Supp. Aesch.*, where the sense is probably obscene; cf. Soph. fr. 171 *TrGF* = 173a *TGF*.

The bored suitors encourage the performance with jovial delight, and the poet takes the opportunity to show how blind they are and how foolish. When Telemachus announces that he will be the enemy of any man who strikes the "new beggar" (18.61–65), he uses conscious irony,[13] but Antinoos is made to propose, without knowing what he says, that the winner shall have a permanent and exclusive place in the house (18.48–49). Then the suitors, with a broader effect, curse themselves by praying that Zeus will grant the victor "all that his heart desires" (18.111–12), and Odysseus marks the double sense of these words by hailing them as an omen (18.117). Finally, when he, the upstart, fells the resident glutton with his first punch, the malicious poet reports almost with a wink that the suitors all "die laughing" (γέλῳ ἔκθανον, 100). They continue to hoot when Iros is dragged out and set up in the courtyard as the deposed Beggar King (100–107), not understanding that this carnivalesque figure represents themselves as they soon will be. Their laughter, indeed, resounds throughout this book (at 35, 40, 111, 350; echoed by the women at 163, 320; cf. 21.376, the suitors' last laugh), an oxymoronic prelude to their coming slaughter.

The Belly War of book 18 comes to its appropriate end with eating (118–21), dancing (304–5), saucy words from a lewd maid called Black Girl, child of Trickster (321),[14] and a final cup of wine (418). Furniture is clumsily tossed about (394), but Odysseus, the Beggar Victor, stands quietly beside a torch that makes his bald head shine out over the brawl, looking for all the world, as Eurymachus notes with truth-telling scorn, as if a god had sent him (351–55). The whole episode thus has the shape as well as the mood and the grotesque look of a satyr play. Here in the epic narrative, however, it comes before the tragic deed instead of after, and as a result the killings to follow are invested from the start with its crude statement that the bad must bleed while the overweening hero gets his reward.

The Iros episode is perhaps a low form of audience reassurance, but encouragement of a more elevating sort comes from the sequence of recog-

13. Conscious irony is characteristic of stage avengers as they make their final preparations for the act of violence—e.g., Soph. *El.* 1451 ff., Eur. *Hec.* 1022.

14. Some deny that her name carries any such sense; see, e.g., H. Erbse, *Beiträge zum Verständniss der Odyssee* (Berlin, 1972), pp. 238–40, where it is argued that there are three men named Dolios, all with slave status rather than trickery indicated in their names. The derivation from *dolos* was reasserted by A. Heubeck, *BiOr* 30 (1973) 481, and recent opinion admits that the man so called may be proposed by the poet as the father, both of Melantho and Melanthios, and also of the six stalwart sons of book 24; see Fenik, *Studies*, p. 192. The sharply differentiated sets of children, the disloyal and the loyal, are usually explained on the grounds of realism, i.e., good fathers do sometimes have wicked children (so Fenik, *Studies*, p. 192). It would seem possible, however, that in archaic thought Dolos was like Eris or Elpis, a concept whose good and bad aspects might be described through good and bad offspring.

nitions that defines Odysseus' progress toward ultimate satisfaction.[15] The report of a meeting of friends long separated is a fictional event that naturally produces joy in an auditor; a god is proverbially present in such a moment, and the world seems to be on the right track. Recognition is moreover particularly important in tales of revenge because it is the opposite of disguise, the dropping of a mask, or in this case of wrinkles and rags (21.221; 22.1). By making himself known, the agent signals that he is about to return to the ordinary world that is not controlled by his plot, there to reclaim his original self, as it was before he suffered injury. Knowing all this, the *Odyssey* poet gives the central deed of bloody vengeance a double wrapping of reunions, as if in this way to absorb the gore. Two great recognitions, one with his son and the other with his wife, flank the avenger's killings so that the palace mayhem is both prepared and followed by powerful emotions of love and delight. In parallel fashion two lesser recognitions, those with Euryclea and Eumaeus, mark and sweeten the inner moments of the intrigue as Odysseus makes sure of his intimate allies.[16] And finally there is the fifth recognition, the greatest of all, which is kept to the end so that the revenger's ugly revelation of himself to his enemies in the moment of violence (22.35–41) may be capped by the kiss he gives to his father when at last he says to him, "Here I am, it is I" (24.321). In this ultimate recognition scene the poet produces the emblem of orchard trees counted and standing in cultivated order;[17] the literal trees are among the recognition tokens (24.336–44), but the tranquil image also works to counteract the powerful previous image of wounded men stampeding in confusion (22.299–309). And in confirmation of this recovered order the poet brings divinity directly into the ultimate recognition by making Athena supervise the bath that rejuvenates Laertes while it marks the end of his self-imposed exile (24.367–69).[18] As the avenger's god-given disguise has let Odysseus kill the enemy suitors, so now its removal brings this old king who longed for death (15.353–55) back to a rich life, and the singer, by noting Laertes' brief loss of consciousness (24.345–48), gives this return a look almost of resurrection.

The paternal recognition that comes after the killings suggests that the vengeance was somehow life-giving, and this notion is related to a second positive motif. Homer has shown how Odysseus passed, by way of domestic

15. On the sequence, see C. Whitman, *Homer and the Heroic Tradition* (Cambridge, Mass., 1958), pp. 301–5.

16. Murnaghan, *Disguise,* p. 19, notes these recognitions as bringing "metaphorical kinship" to Euryclea and Eumaeus.

17. See W. B. Stanford, "The Ending of the Odyssey," *Hermathena* 100 (1965) 7–8, 13.

18. Cf. 16.194–200, where the recognition between Odysseus and Telemachus works like a rejuvenation.

violence, from the condition of city-sacker to that of city-ruler. And he has also shown how Telemachus has concurrently changed from the boy who dodged his mother's eye, from the youth who was checked by *aidos* in Nestor's presence, to one who could serve as his father's ally. Telemachus learned a shared adult secret in the dark storeroom when Athena's golden lamp[19] appeared among the arms (19.33–35), and under that goddess' eye he later received a token wound, a cut on the wrist (23.277), during the melee in the hall. Now, in the sequel to the final recognition, he puts on full armor and is formally received as a member of his *genos*, a man who is trusted now to stand in open warfare beside the patriarch of his family (24.506–9, 510–12, 514–15). Odysseus' recovery of his own full honor and identity thus coincides not only with Laertes' revival but also with Telemachus' advance to manhood.[20] His act of vengeance, in other words, is seen to restore to his father the power to kill enemies (note 24.522–23), while it also promises that same power to his son, bringing the one from senility, the other from boyhood, into the fighting band.[21] And it increases the numbers of that band in another way as well, for the two herdsmen who helped exterminate the suitors have been promised brides, houses in the polis, and the rank of companion and brother to Telemachus (21.213–16; cf. 14.56–71). In some sense, then, the killing of the intruders has worked like the killing of a bogey in an initiation trial, for it has confirmed the status of all concerned as members of the warrior class.

Odysseus' revenge was necessary to his private identity: only when it was done could he lie in his marriage bed and mean "I, Odysseus" when in his tale-telling he said "I." It was also necessary to the preservation of his *genos* and its position in Ithaca. The Iros episode adds the sense that these massive killings were likewise required for a return of Plenty to the land, and the image of the orchard enhances this effect. Nevertheless, if revenge was to be attached only to the survival of a nobleman and his clan in physical security and well-being, the *Odyssey* would surely have ended with the sweet, care-dispelling sleep into which the hero sinks at the close of book 23 (342–43).

---

19. H. Lorimer, *Homer and the Monuments* (London, 1950), p. 429 n. 1, held that this lamp was anachronistic and so a proof that the storeroom scene was an Attic interpolation. In answer, R. Pfeiffer, "Die goldene Lampe der Athene," *Stud. Ital.* 28 (1956) 426–33, argued that here, as at *Batrachomyomachia* 180, the lamp is a Mycenaean actuality remembered in the Geometric period and associated especially with the cult of Athena. If this is true, its mention will enhance the already heavily ritualistic air of Telemachus' visit to a dark place filled with symbols of war.

20. Some of these notions are discussed by C. W. Eckert, "Initiatory Motifs in the Story of Telemachus," *CJ* 54 (1963) 49–57.

21. Compare D. Wender, *The Last Scenes of the Odyssey, Mnemos.* Suppl. 52 (Leiden, 1978), p. 68: "The third purpose of the battle episode is to show the three generations . . . fighting side by side."

And it does not. The *Odyssey* that we have—the poem the fifth century knew[22]—goes on to raise and answer questions about the political and social organization of the Ithacan community before its bard strikes his last chord.

Good omens and positive ritual models are all very well, but violent retaliation in any but a fairy-tale world will probably produce an answering act of violence. The pick of Ithaca's young men were destroyed by the avenging Odysseus (23.111–40), and unless these victims can somehow be rendered beyond revenge (νηποίνοι, as promised at 1.378–80 and 2.143–45), there will be no rest for the returned hero. A counter-revenge is the immediate prospect at the end of book 23, and an endless cycle of violence threatens here in Ithaca just as it does at the beginning of Aeschylus' *Eumenides*. Homer sees the prospective chaos as secular civil war, not invasion by underworld demons, but the problem in both cases is essentially the same. A distinction is needed by which crimes that are gratuitous, unjust, and open to revenge can be separated from answering crimes, acts that restore balance and therefore are not to be returned. The listener has known all along that Odysseus' slaughter of the suitors was a just and god-sponsored return of wrong for wrong, but he needs to know also that the world of this fiction has recognized it as such—that the killing of the suitors will be allowed to stand as a terminal crime, not as a new provocation. Such reassurance is the burden of book 24, where a demonstration very much like that of the later Aeschylean tragedy is offered.

Homer, like Aeschylus, brings his tale of revenge to an end with a three-phased judgment rendered in the underworld, in the city, and among the Olympians. First, in Hades, the complaints of the dead suitors (who parallel the later Furies) are rejected by an Agamemnon judge who candidly admires Odysseus' violent return and, with his praise of Penelope

---

22. The ending of the *Odyssey* seems to have been revised in the sixth century, probably at Athens in connection with the Panathenaic performances. This means that book 24 as we have it must reflect attitudes of that time. Whether or not the changed ending was meant to enhance the power of Pisistratus, the new version would not have found acceptance, would not have become canonical, unless it provided the close that audiences wanted. Thus the argument of S. West, "Laertes Revisited," *PCPS* 35 (1989) 113–43, seems inconsistent: that book 24 was added in the sixth century; that sixth-century opinion demanded punishment for vengeance; that book 24 pleased an Athena-sponsored tyrant by giving divine confirmation to vengeance! The weak link is the assumption that consumers of epic poetry "could not tolerate supermen pursuing private vengeance" (132); the existence of book 24 would seem to prove the opposite. C. Catenacci, "Il finale dell'Odissea," *Quaderni Urbinati di Cultura Classica* 44 (1993) 7–22, notes Else's suggestion (*Hermes* 87 [1957] 36 ff.) that book 24 may have been in position early in the century, ready to be imitated by Pisistratus. Catenacci extends this idea by arguing that a traditional Tale of Return existed, one that always ended with violent punishment of enemies, reconciliation, purification, and the beginning of a new Golden Age; this was the shape claimed by propagandists for the return of Pisistratus, and also the shape that determined the new ending for the *Odyssey*.

(24.194–202), gives implicit recognition to the husbandly act of punishing would-be adulterers. Next, aboveground in Ithaca, the citizens divide (24.463–64) like the jurors of the *Eumenides,* some supporting the fathers of the suitors (24.426–37), others arguing that Odysseus' action was both encouraged by gods and provoked by crimes that were large-scale and outrageous (24.443–49, 454–60). Finally Athena puts the case to Zeus, and he determines that the revenge she has sponsored must not lead to retaliation or punishment of any kind. Instead it is to become the foundation of a new civic order based on reciprocal friendship and productive of riches and peace (24.479–86). And so the *Odyssey* ends, much as the *Oresteia* does, as Athena stops an earthly conflict between those who would punish an avenger and those who see his crime as a necessary and valuable action. She sets the terms of agreement, fixes the oaths on which the institutions of the city will depend (24.531–48), and arranges that Vengeance, with the gods' help, shall have given Ithaca an enduring political order.[23]

II

In the *Odyssey,* vengeance completes and confirms a return from war to peace. It is initiatory and congruent with a rite of Driving Out Want; it is approved by Zeus, and its heap of corpses produces a rich, orderly, and aristocratic city. When revenge is figured by Heracles instead of Odysseus, this same act is at once more primitive and more sublime, its effects reaching downward to establish rules for ordinary behavior, upward to describe a scheme of heavenly order. The Heracles of folktale was a picaresque and often vicarious avenger who worked outside both house and city, answering assaults on any man's plainest rights: to strike back when struck, to keep one's property, to rest, to be paid for work, to sacrifice correctly, and to be purified. Many of the Heraclean retaliations are brutish and not technically revenge, such as returning the blow when his music teacher hit him (Apollod. *Bibl.* 2.4.9),[24] or tying up the Kerkopes when they would not let

23. What is forbidden, at the poem's close, is not vengeance but any retaliation against this act of revenge. This is not, however, the common report; see, for example, J. Svenbro, "Vengeance et société en Grèce archaïque," in *La vengeance,* ed. R. Verdier, vol. 4 (Paris, 1981), pp. 47–63, who claims that the end of the *Odyssey* envisions a simple interdiction of all vengeance which, he believes, is now definitely situated in the past (53–54). It may be noted that Svenbro nevertheless supposes that Odysseus' killing of the suitors would have been classified as justifiable homicide in sixth-century Athens (p. 52).

24. Apollodorus made Heracles justify himself with a rule from Rhadamanthys: "One who defends himself from an initial unjust blow goes scot-free." This episode, which may not be older than the turn of the sixth to the fifth century, is a vulgarized version of Apollo's killing of Linos; it was the subject of a satyr play by Achaios in which Iphicles may also have figured as a pupil of Linos. F. Brommer, *Herakles II* (Darmstadt, 1984), p. 6, lists eight red-figure vases that

him sleep.[25] Such angry returns became favorite subjects with vase painters and the makers of satyr drama,[26] but monstrous and buffoonish as they often were, they worked to define a basic human order. So Lityerses, a field owner who killed his captured laborers when their task was done, was repaid in workmanlike fashion by a Heracles who cut off his head like an ear of grain (Theoc. 10.41 and schol.).[27] And Busiris, when he presumed to use Heracles for a human sacrifice, was slaughtered along with his son by a "victim" who first knocked down a variously reported number of Egyptian priests (Hdt. 2.45; Apollod. *Bibl.* 2.5.1; Hyg. *Fab.* 56).[28] There was moreover a multiform Peloponnesian legend about the usurper Hippocoön that associated Heracles directly with the terminology of vengeance. In return for an outrage offered, Heracles had killed this man and at least ten of his sons, an exploit that he then commemorated by founding a sanctuary in honor of Athena of Vengeance Deserved (Paus. 3.15.3, 6).[29] As to the initial crime that brought such a response, there were at least three versions: in one tale Hippocoön had refused, when Heracles came to Sparta asking to be cleansed of blood taint;[30] in another the sons of Hippocoön had tried to steal brides belonging to Castor and Pollux (Clem. Al. *Protr.* 2.30.5); in a third the Hippocoöntids had perverted the principle of revenge by wounding Heracles and killing his cousin in return for a stone thrown at a dog (Paus. 3.15.3–6; 19.7; 8.53.9). By the first of these, then, purification was added to the list of simple rights guaranteed by Heraclean force; by the second, the custom of betrothal was supported, while the third offered a discrimination between improper and proper acts of retaliation. In all three

---

probably predate Achaios and so disprove Welcker's presumption that the story was invented for the satyr play; see *LIMC* s.v. "Heracles," pp. 1666–73.

25. Nonnus, *Narr. ad Greg.*, Westermann, *Mythogr.* 375; see Brommer, *Herakles II*, p. 28, and Adler, *RE* s.v. "Kerkopen."

26. See S. P. Karouzou, "Ἡρακλῆς σατυρικός," *BCH* 60 (1936) 152 ff.; D. F. Sutton, *The Greek Satyr Play* (Meisenheim, 1980), passim.

27. The story seems to have been used by Euripides in his satyr play *Theristai* (see P. Girard, "La trilogie," *Rev. Et. Grec.* 17 [1904] 149), as it was later in another satyr play, the *Daphnis* of Sositheos, where the motif of a rescue for the enslaved Daphnis was added to the vengeance (Ath. 10.415b; schol. ad Theoc. arg. and 8.93). The tale served as aition for a harvesting song (Poll. *Onom.* 4.54), and probably reflects some form of field magic.

28. See Brommer, *Herakles II*, pp. 42–46, who lists thirty-one pictorial representations, the earliest a sixth-century sherd from Selinunte, all ceramic, almost all Attic, all found outside mainland Greece; in all scenes Heracles attacks a plurality of Egyptians who usually have some attribute of sacerdotal office. On the Euripidean *Busiris*, see B. Snell, "Der Anfang," *Hermes* 91 (1963) 495; also Sutton, *Satyr Play*, pp. 59–61.

29. See Brommer, *Herakles II*, pp. 42–46.

30. Paus. 3.15.3. The motif of refusal to purify also appears in the tale of Neleus as the initial injury that provoked the killing of twelve of that king's sons (schol. *Il.* 22.336; schol. Pind. *Ol.* 9.43; Diod. Sic. 4.31.4; Apollod. *Bibl.* 2.6.2). For the various tales, see D. L. Page, *Alcman, the Partheneion* (Oxford, 1951), pp. 30–33.

there is, to the modern ear, a gross disproportion between provocation and return, but this seeming excess was not marked by the ancient storytellers, and Pausanias notes that this was the one action of Heracles that Hera did not oppose (3.15.7).[31] What is more, Alcman chose this vengeful slaughter of the ten Hippocoöntids as a subject appropriate to a festival song that gave praise to its own ten girl-singers and also to heaven's fated order, as supported by the punishment that comes from gods (σιῶν τίσις, *PMG* 1.36).[32]

Another more notorious and more complex tale offered a clear discrimination between the permissible and the impermissible in vengeance violence. In some tellings of the story of Oechalia, Heracles was denied the bride-prize he had won in an archery contest, after which he was insulted at the table of the king of that place (Hes. fr. 229 M-W; schol. Eur. *Hipp.* 545). Consequently, when Iphitus, one of the king's sons, later came to Tiryns, the hero used a tricky strategy (Pherecydes *FGrH* 3F82b), feigned friendship like the Senecan Atreus, drew the boy into his palace, took him to the top of its great wall, and threw him down to his death (*Od.* 21.13–29).[33] This action provoked Zeus' anger, but not because revenge was wrong, not because Heracles had calculated the boy's lost life as the equivalent of his own lost dignity, and not because a father's wrongdoing was returned upon a son. The excessive repayment and the innocent victim were not the issues addressed by tellers of this tale. Instead, they showed a Zeus who was out-

---

31. One might infer from Pausanias 3.14.6 that the killing entered into the aetiology of certain Spartan ephebic rituals celebrated in that part of the Dromos where there was a tomb of the Hippocoöntid Eumedes and a statue of Heracles.

32. We don't know what he proposed as the initial offense, but Alcman evidently referred to a postponed and covert response in the true style of revenge. E. Robbins, "Alcman's *Partheneion:* Legend and Choral Ceremony," *CQ* 44 (1994) 7–16, esp. 12, argues that Heracles had no part in the myth represented by Alcman, but to reach this conclusion he has to discount the testimony of the scholiast at Clem. Al. *Protr.* 2.36.2. Cf. O. Gengler, "Les Dioscures et les Apharétides," *LEC* 63 (1995) 1–21.

33. For the death of Iphitus, see also Soph. *Trach.* 252–83 and schol. ad 266; Herodorus of Heracleia 31F37 *FGrH;* Diod. Sic. 4.31 and 33.5; Apollod. *Bibl.* 2.611 ff. The punishment under Omphale seems to have been treated in Panyassis' *Herakleia;* see G. Huxley, *Greek Epic Poetry from Eumelos to Panyassis* (Cambridge, Mass., 1969), pp. 177–81. It is the opinion of M. Davies that Creophilus' *Siege of Oechalia* paired the Iphitus killing with the final military revenge; see *EGF* pp. 149–153; "Lichas' Lying Tale," *CQ* 34 (1984) 480–91; also *Sophocles, Trachiniae* (Oxford, 1991), pp. xxiii–xxix. W. Burkert, however, would limit the contents of the epic to what is indicated in Hes. fr. 220: Iole is won, but refused to Heracles, who kills father and brothers and sacks the city, then dies and is taken to Olympus; see "Die Leistung eines Kreophylos," *MH* 29 (1972) 74–85. Vase-painting evidence proves only that a popular connection was made, in the sixth and early fifth centuries, between the Oechalian archery contest, Iole, and the killing of some or all of her male relatives by Heracles. The earliest illustration, a Corinthian column crater of about 600 B.C., puts Heracles inside Eurytus' house as a guest, but there are no representations of the death of Iphitus at Tiryns; see *LIMC* s.v. "Iole I" and "Iphitus I," and also Brommer, *Herakles II,* pp. 23–26.

raged because Heracles had flouted the laws of hospitality while avenging a breach of the same (schol. M ad *Od.* 21.22).[34] The revenge was objectionable, in other words, not because it was exaggerated or inhumane, but because in its replication of the inaugural offense it broke a divine regulation. This is made clear in the design of Zeus' punishment, which required the man who had misbehaved as lordly host to suffer as servile guest, his masculinity enslaved in the house of a female host, Omphale. Once his violation of divine law had been repaired by this temporary assumption of the role of mistreated *xenos,* Heracles returned to Oechalia for a rectified vengeance which included the siege of the city, the slaughter of its king and many of its citizens, and the capture of its princess. The epic versions ended with a magnificent dedication of spoils to a now placated Zeus, and in Hesiod's telling, at any rate, this enormous act of revenge was followed at once by the reception of the hero on snowy Olympus (fr. 229 M-W).[35]

Heracles' angry and sometimes grotesque retaliations were remembered among the inaugural acts of Hellenic culture because they seemed to project the same primitive violence that, in latent form, allowed Zeus to organize the cosmos. Heraclean revenge and the Olympian order stood in a harmonious relation to each other in the popular view, and this was one of Pindar's central tenets. It has its most extensive statement in *Olympia* 10, where the games at Olympia, the terrestrial reflection of the cosmic order, are made to rest directly upon a vengeful Heraclean action. The poet is here celebrating a boy victor in a song whose inner theme is the return of *charis* for *charis,* but he designs his ode so that the actual gracious repayment of song for deed shall derive from, and be juxtaposed with, a return of the opposite sort, one of harm for harm, while he also shows the foundation of the contest itself to have been an act that, like the present ode, contained the reverse passion of anger within its gratitude. The chorus sings of how, at the tomb of Pelops, a hero who is not at first named

> . . . established six contests
> after he killed flawless Cteatus,
> son of Poseidon,
>
> killed Eurytus too. That he might
> with all his will take from unwilling Augeas

---

34. That throwing a guest off the wall was fictional shorthand for a hospitality crime is proved by *Od.* 14.399–405. Sophocles, at *Trach.* 277–78, makes Lichas base Zeus' anger not on the misuse of *xenia* but on the use of *dolos,* but he is explicitly telling a lie.

35. The similarities between the rites described by Bacchylides and Sophocles strongly suggest that there was a final sacrificial scene in their common source, a poem by Creophilus: at Bacchyl. 16.16 the place is ἀμφικύμον' ἀκτάν, at Soph. *Trach.* 752 it is ἀκτή τις ἀμφίκλυστος; at Bacchyl. 16.18 twelve animals are sacrificed (nine bulls for Zeus, two for Poseidon, an ox for Athena), at *Trach.* 760 twelve bulls for Zeus.

an exceeding rough wage for the old service,
waiting in hiding under Cleonae, he—Heracles!—
struck down these two as they moved along, for so
had they ambushed his Tirynthian host
when it lay in the Elean valley,

they, the arrogant Moliones. And it came true:
soon after, the King of Epeians, cheater of guests,
saw his rich heritage sink to the sewer of doom,
victim of grim flame and iron weaponry.
The attack of superior strength
cannot be turned away.
He in his folly held out to the last
but did not escape steep death;

the other, the valiant son of Zeus, assembled his men
at Pisa with all the populace, and there he measured out
a sacred grove as gift to his father, god of power and might.

(Pind. Ol. 10.24–45)

With this as his chosen foundation myth, Pindar makes Heracles' positive gesture of grateful dedication depend immediately and physically upon an act of vindictive reparation. In fact, the ring structure of this passage creates a sacred Olympian rite that, in the listener's experience, contains the bloody revenge, as the sung act of establishment (ἐκτίσσατο, 25 ... σταθμᾶτο, 45, continued in the following verbs, 46–58) is interrupted and invaded by slaughter and siege (26–42). What is more, the narration of this contained causal event is designed so as to make it almost gratuitously vengeful. The irreducible content of the tale is Heracles' victory over Augeas: this provided the spoils that were brought to Olympia, while it also supplied a mythic analogue to the victor's deed, and produced the notion of the ultimate payment of the unpaid wage which was necessary to Pindar's private conceit about the unsung song. The destruction of the king is the core of the mythic example, and yet it is treated in these lines as a mere necessary sequel; the successful siege does no more than flesh out a gnome which subsumes Augeas into a standard type of the fallen ruler and hides Heracles in the plural anonymity of "those with superior power" (30). What counts instead, in this epinician telling, is the preliminary guerrilla attack on the sons of Molione[36] and the finite double killing so emphatically wrought (πέφνε ... πέφνε, 27–28, linking strophe and antistrophe) by a

---

36. Tradition made Cteatus and Eurytus a pair of Siamese twins (Hes. fr. 17a. 17–18 M-W; Ibycus 285 *PMG;* Pherecydes 3f *FGrH*). Pindar, however, does not encourage his listeners to picture them in this way.

hero[37] who had been lying in wait. This sung deed is, by the poet's insistence, a furtive and premeditated act, a true revenge that returns ambush for ambush,[38] an unchivalrous attack upon enemies who are unprepared; indeed the singers may even suggest (with the ἐφ' ὁδῷ of line 30) that the Moliones were on their way to the games and consequently protected by the Isthmian truce.[39] What is more, Pindar causes Heracles' name to come out of hiding just here, so that the hero seems to lay personal claim to his vengeful victory (δάμασε . . . Ἡρακλέης, 30). So far as this song goes, this covert revenge is Heracles' vivid and definitive exploit, and it leads directly to the orderly measurements, the consecrations, the sacrifices, and the future victories that fill the rest of the ode.

In *Olympia* 10 Pindar brings vengeance into a causal connection with the great regulated festival of Zeus, much as in *Olympia* 7 he connects Tlepolemus' vengeful killing of Likymnios with the contests and sacrifices that marked the Heraclid beginnings on Rhodes.[40] At the same time, with his exploration of notions of indebtedness, he gives poetic expression to the fundamental Greek sense that revenge and gratitude are the opposite faces of a single great rule demanding a return of like for like. He, the epinician poet, owes a debt of praise for the boy-victor's fine achievement (*Ol.* 10.3), just as Hagesidamus himself owes gratitude to his trainer (16–21), but the poet has left his debt long unpaid. In this he is like Augeas, who failed to pay another kind of debt, and this congruency, reversed, suggests a solution to the poet's problem. Heracles, in that story, compensated for his own delay in settling his old score by adding interest to his repayment: to the defeat that balanced Augeas' injury (itself a failure to pay), he added his ambush of the king's former allies. What is more, he transformed his delayed retaliation into a magnificent gesture of gratitude to Zeus, and this is just what

37. At Ibycus 285.2 *PMG* the verb for this killing is plural (unless it is first person), which seems to indicate another version of the ambush in which Heracles was accompanied by Iphicles; later stories made him avenge previous injuries to Iphicles, as well as the Moliones' service with Augeas (Paus. 8.14.6).

38. D. L. Burgess, "Pindar's *Olympia* 10," *Hermes* 118 (1990) 273–81, asserts that this action is meant to be "unheroic," but there is no sign of Pindaric denigration; ambush is required, if the debt of injury is to be perfectly repaid, and it is also a youthful form of attack suitable to a hero who decorates an ode for a youthful victor.

39. Later sources include this detail: Diod. Sic. 4.33.3; Paus. 5.2.1.; Apollod. *Bibl.* 2.7.2. If this is what Pindar hints, then the vengeance also included the motif of the perverted religious ceremony, but P. Angeli Bernardini, "Eracle, i Molioni e Augea nell'*Olimpica* 10," *Quaderni Urbinati di Cultura Classica*, n.s., 11 (1992) 55–68, asserts that Heracles' crime is being placed in the category of highway killings, as manslaughter.

40. So also at Delphi, Apollo's revenge upon Telphusa was said to lie immediately behind the organization of cult there (*Hymn. Hom. Ap.* 375–87), though this is not a known Pindaric topic.

Pindar means to do. He appropriates the Olympic foundation as the substance of his own repayment with interest (9), and gives his ode an extra magnificence by filling two triads with a history of the games.[41]

Pindar forced elements of revenge into the Elean campaign and thence into *Olympia* 10 so as to color the radiance of Zeus' festival with Heracles' devious ferocity. Pausanias fussily remarked that the Augeas episode was less than brilliant (5.2.1), and a modern ear may be frankly shocked because Heracles suggests a creature that we greatly fear, the angry man who thinks he is an instrument of god. For Pindar, however, the exploit was perfectly appropriate to an Olympian ode because Heracles was in all truth part of a divine scheme. His outrageous force (τὸ πάντολμον σθένος Ἡρακλέος, fr. 29.4 Snell-Maehler) was a splendid topic which could be hymned next to the joyous rites of Dionysus because from birth his mission had been to "confer doom at its most hateful on all who ignore justice and act with crooked greed" (*Nem.* 1.64). This punitive mission was the explicit subject of a much-discussed choral song that survives only in fragments—the piece about the Nomos Basileus (fr. 169 Snell-Maehler). In their opening act of praise, the singers here announce that under Zeus, a Royal Rule proclaims that extremes of violence, among both gods and men, are dealt with forcibly,[42] and that the raised fist[43] necessary to this Olympian governance is typified by Heracles.[44] Excessive shows of force will arouse a necessary

41. Some of the same observations are made by G. Kromer, "The Value of Time in Pindar's *O.* 10," *Hermes* 104 (1976) 430, and by Burgess, "*Olympia* 10."

42. Reading lines 3–4, δικαιῶν τὸ βιαιότατον / ὑπερτάτα χειρί, as "doing justice to extreme violence with a triumphant fist," i.e., punishing violence with a power superior to it. The alternate understanding of δικαιῶν as "justifying," e.g., "making just what is most violent with arm supreme" (H. Lloyd-Jones, *The Justice of Zeus* [Berkeley, 1971], p. 51) removes the punitive sense which is the tenor of the mythic example. Taking the sense as "justifying," W. Burkert reports that Pindar here comments in sophistic fashion on the curious beliefs of earlier times: "il constate, en s'étonnant, que le Nomos, la tradition, accepte et 'justifie' 'la voie de la violence'" ("Le mythe du Géryon," in *Il mito greco*, ed. B. Gentile and G. Paione [Rome, 1977], pp. 273–83, esp. 283). M. Ostwald, "Pindar, Nomos and Heracles," *Harv. Stud.* 69 (1965) 109–38, esp. 122, asserts that "it is inconceivable that Pindar . . . held 'justice through violence' as an article of faith" (p. 122), but this is to follow Dodds in assuming that we know what "the pious Pindar" could and could not think (*Plato, Gorgias* [Oxford, 1959], p. 270).

43. With the ὑπερτάτα χείρ compare the ὑποχείριος position of the avenger at Thgn. 363. More generally, for the "fist of strenuous vengeance," as Marston has it (*Antonio's Revenge* 5.1), cf. Aesch. *Supp.* 392; Soph. *El.* 1092; Eur. *Andr.* 736, *Bacch.* 897–900; Xen. *An.* 3.2.3; Pl. *Leg.* 683d.

44. The Pindaric song does not propose the axiom that Callicles willfully found in it, i.e., that anyone exercising superior strength was acting in concert with this central *nomos* (Pl. *Grg.* 484b). Nor does it suggest that men should imitate Heracles; that is a straw man set up by Ostwald, "Pindar, Nomos," p. 122.

superhuman response that is likewise excessive, and this threat is the sanction and guarantee of the lesser *nomoi* that control ordinary practices such as the use of domestic animals, the observance of sacrificial rites, and the burial of the dead. As illustration of the Royal Rule at work, the Pindaric chorus (after a glancing reference to Geryon) proposes the tale of Heracles and Diomedes, told so as to derive the regulated sacrificial killing of domestic animals directly from the chaotic eating of man by beast, as it is punished by a return of the same.[45] The Thracian's habit of feeding his man-eating mares on the flesh of visitors is checked as Heracles tosses one of the king's grooms into the stalls, but in this telling it is the horses who return savagery upon the savage as they crunch and chomp (23–25), while the hero struggles to master their unnatural violence and separate them from their evil owner.[46] As soon as the mares have changed hands, the evocation of human dismemberment is replaced by a solemn scene of funeral sacrifice as the singers use the command of Hera, like a gnomic saying, as a device for interrupting their narrative (43–44). The scene shifts magically from barbaric Thrace to seven-gated Thebes, where Iolaus (left behind because Heracles was ordered to work alone) quietly pours out offerings at Amphitryon's tomb (47–48).[47] This instantaneous transit, from animals who eat men to men who sacrifice and eat animals, does not pretend to logic; instead it is a chorally imposed poetic event that draws Hellenic cult and regularity out of a bloody return of outrage for outrage.[48]

For Pindar, Heracles' deeds of anger are the best examples of the inescapable principle according to which actions are repaid in kind. "Do a

45. Ostwald, "Pindar, Nomos," p. 31, detects Pindaric "sympathy" with Diomedes, betrayed by the choral observation (15–17) that men call protection of their property *arete;* this, he believes, is meant to "impair Heracles' glory" (p. 119). Opinions much like these are expressed by W. Theiler, "Νόμος ὁ πάντων βασιλεύς," *MH* 22 (1965) 69–78; Theiler takes the Diomedes example to be a disillusioned and disillusioning use of myth (p. 75).

46. As Pindar shapes it, the mythic example emphasizes neither confrontation between Heracles and Diomedes nor death for the latter. The killing of the Thracian may be stated at 37–40, but this is by no means certain, and it is inaccurate to report, as if part of the song, that "Diomedes hastened to rescue his property and was killed on the spot," as does C. Pavese, "The New Heracles Poem of Pindar," *Harv. Stud.* 72 (1967) 86.

47. A libation is poured and animals are sacrificed (48, 50) in a place which Pindar's audience would associate with the games called Herakleia or Ioleia (Nilsson, *Feste,* p. 446); at *Pyth.* 9.80 ff. this is also the location of Iolaus' tomb.

48. It is notable that Pindar insists on Heracles' trickery, making him enter Diomedes' palace in the dark (19). This does not mark his "sympathy" for the Thracian or his condemnation of the hero, but it does make Heracles' god-imposed action conform to the model of revenge. See the comment of F. Bornmann, "Zur Geryoneis des Stesichoros und Pindars Herakles-Dithyrambos," *ZPE* 3.1 (1978) 34: "Darin liegt kein Tadel, ebensowenig wie in Pindars Ausdruck βίας ὁδός, der sich zweifellos auf Herakles bezieht und eine durchaus positiv Wertung einschliesst."

thing and you will suffer the same" is the gnomic choral comment that follows an account of the knockout punch delivered to Alkyoneus (*Nem.* 4.25). Even when the Heraclean response is frankly vengeful and mercilessly exaggerated, like the killing of the sons of Neleus, Pindar can sing of it (171 Snell-Maehler), because in his view revenge is part of the regulatory system of the cosmos. Benefactions are answered with benefactions, in kind or in praise and gratitude (Heracles on occasion can give back good for good, as in the case of Telemon, *Isthm.* 6.26), and by the same token injuries bring an injurious response, whether open, as with Augeas, or underhanded, as in the ambush on the Moliones. Indeed, Pindar is so easy with the idea of revenge as the reverse of *charis* that he can make it the basis of little jokes. In *Olympia* 9 he announces that his present ode comes as "avenger" (τιμάορος, 84) of an old unsung victory, and in an arch passage at the close of *Nemea* 1 (69–72) he makes Teiresias call Hebe and the bliss of heaven the "punishment" (ποινή) that will be dealt out to Heracles for the violent work that he did on earth. At the end of his vengeful life the hero is to lie above among the gods, praising the august *nomos* that arranges returns of both evil and good.[49]

III

Archaic poets and mythmakers discovered revenge at the roots of Greek political, social, and cosmic order, its greatest practitioners being Odysseus and Heracles. In parallel fashion, men of the ordinary world held that retaliation was the basis of their own everyday order, for justice demanded that an act of outrage had to be returned, harm restored to him who had inflicted it (Pl. *Cri.* 49b–c, etc.). Only a boy like Telemachus would fail to strike back at one who struck first (*Od.* 16.71–72); if he were too weak to take action himself, a wronged man could at least, like old Oedipus, employ a curse and call Hermes, Demeter, Ge, Helios, or special powers named Praxidikai to work damage upon his enemy.[50] Property taken, friendship betrayed (Hipponax 115 W; Carm. conv. 908 *PMG*), personal significance publicly denied (Arist. *Rh.* 1378b18, 1379b12)—any unprovoked action causing shame—demanded a balancing response (*Rh.* 1378b23, 1379a32–34), and it was generally held that he who repaid such an outrage was himself beyond

49. The scholiast evidently found νομόν, which he corrected to νόμον as the song's final word; MSS propose γάμον and δόμον, taken from the lines above.

50. As do the fox in Aesop (*Corpus Fabularum Aesopicarum* I.i, 1.10 ff.), Xanthias at Ar. *Ran.* 746, and many tombstones. See J. H. Croon, "The Mask of the Underworld Daemon," *JHS* 75 (1955) 9–13; D. Jordan, "An Appeal to the Sun for Vengeance," *BCH* 103 (1979) 521–25; H. S. Versnel, "Beyond Cursing," in *Magica Hiera*, ed. C. A. Faraone and D. Obbink (Oxford, 1991), pp. 60–106, esp. 68–75.

punishment. Like the poets, plain men saw no contradiction between piety and a plan to destroy someone who had made one suffer. On the contrary, the presumption was that the gods would help, at least if the angry injured man were of a respectable class.[51] So a dispossessed Megarian of the Theognidean corpus can confidently ask for a supernatural accomplice:

> Olympian Zeus, grant this my request! . . .
> Not yet am I revenged upon those thieves
> who took my property by force. . . .
> Let me drink down their black blood! send
> some Good Power to oversee this work
> and finish it as I would have it done.[52]
>
> (349, 345–47, 349–50)

Nor was a wronged man inhibited by the rules of gentlemanly behavior; rather, an Odyssean deceit was part of the game, and one of the Theognidean songs can urge:

> Sweet-talk your enemy; then,
> when you've got the upper hand,
> Strike!—don't bother with an excuse.
>
> (363–64)

Honor did not suffer if one used guile to answer guile while returning stroke for stroke: such is the assertion of the decent old men of Attica who make up the chorus of Sophocles' *Oedipus at Colonus:*

> Punishment is due to no man who repays
> what he's been made to suffer;
> when he acts, tricks that answer tricks
> respond with pain instead of thanks.
>
> (228–32)

This was a restatement, from the avenger's point of view, of Rhadamanthys' universal rule: "If a man suffer what he has inflicted, / Upright Justice results" (Hes. fr. 286.2 M-W = Arist. *Eth. Nic.* 1132b27).

Most Greek law codes were thought to reflect the Rhadamanthine justice of Crete and the Underworld, and certainly the criminal procedure of

---

51. Active revenge is rare in the Aesopic fables, which usually reflect the idea that a poor man can only wait for an ultimate vindication through chance or the gods; so it is with the Archilochean fox and eagle (179, 180 W).

52. The use of τελεῖν in the closing phrase (350) has the same sinister ambiguity that is found in Clytemnestra's vengeance prayer at Aesch. *Ag.* 973; compare also the lighter use in Sappho's prayer for erotic revenge (1.26–27 V). Such innuendo suggests an almost magical complicity between the supplicant and the power addressed.

Athens took the return of evil for evil as its fundamental notion. Such procedures began, as far as one can tell, when, in cases of homicide, representatives of various tribes took it upon themselves to interrupt, to scrutinize, and then in certain circumstances to sanction the working of private revenge.[53] When a murder occurred before the time of Draco, the victim's closest kinsman seems to have made a public announcement of his intent to avenge by naming the killer, either at the tomb of his dead relative or in the Agora.[54] This accused enemy was supposed to appear before tribal judges, but if he were blatantly guilty he would naturally run while the angry kinsman would as naturally follow, to kill him if he could. And if the accused were taken before the Ephetai[55] and the charges against him were found to be true, the consequence would be almost the same, though governed by a simple rule: the avenger might kill if he could catch the murderer on Attic ground, but he could not do so beyond the borders. In effect, then, the archaic community drew a line, and the avenger, acting from his own kinbred anger, drove the criminal over that line and into exile. As a result, the area inside the boundaries was relieved of the killer's polluting presence,[56] violence was minimized (unless the killer was relatively slow-moving), and the victim's kinsman, though he might lose the satisfaction of taking blood for blood, was honorably utilized as an agent of pursuit and punishment,

53. See, among many, H. J. Wolff, "The Origin of Judicial Litigation among the Greeks," *Traditio* 4 (1946) 31–87: "The archaic magistrate at Athens . . . was an officer charged with supervising the use of private force by individuals; that is to say, as far as homicide cases were concerned, the execution of blood vengeance" (p. 76). Compare R. Maschke, *Die Willenslehre im griechischen Recht* (Berlin, 1926), pp. 42, 51, who concludes that a decision of guilt involved the consequence that blood vengeance would have its way.

54. L. Gernet, "Le droit pénal de la Grèce ancienne," in *Du châtiment dans la cité*, CEFR, 79 (Rome, 1984), 14–15, 22–23; see also *Demosthène, Plaidoyers Politiques*, vol. 2 (Paris, 1959), pp. 189–90. This practice was preserved in the traditional announcement of vengeance that was part of a funeral lament; see E. Reiner, *Die rituelle Totenklage der Griechen*, Tübinger Beiträge zur Altertumswissenschaft, 30 (Stuttgart, 1938), p. 21.

55. See R. Sealey, *The Athenian Republic* (University Park, Pa., 1987), p. 76: "At the much earlier stage when public authority first intervened in the previously private sphere of retaliation and negotiation, it created the *ephetai* as a court for homicide." On the meaning of the designation, see the summary of theories given by H. J. Treston, *Poine* (London, 1923), pp. 264–65; Treston follows Lange and Glotz in understanding οἱ ἐπὶ ἔταις, tribal lords or "sacerdotal nobility."

56. According to Antiphon, *Tetralogiae* 1.1.3, pollution would attach particularly to those who did not act against the killer, but it also threatened the entire land; cf. *Tetralogiae* 2.1.3 and Dem. 23.40, where the pollution would spread throughout Greece if the killer took part in pan-Hellenic games. See D. M. MacDowell, *Athenian Homicide Law* (Manchester, 1963), p. 4, and R. Parker, *Miasma* (Oxford, 1983), pp. 115–26, where the idea of pollution is termed "the imaginative vehicle" of early murder process. On the nature and occasion of Antiphon's Tetralogies, see K. J. Dover, "The Chronology of Antiphon's Speeches," *CQ* 44 (1950) 44–60, esp. 56.

which was important since otherwise he might have been attacked by the angry spirit of the murdered man.[57]

In time, more complex procedures were invented, perhaps in answer to the threat of large-scale vendetta,[58] and a distinction was made between premeditated and unpremeditated killings. Forms of manslaughter were identified,[59] something called "justifiable murder" was recognized (it was perhaps revenge),[60] and acts of bloodshed were allotted to different courts according to their circumstances. The old de facto exile became a formal sentence—one that could be chosen by a defendant before the court reached its decision (Dem. 23.69)—with regulations about the road the criminal should take, and rules about how he should be treated if he returned illegally: he could be killed but not tortured, nor could ransom be extorted from him (Dem. 23.28). Nevertheless, throughout all these elaborations, the victim's kinsmen and natural avengers retained their eminence. They inaugurated murder charges;[61] only they could commute a sentence of exile,[62] and should an exiled killer return illegally they could destroy him and yet be themselves unpolluted and not liable to punishment (IG 1^2.115.30–31; Dem. 23.28).[63] Which is to say that the whole system still depended finally upon the individual man of vengeance. His threat drove

57. Such attacks could drive a man to commit unthinkable acts of sacrilege (Pl. *Leg.* 854b–c5; 734a; cf. *Resp.* 573b1; 577b).

58. R. S. Stroud, *Drakon's Law on Homicide* (Berkeley, 1968), pp. 70–74.

59. Dem. 23.53; Paus. 9.36.8; Ath. 13.569b = Xenarchos fr. 4; see Stroud, *Drakon's Law,* p. 42, and M. Gagarin, *Drakon and Early Athenian Homicide Law* (New Haven, 1981), pp. 31–37, 50–51, 62.

60. It is the contention of E. Carawan, "The *Tetralogies* and Athenian Homicide Trials," *AJPhil.* 114 (1993) 235–70, that the original meaning of "justifiable homicide" was retributive killing. "In the fifth century vindictive killing would appear to be the usual, proper meaning of *phonos dikaios;* a certain moral repugnance is evident but there is nothing parallel to the notion that it was prohibited by law, written or unwritten" (p. 257). Stroud, *Drakon's Law,* p. 56, assumes that there was a subsection of the law on unintentional homicide that dealt with killings considered to be justifiable; this is not certain, but the phrase about striking the first blow, restored at *IG* 1^2.115.33–34, makes it a strong possibility.

61. Thus the killer of a person without relatives as close as children of cousins could not be indicted (Dem. 47.72); see the discussion of Treston, *Poine,* p. 260.

62. Stroud, *Drakon's Law,* p. 41, assumes that *aidesis* could operate only in the class of unintentional and unpremeditated killings, but Sealey, *Athenian Republic,* p. 76, supposes that it was also possible in cases of voluntary homicide, asserting that Demosthenes' statement to the contrary (21.43) arose from misunderstanding.

63. Compare the rules for revenge in pre-Islamic communities: avenger guilty if he does not pursue killer, not guilty if he kills; trickery permissible; enemy not to be killed in his sleep; avenger cries "I avenge X" as he strikes; killing not to be done in month of Rajab and not until four months after the crime; original murderer allowed to ask protection from another tribe, i.e., go into tribal exile; see M. J. L. Hardy, *Blood Feud and Payment of Blood Money in the Middle East* (Leiden, 1963), pp. 16–21.

the killer out, and he watched the border markets hoping to catch his enemy on the wrong side of the boundary line, where the criminal's death would carry no penalty because he was beyond avenging (*nepoinos,* like the suitors of the *Odyssey*).[64] As time went on, a convicted murderer was no longer simply left to the man who charged him, even if his crime was premeditated, but nevertheless the natural avenger, the victim's nearest male kin, still got the essential vengeance reward of public satisfaction, for he was allowed to watch the execution (Dem. 23.69).[65] Presumably he might even laugh and shout insults at his dying enemy; Aeschines imagines just such a scene, though not in connection with the punishment of a homicide (2.181.2).

In the fifth and fourth centuries litigation became a substitute for violent revenge, and plaintiffs could boast openly of bringing charges in order to get even, "moved by the passion of vengeance" (Antiphon, *Tetralogiae* 1.1.7). The man who attempted judicial retaliation was praised, while the one who did not was treated as a coward (Dem. 59.12; Lys. 10.3).[66] And meanwhile the language of revenge continued to color all legal actions. Even in the most humdrum cases plaintiffs who could be called "revengers" (τιμωροῦντες) came before judges, who might also be called "revengers," and the wronged man, as "pursuer" (ὁ διώκων), "pursued" (μετέρχομαι, μέτειμι, μετέξειμι) a defendant who "fled" (ὁ φεύγων). In an ideal murder case, as imagined by Antiphon, the victim, as he died, would indicate his killer and ask his son for vengeance, and in prosecuting the murderer that son would avenge both his father and the city's laws (1.4; cf. Lys. 13.39–42); if he did not prosecute, he was guilty of impiety. All of which was reflected in the scheduling of trials for violent crimes, for they were held on the three days at the end of the month which were sacred to the three Semnai, the powers of revenge under a euphemistic name.[67]

Even in these later times, however, there were still two kinds of enemies against whom one acted with open, private violence. First, those who harmed the state—traitors and conspirators, as well as exiled murderers illegally returned; an assassin who avenged the state against such a one was not simply beyond punishment (Pl. *Leg.* 862b–c), but might be rewarded with honors and crowns (or even citizenship, if he were a metic like Thrasy-

<hr/>

64. Andoc. 1.95; Dem. 9.44; 23.60; cf. Pl. *Leg.* 874c). Even Plato recognized the need for revenge with impunity, should an exiled killer return (*Leg.* 862b–c); see Gagarin, *Drakon,* p. 18.

65. This was "a relic of the time when relatives killed the attacker with or without judicial process" (Sealey, *Athenian Republic,* p. 75).

66. Compare Dem. 24.8; 53.2, 15, 16; Lys. 7.20; 24.2; see R. Hirzel, *Themis, Dike und Verwandtes* (Leipzig, 1907), pp. 190–92, and V. J. Hunter, *Policing Athens* (Princeton, 1994), p. 127; 228 n. 21.

67. Schol. Aeschin. 1.188; see A. H. Sommerstein, *Aeschylus, Eumenides* (Cambridge, 1989), pp. 10–11; B. Weaver, "A Further Allusion," *CQ* 46 (1996) 559–61.

boulus).[68] And second, those who injured the hearth. Thieves (Dem. 24.113), or seducers of a man's wife, mother, sister, daughter, or concubine kept for engendering legitimate children (Dem. 23.53), if surprised in the act, might be killed on the spot in an immediate vengeance (τιμωρία) that was officially labeled "not murder" (Lys. 1.30–31, 34).[69] Such a killer was said to "enforce a justice of the highest sort" (ἔλαβε τὴν δίκην . . . τὴν δικαιοτάτην, Lys. 1.29), and he had his mythic counterpart in Ares, who killed his daughter's rapist (Paus. 1.21.4–7; 1.28.5) and so gave his name to the Areopagus. Even if a wronged man could not take the sexual intruder in the act, the law offered him other pleasures of retaliation, such as holding his enemy as his private prisoner, torturing him, or extorting money from him (Lys. 1.25; Dem. 59.64–65).[70]

Outside the courts, in dealing with public adversaries, it was axiomatic that "to satisfy one's heart with vengeance upon the enemy accords with the best tradition"; such a move was νομιμώτατον, according to one of the Sicilian speeches in Thucydides (7.68.1). At home, Cleon presumably spoke to popular conviction when he urged that retaliation should be quick, while anger is sharp, if an injured party is to achieve a balanced revenge (3.38). And meanwhile private acts of nonbloody revenge seem to have been taken for granted. Athenians were convinced that the return of a first blow was justified not only by the Law of Rhadamanthys but also by the Draconian code (Antiphon, *Tetralogiae* 3.2.3; 4.2.2; Dem. 20.157–58; 23.74; 59.15), and later laws gave tacit recognition to this principle. Anger at injury could be urged in defense of an act of violence (Dem. 21.41), and the *dike aikeias*, the law of hybris, specified that a man could take legal action after suffering a personal attack only if the attacker had unjustly begun the outrage. If, on the contrary, the attack was itself a return—was vengeance, in other words— it was not actionable.[71] Everyday life was evidently rich in such retaliations,[72]

---

68. *IG* 1².110 = ML 85; cf. Thuc. 8.92; Lys. 13.71; Lycurg. *Leoc.* 112.

69. Cf. Dem. 59; Arist. *Ath. Pol.* 57.3; and see D. Cohen, *Law, Sexuality, and Society* (Cambridge, 1991) pp. 99–102, where this law of impunity is distinguished from a law of adultery.

70. Cf. Callias, fr. 1; Ar. *Nub.* 1083; see A. R. W. Harrison, *The Law of Athens* (Oxford, 1968), pp. 33 ff.; K. J. Dover, *Greek Popular Morality in the Time of Plato and Aristotle* (Oxford, 1974), p. 209.

71. M. Muhl, "Eine alte hellenische Gesetzesformel," *Klio* 29 n.s. 11 (1936) 113–15, discusses the proverbial flavor of the qualification, ἄν τις τύπτηι τινα ἄρχων χειρῶν ἀδίκων, that appears in this law. He notes its appearance also in the Law of Draco (33–35; Stroud, *Drakon's Law,* p. 56) and points to the parallel at *Od.* 16.71–72. Compare Hes. *Theog.* 166: Ouranos must be punished, πρότερος γὰρ ἀεικέα μήσατο ἔργα.

72. See A. Lintott, *Violence, Civil Strife and Revolution in the Classical City* (Baltimore, 1982), p. 173; Dover, *Greek Popular Morality,* p. 182. G. Herman, however, argues (admittedly from silence) that in "virtually all cases" vengeance for homicide was limited in fifth-century Athens to malicious legal action; see his "How Violent Was Athenian Society?" in *Ritual, Finance, Politics,* ed. R. Osborne and S. Hornblower (Oxford, 1994), pp. 99–117, esp. 111.

and Thucydides reports that revenge in ever more bizarre forms was in fashion in the late fifth century, the avenger expecting success because he thought of his action as "just" (4.69). The men of Athens, by the historian's report, "would rather receive a wrong, that it might be returned, than never be wronged at all" (3.82.7). It is even possible that such turbulent avengers, if charged with murder, entered pleas of justifiable homicide and asked for trial at the Delphinion,[73] for that court was so swamped with work at the end of the century, and especially with pleas of *phonos dikaios*,[74] that there was a move to limit its jurisdiction.[75]

IV

Vengeance served as a vital model for Attic litigation, just as it provided a mythic foundation for political order, and so it was natural that Athenians should choose a pair of revengers as the founders of their particular civic institutions. As Odysseus' mass slaughter had created peace and plenty at Ithaca, as Heracles' ambush had brought orderly ritual contests to Olympia, so the vengeful action of Harmodius and Aristogeiton had given them their democracy. This was not precisely true, and Thucydides scolded the city for lying to itself, but the citizens of Athens nonetheless said to the world, to one another, and even to themselves, that a pair of avengers had destroyed the Pisistratid tyranny, in this way creating the glorious city that now enjoyed freedom and equality.

73. It is nowhere specifically stated that a fifth-century vengeance killer might claim that his act was done "justly" so as to come under the jurisdiction of the Delphinion. Nevertheless, Demosthenes' emphasis (23.74) upon Orestes' dismissal from that court, his murder judged both *dikaios* and *hosios,* seems to make this an unavoidable conclusion, so that many authorities have taken it for granted; e.g., G. Gilbert, *Handbuch der griechischen Staatsalterthümer,* vol. 1, 2d ed. (Leipzig, 1893), pp. 428–29; C. Wachsmuth, *RE* s.v. "Delphinion"; cf. J. R. King, ad Dem. 20.158, who speaks of "self-defence, or . . . vengeance for an outrageous injury or insult" (*Demosthenes, The Oration against Leptines* [London, 1886], p. 103). Gagarin, on the other hand (*Drakon,* p. 62), would have pleas even of self-defense heard in the Areopagus; at p. 122 he supposes that a revenge killer was first banned from public religious ceremonies (Dem. 20.157–58), then given access to judicial procedure (but where?) which could determine that he was not polluted and might reenter public life.

74. Dem. 23.53 assigns involuntary killings to the Palladion; then at 23.74 he sends all killings done ἐννόμως to the Delphinion; these he says are written down, but he does not list them, though he does make the murder of Clytemnestra by Orestes the founding example. Aristotle, on the other hand (*Ath. Pol.* 57.4), terms "justified" precisely those killings that Demosthenes calls "involuntary," and he assigns them to the Delphinion, which certainly seems to crowd that court.

75. See Carawan, "*Tetralogies,*" where it is argued that *phonos dikaios* was originally the term for retributive killing, but that the Delphinion at the end of the fifth century had to limit this plea to cases where the law explicitly provided for such a defense.

This great Athenian fiction was physically present to everyone who walked about the city in the fifth century, for Harmodius and Aristogeiton stood in the Agora,[76] larger than life, the first mortals to have their images put there (Arist. *Rh.* 1368a18). The original bronze group by Antenor, set up before the Persian War (Plin. *HN* 34.17), had been stolen by the invaders, but patriotic Athenians had erected a replacement as nearly as possible like the first as soon as the war was over (Paus. 1.8.5),[77] the group known to us from the Naples copy.[78] In it two magnificent male figures, one bearded and one smooth, strode forward in perfect harmony, the elder with his sword ready for a body thrust, the younger with his blade raised to cut down upon the tyrant's head.[79] And on the base of the monument were lines composed, so people said, by Simonides (131 *PLG*):

> Great was the light upon Athens when Aristo-
>   geiton killed Hipparchus, he and Harmodius.[80]

76. No other statues of mortals could at first be placed in the vicinity ([Plut.] *X Orat.* 852d), though in 307 B.C. figures of Antigonus and Demetrios Poliorcetes were placed in the environs (Diod. Sic. 20.46.2), as was the original group, when it was returned by Antiochus (Paus. 1.8.5), by Alexander (Arr. *Anab.* 3.16.8), or by Seleucus (Val. Max. 2.20). Then, in 43 B.C., a statue of a second pair of tyrannicides, Brutus and Cassius, was erected nearby (Dio Cassius 47.20.4). Pausanias saw a statue of Demokratia close to the tyrannicides, but he gives no indication as to its date (1.3.3).

77. C. Landwehr, *Die Antiken Gipsabgüsse aus Baiai* (Berlin, 1985), p. 29, argues from the style of the Baiai fragments that Kritios' piece showed a mixture of elements, some proper to the late sixth century, others to the first third of the fifth century. From this she concludes that this second group was as nearly as possible a reproduction of Antenor's original, based upon actual fragments of the old molds which were still in existence. That the later group was, at any rate, a copy of the earlier has been generally supposed; e.g., G. Richter, "The Right Arm of Harmodius," *AJArch.* 32 (1928) 1–5. That, on the contrary, it represented a new departure is the argument of J. H. Jongkees, "Notes on the Coinage of Athens," *Mnemos.,* 3d ser., 13 (1947) 145–60.

78. Landwehr, *Gipsabgüsse,* p. 29, lists all the surviving copies; see in particular the relief from the Elgin Throne, now in the Getty Museum and published by J. Frel, "Some Notes on the Elgin Throne," *MDAI(A)* 91 (1976) 185–88, Taf. 65–67. The group was also represented on coins (see Jongkees, "Coinage of Athens") and on the shield device of Athena, as shown on the fourth-century Panathenaic amphorae (*Arch. Anz.,* 1919, 76–78, fig. 3b–c). Moreover, it is plainly reflected in the fragment of a skyphos by the Pan Painter in the Villa Giulia (C. H. E. Haspels, *Attic Black-Figured Lekythoi* [Paris, 1936], pl. 48, 4a–b) shows a significant variation, for there the assassins move through vine branches toward their victim, and Aristogeiton is made to suggest Dionysus with his full beard. For the whole subject, see Sture Brunnsaker, *The Tyrant-Slayers of Kritios and Nesiotes,* 2d ed., Acta Instituti Atheniensis Regni Sueciae, 4°, 17 (Stockholm, 1971), pp. 107–22.

79. These attitudes were repeated in those of Heracles and Theseus on the south and west friezes of the Hephaisteion; see H. A. Thompson, "Sculptural Adornment," *AJArch.* 66 (1962) 345–46 and n. 26.

80. B. Meritt, "Greek Inscriptions," *Hesp.* 5 (1936) 356–58, attached this dedication to the sculptured group set up in 477 B.C., but he wanted it to be a copy of the original sixth-century dedication and consequently not Simonidean; he allowed, however, for another possibility, i.e.,

The two were thus recorded on stone as saviors of Athens, their victim identified with the tyranny that had darkened the city's freedom,[81] and meanwhile Harmodius and Aristogeiton lived on in everyday speech as proverbial exemplars of true nobility (Arist. *Rh.* 1398a). But where is the revenge in the story of these worshiped tyrant-killers? The shape of the popular tale can be reconstructed by conflating later versions with the scornful objections that Thucydides raises in a notorious digression (6.53–59).[82] His scorn is evidently roused by a popular story of lovers, both from the Gephyraioi clan, the younger of whom—Harmodius—had somehow provoked the spite of the tyrant Hipparchus. That ruler decided on humiliation as a punishment and fixed upon the young man's sister as his token victim.[83] First he had the girl named as *kanephoros,* one of the leaders of the Pana-

---

that the lines are to be ascribed to the poet and that they were composed for the replacement group.

81. They received hero sacrifices annually at their tomb in the Cerameicus (Arist. *Ath. Pol.* 58.1; Poll. 8.19; Paus. 1.29.15), as well as libations at all public ceremonies (Dem. 19.280). It was forbidden by law to speak any evil of them, and their descendants were guaranteed meals at the Prytaneion until the end of time (*IG* 1².97.4.9, ca. 440 B.C.; cf. Isae. 5.47; Din. 1.101), while in the fourth century they were also exempted from taxes. H. T. Wade-Gery, "Studies in Attic Inscriptions of the Fifth Century," *BSA* 33 (1932–33) 123–26, saw the *sitesis* as a Periclean grant, though others have supposed that the Alcmaeonids were "anti-Tyrannicide"; see further F. Jacoby, *Atthis* (Oxford, 1949), p. 159, and M. Ostwald, "The Prytaneion Decree," *AJPhil.* 72 (1951) 32.

82. I take the Thucydidean account that begins in 6.54, is interrupted (by digressions on the moderation of the tyrants and the sovereign position of Hippias), then takes up again at 6.56, to be the historian's retelling of a conglomerate popular tale of the tyrannicides. Jacoby, *Atthis*, pp. 156–62, recognized two previous written versions: the "Alcmaeonid," represented by Herodotus; and the "Official," presumably represented by Hellanicus (see the summary at *HCT* 4:325), where the tyranny of Hippias was forgotten and the rule of the tyrants ended with the death of Hipparchus. It is clear, however, that there was a third, apolitical, doubtless unwritten version containing the erotic details and also the motif of the sister. It was M. Lang's rather unflattering idea that Thucydides had simply invented these matters; see "The Murder of Hipparchus," *Hist.* 3 (1955) 395–407. C. Fornara, "The 'Tradition' about the Murder of Hipparchus," *Hist.* 17 (1968) 400–417, first proposes that Thucydides took the erotic tale from an "oral tradition unknown to Athenians" (p. 403), then later suggests, with Lang, that it was the historian's own "inference" (p. 410). It seems highly unlikely, however, that Thucydides would have risked destroying his point about the relative positions of Hippias and Hipparchus with a blatant invention, even more unlikely that a popular tradition that made Harmodius and Aristogeiton lovers had not long since supplied the "inference" of an erotic motive for the vengeance; the concupiscence of tyrants was after all a storyteller's commonplace (e.g., Hdt. 3.80.5; Xen. *Hier.* 1.26).

83. This episode must have been part of the tradition, possibly an actual event, for its tendency is opposed to Thucydides' purpose, which is to make the assassination as narrow and apolitical as possible. It is the insult to the sister that gives the uprising the color of a general aristocratic resistance to tyranny. Note that the insult to the sister is used as the defining detail of the popular version at [Pl.] *Hipparch.* 229c; it is what "many suppose," the version against which Socrates suggests a pair of purely sexual motives.

thenaic procession; then he took advantage of an open scrutiny of all festival performers to announce that she was unworthy of the position, maligning either her chastity or the status of her tribe (Arist. *Ath. Pol.* 18).[84] The public insult attacked the honor of the girl's brother, that of his family and clan, and, through them, that of all the great Athenian families,[85] and for this cause Harmodius and Aristogeiton decided to take revenge (Arist. *Pol.* 1311a39–40). They found allies and plotted an attack, which was to take place during the Panathenaic festival, and men told one another that there were signs of supernatural approval. In a dream an angelic figure appeared to Hipparchus on the eve of the holiday to announce that he was about to suffer because no mortal man can do wrong and not be made to pay (Hdt. 5.56).[86] Or, if that dream seemed to lack color, a storyteller could recount another in which Aphrodite herself came to the tyrant and dashed blood in his face from a cup that she held (Plut. *Mor.* 555B). The next day the noble conspirators joined the festivities carrying disguised weapons, and though they were denounced, they struck the tyrant down in the midst of the sacred confusion. The Pisistratid bodyguard killed Harmodius on the spot, and Aristogeiton was soon captured and put to death,[87] but Athens was free, thanks to a splendid revenge which had shown all of the favorite motifs: gratuitous insult, discovery of allies, divine sanction, the rescue of a female relative, intrigue and a kind of disguise, and the exploitation of a ceremony.

84. Cf. Ael. *VH* 1 18. It is sometimes supposed that the girl was rejected because she was a member of a "foreign" tribe, the Gephyraioi (so P. Brule, *La fille d'Athènes* [Paris, 1987], p. 303), but if this were a disqualifying objection it is hard to see how Hipparchus could have justified his original appointment. See L. J. Roccos, "The Kanephoros and Her Festival Mantle," *AJArch.* 99 (1995) 542–44.

85. Cf. the slap given by Meidias to Demosthenes when the latter was choregus, which was an outrage not merely upon the injured party but upon all citizens, and note the later laws against summary or humiliating scrutiny of chorus members (Dem. 21.56). Compare the conclusion of F. Frost, "Politics in Early Athens," in *Classical Contributions* (Locust Valley, N.Y., 1981), p. 39: "If the Pisistratids did not respect the philotimia of the Gephyraioi, how long would it be before others were so insulted?"

86. Herodotus had no reason to add the first dream to his account, since he was at work to deprecate the conspiracy; he must have found it already attached to the tale of the death of Hipparchus. The second dream, which clearly belongs to the version of the story that begins with an erotic advance from the tyrant, is reported in the same passage (Plut. *Mor.* 555B) in which the Stesichorean dream of Clytemnestra is set down.

87. Two versions of Aristogeiton's final hours or days were current in the fourth century (Arist. *Ath. Pol.* 18.5–6). According to one he was tortured, betrayed his party, and died miserably. According to the other, asked under torture to denounce his allies, he systematically named all those he knew to be most loyal to the tyrants, so that they would destroy their own party; then he tricked Hippias into a handshake, taunted him with having taken the hand of his brother's killer, and so provoked his own mercifully quick death. In Seneca's version Aristogeiton conforms to the type of the wise man confronting the tyrant; having caused the death of all of Hippias' closest friends, he is asked if he hasn't someone else to name, and answers, "Only yourself; I haven't left out anyone else who cares for you" (*De Ira* 2.23).

Such was the proud foundation of the Athenian democracy according to enthusiastic general opinion.

A more elaborate form of this story added a preliminary erotic outrage from the tyrant, and this was the detail that Thucydides chose to emphasize. Hipparchus had made an insulting attempt to take the boy Harmodius from his lover;[88] Harmodius had refused, and Hipparchus was left in a state of rage, while Aristogeiton was fearful that another approach would be made. The historian thought that by showing the elder of the famous pair as a man afraid of losing his beloved, he could destroy his reputation as a tyrannicide, for by his own strict way of thinking, an action that was personal could not be political. Popular storytellers were of an opposite persuasion, however; among them the demise of tyranny typically had a sexual cause.[89] Furthermore, with this detail added, Aristogeiton had a burning need for revenge because among honorable men an attempt to balk another's erotic will demanded an angry return (Arist. *Rh.* 1378b18; 1379b12). It is plain that Athenians admired the tyrant-killers precisely because their motives were passionate and private, and however they began the tale that formally canonized the noble pair, they regularly hailed them as lovers on sympotic occasions. There was no contradiction; *eros* was by nature antidespotic, and it had educated these two in valor and turned them into heroes (Aeschin. *In Tim.* 140). Indeed, Plato's Pausanias held that the quality of their liaison had entered directly into the great political deed. "Aristogeiton's desire," he says, "joined to Harmodius' love grown strong, destroyed the tyrant's power" (*Symp.* 182c).[90]

Such was the tenor of banqueting songs sung over and over again during the fifth century, and the erotic charm that they lent to the tale of the tyran-

---

88. At *Ath. Pol.* 18 it was not Hipparchus but a younger brother, Thettalus, who propositioned Harmodius and punished him for his refusal, but this figure then disappears in the later phases of the account. Aristotle refers to two different reports, one favorable to Aristogeiton and attributed to demotikoi, the other unfriendly to Aristogeiton and so presumably friendly to the tyrants and attributed to "others." Thettalus, however, would not seem to be at home in either, since his presence takes some of the usual guilt from the elder Pisistratids, while it also renders the conspiracy more theoretical, since Aristogeiton no longer kills a love rival but instead a man who represents a hated power. Thettalus has the look of a bowdlerizing character, since he saves the rulers from performance of the erotic insult; probably he is the invention of some fourth-century schoolmaster.

89. E.g., Smerdis at Lesbos (Arist. *Pol.* 1311b); Antileon at Metapontum, Melanippus at Agrigentum (Plut. *Mor.* 760B); and the special case of Gyges (Hdt. 1.8–15). Cf. Aeschin. *In Tim.* 55, where Krataios revolts from Archelaus because of enforced sexual favors.

90. This became a truism, so that one could argue, "Lovers are a benefit to cities, witness the eros of Harmodius and Aristogeiton, which destroyed the tyrant Hipparchus" (Arist. *Rh.* 1401b9). Later Bion the Borysthenite called the beards that beautiful boys developed "Harmodius and Aristogeiton" because they freed the young men's lovers from the tyranny of love (Plut. *Mor.* 770C).

nicides helped the story to flourish in the face of everyone's unexpressed knowledge that the report was not quite accurate. During the early parts of the century the older men had after all known from experience that Hippias, not Hipparchus, was the real tyrant, and they had seen for themselves how Pisistratid rule actually came to an end. Later everyone will have had first a father, then a grandfather who could have told him about the four years of tyranny that followed Hipparchus' assassination, and about the Spartan invasion that in fact drove the last tyrant out. Even at the end of the century the city was ready to laugh when Aristophanes made a joke about "Spartan liberators" (*Lys.* 1155). And yet, in spite of their knowledge of these actual events, those very same fathers and grandfathers subscribed to the story of the glorious avenging tyrannicides and taught their sons to sing songs about them. It was this that the reasonable Thucydides could not understand.[91]

Athenians chose self-deception, both for themselves and for their heirs, and the mood and thrust of this choice can be felt in the one set of banquet songs that survives.[92] These four stanzas will have been improvised at different times and repeated in various combinations, but they come together by the grace of chance (or according to the taste of Athenaeus) as a kind of villanelle in praise of vengeance-killing and its product, the Athenian city:

> I'll carry my sword in a myrtle branch
> just like Harmodius, Aristogeiton too,

91. There is only a seeming contradiction when Thucydides says that the Athenian populace knew the historical truth "by hearsay" (6.53.3) but also that they believed the tale of the tyrannicides (1.20.2; 6.54.1–2). C. Fornara asserts that the actualities of the end of the Pisistratids became known only after the publication of Herodotus, which he puts after 431 B.C., but this is to suppose that no one ever listened to his grandfather's reminiscences; see Loren J. Samons, *Athens from Cleisthenes to Pericles* (Berkeley, 1991), p. 43 n. 22.

92. These stanzas are sometimes attributed to Callistratus because Hesychius knew a *Harmodiou melos* from that poet, but this was a genre, not a title; to "sing Harmodius" was to sing a traditional banquet song (Antiphanes, fr. 85 *CAF*= Ath. 11.503E). The lines cited are not a single poem but an accidental grouping of stanzas probably owed to an anthologist; on a given banquet occasion, other collocations would have been formed as one guest offered one Harmodius song, and the next responded with another (as at Ar. *Vesp.* 1225). See M. Ostwald, *Nomos* (Oxford, 1969), pp. 123–27, and Fornara, *Athens,* pp. 44–45. It is impossible to determine when these particular stanzas were composed, nor is there any reason why they should all have come from the same period. Some have held that they all originated in the period just after 510 B.C. (e.g., Jacoby, *Atthis,* pp. 152–68; but cf. Fornara, *Athens,* pp. 42–47, where subsequent change is assumed). Others have perceived in them a Cleisthenic attempt to exploit the killing of Hipparchus for Alcmaeonid purposes, in order that the Spartan intervention of 510 B.C. might be overlooked: e.g., V. Ehrenberg, "Das Harmodioslied," *Wien. Stud.* 69 (1956) 57–69; C. M. Bowra, *Greek Lyric Poetry* (Oxford, 1936), pp. 415–21. M. Podlecki suggests that an old aristocratic song was revived in 477 B.C. as a part of Themistocles' move to discredit the Alcmaeonids: "The Political Significance of the Athenian Tyrannicide Cult," *Hist.* 15 (1966) 129–68, esp. 138.

the day they murdered the tyrant and gave
   Athens the rights of equality.
Dearest Harmodius, you didn't die!
You dwell in the Isles of the Blest, they say,
with fleet-foot Achilles the brave, and
   Diomedes son of Tydeus.
I'll carry my sword in a myrtle branch
just like Harmodius, Aristogeiton too,
when at Athena's fair sacrifice
   the tyrant Hipparchus they slew.
May you have glory worldwide and eternal,
dearest Harmodius, Aristogeiton too,
for you two who murdered the tyrant gave
   Athens the rights of equality.[93]

(Ath. 15.695 = 893–96 PMG)

The tyrannicides of these confident verses are not presented as historical figures, nor do they have any motives, either public or private. Instead they are hero agents in a symbolic action that is as timeless as a fairy tale—one in which a monster is slain and men die so that a city may change its condition. Like participants in a ritual, the banquet-singers again and again[94] make contact with this event and magically revive it through the sacred emblem of the myrtle-covered sword. That much is plain, but the song-phrase "in a myrtle branch" has almost withered under blasts of scholarly attention. Some have protested that myrtle would not cover a sword, others that it had no place at the Panathenaia, and these objections have caused modern ingenuity to outdo itself in explanations. It has been suggested that the myrtle of the songs is obscene—that the men of Athens declare that they will go for the ladies with the same verve that marked the mutually devoted Harmodius and Aristogeiton, "when they gave us our equal political rights"![95]

---

93. Fortunately questions about the exact sense, political coloration, and historical moment of the term *isonomia* need not be addressed in the present argument. There is a summary of bibliography and opinion at Fornara, *Athens*, pp. 41–42 and n. 15. All that matters for the moment is that this, the particular virtue of the Athenian polity, was generally seen throughout most of the fifth century as the creation of the revenge killings.

94. That these songs and others like them were constantly repeated is shown by the allusions of Aristophanes, especially at *Vesp.* 1224–27; their performance is associated with banqueting (*Ach.* 980), peace (*Ach.* 1093), respectability (*Eq.* 786–87), and "patriotic courage" (*Lys.* 632).

95. *Myrtos* could signify female pudenda (Hesychius s.v.; Tzetz. ad Ar. *Ran.* 516 p. 840.7 Koster = Hipponax 174 W); *xiphos* could mean penis (Ar. *Lys.* 632; Hesychius s.v.). The obscene meaning is urged by G. Lambin, "Un vers de *Lysistrate*," *Rev. Et. Grec.* 92 (1976) 542–49, who makes it "une plaisanterie fort irrévérencieuse envers les deux héros nationaux, dont tout le monde savait qu'ils avaient surtout été sensibles à d'autres charmes que ceux des femmes" (p. 549). J. Henderson, *The Maculate Muse* (Oxford, 1991), p. 122, with far greater probability locates obscenity only at Ar. *Lys.* 632, which he takes as parody of a serious skolion phrase.

Or worse, that it is the singer who will be "in a myrtle branch," which is supposed to mean "wearing a crown," which in turn must signify "being at table," so that Athenians announce that, whenever they dine, they will carry swords like those of the tyrannicides, which finally must mean that they will boast and pretend to be brave![96] All of which, however, can be put aside because we know that a branch of myrtle could grow large enough to be used for a spear shaft (*Geoponica* 11.8, ed. M. Beckh [Leipzig, 1895]), that the plant did at least have later associations with Athena (ibid. 11.6), and that it was in common ritual use in Attica.[97] We also know that banqueters often sang skolia holding crowns or branches of myrtle in their hands.[98] There is thus no reason why Athenians of the fifth century could not have imagined myrtle branches as passable, even appropriate Panathenaic camouflage for weapons,[99] especially in a story about another time.

There is no reason to distort the overt sense of the Harmodius songs. The disguised swords are their dominant image, an image that stands for deceit and so assimilates the heroic Attic revengers to the type of the devious Odysseus, or that of Heracles in ambush. Special to this trick, however, is the consecration that these imagined swords gain from their leafy dress. Carried in Athena's procession, they have a conceptual similarity to the knife that is cunningly hidden in a sacrificial basket,[100] and this likeness is exploited by the singer of the verses here reported as if they were a third stanza. The myrtle-covered swords, he says, cut the tyrant-victim down "amongst Athena's sacrifices," thus leaving an imagined Hipparchus lying with slaughtered beasts dedicated to the city's goddess. By way of the hidden swords, then, the skolion subsumes the revenge of Harmodius and Aristogeiton into the ritual of the Panathenaia, much as Pindar drew the killing

96. G. Vollgraff, "'Εν μύρτου κλαδί," *Mnemos.*, n.s., 49 (1921) 246–50, followed by Bowra, *Greek Lyric Poetry*, p. 391. This gives a self-derogatory tone which is at odds with the general antique report of the nature of the song; what is more, it is plainly not the way Aristophanes took the phrase; see G. Mathieu, *Rev. Phil.* 50 (1926) 238.

97. Eleusinian *mystai* carried bunches of myrtle and wore crowns of it (Ar. *Ran.* 330 and schol.); myrtle was used in sacrifice at the sending off of the colony in Ar. *Av.* (44 and schol.); and myrtle crowns were a sign of honorable office for generals (schol. ad Ar. *Eq.* 59) and for archons (schol. ad Ar. *Vesp.* 861, where the overt association is with prayer); myrtle was used in second-century-B.C. rites for Demeter on Lycosura (*IG* 5/2.514.14); at Rome it served for purifications (Plin. *HN* 15.29.35), and in Persia in certain sacrifices (Hdt. 7.54; Strabo 15.3). L. Deubner, *Attische Feste* (Berlin, 1932), p. 29, concluded that myrtle at the Panathenaia, though unattested, was not unthinkable; cf. Ehrenberg, "Das Harmodioslied," p. 63.

98. Hesychius s.v. μυρρίνης κλάδος; see R. Reitzenstein, *Epigramm und Skolion* (Giessen, 1893), pp. 24–25, 29, 39.

99. The fact that Thucydides has armed hoplites taking part in the procession (6.58.2) need not render the camouflaged swords ridiculous, for hoplites attended with helmet, shield, and spear, but not with swords or other arms (see *HCT* 4:335).

100. Schol. Ar. *Pax* 948a and b; see U. Schelp, *Das Kanoun* (Würzburg, 1975), pp. 24–25; W. Burkert, *Homo Necans* (Berkeley, 1983), p. 5 and n. 17.

of the Moliones into the games at Olympia. It will be annually revived in the city's greatest festival, as it is whenever this song is sung, so that the city's institutions will rest mythically upon a festive vengeful killing, whatever historians may say. Such is the function of the song, and its success is proved when, centuries later, an enthusiast for Greek independence could still boast, ". . . the myrtle wreathes a sword / Such as Harmodius drew on Athens' tyrant lord" (Byron, *Childe Harold* 3.20.8–9).

When they sang the Harmodius songs, the men of Athens assured themselves and others that they were tyrant-haters, lovers, sword-bearers, tricksters, and citizens of an ideal polity founded upon an act of revenge. Harmodius and Aristogeiton were the iconic proof of these claims, and since indisputable fact had decreed that both be killed, the gentlemen of the city in compensation exaggerated the extent of the damage the two had done. They made the victim the tyrant himself; they substituted immortality for the worldly triumph missed; and they called the result of the revenge by the lovely name of Isonomia. All of which proves that, to the Athenian way of thinking, revenge was far from being a crime that men had to abjure if they were to enter a regulated community. It was not the opposite of order, as we tend to think, but order itself in its original and vital form, the community's power to punish being only a borrowed version of each man's ingrained right to retaliate. Cerainly there was a superstructure of civic law, but this ancient and aristocratic duty was at its base. As an Aeschylean chorus explains: "The sword of vengeance, sharply thrust home . . . props justice at its foundation" (*Cho.* 639, 646).

CHAPTER THREE

Festival Vengeance

Euripides' Cyclops *and Sophocles'* Ajax

I

In early Greek thinking, successful revenge was an orderly justice-bearing action which proved that the world was on the right track. Myths and tales of evil returned upon intruders, monsters, and tyrants satisfied people who had smaller grudges, making them feel—even if the fictional hero should lose his life like the Athenian tyrannicides—that an immemorial law had triumphed. Retaliation meant that the good things of life would continue or even get better, and so motifs of vital overflow like thievery, weddings, drunkenness, and food attached themselves to stories of revenge. Anger, after all, was the reverse face of gratitude—a noble and essential passion—and this meant that the individual avenger was, in spite of his necessary deceit, a simple and almost comic figure. To abstain from vengeance (as Achilles did after Agamemnon's insult) was a problematic nonaction that tested an extraordinary hero, but to perform it was only what any right-thinking man might do. All of which meant that the standard popular tales of achieved revenge which presented themselves to the fifth-century dramatists were fundamentally antitragical because the sufferings their avengers inflicted were deserved (Arist. *Poet.* 53.11–13; cf. *Rh.* 1386b). These stories took an imaginary world a step or two along a path that led from disorder into order, and this was directly contrary to the essential dynamic of Dionysus, whose great festival gave the city a regular though temporary experience of something like chaos.

Consider this notorious genre for a moment, its nature and its possible origins. Attic tragedy was a hybrid dramatic form reputed to have been artificially engendered in the early or mid-sixth century. Whether or not his name was Thespis,[1] its effective inventor was the man who first placed a speaking actor among choral singers, and considering the conditions of early public celebration one can see why he might have done this odd thing. Under the influence of arresting performances to be seen at Corinth and Sicyon,[2] Attic choral celebrations were taking on new forms in the early sixth century. Fresh songs, composed by poet-trainers, began to replace the older traditional chants, and these were made after the pattern of the most musical of all choruses, those of the great Spartan festivals. Attic performers now learned songs that combined invocation, self-description, narrative, and prayer after Laconian and Corinthian examples, and they sang them in an imitation of the artificial Aeolo-Doric of Alcman and his followers.[3] These exotic novelties were evidently in demand, but obviously not everyone will have approved.[4] Some of those who watched, especially the elders, must often have wanted to object, and surely now and then one of them did. Every chorus master must have known that, having made his song and trained his singers, he might lead his chorus out only to see it interrupted.[5]

1. Aristophanes knew a Thespis who took dancing choruses into competition (*Vesp.* 1479), and the Marmor Parium gives him a victory in 534/533 B.C.; see the testimonia at Pickard-Cambridge–Webster, *Dithyramb*[2], pp. 69–72. An alternate supposition follows the *Suda* (s.v. "Thespis") and takes Thespis to be a latecomer in a genre that began in satyr performances in the Peloponnese, as at Hdt. 5.67.5; see, among others, O. Hoffmann, "Das dorische Alpha," *Rh. Mus.* 69 (1914) 244–52. If these performances used an actor and mixed dialogue with lyric, it is hard to explain why, when imitated in Attica, their two parts were not either uniformly Atticized or uniformly left in their original Doric dialect.

2. Arion at Corinth (Hdt. 1.23; cf. schol. Pind. *Ol.* 13.31) composed songs for festival choruses to sing, and these evidently contained some narrative matter since he gave them titles. The preparation of these more elaborate performances was paid for by Pisander, and something similar was arranged by Cleisthenes for the festivals of Sicyon (Hdt. 5.67.5), where the city's choruses for Adrastus were diverted to the celebrations for Dionysus, perhaps taking the mannerisms of heroic praise song with them. See R. Kannicht, "Thalia," in *Das Fest*, ed. W. Haug and R. Warning (Munich, 1989), pp. 29–52, esp. 44–45, where the author posits a general sixth-century trend toward changes in the performance forms of local festivals in Attica.

3. W. Ridgeway, *The Early Age of Greece* (Cambridge, 1901), p. 670, repudiated the idea that the choral lyric of tragedy used borrowed Doricisms, arguing that what appear to be imported forms were actually remnants of ancient pre-Doric cult song. This suggestion has not been accepted; discussion of the nature and extent of borrowed elements is summarized by G. Björk, *Das Alpha impurum und die tragische Kunstsprache* (Uppsala, 1950), who concludes: "Das Dorische ist von aussen wie ein durchsichtiger Schleier um den attischen sprachkörper gelegt . . . ein Stimmungsträgende Glied des poetischen Baues" (p. 222).

4. If Doricisms were already affected by aristocrats, for example in banqueters' toasts, the new songs will have had an "upper-class" or "citified" sound to a countryman's ear. See E. Csapo and M. C. Miller, "The Kottabos-Toast," *Hesp.* 60 (1991) 313–30.

5. Another model of interruption is provided by the ubiquitous Bacchic fantasy in which an individual who spies or breaks in upon the Maenads is attacked by that chorus. Interruption of chorus by bystander would be an informal mirror image of the ritual τωθασμός in which members of the phallus-bearing procession insulted their audience (Arist. *Pol.* 1336b14).

It probably wasn't often that fifty cavalrymen cut through a procession of chanting maidens, causing female spectators to pelt the intruders with apples (as happens at Delphi in Heliodorus' *Aethiopica*, 3.1–3), but some lesser trouble could always be expected.[6] On rowdy holidays a band of dancers would collect random compliments and insults from bystanders,[7] as Anthia does in the *Ephesian Tale of Xenophon of Ephesus* (1.2.2). And even on the most solemn occasions unruly spectators must now and then have broken into the song with disastrous vernacular responses when a chorus made one of its habitual second-person calls to its audience. When the girls of Alcman's *Partheneion* sang, "You won't go asking for Astaphis" (1.73 *PMG*), for example, one of her admirers might well have called out, "Oh, yes I will!"[8] Which is probably why an inventive poet whose name may have been Thespis finally decided to program not only the group-singing but also the interrupting voice.[9] He will have forestalled the rustic participant by posting his double, a disguised and costumed figure[10] (perhaps himself), primed with responses and interjections that the chorus knew how to handle.[11] If the mood of the holiday permitted, the leader of the dancers could

---

6. As extreme examples of disorder and interruption at choral performances, cf. the common stories of girls kidnapped from a dancing group (W. Bühler, *Die Europa des Moschos* [Wiesbaden, 1960], pp. 75, 108, 110 ff.); of sacrificial rites interrupted by Dionysiac representatives (as at Patras, Paus. 7.19.1); of Bacchic dancers spied upon and invaded (*Eur. Ion* 550–53). Another kind of interruption is supposed to have occurred when Persian prisoners were led past a group bent on sacrifice at the time of Salamis (Phaenias of Eresus, fr. 25 Wehrli). And for general disorder during holiday performances, note the story of Alcibiades, who punched a rival choregus (Dem. 21.147), or that of Ctesicles, member of a *pompe* for Dionysus, who broke out of the procession to strike a personal enemy (Dem. 21.180).

7. Perhaps this is what Athenaeus meant when he reported that the invention of both comedy and tragedy came from drunkenness (2.40 A–B).

8. Second-person forms from within a choral fiction, like the call to Helen at Stesichorus 192 *PMG*, might also have provoked waggish responses.

9. "Nothing is more likely than that Thespis should have taken in hand a pre-existing extempore speaker . . . and have made him deliver regularly composed speeches in character" (Pickard-Cambridge–Webster, *Dithyramb*[2], p. 87).

10. He would be disguised (face painted or dyed) to give him anonymity and to protect him from the approach of friends; if he were not marked as something out of the ordinary, his behavior would only encourage others to join him. Thus, in order to displace the real interrupter, he had to become recognizably a False Interrupter. As a precedent for costuming and masking a private figure to take an unannounced part in a public performance, compare the costuming of Phye as Athena in the "court masque" that Pisistratus arranged for his return. W. R. Connor, "Tribes, Festivals, and Processions," *JHS* 107 (1987) 40–56, notes other cases of humans dressed in exotic costumes to suit an unusual function; see also Paus. 4.27, 7.18.7, and the remarks of W. Burkert, *Greek Religion* (Cambridge, Mass., 1985), pp. 97, 186, 279, on humans dressed as gods.

11. He would speak, not sing, and use something close to everyday language, in order to maintain the illusion; later he would be called *hypokrites* because he "answered back" to a chorus, reacting to provocation, challenge, or request. On the sense of the term see G. F. Else,

make a sharp return to this planted commentator; a verbal contest could ensue, or the direction of the song might shift at this point, as if in response to the interruption. In time, the costume and mask of the seeming intruder would be drawn from the choral fiction, his single disguised voice now rendering the cries and bits of direct speech that customarily decorated choral narratives. Each occasion will have elicited its own variants as rural communities brought in the increasingly famous Thespis, or one of his followers, to smarten up a local celebration and "invent new joy for villagers" (*Anth. Pal.* 7.410).[12] Then at last the chorus itself was given the cloak of its own fiction, so that it conspired fully in the illusion, sang from another time, its feet touching another ground. The speaker brought a piece of news, he chased or was chased, but the entire performance was now the epiphany of a bit of myth. Its narrative was fully three-dimensional, and theater as we know it had made its appearance.[13]

All of which is fantasy, like other theories about the origin of Greek tragedy. Nevertheless this tale of a beginning literally improvisational (ἀπ' ἀρχῆς αὐτοσχεδιαστικῆς, Arist. *Poet.* 1449a9) can explain better than most the actual characteristics of the Attic genre, with its improbable combination of diverse modes and styles. At any rate it is certain that in the second half of the sixth century a mixed poetic spectacle, reputed to be local in its origins, became a favorite form of holiday entertainment in Attica.[14] This new performance mode filled its orderly yet unnatural structure with disorderly fictional matter not always perfectly contained. A self-sufficient, narrating, ceremonial group would fall silent while attacks, pursuits, rescues, defeats, and victories were rendered as sustained illusions, thanks to the mimed excitement and firsthand iambic report of a costumed actor using another dialect. After which the unanimous chorus would repossess

---

"Ὑποκριτής," *Wien. Stud.* 72 (1959) 75–107; G. K. H. Ley, "Ὑποκρίνεσθαι in Homer and Herodotus," *Philol.* 127 (1983) 13–29.

12. According to Bakhtin (P. N. Meddvedev and M. M. Bakhtin, *The Formal Method in Literary Scholarship*, trans. A. J. Wehrle [Baltimore, 1978], p. 136), a new genre is called into being by a new "unit of life," which in this case might be recognized in the post-Solonian farmer-villager who permits changes in traditionalist rituals (even as others resist). There was also a new city, whether that of the returned Pisistratus or that of Cleisthenes. Compare the dictum of André Maurois, which allows for the individual artist (in this case, the so-called Thespis): "Les genres littéraires naissent de la rencontre d'un génie et de circonstances" (*Les trois Dumas* [Paris, 1954], p. 233).

13. As an echo of an early actual interruption, one might cite the tragic figure who often arrives saying, "What is this confusion, what sort of a crowd is this?" as at Aesch. *Supp.* 234; *Eum.* 408; [Aesch.] *PV* 115; Eur. *Supp.* 88; *Heracl.* 122; *Andromeda* fr. 125 *TGF.*

14. When Pisistratus wounded himself to justify his demand for a bodyguard, Solon was supposed to have said, "It all comes from performing those tragedies" (Diog. Laert. 1.59–60; Plut. *Vit. Sol.* 29.6, 30.1).

the occasion with sung reflections made in obedience to society's most elegant laws, those of melody, lyric meter, and dance. The single figure increasingly asserted himself—boasting or begging for protection, threatening or rescuing, defying or praising some fictional community—so that ever more direct representations of grief or outrage or contest were embedded in the customary artificiality of the dance. The sound of the tragedy that resulted was discordant, defined by a concatenation of Doric with Attic dialects, of sung with spoken tones, of multiple with single voices, and of religious meters with those of the secular world. And meanwhile for the eye there was the contrast of two kinds of movement, as cadenced symbolic gestures from the group were counterpoised against the fitful mimetic body-signs of a single masker.[15] A contrived and unresolved opposition among its parts was thus the original mark of the tragic genre.[16]

Toward the end of the sixth century the founders of the Greater Dionysia[17] decided to spend city money[18] on this bizarre festival form, placing it beside the traditional procession and phallic dancing that annually celebrated Dionysus Eleuthereus. It is not hard to see why the new genre

15. Cf. W. Rösler, "M. Bachtin und die Karnevalskultur im antiken Griechenland," *Quaderni Urbinati di Cultura Classica*, n.s., 23 (1986) 25–41, esp. 30: "Endlich ist die Tragödie im ganzen, formal betrachtet, etwas das man als die Verbindung von zwei 'Stilen' unterschiedlichen Provenienz bezeichnen kann."

16. In Bakhtin's terms, this was tragedy's "constant specific grouping of devices" (Meddvedev and Bakhtin, *Formal Method*, p. 129).

17. W. R. Connors, "City Dionysia and Athenian Democracy," in *Aspects of Athenian Democracy*, Classica et Mediaevalia, 40 (Copenhagen, 1990), pp. 7–32, proposes a democratic, post-Cleisthenic foundation at some time ca. 501 B.C., but his argument is hard to accept. Essentially it is based in a claim of suitability: that a festival of Dionysus Eleuthereus should be associated with a moment when there was an access of freedom, and should also be contemporary with the annexation of Eleutherae. Nothing, however, connects the country cult with political freedom, nor is there a strong date for annexation of the region. The establishment of the festival was a decision to spend money: would the democracy be any more ready than a reinstated tyrant (or his supporters) to do this? The epigraphical part of Connors' argument is similarly unconvincing, for he removes Boeckh's ἐν ἄστει from *Marm. Par.* 43 (239A *FGrH*) without suggesting any other reading. Furthermore, since the inscription is using whatever it reports Thespis as doing as a well-known date from which to count, it is unlikely that this *post quem* event occurred in some unrecorded and unrecording village. Consequently a date between 538 and 528 B.C. still seems most probable; see the conclusion of M. L. West, "Early Chronology of Attic Tragedy," *CQ* 39 (1989) 251–54: "It is not implausible that Pisistratus should have assisted the process [i.e., the enhancement of the city Dionysia] by some particular initiative of his own. But it should be remembered that this is mere assumption. Books which refer to a reorganization in 533 are relating speculation pegged to a date for Thespis which is itself unreliable."

18. In the beginning this money will have come either from the tyrants or from aristocratic sponsors (as advised at Arist. *Pol.* 1321a35). The city *choregia* with payment publicly assigned began presumably toward the end of the sixth century; see Ch. Meier, "Zur Funktion der Feste in Athen im 5. Jhdt. v. Chr.," in *Das Fest,* ed. W. Haug and R. Warning (Munich, 1989), p. 574.

seemed appropriate, since the enlarged festivities would distantly reflect the rural rites of an upland border village, Eleutherae, and would be celebrated at the turn of the seasons, the life-and-death time toward the middle of March, when sailing had been resumed but the final pruning was just finished and vine stalks stood maimed in the vineyards.[19] This was a time when strangers came to Athens, when responsibilities were relaxed, debts were overlooked, and a lot of money was spent. To bring in a rustic Dionysus was thus to hold a kind of carnival, and those who planned the new (or expanded) festival evidently recognized the suitability of the country-bred, disguised, and innately disorderly Thespian invention. And yet these festival designers must have embraced the ancestor of what we call tragedy with a certain tribulation,[20] for as time went on, the dramatic performances came to be encased, like a dangerous substance, in a leaden box of ceremonies. Generals who poured libations, ephebes in regimented procession, crowned benefactors, armed orphans, and piled tribute were all shown before the tragic performances. And after them, the authority of the city was reestablished through an assembly, an investigation into any illicit festival behavior, and an official scrutiny of the tenor of the entire five-day holiday.[21]

Inside these pompous buffers the new performance was licensed to go about its business, which was evidently to dissolve the foundations of civic

---

19. Hes. *Op.* 564–72 directs that pruning be finished at the end of February, after the heliacal rising of Arcturus but before that of the Pleiades; cf. Theophr. *Caus. Pl.* 3.13.1–2, and A. C. Brumfield, *The Attic Festivals of Demeter and Their Relation to the Agricultural Year* (New York, 1981), pp. 24–31. The scythe of Kronos connected him with the cutting of living branches (Macrob. *Sat.* 1.7), but the pruning of vines was a peculiarly Dionysiac activity, likened in the myth of Lycurgus to chopping off arms and legs, one's own or those of one's children (*Il.* 6.129 and schol.); compare Apollod. *Bibl.* 3.5.1, where the king kills Dryas, thinking him a vine, and "prunes" him; also Hyg. *Fab.* 132, where he cuts off his own foot, thinking it a vine.

20. Any festival might be politically dangerous: Cylon's attempted coup came at a festival for Zeus (Thuc. 1.126.4), and Hipparchus was assassinated at the Panathenaia; see T. Figuera, "The Ten Archontes of 479/8 at Athens," *Hesp.* 53 (1984) 447–73; also R. Osborne, "Competitive Festivals and the Polis," in *Tragedy, Comedy and the Polis*, ed. A. H. Sommerstein et al. (Bari, 1993), pp. 21–37.

21. These regulations developed over the years; see the testimonia collected and discussed in A. W. Pickard-Cambridge, *Dramatic Festivals of Athens*, 2d ed. (Oxford, 1968), pp. 57–125. The end of the festival was also marked by the return of the statue of Dionysus to his temple, but about this nothing is known (ibid., p. 60). The best description of the festival as a whole is by S. Goldhill, "The Great Dionysia and Civic Ideology," *JHS* 107 (1987) 58–76, and "Anthropologie, Idéologie et les Grandes Dionysies," in *Anthropologie et théâtre antique: Actes . . . Montpellier*, Cahiers GITA, 3 (Montpellier, 1987), pp. 55–74, which should be read in conjunction with S. G. Cole, "Procession and Celebration at the Dionysia," in *Theater and Society*, ed. R. Scodel (Ann Arbor, 1993), pp. 25–38; see also C. Sourvinou-Inwood, "Something to Do with Athens," in *Ritual, Finance, Politics*, ed. R. Osborne and S. Hornblower (Oxford, 1994), pp. 269–90.

society in a wave of replicated disorder. Watching from the slopes of the Acropolis, citizens and foreigners, perhaps even women,[22] all indulged by proxy in the same excesses that country people enjoyed on their feast days, city folk more soberly at the Kronia.[23] Through the actors, they disguised themselves and vicariously hobnobbed with monsters, effigies, ghosts, and gods, while they also rubbed elbows with slaves who were inordinately assertive and voluble. As passive celebrants, the members of the audience joined in blasphemies, curses, and insults, or perhaps practiced cunning lies that proved to be effective. They saw the erstwhile great and powerful as bodies slashed, strangled, wounded, blinded, or dismembered—painful images of the disintegration of created form. And at the same time this genre that mixed representation with ritual led the polis as a whole into multiple and outrageous attacks on its own most cherished customs and institutions, as it assisted at the violation of sanctuary, the mock crowning or discrowning of rulers, the murder of military commanders, or the sacrifice of a human victim. Superiors were flouted, burial was refused, hospitality was betrayed, and worship was mocked with sacrilegious parody. Kinship was dismantled by familial imprecations, killings, or sex acts that were tabu, and the most fundamental law of all society was overturned as women resisted, defied, even destroyed men.[24] On occasion the Athenian who sat in the theater of Dionysus could even become a vicarious cannibal, but whatever the particular fiction, he always watched a representation, more realistic than any yet known, of a world where boundaries were lost, any rule could be reversed, and men lived in a confusion they could not control.[25]

22. Whether women were present is still an open question; see J. Henderson, "Women and the Athenian Dramatic Festivals," *TAPA* 121 (1991) 133–47, pro; S. Goldhill, "Representing Democracy," in *Ritual, Finance, Politics,* ed. R. Osborne and S. Hornblower (Oxford, 1994), pp. 347–69, contra.

23. Dem. 24.26; Philochorus, *FGrH* 328 F97; Plut. *Mor.* 1098B–C (unruly servants); Macrob. *Sat.* 1.10.22. On these festivals see L. Deubner, *Attische Feste* (Berlin, 1932), pp. 37 ff.; M. West, *Hesiod, Theogony* (Oxford, 1966), p. 205; also S. Luria, "Die Ersten werden die Letzten sein," *Klio* 22 (1929) 405 ff.

24. This is what V. Turner calls the "anti-structure": "the Nay to all positive structural assertions but . . . in some sense the source of them all and more, as a realm of pure possibility . . . involving the analysis of culture into factors and their free recombination in any and every possible pattern, however weird"; see "Passages, Margins, and Poverty," in *Dramas, Fields, and Metaphors* (Ithaca, N.Y., 1974), p. 255. In Turner's language the Dionysia would be a liminal, not a liminoid, phenomenon, since it portrayed "the inversion or reversal of secular, mundane reality and social structure" but was not truly "subversive, representing radical critiques . . . and proposing alternative models."

25. By contrast with the Spartan, who proverbially stayed away from both tragedy and comedy in order not to hear the laws contradicted (Plut. *Mor.* 239B, no. 33). The Dionysia was a version of those rites founded on a "besoin de violer les règles," recognized by E. Durkheim, *Les formes élémentaires de la vie religieuse* (Paris, 1968), p. 547. Compare J. Baudrillard, *The Transparency of Evil* (London and New York, 1993), p. 66: "No society can live without in a sense

By way of its dramatic representations, the great festival dipped into chaos and touched the creative force that had first brought order from cosmic disorder. Then it sent its spectators back to the city, as if from outside, to give renewed recognition to a revitalized complex of custom and law.[26] The process was, in other words, much like that of initiation except that the populace that experienced it was revived but not changed.[27] The Athenians did not return to the world of the ordinary with new status, nor had they been given fresh information or altered ethical standards.[28] Instead they had been shown a world turned upside down while they vicariously experienced the impermanence of all social structures[29] and the baleful vigor of unsocialized man. Tragedy took its audience into another time, another

---

opposing its own value system; it has to have such a system yet it must at the same time define itself in contradistinction to it." Goldhill expects the tragic attack on institutions to be made in the verbal and paraphrasable parts of a play; consequently he finds that the "transgressive force" of Attic tragedy is always weak and imperfect, always dominated by rationalism, so that "the polis is not seriously challenged" (*JHS* 107 [1987] 68). There are, however, certain actions—killing a ruler, seizing a suppliant, sacrificing a human—that, when imitated, do not rationally criticize the social order but instead simply unmake it.

26. See R. Caillois, who resumes the theory of Durkheim, *L'homme et le sacré* (Paris, 1950), pp. 123–62. Something like the same understanding of the function of festival is expressed by Plato, who says (*Leg.* 653d) that society's rules grow slack but the gods have ordained feasts and thanksgivings so that, after association with immortals, men may set their modes of life upright again (cf. 828 ff.).

27. R. Seaford has argued that tragedy actually derived from initiation rites; see "Dionysiac Drama," *CQ* 31 (1981) 252–75. F. Zeitlin, "Playing the Other," *Representations* 11 (1985) 63–94, holds that the tragic purpose was to alter the members of a male audience by forcing them to identify with female characters, through whom they experienced suffering. To support this thesis Zeitlin must argue that any suffering, indeed any form of passivity, was defined as feminine, so that identification with, say, Ajax or Oedipus would work to feminize the spectator. (And what of Aesch. *Sept.*, where the suffering is reciprocally wrought and felt by an aggressive hypermasculine pair?)

28. J. J. Winkler urged the opposite: "events and characters portrayed in tragedy are meant to be contemplated as lessons" by the ephebes present in the theater; see "The Ephebes' Song," *Representations* 11 (1985) 26–62, esp. 38. This assertion involved him in much distortion and banalization; e.g., the *Medea* teaches "the ephebic proposition that women who have and exercise power are dangerous" (35); *OT* tells of an ephebe who "once and for all proves himself a man in combat" (by killing his father) (67). Max Weber, *Gesammelte Aufsätze zur Wissenschaftslehre* (Tübingen, 1968), p. 192, spoke of the "nomologischen Wissen" of tragedy, but he referred not to information but to a large negative wisdom based on a recognition that institutions, even the construction of the individual self, could come apart.

29. Much current discussion of festival tries to determine whether it finally favors established power (working as a kind of safety valve) or whether it is a genuine expression of popular resistance to custom and law; see, e.g., V. Lanternari, *Festa, carisma, apocalisse* (Palermo, 1983). Obviously the measure of subversiveness will depend upon the particular festival, and upon the particular epoch in which it is celebrated; the Dionysia seems at the outset to have suggested a solidarity among participants that transcended both tribe and city; see the discussion of Meier, "Zur Funktion der Feste," pp. 575–84.

place, and another society, a vague, extrapolitical, aristocratic milieu characterized by war, interregnum, illicit rule, barbarian power, or anarchy.[30] However, where the pan-European carnival of the marketplace leveled all participants in a common debased brutality, the Attic Dionysia, through its tragic use of myth, achieved another kind of leveling. It displayed the brute in man at its highest instead of its lowest form, showing the fearsome vigor of creatures who lived outside the city in an uncomfortable proximity with gods. Both carnival and Dionysia, however, provided an active, simulated experience of excess, reversal, and transgression. And the return from both into ordinary time and causality was usually made by a representation of death, as both holiday-maker and tragic spectator were reminded that mortality is the determining fact of human institutions.[31]

II

For dramas meant to provide a mythicized experience of anarchy and inversion, stories of brothers who killed one another, fathers who cursed sons, women who refused to marry, ghosts who spoke to defeated kings, or commanders slain by women were perfectly appropriate. Revenge, by contrast, was not, because its controlling, justice-bearing agent, its restoration of balance, its affinity with everyday processes of litigation, were all intrinsically orderly. Its imaginary time seemed to lie immediately behind the present, and so its natural place was in the countertragedy that capped each festival day with a touch of the truly carnivalesque. The last play of the day was meant to send the audience back toward the city, not as god-defying heroes but as ordinary creatures in need of food and sleep, while it yet maintained the essential dissolutions that the day's tragedies had wrought. For these contradictory purposes an action that touched the positive revenge tale with lewdness and wild cruelty was wonderfully suitable.[32] Or so Aeschylus

---

30. The Argos of Eur. *Or.* is almost an exception, with its constituted Assembly, but even here the rule of a usurper has only just ended, leaving a power vacuum that waits to be filled.

31. ". . . avec la mort . . . le *cosmos* est sorti du *chaos*. L'ère du tohu-bohu est close, l'histoire naturelle commence, le régime de la causalité normale s'installe" (Caillois, *L'homme et le sacré*, p. 133). Compare the notion of Hölderlin that men and gods from time to time come together, then separate again with a cleaner sense of distinction, and that this truth dictates the death of the hero in tragedy; see the letter to Schutz, cited by R. B. Harrison, *Hölderlin and Greek Literature* (Oxford, 1975), p. 168. As the escape plays show, the hero did not have to die, but he did have to be brought face to face with his own mortality as, for example, is Philoctetes; cf. Orestes, Pylades, and Iphigeneia in Eur. *IT;* Ion in Eur. *Ion,* etc.

32. In the Aeschylean satyr play *Ostologoi,* Odysseus killed the suitors; in Sophocles' *Kedalion,* either Oenopion took vengeance on Orion by blinding him or else the blinded Orion returned to avenge his injury; in Euripides' *Autolycus,* Sisyphus stole Anticleia, daughter of Autolycus, in revenge for stolen cattle; in his *Eurystheus,* Heracles returned from Hades to terrorize his former master; in his *Sisyphus,* Heracles avenged the theft of Diomedes' mares; in the Cyclops plays of Aristeas, Epicharmus, and Callias the revenge of Odysseus was the subject,

evidently believed, for he finished one of his trilogies with a little play about a drunken Heracles who sent sacred messengers back to a tribute-demanding enemy wearing their lopped-off hands, noses, and ears hanging from strings round their necks (frs. 108–13 *TrGF*).[33]

The one complete satyr play to survive, the Euripidean *Cyclops,* depicts a simple, successful revenge in a dramatization that in all its parts reflects its author's perfect satisfaction with his material. The little play in fact functions almost as a warning, a statement from a master dramatist about the dangers of attempting any but a comic treatment of this kind of fiction. In its Homeric form the action against Polyphemus had been more defensive than vengeful, but Euripides, for his *Cyclops,* gives the story all the touches needed to make it a monstrous mirror of the father of all revenges, Odysseus' epic attack on the suitors. First of all, the hero's intention is made physically clear by arranging that Polyphemus' cave shall have many openings (*Cyc.* 197).[34] There is no need for a ram here because, unlike the hero of *Odyssey* 9, this Euripidean Odysseus can get away easily at any time. He stays, not out of necessity, but because, when two of his men have been eaten (one cooked, one raw, 398–400), vengeance (τιμωρία, *Cyc.* 441; cf. 693–95)[35] is his plain duty. As at Ithaca, he is accompanied by a god—here by the real presence of Dionysus in the form of wine (Dionysus "speaks" from the flask, 156)[36]—and this god, like the Athena of Homer, enters directly into the final attack upon the enemy (422, 454, 825). As at Ithaca, Odysseus is disguised, this time by his false name, No Man, while Silenus and the satyrs take the place of Eumaeus and the herdsmen as his assistants; there is even a loving "recognition," played out between Silenus and the contents of a leather wine flask (152–56). The enemy, Cyclops, is not of course multiple like the suitors, but at least he is enormous,[37] and he sets

---

as in the Euripidean play. Other satyr plays titled with the names of notorious villains or monsters may or may not have shown their punishment as an act of revenge; e.g., Aesch. *Kerkyon* (and possibly the so-called "Dike play" if it concerned Cycnus, as supposed by H. Lloyd-Jones, *Aeschylus,* Loeb, 2:577 f.); Soph. *Amykos;* Eur. *Skiron; Syleus;* Achaeus, *Kyknos.* Achaeus also wrote a satyr play *Alkmaion,* but its content is unknown. For discussion and bibliography, see D. F. Sutton, *The Greek Satyr Play* (Meisenheim am Glan, 1980), pp. 14–72.

33. B. van Groningen, "Ad Aeschyli Κήρυκες," *Mnemos.* n.s. 58 (1930) 134.

34. Critics label this a "weakness": "We are not told what prevents the crewmen from escaping together with Odysseus" (Sutton, *Satyr Play,* p. 102).

35. According to the (unlikely) notion of M. Vickers, "Alcibiades on Stage," *Hist.* 36 (1987) 171–97, esp. 195, this announcement of vengeance will have been deformed by a pronunciation that, in parody of Alcibiades, rendered τιμωρίαν as τιμῶλιαν, presumably reminding the audience of Mt. Tmolus.

36. Murray's hunch that the reference in 147 is to a magical ever-full flask is supported by R. Kassel, "Zum Euripideischen Kyklops," *Maia* 25 (1973) 99–106, esp. 100.

37. His size is measured indirectly by the size of his furniture, e.g., his cup that holds the contents of twelve amphorae (388); this was evidently traditional, for in Epicharmus' *Cyclops* the giant's cup was deeper than a kneading trough (fr. 45 Olivieri, *FCGM* = 81 *CAF*). On size

himself to eat, not Odysseus' livelihood, but his very flesh, as well as that of his crew. Finally, as at Ithaca, the means of vengeance is a prodigious weapon, a gigantic burning brand[38] this time, and the opportunity for its use comes as before in an exploited ritual, not exactly a bride contest but still a social rite that promises a bedfellow to one of its members.

The key scene of the *Cyclops*—the one in which deception is practiced and vengeance assured—shows just how sublime vengeance can be when its chorus wears fuzzy trunks and dances the *sikinnis*. It begins when the drunken victim-to-be lurches out of his dining hall in hopes of pulling together a *komos*,[39] a roustabout gang of celebrants, from among his brother monsters. He must be kept apart from any such allies and persuaded back into the cave if the vengeance is to succeed, and these two maneuvers Odysseus contrives through a parody of an initiation that turns into brute seduction.[40] The Cyclops is ignorant of sacred truth, he is marked by *amathia* like Pentheus in the *Bacchae*,[41] and Odysseus offers, like the god of that other play, to introduce him to the mysteries of culture and Dionysus. He plays

---

jokes as expressive of the fundamental carnival notions of excess and greed, see M. Bakhtin, *L'œuvre de François Rabelais* (Paris, 1970), p. 187: "Cette hyperbolisation de la nourriture est parallèle aux hyperbolisations les plus anciennes du ventre, de la bouche et du phallus." Polyphemus was like the "Great and uglie Gyants" of English midsummer pageant, as is easy to see in vase paintings (e.g., the proto-Attic amphora from Eleusis, in P. E. Arias, *History of Greek Vase Painting* [London, 1962], pls. 12, 13, or the oenochoe by the Theseus painter in the Louvre, *ABL* 252.70, which are nos. 1 and 248 in J. Boardman, *Athenian Black Figure Vases* [New York, 1974]). On stage, grotesque size will have been suggested with extra-high shoes and an oversized mask.

38. It should be remembered that this weapon was originally a tree (383), one of the emblems of Dionysus.

39. If the *komos* was the aristocrats' way of showing their disdain for the peace of lesser men, then Odysseus acts to keep an outsider from aping the ways of the privileged class; however, since the *komos* frequently led to outrages, he also acts to avoid the possibility of gigantic displays of *hybris*. See L. E. Rossi, "Il Ciclope . . . *komos* mancato," *Maia* 23 (1971) 10 ff.; O. Murray, "The Solonian Law of Hybris," in *Nomos: Essays in Athenian Law, Politics, and Society*, ed. P. Cartledge, P. Millett, and S. Todd (Cambridge, 1990), p. 140.

40. The scene of giving a lesson was at home in comedy (e.g., Ar. *Vesp.* 1205 ff.); see M. Pohlenz, *Die griechische Tragödie*, 2d ed. (Göttingen, 1954), p. 96. It was also used elsewhere by Euripides in moments of minor comic revenge; so Menelaus and Helen teach false Hellenic burial ceremonies to Theoclylmenos at *Hel.* 1239–77; Iphigeneia teaches false purification rites to Thoas at *IT* 1188–221.

41. The similarity between this scene and Eur. *Bacch.* 923–70 is noted by R. Seaford, "Dionysiac Drama and Mysteries," *CQ* 31 (1981) 252–75, who for some reason holds that the symposium scene of *Cyclops* "serves no function in the story" (p. 273). The parallels between the two plays are extensive because *Cyclops*, like *Bacchae*, is a version of the "god come to visit" tale; Silenus and the satyrs (like Cadmus and Teiresias) recognize the god that Odysseus brings, but Cyclops (like Pentheus) does so only when bedazzled. In addition to the verbal echoes within the scene (noted by Seaford), one may compare the drinking song at *Cyc.* 495 ff. with *Bacch.* 73, 902 ff. Finally, the entry of Cyclops at 203 is much like that of Pentheus at *Bacch.* 215, not in verbal style (which is reminiscent rather of Pratinas, fr. 1) but in content and mood.

host and hierophant as a form of disguise, making a vengeance trick of the hospitable rite as he first misinstructs his victim by teaching him to drink his wine unmixed,[42] then shows him a false Ganymede in lieu of a revelation. The *sacra* of this initiation are ostensibly the attractions of a pretty boy, but in fact whiskered old Silenus is produced, disguised (thanks to the work of Dionysus) in the eye of his amorous beholder. The episode is fast, absurd, obscene, and only in its closing phase, with the victim following his fascinating companion, quibbling over just how his cup should be filled but moving toward the central door of death, does one grasp its devilish likeness to the *Agamemnon* tapestry scene. Here too an Old Queen is drawing a great ruler into the killing spot which is his own home, and here too the bewitched victim insults the gods as he goes. Polyphemus thinks he sees divinities, but no, he will not give a kiss to the Charites! Wine has instructed him, and like Zeus he prefers boys (581–84, 586). This local ruler believes that he and his charming companion are headed for bed, not bath, and Silenus moans in mock despair, "Uh oh! bitter wine ahead!" (589). He is using the avenger's irony,[43] of course, because he knows that the penetration to come will be practiced not by, but upon, the Cyclops and that it will take as its target the monster's eye. The doomed creature has been isolated, and with the beast helpless in the trap Odysseus, like Clytemnestra, speaks the canonical avenger's prayer,[44] this time a call upon Hephaestus, Night, and Sleep for their help in the last phase of retaliation (599–605). He is confident because, in repaying the Cyclops' gross perversion of the ceremonies of hospitality,[45] his own intrigue makes use of the central emblems of the culture that the monster insulted—wine, symposium, sexual *jouissance,* and finally the hearth fire itself.

At this point an Attic tragedy of revenge was always in trouble because of the convention that prohibited visible violence. The infliction of physical harm by one stage figure upon another could not be presented, and yet such infliction was the irreducible substance of a vengeance action. Worse yet, its accomplishment offstage necessarily removed the principal actors,

---

42. Odysseus gave him his first drink at 411, filling the cup from his flask, and knowing that the wine would take vengeance (422). The fact that the Cyclops is throughout drinking his wine unmixed becomes the basis for a series of little jokes: he is called "uncivilized" (ἄμεικτος) at 429; at 557 Silenus tries to avoid filling the cup to the top by objecting that this won't leave space for mixing; at 576, when he is in Odysseus' power, Cyclops cries out ἄκρατος ἡ χάρις.

43. Compare the heavy double sense of Odysseus' ἐν δόμοισι χρὴ μένειν (536, 538), as also of his prediction (575) that Bacchus will leave Polyphemus "scorched."

44. Cf. the prayers at *Od.* 20.112–19; Aesch. *Ag.* 973–74; *Cho.* 479–504; Soph. *El.* 1376–83; Eur. *El.* 809–10; *Hel.* 959 ff.; *IT* 1028 ff., 1398 ff.; *Phoen.* 84 ff.; *Ion* 1048–73 (chorus in behalf of the avenger).

45. At 342–44 Polyphemus, as "irreproachable host," offers Odysseus fire and the paternal cauldron—for the boiling of his flesh.

the avenger and his victim, so that the audience was left at the supreme moment of crisis with nothing but a chorus to look at.[46] This was a cause of serious dramaturgical embarrassment, and in the *Cyclops* Euripides insists that his audience should be fully aware of the scene's innate awkwardness. Hellish things are presumably going on inside the cave, but his avenger nevertheless carelessly pops out again for a moment of comic business as he tries to shush the chorus. The victim is sleeping, he says, shamelessly admitting that he means to take an unheroic advantage. Then he asks for help, setting the satyrs up for a lopsided show of cowardice as they all suddenly discover that they are lame. They split into two parties, both hobbling about to prove incapacity, and in so doing they forever tarnish the memory of a similarly divided chorus of Argives who likewise feebly dithered while the conqueror of Troy was being killed (Aesch. *Ag.* 1346–71). The truant revenger at last goes back to work, and in his absence Euripides gives the coup de grâce to revenge as a serious action. Odysseus has asked at least for encouragement, and so, while the nightmare scene is being played offstage, the idle chorus breaks into a coxswain's cry, with the result that the vengeful spike is "rowed" into Polyphemus' eye to the rhythm of, "Turn it, oh-h! Burn it, oh-h!" (τύφετ' ὧ, καίετ' ὧ, 659).[47] They had offered to chant an Orphic spell that would move the brand telekinetically (646–48), and now, as they mime its manipulation, the great log becomes conceptually like the enormous lance they once used in the battle with the Giants (7), a weapon often depicted as hugely phallic.[48] The mixture of silliness, horror, and obscenity is now complete, and it is a wonder that any tragic poet ever again attempted the scene of the backstage vengeance attack.[49]

The exodus of the *Cyclops* gives a quick, almost ritualistic staging to the success of revenge. The blinded victim displays himself, and the satyrs greet his howls of pain as a paean (664), a version of the song first heard when Apollo's vengeance against a similarly inhospitable dragon had made Delphi fit for habitation. As he stumbles in pursuit of the Greeks who maimed him, the monster is taunted by former slaves who throng about, giving

---

46. On the standard scene of the vengeance killing, see W. G. Arnott, "Offstage Cries and the Choral Presence," *Antichthon* 16 (1982) 35–43.

47. See J. P. Rossignol, "Sur le rhythme d'un chœur du *Cyclope* d'Euripide," *Rev. Arch.* 11 (1854) 165–70, where this is identified as a rowers' song. For a similar song for pulling, cf. Ar. *Pax* 460–72, 486–99, 512–19, and on the general characteristics of work songs, see Rossi, "Il Ciclope," p. 21.

48. See F. Brommer, *Satyroi* (Würzburg, 1937), p. 55. The lance of the Gigantomachy is cleverly associated with the ship of the satyrs' arrival in the opening lines of the play (5, 7; cf. 15, 19).

49. Perhaps few did, if the date of the *Cyclops* was 408 B.C., as R. Seaford believes (*Euripides, Cyclops* [Oxford, 1984], p. 48). Sutton, *Satyr Play*, pp. 114–20, proposes 424 B.C. on the grounds of a relationship with *Hecuba*, but *Cyclops* (if it contains parody of the taunting of Polymestor) should be the later of the two.

wrong directions and probably touching and turning him as in the game of blindman's buff.[50] He who had ruled them is teased and maltreated (687) like a deposed carnival king until Odysseus interrupts the revel. Making the avenger's proper claim (Arist. *Rh.* 1380b22), he insists on being recognized, in his own name, as the agent of a deserved punishment. Vengeance was doubly necessary, he says, first because Polyphemus "had to give a just return for his impious meal" (693), and also because he himself owed it to the fires of Troy to avenge his comrades' blood (694–95). Polyphemus blusters and threatens, but the uneaten Greeks and the rescued satyrs all troop away. The monster's parodic conversion to the customs of the symposium has only confirmed his barbaric blindness to the ways of *charis*[51] (his best effort at gratitude was his offer to eat Odysseus last, 550), and he will go back in darkness to his cave. The Greeks, on the other hand, will go in the opposite direction, sailing with Dionysus toward home and reunion, as civilization (which means knowing how to eat, drink,[52] use guests, and return like for like) visibly draws apart from savagery.

It has been fashionable to discover a sympathy for Polyphemus and a bitter skepticism about Odysseus in this overtly affirmative play, but Greeks of the fifth century B.C. did not admire monstrosity, alienation, and suffering. They did not, like Theocritus, or Trollope's Rev. Crawley, romanticize the Cyclops. Nor did Euripides. His Polyphemus is a caricature of a Calliclean tyrant (210–11, 316–46), one who gives free rein to his natural superiority, explicitly scorns the laws and customs of men, and enslaves weak and shiftless lesser beings. His Odysseus by contrast is a practical man who nonetheless believes in progress and supposes that, if savages are offered *nomos,* they will embrace it. He proposes to deal with the local monster according to

---

50. Cf. Bakhtin, *Rabelais,* p. 208: "ce jeu comporte un protagoniste et un choeur qui rit." At 345 ff. Polyphemus seems to use a staff or stick to force the Greeks into his cave (he has some sort of weapon because he has just come from hunting), and it is tempting to think that the satyrs who reverse this action at the end are likewise prodding him with sticks, in a literal *bastonnade.* See Seaford's note, ad 345, about the staging of an Oxford production. The reverse situation in which chorus tries to catch an actor or actors whom it cannot see is found at Eur. *Rhes.* 674 ff. (and probably also in Soph. *Inachos,* where Hermes wears the cap of invisibility).

51. Cf. 494, where his ignorance of the customs of the *komos* is termed "blindness."

52. In *Cyclops,* wine (= revenge) mediates between two opposite styles of eating. A meat diet that includes human flesh, the most antisocial of foodstuffs, is associated with hunting, keeping animals, and drinking milk, its practitioners being isolated, anarchic, unsharing slaveholders. A second diet, based on grain, goes with sailing and exchange, but also by implication with hierarchy and obedience (119–21, where not cultivating fields seems to explain the fact that there is no authority among the Cyclopes). Unmixed wine is to proper drinking more or less as human flesh is to ordinary meat-eating, and it here causes a cannibal meal to be vomited up again (592), a cannibal to lose the power to seize his prey. By extension, however, wine mixed with water (in combination presumably with a similarly mixed diet) produces easy social intercourse based on hospitality. For further considerations of this sort, see D. Konstan, "An Anthropology of Euripides' *Cyclops,*" *Ramus* 10 (1981) 87 ff.

accepted rules of exchange, hospitality, and suppliancy, but Polyphemus respects only the necessity of his own appetite and forcibly satisfies himself by consuming creatures of lesser strength. And when *physis* takes the form of cannibalism, Odysseus responds with the *nomos* of revenge. Private indignation, respect for his own reputation, and a conviction of solidarity with his crew move him to become the killer of this natural ruler. He does not want to annex the tyrant's power; rather, he wants to keep his own untarnished sense of self, and he also wants to restore the freedom of Hellenes who have been, or might be, enslaved. And so he commits an act of enormous cruelty and then sails away, leaving an afflicted atheistical representative of *physis* with no one to tyrannize over.

In this little play that is at once crude and highly polished, Euripides emphasizes each of the elements that unfits the ordinary revenge action for tragedy. He exaggerates the optimism of the successful retaliation by suppressing the monster's curse, Poseidon's persecutions, and all the coming epic sufferings. He causes the essentially balancing structure to shift toward reversal from bad fortune to good by adding the rescue of wholly undeserving satyrs to the escape of the Greeks. He reifies the support of the divine sponsor by putting it into a flask ("Why would a god want to live in a bottle?" the Cyclops asks, 525). He insists on the deviousness of a hero who is, technically speaking, not very tricky, by making a pun from trick to torch (δόλος to δαλός, 472–76), and he lets the exploited ceremony turn into a lewd sympotic farce. On the ethical side, he sharpens the justice of the victim's punishment by making him not just a host who wants his guests to offer him a feast, not just a cannibal who swallows two men in the course of the action, but also the "butcher of Hades hated by heaven" (396–97). The Cyclops is an enemy of culture who denies the gods, worships his own belly (335), and will not respect either guests or suppliants. And meanwhile the Greeks and satyrs, the party that understands the *nomos* of revenge, become grotesque representatives of all that is best in a civilized Hellenic community: they recognize leaders, they have wine, and they can at least remember Aphrodite (70) and the revels of Bacchus. In this play, then, vengeance keeps easy company with a comic version of an ideal sociability that brings sweetness and *charis* into men's ordinary lives.

III

As cannibalism is to a regulated diet, so is blinding a monster with a burning brand to customary revenge—so says the *Cyclops* action, its two extremes serving to confirm the ordinary human practices of eating and retaliation. Its laughably ugly revenge is a form of *nomos,* and so in its completion it gives promise of safety and regularity, as indeed will any simple and successful stage action wherein like is returned for like. Such deeds, when accomplished, provoke a sense of complacency in an audience, and it is just this radical opposition between an essentially reassuring subject and a form meant to disturb that created the complexities of Attic vengeance drama. The Sophoclean *Ajax* displays the extreme measures needed if a justice-bearing return upon an injurious enemy was to be rendered awesome and disorderly.

The *Ajax* is a revenge play while it is also the most fearsome of all the surviving tragedies, and this anomalous combination of a conventionally promising action with emotions of awe and dread demanded a complex dramatic strategy. To begin with, Sophocles chose a vengeance traditionally ill-conceived and unsuccessful, to which he added a set of systematic inversions even of its failure. The particular story[53] was of an act of violence aimed not at a villain but at constituted military authorities, and to this negation Sophocles brings a divinity who is the avenger's enemy instead of being his ally. The poet well understands, however, that the divinely authored collapse of an unjust revenge would be just as orderly and promising, just as little able to disturb and confound an audience, as the success of its opposite. And so, having taken up the tale of what seems to be an earned disaster, he goes to work on two levels to undermine any complacency that its outcome might encourage. The story already contained motifs of guaranteed chaos-value—madness, mayhem, suicide—and these he exploits by actually putting them on stage. Above all, however, he causes confusion to undermine even the initial negations, so that the hero's failure is after all not absolute, the scheme's injustice is qualified, and the inimical divinity is replaced by imponderable daimonic allies of another sort. Evaluations are proposed and discarded, events are viewed from several standpoints, and ambivalence invades every part of the hero's disastrous retaliation. Then, when the audience has been rendered incapable of either satisfaction or dissatisfaction, an alternate revenge, strangely conceived and dubiously successful, is substituted for the initial attempt, and the drama comes to its end with a celebration of a heroic rage that cannot be classified either as legitimate or as illegitimate and that was after all not quite misspent.

As an example of how Sophocles teases the spectator into attitudes that he will have to abandon, consider the masque of madness at the opening of the play. It is fixed there like a frontispiece as if to give the color of insanity both to Ajax and to the action of revenge, but this small spectacle is full of deceptions. Watching it over Odysseus' shoulder, the audience in a sense steals a revelation meant for that man alone, and because the vision is stolen, it seems to carry a heightened truth. Nevertheless, the audience also

---

53. The only fixed elements in the Ajax story were the hero's chagrin over the grant of Achilles' arms (*Od.* 11.543–47) and the consequent suicide (Arctinus, *Aethiopis,* fr. 2 *EGF*). The maddened attack on the Achaean herds is attributed to the *Little Iliad* (Proclus, *EGF* p. 36), but neither Pindar (*Nem.* 8.23 f.; *Isthm.* 3.337–46) nor Aeschylus (fr. 284 Lloyd-Jones) made use of the motif as far as is known.

sees how Odysseus is being manipulated, how Athena employs the raving warrior as an emblem that tests her selected spectator, forcing him to choose between scorn and pity in his response to the humiliation of a rival. Like a ringmaster, the goddess positions her special audience, excites his appetite for the show, then calls out her lone player to move like a puppet in the proscenium of his tent-opening.[54] (Since Athenians called their stage σκηνή, or "tent," this is a stage upon the stage.) All of which means that the exultant figure who brandishes a whip, rejoices in his own cruelty, and treats a goddess as if she were an enlisted man appears to the audience not as an ordinary character in a play but as an entertainment and a sign to be read.

And yet this is not just an instructive emblem showing how the mighty can be destroyed and deformed by a greater power. What is shown is not a tableau of failure and madness, for what is actually displayed is the revenger Ajax as he would have been, if only he had been allowed to keep his normal eyesight. Athena is absolutely clear about this, explaining with care that it was a sane Ajax who crept out at night with a plan to kill and maim the commanders and the men about them. All she did was give him a diversive push away from the tents of the Atreidai and toward the animal pens, after which she tampered a bit with his vision.[55] Because of her, he saw and still sees animals as men, but it was because of his own rage and hatred that he fell upon them, murdering and capturing.[56] Consequently, since the spectator does not see the animal corpses in this opening tableau, what he sees is not Athena's trick, not the madness of Ajax, but the vengeance that would have been.[57] A visitation of madness is responsible for last night's failure and the present delusion that takes failure for success, but what we (and Odysseus) look at is an ecstasy of rage that belongs to this man's own nature. On this small inner stage, then, there is a deluded madman who in his failure behaves exactly as he would have in success, were he sane. Which means

54. Evidently the tent of Ajax has been set up so as to screen the central door of the scene building, the structure on either side being masked. When, at 814, the chorus departs and the scene shifts to the shore, the tent will be made to disappear, leaving something like shrubbery to mask the opening.

55. See B. M. W. Knox, "The *Ajax* of Sophocles," *Harv. Stud.* 65 (1961) 1–37, esp. 5; and G. Grossmann, "Das Lachen des Aias," *MH* 25 (1968) 65–85, who concludes, "aber seine Ruhm-Rach-, und Ehrsucht, seine Überheblichkeit der Göttin gegenüber, all dies ist nicht im Wahn, sondern im Wesen des Helden begründet" (79–80).

56. This restricted madness of misperception follows the pattern of the Dionysiac punishment of Lycurgus, as does also the madness Hera sends upon Heracles; the intentions of the "madman" are those of his sanity, but he is unable to recognize the objects of his violence.

57. The one objective evidence of madness is his inability to see Odysseus, but Athena identifies this as a fresh failing, not a general symptom (*Aj.* 85). E. Fraenkel objected to her previous promise to distract the glance of Ajax from Odysseus (68–70) as inconsistent with this clouding of his vision ("Sophocles, *Aias* 68–70," *MH* 20 [1963] 103 ff.), but the dramatist needs to insist because this divine trick prepares for the essentially comic situation in which one man listens while another, unaware of his presence, insults him.

that what is shown by Athena in this prologue is the final phase of a revenge action that both has and has not been completed. The avenger's anger has gone through its work to the end, but his victims have been played by stand-ins.

It is polyvalence, not madness, that the prologue fixes as a master theme of the drama to follow, for the one event depicted in Athena's peep show has as many interpretations as it has audiences. A large number of domestic animals (and a herdsman or so) have been butchered: such is the brute actuality. For Ajax, the hero under Athena's enchantment, the pile of bloody flesh marks the triumphant conclusion of his revenge. For Athena, the producer, the same corpses mark the avoidance of a catastrophe and the satisfactory punishment of an irreverent man. For Odysseus, the invited spectator, the gory error means the pitiable humiliation of a magnificent warrior. And for the actual audience out front, the unseen animal bodies provide a puzzle about perception, intention, and the meaning of sanity. And that is only a halfway tally, for as soon as Athena disappears and the first episode begins, the inner theater is reopened and the same event is once again represented. Tecmessa takes the goddess' place now as mistress of ceremonies, and she reveals an Ajax in exactly the same situation, though he is undeceived now and surrounded by visible carcasses.[58] This time he looks at his work and sees not a triumph but a morass of disgusting shame. The mortal Tecmessa looks and discovers an agonized man whom she would comfort, while the Salaminians who have taken Odysseus' place as inner audience see only the destruction of all their hopes of getting home. As for the outer audience, it now sees a man in the depths of a sordid despair, and it is teased by the thought (suggested by Tecmessa, 271 ff.) that perhaps the frenzy and the illusions of the prologue were preferable to this present accurate vision.

A divinely authored deception, then, is proposed as the inaugural fact of this drama and given to the audience as lurid spectacle, while the responses of various inner audiences raise troublesome questions about how far such deception spreads. As to the second great fact, the action that Ajax has just miscompleted, the ambivalence is equally strong, for the poet has entangled its two aspects—intention and achievement—in a knot of confusions from which no clear judgment can emerge. The revenge as planned was to have been a covert, nighttime attack upon Odysseus, the Atreidai, and as many others of the Greek command as Ajax could lay hands on. From the army's point of view, even to plan such a thing was an act of blatant betrayal and treason (726), and so it would have been from the standpoint of any other social organization. Looking for benefit from a particu-

---

58. The scholiast says that Ajax and the butchered animals were on the *ekkyklema,* which would make this scene more than ever a visual parody of the normal display of avenger with victim(s), as at Aesch. *Ag.* 1372; *Cho.* 972; Eur. *El.* 1177.

lar institution, in this case the ad hoc court, Ajax had submitted to its authority; then, disappointed of his prize, he had behaved like an athlete who loses a contest and tries to kill his rival, the other contestants, and the appointed judges as well. (The parallel is implicit in the strong epinician echoes of the first ode in which Rumor has brought news of shame instead of glory, 172–200.)[59] Worse yet, his intention was not simply to take the lives of all concerned; he meant to torture, whip, and maim his enemies and then give their bodies to the dogs, and the audience has watched him mime these very actions.[60] Ajax meant the souls of his princely victims to be forever powerless and cringing in the underworld because of having died like slaves.[61] Such a revenge would have doomed the Trojan expedition, baffled the will of the gods, and stained the glory of Ajax forever, had Athena not interfered.

And yet, in spite of its evident injustice, the poet makes his audience see this outlandish revenge as a superb error, not as a fiendish crime of spite. Ajax is one who (like a failed Stoic) calculates incorrectly when he uses the strength of his hand (he is δυσλόγιστος, 40). He has trouble reasoning as he acts, and this quality is inherited; his father too is δύσοργος, one whose passions go wrong (1017) so that he quarrels too easily. Ajax experienced a negative political stroke, made by a recognized though corrupt group, and misidentified it as a private injury offered by personal enemies. According to his erroneous calculation, the Atreidai and Odysseus seized something rightfully his when they failed to give him Achilles' arms (ἔμαρψεν, 444–46; cf. 100); as he saw it, they willfully attacked his honor (98, 426, 440; cf. the chorus at 196, where their action is called ὕβρις) and therefore owed him repayment in the form of suffering (113, of Odysseus). He made his plan (44) and went out deceitfully, at night (47), meaning to exact repayment for their outrage (304). He attempted a classic act of revenge, in other words, but one based on an inaccurate perception that took a complex (and corrupt) communal phenomenon to be a gratuitous personal outrage. Ajax's anger is thus unjust but understandable, and Sophocles makes it almost admirable by showing that it came from the same passionate source that had moved the warrior to his greatest deeds. His mistaken attack, had it succeeded, would have finished the Trojan expedition (1055), but the

59. Cf. the activity of Phema at Bacchyl. 10.1; 2.1; 9.48. Compare also the judgment of Agamemnon at 1239–45. In a sociologist's terms, Ajax had agreed to compete for a conventional prize by conventional means, so that when he breaks this agreement he is at war with society itself.

60. Cf. 233–44, where Tecmessa seems to report actions that took place just before Athena called Ajax out: through their ram proxies, Menelaus has his tongue cut out and head lopped off, Agamemnon is whipped and covered with invective like a slave.

61. In the fourth century, whipping a free man was a religious crime punishable by death (Dem. 21.180); cf. Arist. *Pol.* 1311b23–26, where the conspiracy against Archelaus of Macedon was caused by his having given over a free man to Euripides, that he might whip him.

identical aggressive rage of ambition has time and again been the army's salvation (1292). Ajax, indeed, is like certain contemporary economies;
expansion is the only phase he can tolerate. He cannot merely maintain a
superlative level of action or of honor; he must constantly raise that level,
and so any failure of increase he marks as a loss. He must win every prize,
otherwise he feels naked (464), hence the misconceived revenge. But he
must also surpass all others, even himself, in battle, and this second version
of his need to expand has made him a tower of protection for the entire
Greek army (1276).

Sophocles thus shows a revenge that is dangerous to the community, ill
conceived, grossly disproportionate, yet closely related to other actions of
undeniable magnificence. It is an error that defies assessment, nor does
Athena's intrusion instruct the audience as to her judgment, for Athena is
not in the least interested in the justice or injustice of last night's attempt.
What she cares about is the persistent irreverence that flowers, like his
courage and his anger, from Ajax's rage for excellence (760–61). Irreverence, unlike revenge, is a religious crime, and she has been waiting for a
chance to punish it by striking at its source, the warrior's enormous self-
esteem. He could best be wounded if he were visited by a humiliation that
he had himself contrived, and his rancor against the chieftains gave the goddess her opportunity. She might have blocked his plot, warned the leaders,
or disarmed the angry Salaminian before he could do any harm, but any of
these tactics would have honored him with her overt opposition. Her purpose was to dishonor, and so, instead of opposing the vengeance, she followed Ajax out into the night and saw to his success in the multiple slaughter that was to give him joy. However, instead of disguising the avenger (as
she did Odysseus for the mass slaughter of the suitors), Athena this time disguised the victims, so that the hero who had mistaken somewhat sordid col-
leagues for arrogant enemies should repeat his mistake in a more grotesque
form. By simply setting his eyesight askew, Athena brought her man into a
ridiculous parody of his own intention, a massive murder of beasts, after
which she arranged for the publicity that would cause him to suffer an
agony of self-wrought and intolerable shame. The punishment was a return
for his overweening disregard for divine power, but it would come from
Ajax himself in the moment that he realized that he, the son of Telamon,
was an absurd object of mortal scorn.

Athena is thus in appearance a divine ally who has become the revenger's
enemy. Nevertheless, since it is a malformed and mistaken vengeance that
she distorts, her participation saves Ajax from committing a colossal crime
from which his reputation could never have recovered. Athena's midnight
activity is thus ambivalent, like everything else here, while it is also periph-
eral to the true action of the tragedy. Her interference occurred before the
play begins, and her punitive purpose has been fully accomplished before
the opening of the first episode, when Ajax knows what it is he has done. At

this point she is satisfied and she withdraws, leaving the hero to make what he will of his newly discovered mortal limitations. Because he has been the object of her wrath, he will continue to be a kind of carrier of that wrath for one more day, a creature dangerous to all, but especially to himself (778). At the end of that day, however, he may be safe, for all the gods care (779).

This, then, is the premise of the Sophoclean tragic action: a man closely crowded between supernaturally determined possibilities of safety and destruction moves in ignorance through a single day that will or will not be his last. Mortals were proverbially creatures of the day (cf. Athena, 131), but the fate of Ajax is somehow in his own hands during these few charged hours, for he is offered a unique instant of openness, when two opposing fates are balanced. And the use that he makes of this unexpected freedom is freely to kill himself. The hero's act of self-destruction is the single deed that is performed in the course of the play, and Sophocles cuts his tragedy so that it should be literally its central event.

The act of self-destruction is the *praxis* of this play, though it is usually treated as a mere pendant to the slaughter of the herds. Some critics, like Seneca, simply join the two acts into one: "frenzy drove Ajax to his death, and vengeful anger drove him into frenzy" (*De Ira* 2.36.5). Others report a self-referential and retrospective suicide, the hero's terminal comment on what has gone before. As such it is described as a final admission of defeat, a recognition of fault, a kind of remorse, an "atonement," even a conversion of sorts, but always as a denigrating and repudiating reflection upon the earlier revenge attempt. No one of these descriptions, however, can account for three importunate peculiarities that are attached to the suicide of Ajax as Sophocles depicts it: first, that it is the single chosen deed performed by the principal; second, that it is acted out on stage; and third, that it has no witness but the audience.

Other suicides occur in Attic drama, and they are indeed mere responses to a more significant action. They are, however, all (with Antigone's as the one exception) performed by secondary characters. Here in *Ajax* the act of self-destruction is a dramatic fact of another sort entirely, performed by the principal, and given a full tragic extension in areas of cause and consequence. This deed is prepared in an analytical decision speech, tested by attempts to dissuade, and threatened by possible interruption. What is more, this suicide, unlike any other piece of tragic blood-violence, is actually mimed by the chief actor, so that it takes on as much reality as the Attic stage can confer. Ajax plants his sword, takes an impossible jump, and skewers himself on the naked point in a gymnastic *tour de force* that, even when it happens only on the page, makes the most blasé heart skip a beat. Nothing like this is done in any other surviving Greek play,[62] and we are bound to

---

62. Closest is Evadne's leap, at Eur. *Supp.* 1071.

think that Sophocles had more than sensationalism in mind when he asked his audience to watch while Ajax turns his living body into a corpse. This demonstration of will and training is the central tragic deed, and as such it must lead somewhere, must press upon events to come. Moreover, such bravado from the hero must describe a passion larger than mere self-disgust; such vital activity must signify more than permanent arrest. There must, in other words, be a second gesture here displayed, one that is contained within the overt act of suicide, and in fact there is. Ajax does not merely destroy himself in his final scene; he also curses, and his curse transforms his death into a renewed revenge.[63]

The hero's curse upon the Atreidai and the entire Greek host is the culmination of a plan that has taken a special inward form, because in this act of vengeance there can be no collaborators. Sitting in a welter of tortured cattle, Ajax comes to a decision and develops an intrigue with only himself as confidant. First he takes stock of his situation in the sort of speech Homeric heroes use when they decide on battle action (457–80). "What is to become of me?" an epic warrior asks himself, then he outlines possible moves with concomitant disadvantages or advantages (cf. *Il.* 11.404–10; 21.552–70; 17.91–105; 22.99–130), and Ajax does the same. "What must I do?" he says (457). To go home would be shameful, to appear before his father intolerable (466); to rush out among the Trojans and be killed would be better, but this would give pleasure to his Achaean enemies (469). At this point in an epic speech the speaker comes to his decision, either going back to the better of his two alternatives, or forward to an emergent third possibility. Ajax, however, first pauses to restate the grounds of his two hypothetical refusals: "(Neither of these is feasible because) I must attempt something that will prove to my father that he has not engendered a lily-livered coward" (470–72). Now he is in a fine rhetorical position for delivering his climactic announcement naming the chosen action that will make his father proud and bring pain to his enemies, but that announcement does not come. From what follows, it is plain that the selected deed is a third alternative—a glorious self-inflicted death (καλῶς τεθνηκέναι, 479)—but just how this is to show his noble birth, please the fierce Telamon, and dis-

---

63. The curse is either a Sophoclean invention or the Sophoclean choice of a very obscure motif, for this is its first appearance. For the revenge curse in general, however, there were precedents in plenty; e.g., the curse of Althaia, *Il.* 9.568–70; of the father of Phoenix, *Il.* 9.454–57; of Oedipus, *Thebais* 2 *EGF.* A curse was the appropriate vengeance weapon for the weak, powerless, or defeated; so the Erinyes, at Aesch. *Eum.* 780–84, would curse the Attic soil; cf. second-century-B.C. gravestones of Delian girls, presumably victims of magic, inscribed with curses upon their killers (J. Bergmann, "Die Rachgebete von Rhenaia," *Philol.* 70 [1911] 503–10). In general, see H. S. Versnel, "Beyond Cursing," in *Magika Hiera,* ed. C. A. Faraone and D. Obbink (Oxford, 1991), pp. 68–75.

please his enemies he does not say. Those around him have heard as much as he will allow (480), but the audience learns from the testament that follows that this death is to be somehow aggressive, for it is his own matchless savagery that he wills to his son (548–49).

Tecmessa sees only that Ajax means to die, and knowing her man, she attempts to prove that suicide will be not glorious but shameful, a desertion of herself and Eurysaces (496–505). Such an act would also be ignoble, since by the laws of gratitude (which are fundamentally the same as those of revenge)[64] he owes her pity (522–24). She appeals to the values that command his fullest faith, but Ajax is firm and cruel against her attempts to dissuade him because he has envisaged a more abysmal shame, should he go home, a more exigent need for repayment, and a recovery of honor. In his opening lament for his lost vengeance he had asked Zeus how he might die damaging Odysseus and the Atreidai (387), and Tecmessa herself had understood this as a kind of imprecation (392). Indeed, the form of his question already held the answer, for death can carry damage if accompanied by a curse. Any curse, correctly made, had its baneful potential, but a suicide's curse—the curse of one dying violently and before his time (ἄωρος καὶ βιαιοθάνατος)[65]—had a superlative effect. Ajax intends that a curse of this sort shall transform his death into a last aggressive slash at his enemies, making it a work of noble anger that he can present with pride[66] to his ferocious father.[67]

64. In comparison with her statement, χάρις χάριν γάρ ἐστιν ἡ τίκτουσ᾿ ἀεί (522), Jebb cites a proverb in Zenobius, 3.328: δίκη δίκην ἔτικτε καὶ βλάβη βλάβην.

65. These are qualities desirable in occupants of graves where curse tablets are to be deposited; see D. Jordan, "New Archaeological Evidence for the Practice of Magic," *Praktika tou xii diethnous synedriou* (Athens, 1988), p. 273; cf. Versnel, "Beyond Cursing," p. 70. On the suicide's curse, see Parker, *Miasma*, p. 198 and n. 48. The Attic belief in the special powers of suicides is reflected in their having a separate burial place, the Kynegion (*Suda*, s.v.), and in the remark of Plato, *Leg.* 865d–e, cf. 873c, that such dead are restless and in search of vengeance; compare the custom of cutting off a hand from a suicide's corpse and burying it separately (Aeschin. *In Ctes.* 244). In theory the only element that could increase the power of a suicide's curse was kinship, as Homer hints in the case of Epicaste (*Od.* 9.280). The idea that the suicide has magical power continues in the present day; see C. W. Wahl, "Suicide as a Magical Act," in *Clues to Suicide*, ed. E. S. Schneidman and N. L. Farbenow (New York, 1957), pp. 23–28.

66. That a suicide accompanied by a curse was an admirable act is explicitly stated by Diodorus; he tells how the widow of Aison went to Pelias' hearth, cursed Pelias, then heroically stabbed herself, "bringing the action off in a way that was manly and worthy of remembrance" (4.50).

67. Marie Delcourt was the first to indicate the importance of the curse of Ajax ("Le suicide par vengeance dans la Grèce ancienne," *Rev. Hist. Rel.* 119 [1939] 154–71). Her observation (though mentioned by Stanford, *Sophocles, Ajax* [London, 1963], p. 289, and by Kamerbeek, ad 835) has not received the attention it deserves because her major emphasis was upon suicide itself as a means of vengeance. Delcourt compared the maidens of Leuctra, raped by Spartans, who with their father killed themselves, in order that they might curse their attack-

His curse is to be Ajax's vengeance weapon, but like any avenger he must scheme in order to put it to use. He must gain access to the place where he will act, and he must block or deflect any who might interfere with his plot. This is the function of the notorious "deception speech," whose difficulties disappear when it is recognized as part of a vengeance scheme.[68] In this special case, it is not his enemy's supporters but his own that the avenger has to fear; against their opposition he must make his way to a particular spot— not a palace interior but the land's edge, the proper location for magical operations. And to effect this he does what other avengers do: he puts on a psychic disguise, choosing a *persona* precisely opposite to his own, that of an apologist for moderation. "I am become a woman, as far as my mouth goes," he says (651), using the irony typical of the revenger whose intrigue is under way. The entire speech is double, as he states his own truth under a mask of rhetoric and false emotion. He begins with a gnome about time and change, to cover the unlikely transformation that he pretends to have undergone. Then he proclaims a pity that is real, though it is the product of his present resolve, not its moving force. He makes his necessary petition in terms both false and true, asking that he be allowed to go alone "where no eye can see" (659), there to bury his sword, purge himself, and, with a rare verb (ἐξαλεύσομαι, 656),[69] avert, guard, or take care of the wrath of Athena. As a kind of mythic example to cover this apparently anomalous treatment of a sword, he refers to Hector and states his genuine conviction that no exchange of good things is possible between enemies (665). He will yield to the gods (in truth, by dying) and learn how to honor the Atreid

---

ers (Diod. Sic. 15.54.2–3; Paus. 9.13.5–6; Plut. *Pel.* 20), but Sophocles nowhere suggests that Ajax kills himself because he wants to curse. He takes his own life because this is the only action commensurate with his nature and his shame, but he seizes the opportunity to curse which suicide offers him. A better parallel may exist at Soph. *Ant.* 1305, where the messenger seems to report that Eurydice, as she died by her own hand, cursed Creon as a child-killer.

68. The speech does in effect deceive; see Tecmessa's explicit statement at 807. Nevertheless a large body of critics insists that this cannot have been its purpose: a) because deception is foreign to the character of Ajax; b) because lies would not be couched in such splendid language; c) because Ajax has no need to deceive since no one would dare to interfere. As for a), the character of Ajax is not a fixed quantity but is being formed within the present tragedy, in which he has already made use of a furtive trick (47). As for b), language and rhetoric are by definition proper to a speech of persuasion; this argument would mean that the speech of the Paidagogos at Soph. *El.* 680–763 could not be deceptive. And as for c), Ajax must avoid even ineffective verbal interference because he has in mind a deed that is verbal as well as physical. For a summary of opinion, see P. T. Stevens, "Ajax in the Trugrede," *CQ* 36 (1986) 327–33; since that sensible review of the question, R. Seaford has put forward the astounding suggestion that Ajax expresses in this speech a kind of internal initiation into the mysteries which makes him desire death passionately because he has glimpsed what lies beyond ("Sophocles and the Mysteries," *Hermes* 122 [1994] 275–88).

69. So codd.; Hesychius E 3546 gives ἐξαλύξωμαι.

rulers (with curses), (dying) as winter gives way to summer or night to day, in full and equal opposition to them (666–76). Then (once dead and having cursed) he will truly know the indifference that lesser people call *sophrosyne* (677, cf. his own version, 586), for he will have no further dealings with either friend or enemy. Then indeed all will be well (684). Winter will as soon fawn upon summer, night upon day, as this man will upon his enemies with the opportunistic cowardice that the world calls moderation, but nevertheless Ajax convinces his listeners with this consummately artful speech.[70] Indeed, his disguise is so successful that he can send Tecmessa into the tent to deliver, in his stead, the requisite revenger's prayer: "Ask the gods to bring completion (τελεῖσθαι, 686) to what my heart longs for."[71] Now he can enter upon the active part of his plan, which is to exploit a pseudo ritual of cleansing—what his shipmates imagine as a πάνθυτα θέσμια complete with sacrifice (712)—in order to give his curse the setting and the strength that it requires.[72]

The deception speech clears the stage, and Ajax is free to arrange his revenge exactly as he will. He inspects the ground, draws Hector's sword, and plants it firmly, tip up, as if for the sword dancer's jump. When this is done he turns to his real task, which is to damage his enemies. He needs divine aid, and so, for the first time in his life, he assumes a posture of reverence.[73] He has not undergone a conversion, nor is he repentant over his

---

70. Taken at face value, his speech is internally inconsistent because it pretends to illustrate one action by another that is wholly unlike it. To dissolve and deny disagreement by yielding to and behaving toward enemies as if they were friends is an act essentially opposite to that of balancing and perpetuating disagreement in an endless series of defeats and victories. Ajax knows the difference between the gray of shifting definitions (679–80) and the black and white of fixed entities like Night and Day that alternate eternally but do not mix. His listeners, on the other hand, suppose that submission and compromise are somehow figured by the ever opposed activities of storm and calm.

71. On τελεῖν in such prayers, see chap. 2, n. 52.

72. The shore is not just a poetic setting for despair; it is the required locality for certain magical transactions. Cf., e.g., *PGM* xi a 3: "go to a place by a river, to the seashore, or to a crossroads . . ."

73. What posture exactly? He says προστρέπω(831), and it has been argued that he is on his knees on stage, as he is on a red-figure lekythos in Basel from the 460s; see K. Schefold, "Sophokles' Aias auf einer Lekythos," *AK* 19 (1976) 71–78. This painted figure has both knees on the ground, both arms stretched out, whereas when he is shown planting the sword Ajax has only one knee down. Since other kneeling figures from vase paintings have fallen or been forced, the Ajax of the lekythos is unique, and Schefold concludes that the painted gesture reproduces that of the Sophoclean hero. This, however, seems unlikely because of the previous business of burying the sword, which would have required the actor to stoop, after which it would be extremely awkward to rise, come away from the shrubbery, and then fall to one's knees. For a male stage figure a kneeling posture is almost unheard-of; Oedipus is reported to have knelt to be gathered into the earth (Soph. *OC* 1654), but he was not visible; only Orestes and Pylades seem to kneel before entering the palace at Soph. *El.* 1374. In general, kneeling is a gesture associated with women or with powerless lower-class men; see F. T. van Straten, "Did

lifelong stance of equality with the Olympian deities. It is simply that the one heroic action left to him demands the collaboration of the supernatural. After a firmly stated request that Teucer should take charge of his corpse, he makes his formal submission to Zeus (προστρέπω, 831) without a single worshipful word, without even a cult epithet. And with Underworld Hermes he is equally terse as he asks for a lucky jump and a quick death.[74] So much for the Olympian preliminaries; the way is clear and he can get to work.[75] Ajax lifts his voice[76]—the enormous voice that Homer says could be heard in the skies (*Il.* 15.686)—and calls upon the Erinyes, invoking them in a high liturgical style that contrasts significantly with his plain address to Zeus and Hermes.[77] He summons the Furies as his battle companions, his ἀρωγοί (835),[78] and he praises them as ever virginal, ever overseeing the sufferings of mankind (836).[79] Then he adds two august epithets in order to please them, the last specifying the particular aid that he wants; they are to come τανύποδες, on swift feet, which is to say as pursuers and persecutors (835–37). Invocation finished, Ajax begins upon the actual vengeance curse, first denouncing the Atreidai as his destroyers (838),[80] then demand-

---

the Greeks Kneel?" *BaBesch.* 49 (1974) 159–84. The question of the actor's posture during the curse is closely related; I would rule out beating on the ground like Althaia (*Il.* 9.568–70), for the reason just stated. It seems possible, however, that the actor, though standing, may have stretched out his arms like the figure on the lekythos; at any rate, Teucer makes a gesture toward the sky as he reformulates the curse at 1389; cf. Creon's similar gesture when taking an oath, at Soph. *Ant.* 758. The priests and priestesses who cursed the desecrators of the herms stood and faced east, "according to ancient custom," but their gestures are not specified ([Lys.] *Andocides* 51).

74. It is worth noting that Chthonian Hermes is the most frequently addressed divinity in the curse tablets; see E. Kagarow, *Griechische Fluchtafeln, Eos* Suppl. 4 (Lvov, 1929), p. 59.

75. An almost equally elaborate curse is spoken at Soph. *OC* 1375–92, where Oedipus first calls his former curse demons to come again as his allies; next he turns aside to spell out the contents of his curse to its recipient; then he makes a triple call upon Tartarus, the curse demons, and Ares as witnessing powers. At Soph. *El.* 111, Electra voices a much simpler prayer-curse, calling Hades, Persephone, Underworld Hermes, Lady Curse, and the Erinyes who watch over unjust deaths and adulterous beds to come to her aid and repay her father's murder.

76. On the voice of Ajax, see P. von der Mühll, *Der Grosse Aias* (Leiden, 1930), p. 21.

77. Note the formal repetition of ἀεί τε . . . ἀεί θ' at the opening (835–36), and compare the repeated use of καλῶ in the curse invocation of Oedipus (*OC* 1389, 1391). On the use of prayer formulae in curses, see C. A. Faraone, "The Agonistic Context of Early Greek Binding Spells," in *Magika Hiera*, ed. Faraone and Obbink, p. 6; Kagarow, *Fluchtafeln*, pp. 41–44. For use of a highly decorated style in the curse tablets, see ibid., pp. 34 ff.

78. Oedipus, at *OC* 1376, calls for his curse demons as ξύμμαχοι; in magical spells such assistants may be called συνεργοί—e.g., *PGM* xii.237.

79. With his phrase ἀεί θ' ὁρῶσας πάντα τὰν βροτοῖς (836) compare the examples of empowering participles used in curse-tablet invocations, as cited by Kagarow, *Fluchtafeln*, p. 41. Compare also Electra's description of the Erinyes at Soph. *El.* 113, and the frequently used τὸν πάντα ὁρῶντα of a magician's daimon—e.g., *PGM* xiii.63.

ing that evil should come to them in phrases that show close regard for the rules that shape such magical utterance. He gives the call, "Come!" (843); he appends further instructive epithets, "O ye swift[81] and punitive Erinyes" (843); he continues formally with the ritualistic positive/negative pleonasm, "Devour! Do not spare!" (γεύεσθε μὴ φείδεσθε, 844).[82] Last of all comes the designation of those who are to be attacked by this curse: the whole body of the army (844). The destruction of the Atreidai named at the beginning is to carry with it a general debacle, for this anger is broader even than the wrath of Achilles.[83] Having spoken his curse, Ajax gives the Sun an assignment to perform for him (he is retiring, like an equal Night, before the Day);[84] he speaks his farewell to the landscapes that have nurtured him, and with his last words he promises to tell over his injuries and his curses in the underworld (865). Then he steadies himself like an acrobat and makes an ecstatic leap (πήδημα, 833), not over but onto the point of his sword.[85]

---

80. Compare the curse formula ἀδικούμενος γὰρ ὑπὸ . . . , discussed by Kagarow, *Fluchtafeln*, p. 39. Lines 839–42 should be deleted, as by Lloyd-Jones and others; see D. L. Page, *Actors' Interpolations in Greek Tragedy* (Oxford, 1934), p. 117. The scholiast at 841 notes their doubtful reputation; the infinitive followed by a third-person optative (840) is anomalous; the word φίλιστος appears only here, at 842. The magical statement is moreover skewed; "as I fall, let them seize" will not trigger any sympathetic destructive mechanism, which would require either, "as I fall, let them fall," or, seizing some object, "as I seize," etc. It might be noted that Quintus Smyrnaeus, who reports the Sophoclean curse though not the leap, obviously did not have these lines.

81. For the frequent magical demand for swiftness, see A. Cameron, "Sappho's Prayer to Aphrodite," *Harv. Theol. Rev.* 32 (1939) 9; cf. *PGM* vii.835a, ἵνα τάχει ἔλθετε, and the discussion of Kagarow, *Fluchtafeln*, p. 44.

82. For asyndeton in magic spells, see, e.g., *PGM* vii.659, and, closer to home, Soph. *El.* 115; cf. Kagarow, *Fluchtafeln*, p. 36, who finds it typical of curse style.

83. Sophocles had to construct a curse that would seem to his audience to have been in some degree effective; so, this general malediction which can claim a part in all the losses still to come here at Troy, and in all the disasters of the various returns. The blanket curse is also characteristic of Ajax because of its godlike unconcern for particular human lives.

84. The address to Thanatos and the second address to Helios should be deleted; Fraenkel noted 854–58 as a blatant interpolation, with its repetitions from the previous lines, its echo of Soph. *Phil.* 797, and its absurd premonition of a conversation in Hades; see *Due seminari romani di Eduard Fraenkel*, a cura di alcuni partecipanti (Rome, 1977), p. 30.

85. Both boys and girls were trained in acrobatic dances in which the performer leapt out of a circle of swords, or over a single sword set in the ground. For descriptions, see Xen. *Symp.* 2.11, 7.3; Pl. *Euthydemus* 294e; Ath. 4.124d. The funerary and Dionysiac associations of such performances are discussed by W. Deonna, *Le symbolisme de l'acrobatie antique* (Brussels, 1953), pp. 82–95, 105–8; for illustrations, see M. Davies, "The Suicide of Ajax," *AK* 14 (1971) 148–57, also "Ajax and Tecmessa," *AK* 16 (1973) 60–70, where it is supposed that Ajax did not jump but fell upon a sword that he still held in his hand (p. 65 n. 28). Certainly there are graphic representations that seem to depict a forward fall from a standing position, but the scene on the Brygos cup (*LIMC* s.v. "Aias I," 140) shows an Ajax who has been pierced back to front,

The unexpected violence of his final gesture gives extra power to Ajax's suicide curse.[86] There is no cry, for Hermes has granted accuracy to this ultimate show of strength, and the pierced corpse lies just out of sight. Nevertheless the arc of its fall (a literal fulfillment of Calchas' prophecy at 759) forces the spectator to imagine what will soon be described, then seen— black blood gushing from the nose and boiling out of a gigantic wound (918–19, 1411–12). And meanwhile, in the gaping silence that follows the thud of the body's contact with earth, the echo of Ajax's imprecation brings visionary curse demons toward the sacred attraction of gore. The death and the curse are thus one, in dramatic effect as in intention, but the physical shock of Ajax's leap is so intense (and the problems of its staging so flagrant)[87] that many scholars have overlooked the accompanying magical act.[88] Sometimes the curse goes unmentioned, as if it had not been spoken; more frequently it is loosely described as a "prayer," which may then be taken as a proof that Ajax is "reconciled with the gods."[89] And yet this staged curse is as anomalous and almost as sensational as is the staged suicide. Other tragic characters may use short vernacular phrases that invoke

---

which could only result from an acrobatic flip in the air. It is interesting to note that dances with swords were common at medieval carnivals; see P. L. Jacob, *Mœurs, usages et costumes au moyen âge* (Paris, 1878), p. 240, fig. 169.

86. In that it is like a dance figure, the leap is an act of skill misperformed, a perversion of a ceremonial gesture, and so it is conceptually analogous to a curse, since it stands to dance as curse does to prayer.

87. It is generally assumed that the opening in the scene building, dissimulated behind bushes, is the place where the sword is fixed and into which Ajax jumps, so that only his ultimate contact with the weapon will be invisible. A dummy is presumably then positioned in the same place, there to be discovered by Tecmessa when she is still just offstage (891) and brought onstage by Teucer (988). See, among many, P. Arnott, *Scenic Conventions in the Greek Theatre* (London, 1962), p. 131; S. P. Mills, "The Death of Ajax," *CJ* 76 (1980–81) 129; O. Taplin, "Spazio," *Dioniso* 59.2 (1989) 103–5; S. Stelluto, "La visualisazzione scenica," *Civiltà Classica e Cristiana* 11 (1990) 33–64; L. Pollaco, "Problemi di scenografia," *Numismatica e Antichità Classiche* 19 (1990) 77–97.

88. One reason for the accumulation just here of interpolated lines (839–42, 854–58) was that later actors and producers wished to emphasize the suicide over the curse, as more obviously sensational. The interpolations would make the curse ridiculous with specific details notably unfulfilled, while they would render the suicide sentimental and similar to "sacrificial" deaths like those of Antigone (Soph. *Ant.* 808–9), Polyxena (Eur. *Hec.* 435), Alcestis (Eur. *Alc.* 244), Iphigeneia (Eur. *IA* 1505), etc.

89. C. M. Bowra, for example, ignores the curse, though he has invented a "curse of Athena" (*Sophoclean Tragedy* [Oxford, 1944], p. 61); J. D. Mikalson suggests that Ajax's words are "really an intense wish," though he treats them as a prayer in "Unanswered Prayers," *JHS* 109 (1989) 81–98, esp. 93; O. Taplin concludes, "Ajax has made his peace with the gods and that is why he is able to spend much of his death speech in prayer" (*Greek Tragedy in Action* [Berkeley, 1978], p. 131). On the other hand, for full appreciation of the curse, see H. Weinstock, *Sophocles* (Wuppertal, 1948), p. 44: "Rachgier als verletzter Ehre—das ist Todeswort und Todestat."

destruction—"Be damned to him!" or "Rejoice in hell!"—but no other figure utters a full imprecation with its formal call, denunciation, petition, and
plea for swift action[90] (magical phrases were felt to be dangerous even in
imitation). Only Ajax, which is to say only Sophocles, risks daimonic activa-
tion by reproducing formulas that can be found in the magical papyri, and
from this we must conclude that the curse of this hero was indispensable to
his play.[91] It serves mechanically as the weapon of the second vengeance,
the means by which Ajax ransoms his honor. In the larger dramaturgical
scheme it is the device by which the audience both sees and hears the undi-
minished anger of Ajax. And on the transcendent level the curse works to
show Ajax's characteristic arrogance as it finally identifies itself with forces
more than human (though not, be it noted, Olympian). With his destructive invocation he claims a new set of immortal allies as replacement for
Athena, and for the first and last time in his life he transfers responsibility
for his own success to a stronger power. He hands his rage and his revenge
over to the crude justice of bloodsucking demons who will strike the
Achaean army at their own discretion.

Sophocles made the suicide's curse the central event of his play, a poetic
innovation unique in its represented violence and also in its perfect separation from all context. It is a secret action that depends upon a deception
of friends and closest kin; it is performed in solitude at the edge of a continent; and its full sense is never known within the play. Everyone on stage
sees the body, some even touch it, and they all understand that there has
been a suicide (906–7), but no one of them knows about the curse,[92]
though for Ajax it was this that made his a noble instead of a shameful
death. This audience, then, is in possession of exclusive knowledge shared
only with one another and the poet, and throughout the rest of the action
they nurse a piece of information that sets them apart from the speakers on
stage. Odysseus was granted a view of the frenzied Ajax with the beasts, but
they alone have received an eclipsing revelation in which the same man did
the same work over again with resolve and control, his action fully his own.
Only they recognize the self-drawn black blood as an active force that
engages the daimonic world, and only they know that the suicide has effectively revived the honor of this fallen Ajax.

90. Closest is Oedipus at *OC* 1375–92, see above, n. 75; next in fullness is Electra's curse-
prayer, Soph. *El.* 110–17. Oedipus may have given a complete curse in the Aeschylean play that
preceded the *Septem;* cf. A. P. Burnett, "Curse and Dream," *GRBS* 14 (1973) 343–68.

91. Another indication of the importance of the curse to Sophocles is the price he paid
for it: he had to give up the fairy-tale motif of invulnerability that Aeschylus had used in his
Thressai (schol. Soph. *Aj.* 833; Eust. *Il.* 14.404).

92. The motif of unattainable knowledge is accompanied here, as in other Sophoclean
plays, by that of the obscure oracle: just as no one on stage knows what Ajax has actually done,
so no one knows what it means that he might be "saved" (779; cf. 692).

In the first half of his tragedy Sophocles has thus constructed a bizarre second revenge for Ajax, one that defies the norms for this action and obscures all questions of justice. The deed of vengeance is complete, leaving the avenger's enemies demon-pursued, yes, but nevertheless they are alive, while he is a corpse—is this success or failure? The spectator is numbly convinced that he has seen what Ajax promised, a "fine death," but he has also viewed the hero's madness, learned of his error, and enjoyed the actor's shocking breach of stage conventions. He must somehow treat with the giant corpse that the action has left behind, but he doesn't know whether to blame or admire, and so, to help him find a place in his mind for this hero who is both destroyer and destroyed, Sophocles provides a review in which disputing characters come forward with opposing judgments. On one side Ajax is proved to have been a traitor, a villain, an enemy to all Greeks; on the other he is shown to have been a defender and savior. This only dramatizes the spectator's uncertainty, but Sophocles then produces the Odysseus who has been forced by the prologue's goddess to discover his own humanity. He does not come as mediator; he does not weigh the two arguments and proclaim a victory for one or the other. He comes rather as an antijudge, one who renounces all attempts at finding any ordinary right or wrong in the present case, urging instead that, in considering Ajax, the idea of justice is irrelevant.

All during the long final debate its material subject is visible, and the shrouded corpse grows in importance when it is flanked, halfway through, by the suppliant figures of Tecmessa and Eurysaces. The practical question is whether this dead body shall be buried or left to the dogs, but for those who speak, the true subject is the Ajax that once was alive. What is the ethical sum, when his criminal acts are added to his acts of courage? The contest is passionate, shaped by defensiveness and vindictive anger on one side, by pride and fierce resistance on the other. It is also sordid, wonderfully designed to make a listener feel how different Ajax was from men of this sort;[93] as Teucer says, one is ashamed to listen to this cheap vocal gesticulation (1161–62). At bottom, however, the long dispute proves to be an indecisive discussion of the conflicting rights of group and individual. The military organization, sometimes called the city (e.g., 1073, 1082) demands moderation and obedience from each citizen (1352), whether because it has superior physical strength (so Menelaus, 1062, cf. 1160) or because it is directed by men of superior sense (so Agamcmnon, 1252). This group takes to itself the right of revenge (1086); if an unruly member refuses to submit, causing the group to suffer, the community will make him suffer in return, because in a city as in an army, order depends upon fear (1074) and

---

93. This effect is intensified by the implicit allusion to the struggle over the corpse of Patroclus at *Il.* 17.128 ff.; see the discussion of R. Garner, *From Homer to Tragedy* (London and New York, 1990), pp. 60–61.

its partner, conformity to custom (1076, 1079, 1084). Teucer, from the opposite camp, asserts the continuing sovereignty of a powerful individual, even after he has entered a group (1096–1106). The army has survived only because of Ajax's extraordinary exploits (1272), and consequently he, as its benefactor, is outside its jurisdiction. In its final phases the dispute degenerates into a hurly-burly exchange of insults between a king and someone he chooses to regard as a slave, but the two arguments nevertheless continue to be equally destructive, each of the other. It is plain that the moderation of an ideal citizen has a dangerous likeness to the total submission demanded by autocrats, and that *sophrosyne* may come to mean responding to a whip like a patient ox (1253–54, 1259). And yet it is likewise plain that a single insubordinate individual, though he may be its savior, can threaten the continued existence of a community.

There is deadlock, and the bastard bowman is threatening the royal commander in chief with physical harm when Odysseus interrupts. His first remark seems to be an appeasement for both sides, but this is festival theater, not a lecture on citizenship, and Odysseus brings anything but a reasonable resolution to this conflict. Rather, it is a new transpolitical way of thinking that enters with him. Odysseus recognizes the law of revenge and reparation that moved Ajax and now moves the Atreidai (1323); he too gave back hatred for hatred, when to do so was fine and fair (καλόν, 1347), but such a return can sometimes cause a man to trample on another sort of right balance (1335). To begin with, the laws of the gods do not allow a living man, though he hate with the best cause in the world, to harm another who has died (1345). And on the other hand, in the case of a dead man who was noble and worthy, a failure to act out the positive reverence that superlative excellence must always produce undermines the laws of the gods (1342). To one who was made of noble stuff (1354–55), honor must be freely and positively given as *charis,* not merely in repayment of benefaction but in gratuitous celebration of innate quality, and this rule takes precedence over the ordinary practices of friendship and enmity. Men move in and out of those definitions, after all (1359, as Ajax had seen to his disgust), but the splendor of a truly fine nature is fixed beyond alteration. To recognize such splendor—such *arete*—wherever it appears is to act in a way ultimately right (it makes a man ἔνδικος in the eyes of his peers, 1363), and Odysseus himself provides such recognition for Ajax when (repeating the judgment of Homer) he says, "He was the finest man to be seen here at Troy, excepting only Achilles" (1339–41; cf. *Il.* 17.279–80). These are the words that, spoken earlier, would have awarded the arms to Ajax, but such magnanimity can be practiced, as Odysseus well knows, only toward the dead. Even spoken late, however, they constitute a kind of reparation.[94]

94. This restitution becomes material in later stories; Pausanias was told that when Odysseus was shipwrecked the arms were lost and that they finally washed up at the tomb of

In effect Odysseus says of Ajax: Don't try to classify his actions, ethically as injurious or beneficial, or judicially as initial provocation or answering revenge. Do not investigate his intentions, do not assess his success or failure. Look away from his particular actions and consider instead the inner force that impelled this man, in his revenges, in his impiety, as also in his courage. Whatever it produced, that force must be treated with reverence because of its excess, its sheer peloric thrust and magnificence. ("The tygers of wrath are wiser than the horses of instruction," as Blake had it.) Agamemnon of course can't understand this Pindaric imperative, and he yields only because he owes Odysseus a favor (1370–71). Teucer, too, still follows the lesser law of reparation, and the Atreid intention to outrage the corpse draws from him a pale echo of Ajax's great curse (1389–92).[95] The spectacle, however, follows Odysseus' exhortation, for Sophocles arranges the closing scene of his tragedy so that reverent honor shall be visibly paid to this suicide who attacked both enemies and companions with a superb rage.

The exodus scene is not long, but it predicts in action the cult that will be established for Ajax,[96] first on Salamis and then in Attica; each present regulation and gesture sketches an aspect, either of the heroic *dynamis* or of the rites that will give it recognition. To begin with, Teucer, as hierophant, directs that a hollow shaft be dug.[97] He also asks that implements of ritual

---

Ajax (1.35.4). Philostratus (*Her.* 11) reported that Odysseus offered to set the arms on the tomb as funeral decoration but that Teucer refused to allow it. The same passage of Pausanias (1.35.3) also preserves the tale of the miraculous flower that sprang up on Aegina at the time of Ajax's death, each petal marked AI.

95. It is interesting to compare this ordinary vengeance curse with the product of Ajax's rage. As administering powers, Teucer names Zeus, Erinys, and Dike, each with a single neutral epithet, a trio that Kamerbeek calls "maintainers of a moral world order," ad 1390. These three are asked but not commanded to oversee the destruction of Agamemnon and Menelaus in an optative construction that takes just two and a half lines.

96. Because there is no formal announcement, it has been said that nothing in the play points to future cult status for Ajax. This, however, is to overlook 1166–67, where the chorus predicts that Ajax will occupy a moldy tomb ever remembered by men (ἔνθα βροτοῖς τὸν ἀείμνηστον / τάφον εὑρώεντα καθέξει). It is in this context that Teucer assigns the double role of mourner and suppliant to both Tecmessa and Eurysaces, inaugurating offerings of hair and adding a particular curse to the protective power of the corpse (1171–84). For a full exegesis of the first of these passages, see A. Henrichs, "Aias and Hero Cult in Sophocles," *Cl. Ant.* 12 (1993) 165–80; for the second, see P. Burian, "Supplication and Hero Cult in Sophocles' *Ajax*," *GRBS* 13 (1972) 151–56. Henrichs takes issue with Burian for understanding φύλασσε in 1180 to mean that the protection is reciprocal, but in fact the suppliants do protect, in that their presence increases the potential ritual crime of disturbing the corpse: harm to them would activate the curse of 1175 ff. Further details intensify the sense that Ajax is invested with more-than-human powers; e.g., the uncanny rumor that passes through the host at the moment of his death (998–99), and the highly ambivalent choral phrase at 1214–15, where Ajax is said to be a free-roaming spirit consecrated to Hades, νῦν δ' οὗτος ἀνεῖται στυγερῷ δαί- / μονι.

97. The phrase κοίλην κάπετον occurs at *Il.* 24.797, of Hector's grave; see Garner, *From Homer to Tragedy*, p. 54.

purification be brought to the place of burial, in particular a tripod for sacred lustrations (1403–6), for Ajax is to be purified, as he said he would be in the deception speech. Some of the Salaminians are employed in these ways, while others are sent to bring the arms of Ajax as panoply for his tomb, as he had commanded in his farewell words (577). Teucer then formally breaks the contact between the two suppliants and the corpse that has been protecting them with its sacredness. He raises them, and Eurysaces, somehow no longer an infant (having drawn physical strength from the heroic corpse?), lifts the heavy body from one side while Teucer takes the other (1409–11). Together they proceed with it toward an invisible bier, with Tecmessa to follow as mourner, and from this procession Teucer calls out to all those who would name themselves friends of Ajax. They are to join in honoring this man who was in every way better than any other (1415–16). He seems in fact almost to command the formation of a chorus with his ritualistic pair of imperatives in asyndeton: "Move! Step out!" (ἄγε . . . σούσθω, βάτω, 1413–14). The black blood that still spurts from the hero's veins (1411–13) will be washed away, but the aggressive power that crested in the curse and the suicide now goes with Ajax to his tomb. And because they heard his words and saw his death leap, the spectators know that this huge anger—source of battle rage, of insults to gods, of slaughter of herds, and perhaps of disasters for erstwhile allies—is now in the keeping of the Erinyes. It endures, vital and accessible to men like themselves who have cherished the cult of this hero and enjoyed his answering protection.[98]

An *Ajax* tragedy did not have to be a play of revenge. Sophocles freely chose the fiction of a failed attempt on the Hellenic chiefs, then added his own invention, a second revenge by way of a suicide's curse. This allowed him to replace an image of frantic and foolish beast-slaughter with another in which a disciplined athletic feat is dedicated to supernatural powers. The first represented a wild and unjust return, divinely deformed, and it was presented as a peep show meant to give instruction to a fictional character. The second displayed the same intention, fired by the same angry passion but transferred to supernatural agents for its accomplishment. And it was presented directly to the audience, like a sacred drama shown to a group of initiates. This second image was then in turn overlaid with that of a corpse around which lesser creatures gather to lament, dispute, find protection,

98. Every Athenian in the audience will have taken part during his ephebic years in the annual celebrations at the Aianteion on Salamis (Paus. 1.35.3–4), having rowed over and raced there (Hesychius s.v. "Aianteia"; Deubner, *Attische Feste*, p. 228; see C. Pélékidis, *Histoire de l'éphébie attique* [Paris, 1962], pp. 225–47). There was also a place of worship for Ajax at the Eurysakeion in Melite; see W. S. Ferguson, "The Salaminioi of Heptaphylai and Sounion," *Hesp.* 7 (1938) 18, and inscr. no. 15, p. 94 of same vol. All will have been familiar with the statue of Ajax that stood among the eponymous tribal heroes in the Agora (Hdt. 5.6.6; Paus. 1.5.1), and roughly one-tenth of the citizen audience will have belonged to the Aiantid tribe.

and finally to pay ritual honors. The audience has thus witnessed the bare rectification of the central error that made this man what he was—his belief that he had no need of the gods. It has also watched the award of that honor from peers which both revenges were meant to repurchase. And above all it has seen, in a secret revelation, an expense of physical valor of such dreadful beauty that the hero's future cult status becomes almost comprehensible to the mortal mind.

For festival purposes, Sophocles has entirely dismantled the regularity of the revenge mechanism, everywhere baffling its tendency toward order. At the same time, however, his play has expanded the basic revenge passion, causing a ferocious demand for honor to swell into an eternal and unappeasable force. The anger of Ajax has been heard praising itself as the best legacy for a son and directing that Eurysaces be trained up in the savage habits of his father (548; cf. 556–57). It has, moreover, been seen extending its daimonic protection over a pair of suppliants. This anger has been staged as cruel madness and misguided slaughter, but it has also been given two unparalleled dramatic forms, one a full and solemn imprecation, the other an incredible acrobatic feat. And finally it has been imaged in the boiling rush of Ajax's own blood. This infinite rage of retaliation is nothing like the furtive and guilty resentment of a Vindice, and it is almost equally far from the practical sense of outrage that moved Odysseus against the suitors in the *Odyssey*. It is certainly not the justifiable indignation that Aristotle could admire (*Eth. Nic.* 1125b–1126b) but is instead something like the erroneous *ira* that Seneca condemned, in that it interferes with perception and is beyond the control of reason. Nevertheless, whereas Seneca's *ira* is an ugly mental crime (*delictum animi, De Ira* 1.16) that puts a man in opposition to Nature, the rage that moves Ajax is the same passion that made him *aristos* and *gennaios,* a preeminent man and a noble one. It transcends the particular excess or crudity of its own effects, and so it is similar to the fury of Heracles, a force closely related to the daimonic side of creation and one that is for any city both essential and dangerous. It lives in individuals who are necessarily savage but fortunately rare, and it is stored in the tombs of heroes—a current of primal energy that citizens can tap in time of danger and tragedians may regularly revive as part of Dionysus' chaotic celebration.

CHAPTER FOUR

Ritualized Revenge

Aeschylus' Choephori

In the Renaissance it could be said that where the bad bleed the tragedy is good, but this was not true at the Dionysiac festival. Simple, successful revenge was unsuitable for Attic tragedy, and yet its disguises, its deceptions, and its final principled burst of violence were attractions too strong for a poet to resist. In consequence the Attic dramatists turned to revenge fictions that could supply saving perversities—cases where the vindictive action failed, or where an improper agent performed it. Best of all were stories in which the vengeance duty was crossed by a contradictory imperative, and this is why all three of the greatest poets made tragedies about Orestes. Here was an avenger who was at one and the same time the most proper agent of death, according to the commands of masculine society, yet also the most improper, according to a fundamental human tabu. Orestes was a secondary avenger, in that he responded to an outrage against his father, but since it was his mother who was author of that outrage, the supreme honor that he was expected to pay to his male parent meant destruction for the female. He was thus in a sense a mirror-opposite to Oedipus, but this son who *under*valued his mother to the point of killing her had to break one of nature's oldest and strongest laws, not blindly like Jocasta's son, but with full intention and according to a cunning plan. The consequent tangle of contradictory duties, necessary atrocity, active resolve, and full knowledge made Orestes an irresistible subject for the poets of tragedy.

None of which was present in the story that the *Odyssey* proposed as a model for filial behavior. There Orestes' action against Aegisthus was simply the best available example of the right expression of one's duty as a son. Indeed, in the imaginary world of that poem, secondary revenge was the criterion that marked the boundaries of a kin-group. Each individual was a potential avenger who had to know how far his particular net of loyalties extended and what his own position was in relation to every other member. By the same token the group knew each man and would, when injury occurred, designate the correct seeker of repayment and insist that he act.[1] (Such pressure could come even from peers who were outside the kin-group, as Nestor shows in his advice to Telemachus.) Kin revenge was a plain social duty, and it was also inevitably political since, whether committed or omitted, it affected the inner organization of an agglomeration of human beings. The man who offered injury stole or at any rate altered another man's proper position, and the communal structure would return to normal only when the injury was given back. This public truth was expressed in the mythogram of the prince who avenges his murdered monarch-father by killing a usurper-assassin, and it marked all such tales with certain generic characteristics. First, the retaliation is not freely chosen (as is the primary defense of one's own honor); instead it is imposed by an abstraction, the agent's position within a particular group. Second, the agent is of interest to underworld powers (as a primary avenger is not) because unless he moves, he is open to curses from an injured kinsman who lives or to ghostly perse-cutions from one who has died.[2] Consequently the hero of such a story risks something like religious guilt, not (like a Jacobean) for taking revenge but rather for any failure, or even tardiness, in its fierce performance.

It is obvious that a successful revenge of this dutiful kind would not lend itself immediately to tragedy.[3] The Homeric Orestes who performed a clean Zeus-sponsored task assigned by filial duty (*Od.* 1.40 etc.) did not belong at the disorderly Dionysia, but there was another Orestes who did. The epic revenger had been asked to kill his father's cousin in a deed that society admired, but the chemistry of storytelling also created a slightly altered son of Agamemnon whose uncomfortable vengeance reflected men's questions about the hierarchy of kin. Of course Agamemnon's heir would kill an Aegisthus-assassin, but suppose his father's murderer had stood closer? Sup-pose (since myth's task is to touch extremes) that the assassin had been the closest of all, the avenger's mother? Storytellers[4] had put this question at

---

1. In some cultures artificial vengeance-groups are made through blood-brotherhood rites; see B. Heiderich, *Genese und Funktion der Rache* (Cologne, n.d.), p. 31.

2. Antiph. *Tetralogiae* 1.1.3; Pl. *Leg.* 734a; 854b–c5; 871a, cf. *Resp.* 573b1; 577b. The injured man looks to his avenger for a kind of rescue, much as a suppliant looks to his cham-pion, and in both cases the curse is the potential sanction, impelling a designated agent to action.

3. The secondary filial revenge action of Euripides' *Cresphontes* was presumably rendered disorderly by the blind attack of a mother upon her son; see A. P. Burnett, *Catastrophe Survived* (Oxford, 1971), pp. 18–21.

4. The process need not have been exclusively bardic; people everywhere were telling stories, whether they used epic formulae or ordinary speech, as Herodotus makes clear. For a convenient summary of the literary evidence, see A. F. Garvie, *Aeschylus, Choephoroi* (Oxford, 1986), pp. ix–xv.

least as early as Hesiod (fr. 23a30 M-W) and had answered that even in this extreme case Orestes would kill.[5] From this premise masters of oral narrative wove unrecorded but ever more elaborate fictions that can be glimpsed only in graphic representations.[6] The radical change, the mother-killing, doesn't appear in any surviving early depiction,[7] but there is, on a proto-Attic vase by the painter of the Ram Jug, a determined sword-bearing Orestes who pushes Clytemnestra as well as Aegisthus toward certain slaughter.[8] He has seized Aegisthus by the forelock (unless he bathes his hand in blood from a wound in his enemy's head), and he seems to be urged on by demonic creatures who throw stones.[9] Meanwhile the necessity for this killing of a mother was evidently made plain in accounts that now gave Clytemnestra a primary role in the murder of Agamemnon,[10] for on the Gortyn pinax (from the end of the seventh century) she actively assists, and in a bit of early-sixth-century metalwork from Olympia it is she who thrusts a sword into her husband's back while Aegisthus merely holds him in position.[11] Later yet, the preferred image came to be one that conveyed the

5. It is possible that in Hesiod, Orestes killed Clytemnestra as adulteress, not as murderess. It has been argued that matricide is implicit at *Od.* 3.305–10; according to Proclus, Clytemnestra was joined with Aegisthus in the seventh-century *Nostoi*, both in the murder of Agamemnon and as victim of Orestes' revenge, which was taken with the help of Pylades; see A. Lesky, "Die Schuld der Klytaimnestra," *Wien. Stud.* 80 (1967) 5–21.

6. These are most easily seen in the collection made by A. J. N. W. Prag, *The Oresteia: Iconographic and Narrative Traditions* (Chicago, 1985), where even the dubious representations are reproduced. See also D. Knoepfler, *Les imagiers de l'Orestie* (Zurich, 1993).

7. Unless this is the event pictured on a South Italian silver-gilt relief strip of 540–530 B.C. (Getty 83. AM 343), where a sword-bearing male steps over the fallen body of a man (Aegisthus?) to attack a standing woman (Clytemnestra?). Another scene on a bronze strip from Olympia of about 570 B.C. is identified by K. Schefold, *Frühgriechische Sagenbilder* (Munich, 1964), p. 89 and pl. 80, as the death of Clytemnestra, but see Prag, *Oresteia*, p. 35, for legitimate doubts.

8. Prag, *Oresteia*, pp. 6–7 B2 and pl. 5 b–c; Schefold, *Sagenbilder*, pl. 36; see J. D. Beazley, *Development of Attic Black-Figure* (Berkeley, 1951), pp. 8–9. Compare the later shield-relief from Olympia (Prag, *Oresteia*, pl. 22b; Schefold, *Sagenbilder*, fig. 44) where Orestes likewise takes Aegisthus by the hair. M. I. Davies, "Thoughts on the *Oresteia* before Aeschylus," *BCH* 93 (1969) 214–260, takes up Beazley's rejected suggestion and sees Aegisthus killing Agamemnon in the (unlikely) presence of an insignificant female; he reads the forelock or gushing blood as a "delicate hair-like net" drawn over the victim's head.

9. Beazley reported these as wild men of the woods (*Attic Black-Figure*, p. 9); Prag, *Oresteia*, p. 8, calls them a "hint" of Clytemnestra's Furies, but they might also be seen as demons demanding revenge for Agamemnon's murder.

10. It is strongly implied at *Od.* 24.200 that she did more than kill Cassandra. Davies ("Thoughts on the *Oresteia*") supposes that Clytemnestra was chief killer in the *Nostoi* and that this was the "Standard Version," but there is no proof.

11. For the pinax, see Prag, *Oresteia*, pp. 1–2 and pl. 1; Schefold, *Sagenbilder*, pl. 33; cf. Doro Levi, "Gli scavi del 1954 sull'acropoli di Gortina," *ASAA* 33–34 (1955–56), 275 and fig. 56. For the shield-strap decorations, see Prag, *Oresteia*, 2a; Schefold, *Sagenbilder*, fig. 43.

whole story of adultery, murder, and revenge in the figure of a Clytemnestra ready to defend her fellow assassin by smashing her son's head with an axe.[12]

Orestes' revenge certainly required mother-killing in the Stesichorean *Oresteia*, for that early-sixth-century poem told how Clytemnestra dreamed of a son-avenger who appeared in the form of a snake from the gash she herself had made in her husband's head (*PMG* 219).[13] And meanwhile this initial crime, the murder of Agamemnon, was being elaborated by storytellers who sharpened the gender conflict by making the wife kill her husband in behalf of her daughter,[14] while she herself threatened their baby son who had to be smuggled away by a herald or a tutor or a nurse.[15] With touches like these the maternal revenge victim was rendered more and more unnatural, so that she became not merely an adulteress and regicidal husband-killer but a more generally fearsome and monstrous female who attacked the male. And meanwhile the same fictional details urged the consumers of these elaborated kinship legends to think of the matricidal avenger as an innocent infant or a deprived exile. By such means the weavers of tales were able to treat this new mother-killing Orestes as one who had acted with something like the ethical simplicity of his Homeric prototype.[16] Nevertheless, as Clytemnestra became more threatening, it was inevitable that the tellers of Orestes tales should also give more attention to the young avenger and the atrocious side of his crime. The deed that Homer led one to imagine was easily described as an attack on a foppish Aegisthus, but how explain

12. The first appearance of the axe is in a metope from Foce del Sele, ca. 540 B.C.; see P. Zanconi Montuoro and U. Zanotti Bianco, *Heraion alle Foce del Sele*, vol. 2 (Rome, 1954), pl. 86; Prag, *Oresteia*, pl. 7a. For the axe on red-figure vases, see Prag, *Oresteia*, pls. 9c, 10a, 11b–c. In general, see E. Vermeule, "The Boston *Oresteia* Krater," *AJArch.* 70–71 (1966) 1 ff.; P. Ghiron-Bistagne, "Iconographie et problèmes de mise en scène," *Rev. Arch.,* 1978, pp. 39–63.

13. On the dream, see H. Eisenberger, "Der Traum der Klytaimnestra," *GB* 9 (1980) 11 ff., and bibliography cited there.

14. Pindar, at *Pyth.* 11.21–23, refers to this murder motive as if it were well known to a Theban audience of either 474 or 454 B.C. It may be that Clytemnestra mourns the sacrificed Iphigeneia in a Simonidean fragment (*PMG* 608), but nothing in the lines suggests that there was any connection with the murder of Agamemnon.

15. For Stesichorus (218 *PMG*) the female rescuer was Laodameia, as also for Pherecydes (3.134 *FGrH*); for Pindar she was Arsinoe (*Pyth.* 11.17); for others, Cilissa (Schol. Aesch. *Cho.* 733), while the male rescuer was later often identified as Talthybius; evidently there were at least three influential versions of the incident current at the beginning of the fifth century. For the emergence of Talthybius, see C. Robert, *Bild und Lied* (Berlin, 1881), pp. 149–91, and in general on the development of the legend see M. Delcourt, *Oreste et Alcméon* (Paris, 1959), pp. 22–24.

16. In one of the reliefs at Foce del Sele, Orestes coolly puts a blade into the back of a pleading Aegisthus; see *Heraion,* vol. 2, pl. 87. The sculptors, however, were presumably following a version of the story that also contained the matricide for there is a snaky form that seems to represent an Erinys on another metope (pl. 89).

the success of a mere boy against a queen armed not only with the curse of her maternal blood but also with a sizable axe?[17] No companion human or divine had been named in the *Odyssey,* though in the *Nostoi* (25–27 Davies, *EGF*)[18] the mortal Pylades seems to have lent a hand against Aegisthus. This later Orestes, however, clearly needed supernatural support as well, and so some genial poet—Stesichorus, or perhaps Xanthus, his predecessor[19]— named Apollo to the post of divine sponsor. Certainly the Delphic god offered Orestes a magic bow for repelling the demons of his mother's blood in the Sicilian *Oresteia* (Stesichorus 217 *PMG*), and with Phoebus in place the old story was ready to move into classical times. The revenge tale could now develop easily because, as son of Zeus, Apollo was the right god to reinforce a paternal claim for the loyalty of a son; as Paean, he was the right god to protect the avenger, should his mother's furies attack; and above all, as a divinity who watched over young men's coming of age, he was the right god to see a young man through a dangerous trial.

The story of Orestes as it had developed in the sixth century B.C. measured the furthest limits of duty toward a father, stretching them to include even a possible matricidal imperative. It also established the necessary and absolute hierarchy of the sexes, while at the same time fixing another sort of hierarchy in which both husband-killing[20] and disloyalty to a father were defined as crimes more heinous than matricide, while patricide was fixed by implication as the worst of all human transgressions.[21] Reversed to read positively, the tale of Orestes asserted that the artificial, culturally determined,

17. In Etruscan art the axe signified daimonic power; see Vermeule, "*Oresteia* Krater," p. 6, where it is described as "primarily a literary invention," suitable "not simply because it is the weapon of hybrid monsters and Amazons . . . but because it indicated character—the kind of woman who would kill her son to save her lover."

18. Likewise in Pind. *Pyth.* 11.15–16; cf. the painting that Pausanias saw in the Pinacotheca of the Propylaea (1.22.6). There are however no early pictorial representations of Pylades.

19. Xanthus of Locri was reputed to have been the source of some of Stesichorus' work, most particularly his *Oresteia,* according to Athenaeus (12.513 A). The association of Orestes with Apollo could of course be older; Artemis is shown on the Berlin vase by the Ram Jug Painter, and it is possible that Apollo was also there; see Beazley, *Attic Black-Figure,* p. 9. Wilamowitz and others supposed that the significant role for Apollo could only have developed at Delphi; see below, n. 61.

20. Compare the Alcmaeon myth, in which a wife's betrayal of a husband is likewise punished by matricide. Wife-killing was a lesser crime; so Periander's murder of his wife, in the telling of Herodotus (3.50–53), did not demand that his sons avenge her upon their father: Lycophron considered killing Periander but decided against it. When A. Lebeck termed Orestes' matricide "a greater crime than that which it must punish" (*The Oresteia* [Cambridge, Mass., 1971], p. 116), she applied modern culture-bound standards.

21. See the admirable discussion of C. Sourvinou-Inwood, *Theseus as Son and Stepson, BICS* Suppl. 40 (London, 1979), pp. 8–17. Patricide was literally unthinkable: Aristarchus wanted to expunge even the passing notion of such a thing from the mind of Phoenix at *Il.* 9.458–61; see Plut. *Mor.* 26F.

potentially aggressive honor owed to a male parent was ultimately of more value than the natural, instinctive, cherishing impulse that defined a mother as the one creature a man could never attack. All of which was very well as patriarchal theory illustrated by human figures who were mere mythic signifiers, but as soon as the story was told with fullness and decoration, as it certainly was by Stesichorus, its closure would seem to be challenged by its own contents. Greek society was not crudely patriarchal and in any case reverence for one's father was an intangible good, whereas one's mother's blood was a threat that was real and beyond all things polluting, when spilt. Consequently, as Hellenic society became more sophisticated, the two imperatives at work in the Orestes story came to press with almost equal force, so that its outcome no longer carried the simple, implacable truth of mythic demonstration.

At the beginning of the sixth century the Orestes fiction had attained a perfection of inner disorder. It turned upon two chaotic crimes, a husband-killing that made woman the master of man, and a mother-killing that dissolved bonds formed in the womb. Its hero defended the human household by attacking it and removed pollution by incurring more. And finally, with Apollo as sponsor, the story juxtaposed matricide and Delphi so that the most impure of commands originated at the Navel of the earth, the sacred place from which rites of purification were disseminated.[22] The material was potentially paradoxical enough for the Dionysia, and yet no early tragedy that we know of made use of it. Unless the matricide was somehow depicted, Orestes would be too virtuous—a pattern hero who attacked a tyrant, as he was shown on vases[23]—but let the mother-killing be too strongly present and he became vicious. And meanwhile the traditional presence of Apollo drained the human dynamic from the great patriarchal choice by robbing the avenger of independence. How was a tragedian to make a vital stage-figure of a man who was at once a knowing mother-killer and a servant of Apollo? Given any appetite for his work, he became a psychopath, but deprived of will, he was no more than a cardboard puppet, a sign that Del-

22. Cf. the summary of Sourvinou-Inwood, *Theseus*, p. 10: "The act of matricide is at once one of loyalty to the oikos and of disloyalty to it. It restores social order by punishing and eliminating the generator of disorder, and itself brings about new disorder. It both avoids and incurs pollution; it stimulates both divine help and divine persecution and punishment."

23. In the first decades of the fifth century a number of red-figure representations of Orestes' revenge appear (Prag, *Oresteia*, pls. 9c–d, 10, 15, 16, 17, 19, 20); see Vermeule, "*Oresteia* Krater," p. 14, who supposes a model or models "in fresco or poetry." All show a beardless and confident Orestes in the act of killing an Aegisthus who is throned (as usurper), effeminate, and sometimes supplicating; only the Boston krater of the Dokimasia Painter adds its unique scene of Agamemnon, murdered within the net (Vermeule, "*Oresteia* Krater," pp. 1–4, pls. 1–3). The first certain representation of the death of Clytemnestra is on a silver seal from Kerasa, late fifth/early fourth century (Prag, *Oresteia*, pl. 28c); here Clytemnestra is seated on an altar like Creusa, trying to protect herself from an Orestes who attacks with a dagger.

phi and patriarchy must prevail.[24] Such was the challenge, and at last, toward the middle of the century, Aeschylus took it up.

II

For Aeschylus the Atreid myth showed patriarchy challenged and restored, while it also reflected mankind's passage from enslavement to Nature, into a civic structure that held natural forces in fruitful bondage.[25] This was a move away from an initial, wild, and woman-wrought justice and toward a final institutionalized system of punishments administered by a court of men. This great human shift was, moreover, to be understood as reflecting a similar change in heaven's dominion, as the divinities of the sky first challenged a covey of irregular underworld powers, then brought those female demons into the Olympian system. In this grand double transit, the Apolline revenge served on both levels as middle term, a stepping-stone by which both men and gods passed from female threats of disorder into the security of male domination.[26] The fact that vengeance was a bridge was made manifest in the tripartite structure of the *Oresteia,* where Orestes' god-sponsored matricide stood as a refutation of the curse-driven female crime of the *Agamemnon* but also as an imperfect premonition of the new mode of punishment established in the final play. All of which meant that, for this middle piece, Aeschylus had to create an Orestes who murdered his mother without depravity, who embodied the premise of a Delphic punitive system without servility, and yet proved without failing that such a system was not a workable model for the achievement of secular justice.

The *Oresteia* as a whole represented a passage from wild to tame, from feminine to masculine, and its language painted this as a shift from monstrous to normal, from hunt to pasture, from dirty to clean, and from sickness to health.[27] This being the case, it was natural that Aeschylus should use the same notion of passage as he dealt with the special problems of Orestes' act of revenge. He saw that a principal made after the Telemachus model— one who moved out of boyhood by standing beside his father in an act of

---

24. This is how Orestes appears to the chorus at Aesch. *Cho.* 935 ff.: he is a creature moved by the oracle (940), a Poine touched by Dike, and the representative of all that is holy (935–36), a savior who cleanses the house and opens it to Time and Good Fortune, the supporters of legitimacy (965 ff.).

25. For a discussion of the *Oresteia*'s reflection of particular ritual models, see A. M. Bowie, "Religion and Politics in Aeschylus' *Oresteia,*" *CQ* 43 (1993) 10–31.

26. As S. Goldhill puts it, "the middle play . . . marks the *limen*" (*Language, Sexuality, Narrative: The Oresteia* [Cambridge, 1985], p. 207).

27. The systematic revisions in imagery were observed by Lebeck, *Oresteia.* Subsequent studies have carried her work further; thus Goldhill has noted a shift from a feminine *doxa*, as guiding principle in knowledge, to a masculine *phren*, from fleeting perceptions, *phasmata*, to permanent principles (*Language*, p. 37).

violence—could accommodate both the lack of freedom and the grotesque crime that his fiction demanded. And so the Aeschylean Orestes enters the *Choephori* as a very young man, one who is not yet the vase-painters' ephebe and certainly not yet a Hamlet, because he does not judge, or think, or feel. He and his friend have already been to Delphi and his instructions are plain: he is to become bestial in his anger (ταυρούμενος, *Cho.* 275)[28] and commit a cunning crime (274; cf. 556). Coming directly from the exile of childhood, however, it is impossible that he should follow this program. He has no general convictions about injury and retaliation, and what is worse, he has no wrath because he has no memory of his murdered father; the crime that he is to repay is only a tale told about another time and another place. And so Orestes moves ahead only because of a general wish to behave like a man, and also out of a particular fear, because he has been threatened with horrid persecutions if he does not act according to the Apolline command (278–90).

Orestes enters as a youth called to play a part for which he is not prepared, but he walks directly into a complex ritual that both empowers and instructs. He interrupts what is already a "contaminated" ceremony, a topsy-turvy rite originally meant to paralyze the anger of the dead Agamemnon but reformulated by Electra and the chorus so as to become a call for help from underground powers. Now it is given yet another aspect,[29] as chorus and solo singers ask the roused magic of the tomb to give young creatures, figured as eaglets, the right to hunt like adults (246–51).[30] The long cantata usually called the kommos is not, however, an imitation coming-of-age ceremony, nor is it a vehicle for decision or persuasion. Instead, it is a rite of transformation invented by the poet specifically for this stage, in order that his audience may witness a change that is not psychological but func-

---

28. I would leave line 275 in MS position. The difficulties of the passage stem from its mixture of positive and negative exhortation (particularly from the fact that τάδε in 276 must refer to εἰ μὴ μέτειμι at 273), and they are not solved by moving 275. As Garvie remarks, ad loc., the only real objection to leaving this line in its traditional position is "the intrusion of personal motivation into the description of Apollo's command." But since Apollo prescribes the mode of action (τρόπον τὸν αὐτόν, 274) why should he not specify spirit as well, especially as the importance of motive is a central theme of the trilogy? The god directs that Orestes should kill in anger over his stolen inheritance, an anger like that of a wild bull who defends his territory. (This, incidentally, is the same kind of anger that Aristophanes puts into Aeschylus' eye when he defies Euripides, at *Ran.* 804.) As a parallel Delphic command concerning the emotional concomitant of an action one might cite from the traditional oracles 163 Parke-Wormell = Paus. 8.9.3, spoken to the Mantineans about the bones of Arcus: ἔνθα σ' ἐγὼ κέλομαι στείχειν καὶ εὔφρονι θυμῷ . . . κατάγειν, κτλ.

29. Cf. Lebeck, *Oresteia*, p. 121: "The old form is put to new purpose. Motifs associated with invocation to the dead are used here to rouse the living."

30. K. Reinhardt long ago compared the kommos to rites that prepare a savage for the hunt; see *Aischylos als Regisseur und Theologe* (Bern, 1949), pp. 110–40.

tional.[31] According to Orestes, its central practicant, the purpose of the ceremony is simply to make contact with the dead (315–22). It is the chorus, however, that is in hierophantic position,[32] and according to them this great ritual is meant to extract from the Moirai a punishment for old crimes, a punishment that will take the form of an actual "bloody stroke" (312–13). And in fact such is its effect, for at the close of the rite Orestes is invested with new powers that make him the embodiment of that fateful "stroke" (458), one who is ready to bring Stasis (458) and savage, gory Eris (474) to this house. (By further describing their song as prelude to the paean that regularly welcomes a new-pledged household member, 342–43, the chorus also suggests a full reinstatement for this boy-exile, but other rituals will have to be performed at Delphi and Athens before the poet is ready to install Orestes on his father's throne.)

Consider the procedure of this transformation, as it is staged. First, the celebrants identify the dead Agamemnon as the source of an illuminating anger, fuel for coming action that Orestes must take into himself (324–31). They provoke that anger, reminding the dead man of his unheroic death but also of his kingly power (345–71); then the performance describes the present situation in which the young man must now exercise the new status he hopes to achieve. The contest ahead is with strong enemies who are also parents, and this reminder induces in the boy from Delphi a sense of helplessness and total reliance upon Zeus (380–85, 405–9). Meanwhile, however, as neophyte he is given lessons in hatred (386–92) and instruction in the theory of retaliation (400–404), while he himself calls upon the invigorating curses of the dead (406). He is then brought back from the point of self-negation by way of a particular set of teachings designed to convert his abstract, underworld-inspired anger into an explicit and directed wrath.[33] First Electra points to the persecutions she has endured, describing their wolf-mother[34] by her works, so that Orestes may know his prey (418–22).

---

31. This transformation is formally expressed in the song's description of itself, for it begins as a *goos* (320, 330), becomes a *threnos* (335), then a *hymnos* (475), a song of praise which will develop into a *paean* of victory (343, 478).

32. In a vendetta culture, women perform a mixture of lamentation and accusation which sets the masculine band in motion; for Mani, see B. Vlavianos, *Blutrache* (Jena, 1924), p. 63; for Sardinia, I. Tetzlaff, *Einladung nach Sardinien* (Munich, 1965), p. 153; in general, Heiderich, *Genese und Funktion,* p. 85.

33. This section is similar to the ritual denunciation (of an unknown killer) at the burial place of a victim, where the call was upon Zeus Areios (Harp. s.v. ἐπενεγκεῖν δόρυ). L. Gernet, *Droit et institutions en Grèce antique* (Paris, 1968), p. 78, calls this "une action magico-religieuse," having explained that "par le rite le vengeur se trouve participer d'une force par quoi l'accomplissement de la vengeance est assuré."

34. At Aesch. *Sept.* 898–99 the πότμος ἐκ πατρός is a fate that emerges from the father; cf. ἐκ θεῶν at Aesch. *Pers.* 373. Even closer to *Cho.* 421–22 is Soph. *El.* 619, where Electra reproaches Clytemnestra with her enmity, ἡ γὰρ ἐκ σοῦ δυσμένεια; cf. Paus. 9.14. The only reason for not taking *Cho.* 420 in this easiest sense ("Like a savage wolf the *thymos* that comes

Then the dishonorable funeral and unspeakable maiming of Agamemnon are held up like *sacra:* this is the knowledge that Orestes must carry branded upon him forever. His sister's suffering and his father's filthy dishonor are to mark him, as if cut into his flesh like an initiand's tattoo. "Write this on your heart," sings Electra (450), and the chorus repeats, "Let this tale bore its way through each ear and into your heart's still depths. These were their crimes: your own anger is for you to learn. The contest must be undertaken with unswerving rage" (451–55).

When the kommos is finished, Orestes has found within himself the same paternal daimonic anger that would have struck at him from outside, had he refused to act for his father. He will not suffer it, however; he will use it, for this implanted anger is to be directed explicitly against a mother (385, 421, 435) who is now known, as if by Orestes' own experience, as his sister's tormentor and one who hacked his father's corpse. Furthermore, this new anger does not answer to Apollo alone; it partakes of an Ate sent by the Underworld Zeus (382–85); it is supported and witnessed by curses of the dead (406), and it lives inside a filial agent who now has Ares and Dike (461) and the Moirai (306) as his further guardians. Orestes began by asserting that, even without a hint from Delphi, the political situation and the fate of his father together fixed vengeance as his unavoidable responsibility (297–305). Now the kommos-song has presented him to the father whose murder claims him as its avenger, and also to the powers that support that claim, and its ritual has invested him with the force he needs to carry out their demand.

All of this is made plain as soon as the singing stops. The newly empowered Orestes claims his father and Dike as his allies (479, 497–99), and then, still full of the underworld, he asks about the dream that inspired the ceremony from which he has just emerged. His question provokes a revelation, and the revelation in turn excites a solemn public vow by which Orestes formally assumes his new office. Her murdered husband's anger had formed a serpent in Clytemnestra's dreaming mind, and, hearing this, the vengeance initiate knows his special sign.[35] "I will be a snake," he says,

---

forth from our mother is not to be placated") is the general conviction that Electra should not say this. Thus Tucker announced that to read this way would be "disastrous," and Garvie states as fact that "Electra could never, even for a moment, imagine that her troubles would abate if she were to flatter her mother." What Electra says, however, is that the aggressive spirit of their mother is implacable and savage and that she suffers from it. There is nothing shocking in the notion that she might, at one time or another in all these years, have tried to mitigate the queen's persecution (or have seen another make the attempt), but in fact the clause containing the verb σαίνειν is impersonal and hypothetical: "one may make gestures of appeasement," she says, "but the torments are not charmed away" (420).

35. In late magicians' initiations, a falcon flew down, flapped its wings, and dropped an oblong stone, at which the initiate was instructed: "You should pick up this stone" (*PGM* 1.64–66); see F. Graf, "The Magicians' Initiation," *Helios* 21 (1994) 161–77.

"and I will kill her as the dream commands" (549–50). These words mark his intention to proceed; with them he actively chooses to go on to the next phase of the contest that has been set by Apollo and by Agamemnon.[36] What is more, these words also mark Aeschylus' solution to the potential problems of the puppet principal, as Orestes with them freely claims the double function that is thrust upon him. He will be a patriarchal avenger in the secular world and a Delphic erinys in the daimonic realm (cf. 402).[37] Thanks to the kommos and its magic, however, Delphi has temporarily sunk into the background so that Orestes now goes to work like his Homeric counterpart, as a son who freely chooses to avenge his father.

Orestes' obedience to Apollo has been reformulated as a willing entry into a secular contest set by father and city, and as such it is likened to the many forms of active submission through which mortals everywhere move from one phase of life to another. What is more, the mother-murder becomes, in this metaphorical context, the trial through which a ritually prepared candidate must pass (κίνδυνον περᾶν, 270),[38] and this helps the poet to solve his second great dramaturgical problem—how to help his audience to tolerate an intolerable crime. As contest, the matricide is now congruent with the fairy-tale dragon-battle on which a hero's power is based, and in support of this effect the poet gives his Clytemnestra strongly monstrous qualities.[39] Already in the *Agamemnon* the husband-killer has been figured as a sea monster—a stinging double-headed serpent, a devouring Skylla (*Ag.* 1233–36)—or yet more horribly as a disembodied pair of biting jaws (1232). Here her first image is that of a coiling snake who attacks the children of the Agamemnon-eagle (ἔχιδνα, *Cho.* 248–49), and this figure is confirmed at the end when Orestes stands over her body. He is making, before gods and men, his public claim to his own just act of revenge, and he needs to identify his female victim. He has referred to her as mother (989) and one who carried him in her womb (992), but these terms miss the mark and he struggles for greater accuracy. Say rather a water serpent so aggressively evil and so poisonous that, without even biting, she causes whatever she may touch to rot (994–96)! The chorus renders the same idea as folk legend when it sings of a champion who frees the land by cutting off the heads of a pair of dragons (1046–47). And so, whatever we thought while watching the *Agamemnon,* it is plain that we are now to see this woman not as a human being but as the hero's monstrous opponent, and this

36. The τείσει that refers to Clytemnestra at 435 (or τείσεις, if one prefers Herwerden's correction to that of Kirchhoff) now becomes κτείνω νιν (550).

37. See J. E. Harrison, "Delphika," *JHS* 19 (1899) 213; note that at Aesch. *Eum.* 127 the collectivity of Clytemnestra's Erinyes is termed δράκαινα.

38. Cf. 455, καθήκειν with ἀγῶνα understood; also the ξιφηφόρους ἀγῶνας overlooked by Hermes at 584 and 729; more generally the metaphor of a chariot race at 794–800.

39. See N. S. Rabinowitz, "From Force to Persuasion," *Ramus* 10 (1981) 159–91.

instruction is made specific in the icon of Perseus and Medusa. It is under that sign that Orestes enters the place where he must kill, the chorus singing as he disappears, "Keep the heart of Perseus in your chest and deliver to friends living and dead what will give them joy—a bloody Gorgon-fate for enemies within" (831–36).[40] With Medusa as her doublet, Clytemnestra is confirmed as one of nature's horrors, a female sprung from the copulation of chaos monsters, and one so ugly and evil that her mere picture could keep bad spirits at bay. By the same stroke her killer becomes a young hero of interest to the gods, and one whose exploit will eventually establish him as ruler of a city.[41]

And yet Clytemnestra must also remain a woman if the patriarchal thrust of the myth is to keep its force. If she becomes wholly monstrous, then Orestes' choice will be not of male parent over female but of human over nonhuman. Consequently, as soon as the revenge plan is plainly stated, the chorus sings an ode that makes Clytemnestra the prime representative of a male-destroying passion that is typical of human females and the crowning horror of the universe. She is a woman whose aggressive evil surpasses that of storms or comets of the air, or all the dreadful creatures known to sea and land (584–651). In this way Aeschylus does all that a poet can to identify his vengeance victim as the embodiment of a threat offered by an entire devouring sex, but nevertheless when she actually appears, Clytemnestra can of course have only the commonplace stature of the other figures in the playing area. She will speak as they do, move as they do, and once she is reduced to this ordinary scale, even her poet will no longer be able to dissimulate the essential mythic fact about her—that she is a mortal woman who gave birth to the young man who must kill her. Before the trilogy is over, the audience will be told that mothers have no blood relationship with their offspring, that they are, as Egyptians and Pythagoreans had taught,[42] only the soil in which a father's seed is sown. That, however, must be left for Apollo to explain (*Eum.* 658–61). Here in the revenge play Aeschylus is not ready to suggest that mothers are not kin to their children, because that would palliate the awesome irregularity of his chosen tragic crime.

40. The last phrase, 836–37, looks like a typical Aeschylean simplification or qualification of a possibly too-elaborate previous statement; for this reason a second imperative in 837 seems best. If Murray's ἐξαπόλλυ' εἰσορῶν is right, then the sense is: Behead your enemies, as Perseus did the Gorgon, but destroy with your eyes wide open (since your opponents have no magic)!

41. By imposing the inevitable image of the Gorgon's threatening mouth/vagina (explicit on a bronze chariot-fitting from Perugia, ca. 540 B.C., *LIMC* s.v. "Gorgones," 89) the comparison also supports Orestes' identification of his mother as lecherous adulteress (894–95, 917), while it blocks the effect of her own appeal to her nurturing breast. Since the Gorgon was nonetheless markedly androgynous, the image also serves the identification of Clytemnestra as a man-woman (Aesch. *Ag.* 11, 351, etc.).

42. A. Peretti, "La teoria della generazione patrilinea in Eschilo," *PP* 11 (1956) 241–62.

The killing of Clytemnestra must remain viscerally appalling, while it is yet in this particular instance not ethically repellent, and Aeschylus achieves this contradictory effect with an appeal to the rules of reciprocity that governed parents and children. A child was not to harm a mother because that child owed the exact opposite, benefactions, as a return for the nurture she had given.[43] If there had been no such nurture, then obviously the child was not bound to make beneficial return and might instead show loyalty to his other parent. Ritually speaking, the blood of an unnurturing mother would still pollute, but a crime against her would no longer have the ethical stigma of ingratitude. And so it is on this point of nurture that the dramatist makes his preliminary attack, not yet upon maternity in general, but upon the maternal status of this particular woman. He takes the storytellers' motif of Orestes' childhood separation from his mother and pushes it back to the moment of birth, destroying Clytemnestra's claim to mercy owed in return for nurture. He does this, moreover, in three-dimensional stage terms by displaying the mother's replacement, the woman who actually gave food and protection to this present avenger. The Nurse is an almost carnivalesque figure,[44] a fearful, loving, complaining, Shakespearean old nanny who is a fresh surprise each time one turns to this play. She appears at a moment of melodramatic tension,[45] for Orestes and Pylades are inside the palace in company with a suspicious Clytemnestra, while Aegisthus and his armed men are not far away. More important, this is a moment of doubt for the spectator who, though he expects to see Clytemnestra's body before the play is done, does not know what he ought to feel about such a spectacle. This old lady, however, is come to give his mind the right set. First, she is validated by a somewhat unconventional announcement of her office: she is Nurse to Orestes (τροφὸς 'Ορέστυυ, 731).[46] Then she explains what this means. On the day of his birth, she took the infant directly from his mother's womb (she may have delivered him, μητρόθεν δεδεγμένη, 750), after which she was appointed to his care by his father (762). It was she who fed him, she who changed his diapers, she who did all the things that must be done to keep a newborn alive, using up her own life to do so (749–50). Naturally, then, it is she who now mourns him at the (false) news of his death, while his so-called mother smiles into her sleeve (738–39). And naturally

43. Which becomes the debt owed to a father- or motherland for its nurture; e.g., Soph. *OC* 795; Isoc. 4.24.

44. On babies, and especially on the motif of urination, see M. Bakhtin, *L'œuvre de François Rabelais* (Paris, 1970), p. 151. For wet nurses in classical Athens, see H. Ruehfel, "Ammen und Kinderfrauen," *Antike Welt* 19.4 (1988) 43–57, where Abb. 17, a Tanagra figurine (Vienna, Kunsthist. Mus., Antikensam. V.1400), might almost be the *Choephori* nurse.

45. The episode serves ethically much as the Belly War does in Odysseus' revenge, giving the hero a happy positive color and thus promising success. Here, however, the comic figure also functions in the intrigue, as a lure to draw one of the victims into the revenge trap.

46. See O. Taplin, *The Stagecraft of Aeschylus* (Oxford, 1977), pp. 345–46.

too it is she who unwittingly works as his ally in vengeance by distorting Clytemnestra's message and drawing Aegisthus unarmed into the palace trap.

The Nurse makes the revenge mechanically possible by suppressing Clytemnestra's request that Aegisthus come with a company of armed retainers (769–70), but that is the sort of thing an apprentice playwright might have arranged. The real function of this figure is to make the revenge ethically possible by destroying Clytemnestra's right to use the maternal breast as her shield and sign. Consider the sequence of scenes. First we are shown a devious Clytemnestra alerted by her dream—one who hides her rank, pretends grief at a report of Orestes' death, and at once sends for the soldiery.[47] The next time she appears, Aegisthus is already struck down and she is facing the prince whose vengeance is not yet finished. She has solved the riddle of his identity, and her first act of recognition is to call for her notorious axe so that she can kill this returned son (887–91). She means to defend to the death the palace and lover that are hers, but when she realizes that Aegisthus is beyond help, she thinks of herself and chooses an alternate weapon. Opening the shoulder catch of her dress, she turns full upon Orestes and calls, "Stand back at the sight of this breast where so often you sucked good milk and slept" (896–98).[48] And for an instant that one breast fills Orestes' entire vision; he no longer sees either his father's tumulus or Apollo's distant temple but is as frozen as if he had looked straight at Medusa. "Should I stand back from killing a mother?" (899) he wonders, but Pylades reminds him that even a mother may be treated as an enemy, if thereby one saves the friendship of Apollo (902).[49] Orestes is satisfied, because he has recently heard the voice of that very god, demanding the death of this woman. And we who have not been to Delphi are also satisfied, because we have just heard the Nurse in the preceding scene. We know that

47. Many critics, in search of psychological drama, insist upon softening Clytemnestra; thus Garvie again and again notes her "sincerity," finding, for example, "the sincere and natural reaction of a mother" at 691–99, in spite of the immediate fact that in this scene the queen is denying her own identity (716), in spite of her subsequent call for armed men, and in spite of the Nurse's plain announcement of the falsity of her lamentations (737–40).

48. Speculations about the staging of this gesture are sometimes amusing. Recently it has been fashionable to say that Clytemnestra sketches a tasteful indication: "lays her hand on her breast," "a mere gesture towards the costume" (so O. Taplin, *Greek Tragedy in Action* [London, 1978], p. 61; cf. J. M. Walton, *Greek Theatre Practice* [Westport, 1980], p. 191). The reasons for this are supposed to be "decorum" and the fact that actors were male: "One can hardly imagine that a male actor would have opened his dress to display an artificial bosom!" (Walton, *Greek Theatre Practice*, p. 191). There is, however, no need for such anachronistic imaginings, given the distance between audience (without opera glasses) and players, and given also the highly conventionalized nature of Attic representation: a body painted white to signify femininity might have marked on it in an earth color the same near circle that indicated a woman's breast in some schools of vase painting; cf., e.g., *LIMC* s.v. "Amazones," 92 (c); 302(c), (d).

49. Or perhaps "if thereby one avoids making an enemy of Apollo."

this melodramatic move of Clytemnestra's[50] is as fraudulent as her crocodile tears over the death of her son. We know that only in the dream did Orestes suck at this breast. Clytemnestra cannot demand a return of nurture for nurture, of care in old age for care in infancy (ἔθρεψα, 908), because it was not she but the old woman, his *trophos,* who gave milk to Agamemnon's son and kept him alive.[51]

The chorus had counseled, "When she says 'Child!' do you answer, 'Yes, my father's!'" (829–30),[52] and that is exactly what Orestes does in this unparalleled scene. Clytemnestra pleads for her life, four times addressing Orestes as "child" (*teknon,* 910, 912, 920, 922), but when she pretends to have cared for him, he answers that she killed his father and reminds her that a wife owes a return to her husband for nurture (921). His essential choice, however, that between male and female parent, has nothing to do with practical benefits. When Clytemnestra sees that no appeal to the laws of gratitude will touch Orestes, she threatens him with her curse (924). "Beware of a mother's demon dogs!" she screams, but his answer is sharp and firm. "Better yours than my father's!" he says (924–25). A mother's anger has weight in the demonic world, but a father's has more, and that in effect settles the question. Clytemnestra formally recognizes Orestes as the punitive snake-son of her dream, but while they move off, his exit line defines the unseen killing-spot as the meeting place not of mother and son but of a pair of abstract prohibitions: "You killed one who ought not to be killed, so you suffer what ought not to be suffered" (390).

The *Cheophori* is half over before its mechanical revenge begins, but the extremely efficient intrigue is nonetheless perfectly conventional in its details. There has been a recognition, with the motif of a female relative to be rescued; there has also been a denunciation (in the kommos), and even a replay of the original crime, for Clytemnestra's attempt to disempower Agamemnon with placations (impious because as his killer she is forbidden all ritual contact with him) repeats her original attack on his corpse. This quick revenge has used disguise (at least of tongue, 564) and falsehood (674 ff.), the whole being defined as a piece of deceit (566–67, cf. 274; 726, 888, cf. 947, 95). And as for divine aid, in addition to the great call upon

50. The gesture is a conventional one, but in its best-known instances it is used not by a woman who wants to save her own life but by one who begs her son to save himself; e.g., Hecuba, *Il.* 22.80–82; mother of Geryon, Stesichorus S 13.5 Page, *Suppl. Lyricis Graecis;* Jocasta, Eur. *Phoen.* 1567–69. The other prominent parallel will not make Clytemnestra's move here any more admirable, for it is supplied by the notorious show of Helen's breast, when pleading with Menelaus; cf. Eur. *Andr.* 629, Ar. *Lys.* 155–56. I cannot, however, recognize as Aeschylean the sexual overtones discovered by N. Loraux, "Matrem nudam," *L'Écrit du Temps,* no. 11 (1986) 90–102.

51. Cf. Loraux, "Matrem nudam," p. 97: "c'est la nourrice et elle seule qui a nourri l'enfant."

52. Reading θροεούσαι with Murray and Rose.

Agamemnon and the underworld powers in the kommos, there are two revenge prayers uttered by the chorus, a short one to Tricky Peitho and Underworld Hermes (726–29) and a full-scale petition addressed to Zeus, with a nod to Hermes as well (783–818). Access to the victims is gained by the familiar means of a distorted ritual, this time the stranger's formal claim to hospitality (656, 662).[53] And finally, the offstage violence is indicated to a waiting chorus by cries from within (869), then consummated in a display of bodies that allows the revenger to claim his work and to recommend it as justly done (972 ff.). Such a brisk unrolling of the expected gives the event a breathless inevitability, while it also leaves the two dramaturgical innovations strongly emphasized. First, the long delay between recognition and intrigue adds an aesthetic suspense to the ritual dynamic of the kommos. And second, the unusual choral intervention when the Nurse is subverted allows that wonderful woman to destroy Clytemnestra twice over, by falsifying her message as well as by telling the truth about her uncaring maternity. And finally, the extraordinary confrontation of victim with unmasked avenger—of Clytemnestra with the recognized Orestes—distills the entire action into its essential material: a conflict between the command of Zeus' son and the appeal of a mother's breast.

This tightly regular but tellingly distorted vengeance action is accompanied by some of the plainest rationales for revenge that can be found anywhere. The chorus is quick to suggest Orestes' name (115) and his coming as an avenger (121) as suitable subjects for Electra's revised prayer; they are proud of their own anger (386–92) and strong in recommending that same passion to Orestes (454), and they have never swerved from their conviction that the old blood crime must be answered with a duplicate of itself (312–14, 400–404, etc.). A vengeance killing is in their words a *charis* owed to friends who have suffered outrage (834; cf. 44, where it is *charis acharitos,* a benefaction, albeit an unlovely one), the ultimate act of gratitude in a society knit together by kin obligation. Moreover, in this present case it is also an attack upon a monstrous evil that has come in the form of female passion, and so its work is the work of Justice itself:

> A sharp sword thrusts
> right through the breast
> —such is established law—[54]
> where Dike is found trampled
> and men step off the path
>   of reverence to Zeus.

> That sword props Justice at its base;
> Aisa, weapons-maker, hones it sharp;

53. Orestes was also ready to use false suppliancy if necessary (569).
54. Reading θέμις γὰρ οὖν at 641 with Garvie (after A. Ludwig).

so now a famed deep-thinking Fury
sends at last a child into this house
to recompense the filth
    of ancient bloody deeds.[55]

(639–51)

Such were the reflections of the chorus when the murder plan was made, and their view does not change. When Clytemnestra is forced back into the palace where her throat will be cut, they burst into a hymn because they recognize Dike and Poine, Justice paired with Vengeful Requital, in joint epiphany (935, 946–47). It is finally Apollo whom they salute, however, for it is he who has sent these sacred powers to destroy a pair of polluted victims (944), supplying a mortal agent (940–41) so that the house might revive and be cleansed. And in time, when the purification has been completed, they expect a return of good fortune after this revenge, not just for the palace but for all who dwell around it (965–71).

Unlike the vase painters, Aeschylus has chosen to confront the mother-killing directly, coming as close to its actual depiction as theatrical convention would allow. True, he spares his audience any overheard cry, but that is because his Clytemnestra has made her desperate life-and-death appeal on stage and each spectator has received the direct shock of her bared maternal breast. And meanwhile, with the horror of the matricidal sword-thrust so intimately represented, the dramatist has underlined the regularity of the revenge thus achieved, so that the disorienting paradox of the myth should have its sharpest outline. Orestes is both savior and deadly doom (σωτήρ and μόρος, 1073–74). Neither of these definitions has any flaw in it, and in consequence this rescuer who is a mother-killer challenges the very notion of ethical definition. And since he is also a pawn in a game being played by daimonic powers, his deed makes one wonder about the gods' ability to discriminate in these matters. Can even immortals find their way in a creation where opposites melt into one another?

The chorus has found something called justice, yet ethical confusion has spread to become theological concern, and Aeschylus chooses to give this unstable situation dramatic form in Orestes' wild retreat before an attack of invisible Furies. This, the play's final event, is usually spoken of as a scene of madness;[56] indeed the one thing everyone thinks he knows about this play

55. Garvie insists (ad loc.) that the sense cannot be "Erinys brings child to avenge" because that would require τίνεσθαι, and consequently he hears an assertion that Orestes is brought in to pay by his own suffering for the crime he will commit! It is true that the active is used of him who pays, but it is also true that the avenger owes his enemy an injury (just as the victim owes the avenger suffering), so that he too may "pay." This is most clear at Soph. *OC* 230, where τίνειν means to repay suffering to someone who has made you suffer.

56. So Lebeck, *Oresteia*, pp. 107–9, who describes Orestes as "the child whose birth ends in his mother's death and his own madness." It would be more correct to say that his birth ends in the formation of the Areopagus and his own return as ruler to Argos. Goldhill, *Language,*

is that Orestes runs mad in the end.[57] Which is astonishing, because in these final lines the poet specifically denies that his hero is insane. The situation must be considered closely. Orestes has shown the bodies of his victims and spread out the bloodstained bit of tapestry that accuses them of Agamemnon's death. Then, letting go of the cloth whose pollution he now shares (1017), he suddenly makes an unexpected and incomprehensible gesture—he leaps, or shudders, or whirls. In response to an unexpressed choral question he explains (ὡς ἂν εἰδῇτ᾽, 1021) that he has been invaded by a sudden fear, a Phobos that wants to sing and dance within him. This is what drives him off course, and it makes him doubt whether he will long be in control of himself (1022–26), but while he is he has a statement to make, as head of the House. The matricide was just, because Clytemnestra was polluted and hateful to the gods; moreover, he was given strength to do it by Apollo, who assured him that he would not be charged with evildoing (1027–32). This announcement made, Orestes for a second time today changes costume; earlier he took up the false baggage of a peddler (560, 661), but now he grasps the tufted branch which transforms a man into a suppliant (1035). With it in hand he can approach the untouchable sanctity of his patron god, but there is no knowing how long he will have to wander as an exile. Should Menelaus return first, he is to be told the reason for Orestes' absence (1041–43).[58]

Orestes is thinking sanely about the future rule of Argos, but in the middle of his practical words he gives a double shriek (between 1047 and 1048). Creatures like Gorgons crawling with snakes (1048–50) have suddenly appeared, and in abject fear he runs toward the parodos that leads away from home. Only he can see these monsters, and the chorus leader assumes that they are phantoms, private symptoms of an insanity caused by

---

pp. 99 ff., seems to take Orestes' madness both as clinically genuine and also as a metaphor for the inevitable disjunction between one man's perception (and so language) and another's. Finally, however (p. 202), he will have it all ways at once: "For how/when is Orestes mad (if he is)? Can we define the point when he becomes mad? His (mad) language seems logical enough, without even the 'symptoms' of madness one might expect from, say, Shakespeare (not to mention Artaud or Nietzsche)."

57. Euripides will give his Orestes bouts of raving madness, and countless legends in the Peloponnese and Magna Graecia told how his madness was healed in some local shrine; e.g., Arcadia (Paus. 8.234 1–3), Rhegium (Hyg. *Fab.* 261). At Taurus the final cure was associated with the end of the practice of human sacrifice, so that in this mythic model Furies and gods simultaneously distanced themselves from human blood.

58. The sense of these perhaps damaged lines is that Menelaus, as normal regent in Orestes' absence, should know his, the true ruler's, status: that his action was just and that he is engaged in a purification which may eventually allow him to return. It is notable that everything that Orestes says in this so-called scene of madness is marked by plain common sense, in sharp contrast to Renaissance mad-scenes which were used by poets as an excuse for strained language, grotesque comedy, and the portrayal of extremes of passion, most commonly grief.

the blood that is now on his hands (1055). In pursuit of this idea, she predicts that Apollo will cure the sufferer as if from a disease, by a simple touch of his hand (1059–60). To all of which Orestes objects stubbornly. True, his fright is within him, but these new horrors are *not* visions and they are *not* internal: they are actual demons materialized from his mother's curse (1053–54). He calls Apollo to witness how they swarm around him (1057), but he knows that creatures whose eyes drip real blood will not be defeated by mere purification. They are not emanations from his own strained mind, not simple reifications of miasma, but particular demonic presences— maternal Furies, and as such powerful representatives of that mother- oriented section of creation which has been challenged by his act of Delphic vengeance. With heightened perception he sees what those around him do not,[59] but he sees truly, and the next play will give ocular proof that sane men can also look upon the Furies.[60] Meanwhile Orestes ends this play in a psychic condition more disturbing than madness, for he runs off in stark, intolerable fear before an attack by creatures who swarm and multiply, embodied horrors with hatred oozing from their eyeballs (1057–58).

The *Choephori* thus does not end in madness, but it does produce panic and a political vacuum because, in the scheme of the trilogy, Orestes' adventure represents a rejected hypothesis. It might seem that deeds of loyal masculine vengeance, sanctioned and purified by Apollo, would be the logical alternative to the curse-driven work of a Clytemnestra, but to the Aeschylean way of thinking a Delphic erinys is a contradiction in terms. In his three-part story of the great shift from wild, woman-made vengeance to the city's Olympianized revenge, Orestes' return paid to his father's killers represents a Delphic bid for the punishment function, seriously proposed and seriously rejected.[61] It is not simply that an overtaxed punishment agent

59. Attic dramatists were alive to the effects to be got when an actor worked against an invisible stage presence, as witness Io's dance passages, [Aesch.] *PV* 561–607 and 877–86 (unless one supposes a mute dancer who pursues). There were also scenes in which the audience could see what an actor could not see, as at Eur. *Rhes.* 675 ff., and apparently in Soph. *Inachus* (Hermes in his cap of invisibility).

60. Contrast the cases of Ajax (in Soph. *Aj.*) and Heracles (in Eur. *HF*). Ajax looked at what others saw as sheep, saw them as men, and treated them not as others would treat either; Heracles looked at what others saw as his own children, saw them as belonging to Eurystheus, and treated them as no one's children are ordinarily treated. In the first case the audience is permitted to see the actual sheep, in the second the actual children, so that it has direct experience of what is labeled as the sane perception. Here Orestes looks at what others see as nothing, sees demons, and runs from them as anyone would from pursuing tormentors; at the beginning of the next play the audience is allowed to see, not the emptiness that this chorus saw, but the same demons here described by Orestes, from which they can only conclude that he is as sane as themselves.

61. There is no need to posit an actual Apolline claim to supervise earthly justice, put forth in a Delphic *Oresteia*, as did Wilamowitz, *Aischylos-Interpretationen* (Berlin, 1914), pp. 192–93; *Griechische Tragödien*, vol. 2 (Berlin, 1900), pp. 135 ff. Cf. A. Lesky, "Die Orestie des Aischylos,

might run mad—that is a flaw in any system of human justice—but rather
that mortal order depends upon a kind of abject horror that could never
live at Delphi (*Eum.* 192–95).[62] Punishment can only do its real work of
holding off anarchy and preventing crime if it inspires a sordid and degrad-
ing fear which can paralyze the worst as well as the best of mankind,[63] and
phobos and Phoibos cannot cohabit (*Eum.* 194–97). This is why the visible
Erinyes of the next play, Clytemnestra's "dogs," are driven away from Delphi
as loathsome monsters but cajoled into settling under the Areopagus at
Athens. And this is also why the unseen but all too real demons of the
Choephori must implant an unreasoning Phobos (1024)[64] in the sane
Orestes of the final scene of this, the vengeance play. By so doing, they make
him the errant, impassioned and individual forerunner of jurors, plaintiffs,
and defendants—all who will frequent Athena's impending establishment.
For the moment the Furies are still in opposition, but eventually a city, and
within it a court backed by Olympians but rooted in a covey of demons, will
inflict retaliations. These will be determined by the judgment of men, but
will be dreadful as the Furies are dreadful and consequently effective. "What
man, what city, honors Dike who does not feed his heart on fear?" (*Eum.*
522–25).[65]

Hermes 66 (1931) 195–214, esp. 194; and J. Dufradas, *Les thèmes de la propagande delphique*
(Paris, 1954), pp. 160–204, who urged that the Orestes story as we know it "n'a pu être créé
qu'à Delphes" (p. 164).

62. So Apollo used the Erinys-threat (having none of his own?) when imposing the duty of
revenge upon Orestes (278–85).

63. All this is made explicit in *Eum.*, first by the Furies (490–565, esp. 516–24) and then
by Athena, who makes *phobos* and *sebas* brothers that restrain the citizens both in open daytime
activities and at night (690–706).

64. T. G. Tucker, *The Choephori of Aeschylus* (Cambridge, 1901), was perhaps the first to perceive Aeschylean play between *phobos* and *Phoibos*.

65. Reading Thomson's ἐμφυεῖ καρδίαν φόβωι τρέφων at 522–23; see A. Sommerstein,
ad loc.

CHAPTER FIVE

Delphic Matricide

Sophocles' Electra

For Aeschylus, Orestes' revenge was part of a giant process by which human institutions came to reflect an Olympian design. For Sophocles, the same event occurred within an individual psyche in that area where decision is crystallized into action. The killing of the killers of Agamemnon was not a step along a path, nor was it a hypothesis rejected in the course of a great social change. It was instead a discrete deed that served as a paradigm for all forms of mortal action. All men, like the pattern avenger, were incomplete if they did not move; all, like him, were somehow tainted if they did. All actions, like his, required memory for a preliminary resolve, but forgetfulness in the heat of their doing. And so revenge, as a conscious, retrospective, self-defining impulse that leads to injurious action, seemed to be an ideal dramatic vehicle for the notion that intention must always be sullied as it is externalized to become achievement. Or might revenge be paradoxically the one action that denies this rule? Here was a deed dedicated to restoring the past. It was one man's imitation of what another had done, its curiously negative purpose being to *de*-create a former tainted deed. Might this mean that this reenactment that erased could issue into reality without any taint of its own? And yet was it not absurd to assume that impurity could be imitated in a way that was pure? The Orestes tale, with its seemingly unbridgeable gap between radiant Delphi and the tub where Agamemnon was slain, stirred up all these questions, especially the last. The original murder had been loathsomely unnatural and unclean, a parody of a homecoming rite and the destruction of a commander/husband/king by a wife warm from another man's bed. How could any second action of revenge maintain the total purity of Apollo while it reduplicated the total impurity of Clytemnestra's crime? Questions such as these shape the Sophoclean play that treats Orestes' vengeance through an agent who did not perform it, his *Electra*.[1]

I

In this play Sophocles asks whether or not there can be a human impulse that is clean, and if so, whether this quality can persist as psychic thrust finds external fulfillment in a deed. His largest move, in addressing this question, is to separate intention from achievement. And his second is to study intention, the initial element, in two forms that are sharply discriminated (though they will finally combine). The first version of the revenge impulse is masculine, divinely inspired, forward-looking, and unfree; it includes the matricide, and it will eventually be effective. The second is feminine, oriented toward the dead, backward-looking and wholly free; it aims only at Aegisthus, and it is technically unfulfilled. These two intentions mingle in the end in the slaughter that is actually performed—the deed that is being tested for purity—but in their potential phases they are displayed apart from each other, so that each may be extensively analyzed.

As host to the externally imposed, masculine revenge impulse, Orestes is the obedient creature of opportunity and his surroundings as he arrives at the decisive spot. His task is a road to be traveled (68), and he is in training for it. The Tutor says, "I took you, I kept you alive, and I brought you to your present age to be the avenger of your father's murder" (τιμωρός, 13–14). What is more, Delphi has told Orestes exactly how to proceed with his mission (37); each movement on this particular day has been fixed by the oracle (51), and the young man is to have no scruple about methods (47, 61), for the god has told him to use trickery.[2] Orestes also has behind him an unspecified secular community made visible in his two male companions, and this masculine group will support him as he kills a tyrant and brings legitimacy to Argos.[3] As revenge agent, Orestes is thus ready in his muscles,

---

1. For a precisely opposite opinion, see D. A. Hester, "Sophocles the Unphilosophical," *Mnemos.* 24 (1971) 11–47.

2. One might compare Soph. fr. 247 Pearson: κἂν ἔξω δίκης / χωρεῖν κελεύηι, κεῖσ' ὁδοπορεῖν χρεών. / αἰσχρὸν γὰρ οὐδέν ὧν ὑφηγοῦνται θεοί. C. Segal, "The *Electra* of Sophocles," *TAPA* 97 (1966) 510–11, asserts that Orestes' use of *dolos* must mean "from the author of *Philoctetes,*" that he is offered to the audience as base and nonheroic. There is, however, an absolute difference between a trick urged by Odysseus as part of stealing from a friend, and one commanded by Apollo for use against an enemy (cf. Thgn. 415–18). In real life, "stealth" was always appropriate in actions taken in defense of honor (see R. Parker, *Miasma* [Oxford, 1983], p. 132); on stage it was expected of the avenger and has already characterized the Orestes of Aeschylus (*Cho.* 569).

3. M. W. Blundell, *Helping Friends and Harming Enemies* (Cambridge, 1989), p. 175, argues to the contrary that the presence of Pylades indicates Orestes' cowardice because two men are

ideologically prepared, and a bit impatient—this is his chance! (75–76)—but he is somehow mechanical. He has brought no passion with him, and his sense of the past reaches back only to Delphi. Certain critics find him odiously jaunty, even "obnoxious,"[4] but this is a picture of a condition, not a personality.[5] What Sophocles shows in the Orestes who enters this play is a man whose dutiful intention is in every ordinary sense irreproachable, but one who, should he act now, would not be able to call his deed his own, nor would he be responsible for it. He understands what he is to do, but he has nothing of self to invest, and so, having been described, Orestes is sent to the wings in order that we might consider a figure who embodies all that he is not.[6]

Electra is a being of another sort entirely. She has not been educated or called to any career. She has no director of conscience, nor has she heard a voice from the *adyton* at Delphi, and no law of kin solidarity fixes her role. Unlike the strongly socialized Orestes, she is alienated from community and family, and her external identity has been erased by a set of counterdefinitions laid down by her father's murderers. She is a princess enslaved, a pauperized heiress, a beauty turned into a hag (187–92). She is an unmarried woman of marriageable age (164–65, 185–86), and she is also a citizen who lives like an exile (189), a sister with no brother, her mother's child and yet an orphan.[7] Electra knows herself only as her father's daughter or, figuratively, as a quiet domestic animal who is out of doors howling. With no identity, she is naturally passive; the one form of action she allows herself is the negative one of disturbing others with an exaggeration of her own suffering. Her boldest deed is only a matter of breath, as she voices a vague curse-prayer that asks for divine response to her father's murder (110–16). She

---

to attack one woman. This one woman, however, is paired with a warrior-ruler who lives in a fortified place, in the company of his own men and surrounded by dependent subjects.

4. J. Kells, *Sophocles, Electra* (Cambridge, 1973), p. 10; cf. S. Schein, "Sophocles' *Electra,*" *A&A* 28 (1982) 79. T. M. Woodard is much closer to the actual Sophoclean effect when he says that Orestes is "like Apollo: detached, confident, remorseless, rational, lucid" ("*Electra* by Sophocles," *Harv. Stud.* 70 [1965] 211).

5. For the common view according to which Sophocles, in this play, was entirely "preoccupied" with personality, see, e.g., F. Solmsen, *Electra and Orestes,* Mededelingen der Koninklijke Nederlandse Akademie van Wetenschappen, Afd. Letterkunde, n.s., 30.2 (Amsterdam, 1967), p. 52 n. 1.

6. There is a distant later parallel to this kind of split in *Spanish Tragedy,* where Hippolito carries the intellectual burden of the revenge, while Isabella embodies the grief, madness, and suicide that are its emotional cost. Hippolito, however, has his own passion and does not need to borrow from his wife.

7. Compare Hofmannsthal's Elektra, who says, "Ich bin nicht Mutter, habe keine Mutter, / bin kein Geschwister, habe keine Geschwister, / lieg' vor der Tür und bin doch nicht der Wachhund" (*Elektra* [Berlin, 1904], p. 67).

has been thrust outside the area in which *aidos* (respect for status) operates, and so she makes aggressive use of the only social quality left to her, her shamelessness (τὸ μὴ καλὸν καθοπλίσασα, 1088–89),[8] giving it the form of public scandal (605–9, 616–21, 254).[9] Rejecting all modesty and proper behavior (307–9; cf. 607, 615), she attacks her mother with insults, so that Clytemnestra, in self-pity, says that her unfriendly daughter has "sucked her mother's life blood" (758). Electra chooses also to live outside of time,[10] filling both nights and days with the same funereal motions and sounds (105–6, 259). "I scream; I sob; I wail," she says, describing the varieties of her experience (283).[11] And yet, precisely because she is alienated, Electra is free. Her endeavor is all in her mouth, which is entirely under her own control, and her song, which is a kind of testimony, is also a form of flight (242–43).

When she is first shown, Electra has no wish to use her freedom to do anything. Her impulse is all spent upon being, on feeling and embodying the manifold passions that occupy her. She has a brooding anger (χόλος, 176; ὀργή, 222, 369, 1011), but she is loudest in outbursts of grief for her father (e.g., 86–91, her first consecutive words), outrage at the desecrations practiced by his murderers (97 ff., 201 ff., 244–50, 439–47), and horror and loathing for the contamination that the palace exudes. Like Hamlet, she senses an infection that spreads from the royal act of adultery (261–92);[12] and like him, she is prey to constant fluctuations of mood.[13] Snarls of exas-

---

8. Many emendations have been offered for this phrase, but it responds to οὐκ ἐν ἐσθλᾷ in the antistrophe (1094), and it perfectly describes Electra's strategy of attack with weapons of impropriety. If one can "arm" popular outcry, as at Aesch. *Supp.* 685, then one can "arm" one's degraded position. Objections have come from those who, like Jebb, want the chorus to say that Electra "spurned dishonor," but that is exactly what she has not done. She has courted dishonor in the world's (Chrysothemis') sense.

9. Electra's demonstrations follow the underlying pattern of suppliancy, since what she does is put herself in the wrong place; behavior that is forbidden threatens the community and its rulers with disorder and possibly with pollution. Aegisthus' response is a threat to remove her by force (like Hermione's threat to use fire or sword against Andromache), and to this Electra responds like a suppliant heroine: "Then I shall fall paying honor to my father!" (399; cf. Eur. *Andr.* 258, 260).

10. In Woodard's phrase, which picks up the Niobe image at 150, she lives "in petrified time" ("*Electra* by Sophocles," p. 198); R. Seaford, "Sophocles' *Electra*," *CQ* 35 (1985) 317, puts it more modishly as a "permanent liminality of mourning."

11. Her *threnos*, like that of Procne, is never-ending (104–9, 147–49; cf. 78, 94, 107–8, 231–32, 850).

12. For actual fifth- and fourth-century views of adultery as a source of pollution and a form of *hybris* for which revenge was appropriate, see D. Cohen, "The Athenian Law of Adultery," *RIDA* 31 (1984) 147–65.

13. A general likeness between Electra and Hamlet was noted by W. Schadewaldt, *Hellas und Hesperien*, vol. 2 (Zurich, 1970), pp. 7–27. Hofmannsthal too felt the kinship between the two figures, especially as doers of deeds not done; see *Aufzeichnungen* (Frankfurt, 1959), p. 217.

peration (169–70, 376–77), groans of despair (119–20, 230–32, 303–6), and sharp touches of sarcasm (403, 591–92, 608–9) break the mixed flow of vocal sound as she proclaims her own loyalty to her dishonored father (236–43, 349, 355–56, 399, 457) and protests against her mother's treasonable sensuality (608–9).

For five or six years Electra has been in this passive state of disgust and grief. On this day her inchoate emotion will sharpen into a resolve, but before it does, Sophocles tests the quality of her longtime resistance with two characteristic devices: the rumor of a threat and the report of a dream. They are equally insubstantial, but both establish facts about Electra. Her defiance of the airless underground prison (380–81)—whether or not it actually awaits her—proves that she will not buy her way out of even the greatest physical suffering with even the smallest gesture of complicity with her father's killers. And meanwhile the dream with its budding scepter (417–23) lets her demonstrate that her hope, like her defiance, is inextinguishable and ready to be translated into action.[14] With her instructions to Chrysothemis she makes her first positive move, diverting the libations, substituting the sisters' own dedications, and articulating a prayer that imagines another mode of dealing with enemies. Howling shamelessness has been forced upon her, but Electra can conceive of a direct attack, to be made by an Orestes who will come as her father's champion (453–56). These are only preliminaries, however, for as principal of this drama Electra will have to convert her long passive defiance and her vicarious hopes into an actual intention to destroy. That conversion, though internal and impalpable, will be her "tragic deed," the play's inner act of disorder and its measure of how far a heroic human soul may stretch. The spectator knows always that Electra will not carry out her aggressive intention, but that is exactly as it should be if they are to be shown an abstraction—the Impulse of Revenge in its pure state, untainted by contact with its goal.[15]

It is the forward progress of the pragmatic, masculine revenge plan that, with characteristic situational irony, persuades Electra that her brother will never come and that she herself must act. Her psychic adventure is thus based on a lie, and the audience is aware of this, having themselves seen the living Orestes. They hear the speech that describes dismemberment at Delphi, knowing it to be false and admiring its gorgeous deceptions, while they also watch Electra take the same words as truth and build her resolve upon

---

14. The dream also allows her to go strong into her scene with Clytemnestra, where she will enunciate the rules for revenge before her temporary collapse at the Paidagogus' news.

15. Note the contrast with Hofmannsthal, who wished that the myth might have allowed him to make his Elektra an actual avenger; in a letter to E. von Bodenhausen he claimed that his tragedy "ein schöneres Werk und ein reineres Kunstwerk wäre, wenn der Orest nicht vorkämt" (*Briefe* 2:168).

them. It is with this great central lie, then, that Sophocles contrives to keep the disengaged and hypothetical nature of Electra's project uppermost in our minds, even as he stages her decision and investigates its inner sense.[16] And among the many things we learn is that a single deception or *dolos* can lead a guilty woman toward her death, while it tricks an innocent Electra into heroism. Told that her brother's body has been torn apart at Delphi, the heroine's first response is to restate her old resolve. She will never collaborate, and she longs to die (817–22); the only action she could wish to perform is the burial of her dead brother (868–70), the only passion she can entertain is grief. What first rouses her from this paralyzed despair is scorn for her sister's ignorance (scorn based upon a false report and leveled against one who in effect knows the truth). After which the aggressive experience of destroying another's hopes, just as her own have been destroyed, transforms her. As soon as Chrysothemis has been brought from joy to grief (Orestes from life to death, in her imagination), Electra demands that this newly created companion in loss shall join her in an action that will take daring. Her genuine ally is hiding, and the need to persuade this substitute (who will refuse)[17] ripens her resolve, while it lets the poet display an isolated creature in the act of taking a principled and wholly elective decision.

Chrysothemis thinks about results, and she can see in Electra's proposal only disastrous foolishness. The revenge plan is angry, incautious, bold, masculine, and certainly doomed because aimed from feminine weakness against a man who is strong (994–97, 1011). Electra, on the other hand, cares only about the inner sense of the project. As she tries to recruit Chrysothemis, she describes the deed that is in her mind, and we learn that she would take over the large, clear patriarchal vengeance of the Homeric Orestes. She has no interest in means, no tricky intrigue to suggest, nor does she imagine the satisfaction of physically doing the deed. What she sees instead is the innate splendor and unmixed glory of a courageous act of loyalty, and her new vision does away entirely with the (downtrodden and

16. Critics have often accused Orestes, even Sophocles, of cruelty, because the Tutor's deception makes Electra suffer "unnecessarily." This, for B. Vickers, is a major fault of the play: "the *Electra* seems to me a failure because, when we become conscious of how false and unnecessary Electra's sufferings are, this can only detach us from her situation and make us regard it clinically or indifferently" (*Towards Greek Tragedy* [London, 1973], p. 573). Before condemning the play as a failure one might entertain the idea that it is not Electra's sufferings but her decision which we are asked to watch with engagement.

17. The episode in which the avenger approaches the wrong ally is not found elsewhere in surviving tragedy, but this is a possibility that haunts all revenge stories, explaining the extreme circumspection of the standard Odysseus-style revenger. He must not risk revealing his plan to an informer, as we are reminded here by Electra's challenge: "Go ahead, go in and tell your mother!" (1033). The nonrevenge parallel is of course Antigone's revelation of her plan for civil disobedience to Ismene.

female) language of grief. There is now a virile, epic flavor to her words as she proposes an entirely new set of images for the sister-avengers. The dead Orestes and Agamemnon will know them as active comrades in the work of battle (986–87; cf. 968–69), and the whole world will recognize them as champions of the fallen, saviors of their paternal halls—in sum, as women who have exercised *andreia,* the virtue of men (983). There is even an epic-style fantasy of praise, complete with imagined direct speech, as future neighbors cry out, "Look at that pair! . . . they should be honored with festivals!" (975–83).

Electra's apprehension of triumph is so full-throated and unwomanly that most modern critics turn away in embarrassment, some suggesting that the heroine is suffering from a fit of insanity.[18] (Why do our contemporaries want so much to see insanity on the ancient stage?) Such exaltation is inappropriate, they say, in a woman who is urging mother-murder, but they would do well to look more closely at the terms of Electra's proposal, for they have missed a negative fact of highest significance. Her intended revenge is to take Aegisthus, and Aegisthus alone, as its victim (strongly enjambed at 957; cf. 965), and this Chrysothemis perfectly understands (1001).[19] Electra does not have matricide in mind because she means to perform the epic version of her chosen act. Earlier she had said that if Agamemnon's death were not punished, Aidos and Eusebeia—right regard for profane order, and true reverence for the sacred—would disappear from earth (ἔρροι τ' ἂν αἰδὼς ἁπάντων τ' εὐσέβεια θνατῶν, 247–48).[20] Now, by reversing that premise, she can reestablish these two eternal principles. "If we kill Aegisthus," she says in effect, "normalcy and piety will return, and we will regain our proper places and exercise the freedom to which we were born" (968, 970–72; cf. 1510). If they fail, harm of course will come, but it is ignoble to shrink from a just action simply because it may be costly. The only real evil would be to waste noble lives in the baseness of cowardly caution (988–89), for it is finally the quality of a deed, not its result, that makes it preferable to inaction. Chrysothemis cannot agree, but the chorus sings an ode that roundly blames her timidity while it prais-

---

18. E.g., Kells, *Electra,* p. 10.

19. Electra's concentration on Aegisthus is sometimes dismissed as deception intended to entrap Chrysothemis; so H. Lloyd-Jones: "Naturally she makes no mention of her mother for her aim is to persuade her sister" ("Tycho von Wilamowitz on the Dramatic Technique of Sophocles," *CQ* 22 [1972], 224). When, however, a tragic character practices deception, he or someone else marks the falsity as such for the audience; so for example here, at 807, Electra tells us that Clytemnestra actually smirks, though she pretends to weep.

20. There is an obvious allusion to Hesiod's lines at *Op.* 197–200, but a more interesting parallel is found at Soph. *OT* 906–10, where, if oracles are not honored, everything holy will disappear. Punishment of crime would seem to be generally congruent with faith in oracles, both being necessary to right relations with the gods.

es Electra's exalted resolve to honor her father. With the only surviving Sophoclean reference to Themis, they swear by that goddess and by lightning-bearing Zeus that this revenge will be accomplished (1063–65), and they pray that, though the sister pair have separated and Electra is alone (1074), the pair of victims will yet suffer, one by violence, the other by poverty, when this, the best of daughters, has her triumph (1058–97).[21] Indeed, they bring immediate poetic fulfillment to Electra's fantasy of acclamation by singing, "What mortal ever born was as loyal as she to a father?" (1081).

Chrysothemis' defection crystallizes Electra's decision; it works upon her as the report of the snake-dream does upon the Aeschylean Orestes, making her recognize herself as an avenger. "Then I must do it alone, with my own hand," she says without hesitation (1019). Freely and in a matter of minutes[22] she has chosen to do this deed that her brother would have been compelled to perform, though in her case this means the violation of her

21. They ask that Electra shall in future dominate her enemies, with superior hand and wealth, as she is now dominated by them (1090–92); the "hand" of successful violence (see above, chap. 2, n. 43) will be appropriate to the usurper who meant to imprison his wife's daughter, the crushing "wealth" to the decadent Clytemnestra. In the same song an earlier phrase, "taking the double Erinys" (1080), avoids any specific suggestion of blood. R. P. Winnington-Ingram, "The *Electra* of Sophocles," *PCPS* 183 (1954–55) 20–27, made strong complaints against the rhetoric of this ode, arguing that Sophocles should have formed it so as to say: "As once you chose your life of lamentation, so now you choose to risk your life by destroying enemies." He wanted a clear "then/now" contrast to be achieved before the end of strophe 2, and so failed to see that the "now" member of this lyric statement actually follows in antistrophe 2 (where it is closed by a return to the past at 1093–95). The sequence is: Str. 2, "no person of nobility chooses to shame a fair name, and so you chose your former renowned life of lamentation, making your lowly situation aggressive, and won the double fame of wisdom and filial loyalty"; Antistr. 2, (now that you have chosen action) "may you live in triumph of hand-strength and wealth, as superior to your enemies as you are in this moment subordinate, for I have seen you, though in misfortune, take the prize in the category of the highest laws, with your reverence for Zeus." The *megista nomima* (1095–96) are those that command loyalty to a father (cf. 1081).

22. When she says at 1040 that her resolve was long since taken, she refers to the resolve to resist with all her powers; she has now made a new assessment of those powers. In her early speeches Electra does not specify direct personal revenge (by any agent) as what she longs for. In her prayer to the underworld powers she asks separately for two boons, daimonic retribution upon her enemies, and the coming of a brother who will share her troubles (110–20); cf. her wish that Zeus would punish the killers (209–12). The idea of murderous mortal retaliation is expressed only after the report of Clytemnestra's dream, when Electra imagines a triumphant Orestes with his foot set on the corpses of the killers (455–56). Clytemnestra has often accused her of preparing an absent Orestes for a return as avenger (μιάστωρ, a punishment agent brought into being by the pollution of a crime), and at the height of their quarrel Electra's anger makes her boast that she would have done so if she could (603–5). In her lamentation, however, when Electra gives Orestes' lost function a positive name, she calls him only μελέτωρ (846), one who would have comforted her. She has not, in other words, been as vengeance-minded as usually reported.

own nature. She will end what has been her eternal nightingale's lament (103–9), stop using shameless behavior, employ the hand of violence instead of her witnessing tongue, and crown the anomalies her enemies have forced upon her by becoming a woman who kills like a man (so Chrysothemis, 997). Had she been her father's son, Electra would have been bound by kin-duty to do what she now proposes, but for women there was no such responsibility (as Chrysothemis reminds us). And this means that Sophocles has placed in the mind of Electra a secondary revenge like no other—one that is undertaken not as a social duty but as a freely determined, other-oriented act that expects no mortal or divine aid. Her anger is a fresh inner creation, her need to honor her father an autonomous obligation invented in opposition to the pressure of society,[23] its independence expressed by the crossing of gender boundaries as she—a nonwoman who has no hearth—nevertheless imposes on herself the patriarchal imperative in its extremest form. Electra's exemplary deed is also, however, an action caught in a state of pure potentiality, for she has not even considered how she will strike Aegisthus, or when, or where. Her intention is a container that must be filled with practical action, according to her own metaphor (it is κενός, 1020), but she has no plan, no ally, no disguise, no patron god, and no strength in her female arm (998). Her passion now has a form, but it is empty of content.

Electra is still innocent of doing but nevertheless given over wholly to her free and passionate resolve, when Sophocles at last brings her into contact with her brother, the passionless agent of Delphi. Her unconsidered, impossible, nonmatricidal choice is in many ways the direct opposite of his practical, dutiful, divinely sponsored program of mother-killing, but in combination these two contrasted intentions will produce the action that ends the play. Electra's adherence will color the otherwise automatic performance of the Apolline plan with free human heroism, while at the same time Orestes' simple obedience will ensure the performance of a matricide now cleanly defined as a killing imposed by the god, but not passionately intended by either of the avengers. Put in these terms, the play's solution to the central dramaturgical problems of the Orestes tale—its unfree avenger and its intolerable crime—may seem arid and overanalytical. Sophocles, however, has found a way to stage this schematic juncture of passionate will with reverent obedience as dynamic spectacle. Brother and sister embrace in what is the true climax of this tragedy—the most theatrical, yet also the most inward and analytical, of surviving recognition scenes. The audience watches as, before its eyes, mutual knowledge becomes mutual decision and

23. Compare C. Whitman, *Sophocles* (Cambridge, Mass., 1951), p. 171: Electra finds, "beyond hope, in herself the ultimate extension of that *arete* which Sophocles considered to be the divine in man."

incomplete impulses, created by various stimuli, join to give the muscles a command. And at the same time, it is shown the unfreedom of all human resolution, for every gesture of these players is determined by a visible object that represents god—the Delphic urn that pretends to contain the ashes of Orestes.

This urn is a bronze vessel about eighteen inches high.[24] It has been brought from Delphi (54–55), and it is the deceit recommended by Apollo, the Paidagogus' lie, in solid form. (As such, it signals the direct working of god in the revenge intrigue, exactly as the wine flask does in *Cyclops*.) In a sense this vessel contains the matricide since it contains the means to that deed; it will work the avengers' entry into the palace, and it will play a part in Clytemnestra's slaughter there, for she will be murdered as she pays false honors to its false remains. Nevertheless, Apollo's ash-urn has a saving function as well, and Sophocles insists on this brighter aspect by giving it a major role in the reunion of Orestes with his sister. Indeed he makes this spurious and deadly urn bring joy and truth out of lies and misunderstanding as, like the magic ring in a fairy tale (or like the bow of Heracles, in his own *Philoctetes*), it moves from hand to hand. At the scene's start, each of its figures is falsified, for Orestes is disguised as a man from Phocis, Electra seems to be just any household drudge, and the urn claims to hold the remains of Agamemnon's son. All of which is preparation for a wondrously complicated process of unmasking that turns always on one conspicuous stage prop, the likeness of a fake artifact. First, Electra catches sight of it, asks to hold it, and Orestes orders its bearers to pass it to her. He supposes that he offers a sham object to a stranger, while she believes that she takes the dust of her dead brother into her arms, but in spite of such various delusions the discovery of their actual relationship at once commences. Unlike her mother, Electra responds to these bogus remains with a grief that is real; the anguish of her lament is the voice of her sisterhood, and by that anguish Orestes knows how he stands to her, and who she must therefore be.[25]

---

24. D. C. Kurtz and J. Boardman, *Greek Burial Customs* (London, 1971), p. 53, report that ash urns from early Athenian burials normally had "modest proportions" and were shaped like neck-handled amphorae. A descendant of this particular urn can be seen on a fourth-century Lucanian bell krater in Vienna, *LIMC* s.v. "Electra I," 48.

25. A partial model for this recognition is found in the scene between Odysseus and Laertes in *Od.* 24 (esp. 316–17), where the old man's gestures—sinking to the ground and covering his head with dust—so move Odysseus that he reveals himself. This being so, it is likely that Electra here similarly sinks to the ground with the urn; see T. C. W. Stinton, "Allusion in Greek Tragedy," in *Greek Tragedy and Its Legacy*, ed. M. Cropp, E. Fantham, and S. Scully (Calgary, 1986), p. 96 n. 74; J. F. Davidson, "Homer and Sophocles' *Electra*," *BICS* 35 (1988) 43–71. The urn itself may be a kind of *hommage* offered to Aeschylus; as R. Garner puts it, "An Aeschylean image which never makes an actual stage appearance has been developed into a

Electra's grief, excited by the urn, serves as the efficient "token" in this recognition,[26] but meanwhile her emotion, combined with the Apolline prop, strongly suffuses the moment with a further sense of love and revival. Consider what she does. She gets hold of the ash-urn, and for the length of one line she remembers that it is (supposedly) a piece of funeral furniture (1126). Then, with it cradled in her arms (1130), she begins to call this rounded, baby-sized object "You" and "Child"! She remembers the last time she held this child; he was heavier then, when she stole him from death (1129–35). Next, she goes deeper into the past, to the time when she was his nurse because he was not loved by their mother, and her reminiscence continues to address itself to the urn in the syntax of "I" to "thou." She knows that there is dust inside (1159), yet she calls the urn-child "you piti-ful bit of flesh" (δέμας οἰκτρόν, 1161), "dearest" (1163), and "brother of mine" (1164). We in the audience know even better than she that this illu-sory baby is just a hollow pot, but all the same, given the size and shape of a stoppered ash-urn, we too momentarily fancy that Electra's swaying figure is that of a mother with a dead child.[27] And consequently—because of an urn full of Delphic trickery—we find ourselves in the presence of an emotion entirely new to this play. This is not the harsh, almost theoretical grief that caused Electra's lamentations for her father. This is a living anguish that bespeaks a tender and cherishing love.

Electra's grief transforms false ashes into a remembered child; Orestes recognizes himself in that child, and in this way he comes to know his sister. At the same time, her grief also transforms him, for the Orestes who watch-es her bereaved tenderness is no longer a vengeance automaton bereft of emotion. He feels pity, and finds a new dimension in himself as he groans over someone else's sufferings as if they were his own (1179–85). And his marked pity in turn works to make Electra suspect his identity, since no other person has ever shown her commiseration. All this the urn achieves even before it passes back into Orestes' hands, there to provoke his formal revelation of himself as lost brother and true avenger (1221). Consequent-ly, when this revelation does at last occur—when after her own revelation of love Electra learns that Orestes is not dust but alive—the event is for her a miracle. The urn, like a womb, seems to have produced a living being, for the dead child now stands visible before her, brought back to life by the

---

vivid focus of attention in Sophocles' play" (*From Homer to Tragedy* [London and New York, 1990] p. 121).

26. The formal token, the signet ring, is used only to confirm Electra's already felt convic-tion as to Orestes' identity (1222).

27. She has been associated with other such maternal figures: Procne, at 107–9 and 147–49; Niobe, at 150.

same Delphic deceit that had killed him. "Dead by trickery and now by trickery revived!" Electra calls out to the chorus (1228–29; cf. 1314–15).[28] The sister greets the brother as "fairest light!" because he is come godsent, like a day of salvation (1266).[29] He is already on the path of revenge, and she understands now that the unknown, the daimonic, the unpredictable has come with him into the vengeful purpose that was once all her own. Indeed it even seems to her that Agamemnon might now return from the dead (1316–17; cf. 453), and so when the Tutor comes out of the palace to insist that the plot must proceed, she knows him as her brother's companion and savior, but she sees him as the parent whom they both would honor with their loyal action. Touching his hands, kissing his feet, she calls him "Father!" (1361)[30] because she has been instructed by the trickery of Apollo. It has brought her the brother she wanted; it will bring Agamemnon the retaliation that he demands.

In the recognition duet (1232–87) Electra's passionate resolve mixes audibly with Orestes' objective determination (the Tutor calls it his *nous*, 1328) as her jubilant melodies and unruly tongue mingle with his spoken obedience to *kairos* and god (1259, 1263). And in the same way their once-separate impulses mix. Electra is ready now to take part in the matricide, the urn having taught her a sharp regret for an Orestes who would punish their unmotherly mother (1154–56). On the practical side, the passionate joy she feels at his seeming resurrection joins with her ancient hatred to provide the tears needed for their plot (1310–13), and above all, because of the urn, she now knows this to be a day in which a daimon is present (1306). Meanwhile Orestes' obedience also takes on a new quality. Before, he meant to avenge his father dutifully but without expense of self, but now he has memory; he shares the pain of Electra's past degradation and is moved by a wish to be his sister's protector (1278–79). His enemies are no longer simply creatures who outraged an unknown father; they have mistreated this

---

28. Orestes is like an initiate invigorated by a ritual death. This effect was hinted at early in the play, when the chorus called him "blessed" (*olbios*, 159) for being about to return from his secret youth. Elsewhere the idea of return from death has been broached at 61 (Orestes' light reference to followers of Pythagoras); 139 (Electra will not revive Agamemnon with lament); 418 (Agamemnon seems to return to life in Clytemnestra's dream); 940–41 (Chrysothemis scorns notion of raising the dead). In the actual killings the motif is continued with references to what must have been a well-known conundrum about risen dead who send the living underground (1419, 1478).

29. R. Seaford, "Sophocles and the Mysteries," *Hermes* 122 (1994) 275–88, notices the "mystic" quality of the business with the urn, supposing that it is meant to suggest the birth of a sacred child. He, however, argues that these allusions have been planted as foil to the horror of the play's ending, which offers "release" by way of a "death ritual in hideous revenge for the perversion of the death ritual of Agamemnon" (p. 281).

30. This is "delirium," according to Kells, *Electra*, p. 11.

present sister, and so he promises that after the revenge he will belong to her (1280). A new intention, generated by a vital passion of his own, now hurries him on to the patriarchal and Delphic act of revenge.

This union of complex qualities—of freedom and duty, emotion and reason, clean impulse and dutiful criminality, in a word, of sister and brother—is made visible in a fraternal embrace. Then the Tutor signals that the time for action has come. The young men prostrate themselves before the house gods in the rare gesture by which Greeks attempted to turn away non-Olympian wrath (1374).[31] Then, taking the urn, they go in to kill Clytemnestra while Electra stays outside to beg the palace Apollo, the Argive Wolf-Killer deity, to act as their defender (1376–83). Her posture repeats that of her mother, earlier, reminding us of Clytemnestra's gross petition to this same god that she might continue to enjoy all her blood-bought pleasures of wealth, power, and Aegisthus' love (648–53). Indeed, Electra's opening formula (ἵλεως . . . κλῦε, 1376) repeats the phrase that had introduced Clytemnestra's covert request that Apollo should bring evil upon the son who threatened her (655).[32] Clytemnestra had supposed that her sinister petition was answered in the news of Orestes' death, but in fact it is the present revengers' prayer that will be fulfilled. Apollo does act as their ally in their intrigue (1381), and its success does show the world the wages of impiety (1382–83). Clytemnestra, on the other hand, is touching Apollo's trick, the Delphic urn, when she is struck down. She echoes Cassandra's Aeschylean pun when she says that the house is filled with (Apolline) destroyers, ἀπολλύντες (1405), and when she is dead Orestes confirms that all has gone according to the god's prophecies (1424–25).[33]

31. The gesture seems to be fundamentally apotropaic, meant to check the threat of greater power, as in the popular practice referred to at Pl. *Resp.* 451a; at *Resp.* 398a it is the ritual version of driving the sorcerer out, but this of course is a joke, because Greeks were proud of not kneeling before other mortals (e.g., Hdt. 7.136). At Soph. *OC* 1654, Theseus falls to the ground at the chthonic miracle of Oedipus' disappearance; at Soph. *Phil.* 776, Neoptolemus is to kneel to Phthonos before he takes the magic bow, and at 1408, he and Philoctetes will depart after bowing to earth to avert daimonic wrath; at Ar. *Eq.* 156, someone about to be told incredible news is told to bow down. Finally, at Aesch. *Pers.* 499, Persians terrified by a storm bow down to earth and heaven, but this may be meant as typically oriental behavior.

32. Clytemnestra feels threatened because of her dream, and her prayer begins with a conventional plea: if this sign should denote good, let me have that good, but if evil, turn it upon my enemies (646–47); cf. Aesch. *Pers.* 217–19, and for Near Eastern parallels, see H. Jacobson, "Ritualistic Formulae," *CQ* 32 (1982) 233–34. Next, by specifying that for those of her children who are not ill-disposed she would have goods (653–54), she prepares for the unspeakable request (656–57) of her closing lines, which is obviously that evil should come to any of her children who are ill-disposed.

33. These lines are usually supposed to mark a terrible doubt that has just assailed Orestes: "if the god's prophecies were fair [but, oh horror, perhaps they were foul!] . . ." The "if" clause is far more probably a form of asseveration: "affairs indoors are fine, if Apollo's prophecies are

Nor is Apollo the only daimonic power associated with the success of this revenge plot. Electra's early-morning call on the Other Powers of the underworld (110–20) is now fulfilled, for the killers are said to enter the palace like a pair of erinys-hounds (1378) led by Trickfoot Hermes (1392; cf. 115). Old curses are also finding their completion, according to the chorus (1419), as city and family enter at last into a new dispensation (1413–14). Every power, from Olympian to ghost, is thus on the side of the avengers, and so the killings follow rapidly without hindrance or suspense. Clytemnestra's takes place in conventional fashion, behind the scenes, while a visible Electra (impulse apart from action) assists with voice but not with hand (1415). Aegisthus, however, demands a little more time because he must perform a grisly bit of business in which, thinking to uncover his dead enemy, he unveils instead the fresh corpse of his "bride" (1468–75),[34] thus replaying his old adulterous crime. He turns out to be as tough and sardonic as a Jacobean villain,[35] but nevertheless the play closes with all speed as Orestes pushes a defiant and viperish usurper toward his death site, the exact spot where Agamemnon had died (1495–96).[36] Only one figure is thrust along to his death, but nevertheless the archaic confidence of this last tableau is strongly reminiscent of the rough scene that was depicted by the Ram Jug Painter.[37]

II

Aegisthus is last seen not as an inert body but as a man being pushed toward extinction, for the play breaks off while it is in motion. Such an unrestful ending is a reminder that quiet will not settle at once, that there must be a cleansing before Orestes can take part in the life and the rituals of this palace. More important, this premature finish denies any visible profit to Orestes and Electra. Their revenge is frozen while it is still dynamic, its end never shown, because their drama is concerned with action, not with

---

fine (as we all know they are)." The effect is like, "as God is good," or the popular "if the pope's a Catholic"; for extended examples of artful doubt used for emphasis, see T. C. W. Stinton, "Si credere dignum est," *PCPS* 22 (1976) 60–89 = *Collected Papers* (Oxford, 1990), pp. 236–64.

34. The "Stück" is the same as that of Rigoletto uncovering the body of Gilda, but here it is the labeled villain who undergoes the grisly deception.

35. Thus, when Orestes says, "In your case I am a prophet of surpassing power" (1499), Aegisthus answers, "That wasn't your father's strong point!" (1500).

36. For the convention of the revenge death on exact spot, with same weapon, as the original crime, see R. Hirzel, *Die Talion, Philol.* Suppl. 11 (1907–10) 442–56.

37. For an opposite opinion, see D. Seale, *Vision and Stagecraft in Sophocles* (Chicago, 1982), pp. 77–78, where the avengers' "calculated cruelty" is said to present "a picture of physical and spiritual destruction" for themselves.

achievement. Or rather, it is concerned with two actions, the present Delphic killing and the past regicide to which it responds. A revenge, after all, has its beginning and its end according to the outrage that brought it into being, and Sophocles makes certain that his audience shall constantly measure the deed that he stages against its doublet in the past. The old crime, the murder of Agamemnon, is ceaselessly reenacted in Electra's memory (47–99), and through her it becomes almost as immediate to the present audience as anything actually mimed. Its lewd motives are reviewed (197–200), and its scandalous means are spoken, sung, and rendered in symbolic form—most notably as a gobbling bloody axe that chops down a giant oak tree (98; cf. 484–86, where the very axe accuses its employer). And finally the malicious violence of this unseen outrage has been fixed in each listener's mind by two unforgettable gestures attributed to Clytemnestra: the lopping off of the dead king's limbs (444–45)[38] and the wiping of her gory hatchet on her victim's hair (445–46).[39] A crime so unclean cannot be contained by the past, and the spectator is told that in this present day it "blossoms" (260) in the infection brought by flourishing killers to the dead man's hearth, throne, scepter, altars, and bed (258–70).

Pollution must spread when murderers eat and worship where their victims did,[40] but nevertheless a debauched Clytemnestra now sits in the palace, feasting and laughing (277) like the suitors of the *Odyssey*. Her continual laughter is a final insult offered to the dead Agamemnon, and each month she calls the public in to laugh and dance with her, as she celebrates the day on which she and her paramour murdered the king (278–81).[41] Indeed, Sophocles has even arranged it so that Clytemnestra is jeering at

38. Jebb's note, Appendix, p. 211, cites the ancient information about *maschalismos*, which suggests two possible motives for the practice: 1) desire to cripple the ghostly anger of the dead (second and third scholiasts and Ar. Byz., ap. Photius and *Suda*); 2) attempt to get rid of pollution (*Suda; Etym. Magn.;* schol. Ap. Rhod. 4.477). Since Sophocles specifies the separate act of wiping the sword in order to return the miasma, he evidently saw the maiming as an attempt to disempower. The idea is to make the dead as unlike as possible to the many-handed, many-footed demon of punishment (πολύπους καὶ πολύχειρ, Soph. *El.* 489).

39. This kind of mechanical return of pollution to its source is at the root of the proverbial "be it on your own head" (e.g., Pl. *Euthydemus* 283e; Ar. *Pax* 1063; cf. Dem. 18.290). On gestures by which one rids oneself of pollution after a justified killing (taking blood into the mouth and spitting it out, etc.), see M. Delcourt, "Le suicide," *Rev. Hist. Rel.* 119 (1939) 162.

40. By Drakon's law Clytemnestra and Aegisthus would have been excluded from "lustral water, libations, mixing bowls, shrines, agora" (Dem. 20.158; cf. Oedipus' proscription at *OT* 236–41). The killer who takes his victim's house or wife is at the ultimate extreme of impurity (Pl. *Leg.* 865e; cf. Aesch. *Eum.* 655–56); see L. Moulinier, *Le pur et l'impur dans la pensée des Grecs* (Paris, 1952), p. 185.

41. Encouraging others to laugh at someone you have injured is typical of the author of *hybris* (Dem. 54.8–9), and it represents the kind of exacerbated injury that may be admirably avenged according to Aristotle (*Rh.* 1374a13.5; 1378b23.5).

her husband's would-be avengers in her last staged moment. She has just heard of Orestes' death and classified the news as both gladsome and fearful, but certainly profitable (766–67). She has felt a twinge of maternal emotion because it is hard to hate one's own child (770–71), but from this she easily recovers.[42] When the Tutor suggests that perhaps regret for her son makes his own coming fruitless, she joyfully remembers that all the advantages she killed for in the past, prayed for today, are now safe. "Fruitless!" she says. "How could you suggest it?" (773). Not if he has brought certain proof that Orestes (the vile son who deserted and slandered her) is truly dead (773–82)! And when Electra makes an indignant objection to such indecency, Clytemnestra compounds it by reminding her daughter that her brother, though dead, is far better off than she is going to be (791). After which she assures the Tutor that he has truly won a reward if his message has not only reported the death of her male, but also stopped the raucous mouth of her female, child (798). Thus self-reassured in what she thinks will be unchallenged power, Clytemnestra leads her guest away with a mocking laugh (as reported by Electra, ἐγγελῶσα φροῦδος, 807; cf. 1153 and 1295 for later, offstage laughter). She will not be seen again until she is a corpse.

Against this bizarre foil, today's killings are shown to be appropriate but austere. The filial revenge is given a positive symbolic color by the dream that Agamemnon sends, for there it is figured as a fresh green sprout from the dead king's scepter, a branch that frightens those who cut the parent stem but offers shade to all the Mycenaean land (422).[43] In its accomplishment, moreover, the revenge has a tight Delphic symmetry—trick for trick (37, 197, 1391), slaughter for slaughter (37, 1420), and murder site for murder site (1495–96). The new killings are exactly as merciless as the old, so that, when Clytemnestra cries, "Child, pity your mother!" Electra can answer, "Our father got no pity from you!" (1410–11; cf. 100).[44] At the same time there are certain stern differences. The young killers have no extraneous motives, being legitimate heirs, not lawless usurpers, and being, moreover, a fraternal instead of a copulating pair.[45] They are not moved by

---

42. On this speech, see I. J. F. de Jong, "Πιστὰ τεκμήρια," *Mnemos.* 47 (1994) 679–81, where Clytemnestra's "brief moment of 'weakness'" is noted as "surprising" (or perhaps hypocritical) but is not discussed.

43. The dream also affirms the revenge by unmothering Clytemnestra: the paternal scepter has only to be thrust into the hearth in order for it to bring forth the ominous but promising child-twig.

44. There is no overpayment: Clytemnestra receives two blows for the three she notoriously gave (1415; cf. Aesch. *Ag.* 1348).

45. Note the description of the murder of Agamemnon as the hideous child generated by Dolos and Eros (197–98).

lust, nor are they looking for pleasure of any sort, and their idea of profit is not to hear of an enemy kinsman's disaster (as Clytemnestra, 767) but rather to give honor to the beloved dead (353; cf. chorus at 370).[46] Electra hopes only to live in a world where respect and piety are practiced, and to hang garlands on her father's tomb (457–58), in reverse imitation of her mother's scandalous monthly festivals. Above all, the young revengers do not laugh as they work. If in future they smile, it will not be in celebration of the horrors they have done but, according to Orestes' promise, because at last they enjoy each other's company in freedom (1300).

Clytemnestra's jeering works to block any sympathy a spectator might be tempted to feel for her as a human being, while it also gives the measure of the secular, psychic difference between the agents of the old outrage and their counterparts in today's revenge. The fates of the old and the new corpses, by contrast, describe a ritual difference that will affect the fictional community in its relations with the gods, and so by extension will determine the reaction of a city audience to these tragic events. Clytemnestra maimed and insulted her husband's body, then substituted a monthly carouse for all funerary honor, but Electra has quite another plan. Unlike her mother, she is not concerned about a magical removal of gore from her own person, but she does hope for a radical cleansing of both palace and community. And for this purpose the corpse of Aegisthus can be useful. He has been killer, usurper, adulterer, bearer of old curses,[47] hierophant in unholy rites, polluted carrier of pollution (μιάστωρ, 603)—in sum, he is an anthology of all the crimes that have made the race of Pelops notorious (1497–99).[48] This being so, Electra decides to treat his remains as a housewife would a tainted rag, or a Hecate puppy loaded with uncleanness (Plut. *Mor.* 277).[49] Defilements such as these were carried out over a boundary, perhaps to a crossroads, and left in the open air where their pollution could do no harm, and

---

46. For the Orestes who enters, profit is success in an assigned task (61).

47. There is no reference in this play to the curse of Thyestes, but as a Pelopid, Aegisthus is under the baleful influence of Myrtilus (509–15).

48. This is initially suggested by the structure of the first stasimon (472–515), where the coming vengeance occupies the strophe, the adultery of Aegisthus and Clytemnestra the antistrophe, and the death of Myrtilus the epode. Aegisthus' crimes are there made analogous to those of Pelops by the use of the word ἁμιλλήματα, (chariot) races (494), to describe his sexual activity.

49. Plato proposed that in the case of kin-killers the magistrates should put the murderer to death, then cast him out naked at the crossroads where each one would drive off the pollution by casting a stone at the culprit's head (*Leg.* 873b–c; cf. 773c for similar treatment of authors of religious crime). When the Corinthians rose against Cypselus and killed him, they razed his house and threw his body over the border, unburied (Nic. Dam. *FGrH* 90 F 60). In general, see Moulinier, *Le pur et l'impur,* p. 93.

so it shall be with Aegisthus.[50] His corpse will receive no injury, but it will be borne away out of sight (1489) and left where it can no longer infect the community. Should anyone want to give the body some form of burial out there, he may do so (1488),[51] for exclusion will suffice.[52] "In my view," Electra concludes, "this one act will serve as a cleansing rite for the evils of the past" (λυτήριον, 1487–90). This proposal brings a conceptual fulfillment to Orestes' entering wish, which was that he might be a purifier here in Argos (καθαρτής, 70).[53] And it also leaves the word *luterion*, ritual of cleansing, as the last sound uttered on this stage by the impassioned voice that has been Electra's sole weapon of revenge.[54]

These two responding crimes that repeat, yet diverge so widely from each other, are discriminated in theoretical terms as well, for the one is defined as wanton and self-advancing destruction, the other as balanced and justice-bringing revenge. This distinction is established as soon and as sharply as possible, by means of a set debate between Clytemnestra and Electra in the second episode (516–608).[55] Clytemnestra claims that she has nothing to be ashamed of in the matter of Agamemnon's murder, because she acted as an avenger according to the aristocratic rule of honor. She killed because of

50. Electra speaks no word about her mother's body; presumably her corpse will lie beside Aegisthus' remains in fulfillment of the constant theme of adultery.

51. One might compare *Od.* 23.417–20, where kinsmen are allowed to tend the suitors' bodies, except for that of Melanthius. There are no dogs or birds in the lines Sophocles wrote for Electra, nor should they be imported from Nestor's description of what Menelaus would have done, had he found Aegisthus alive (*Od.* 3.258–61). It is true that Aeschylus can say "buried by birds" at *Sept.* 1020–21, but that does not mean that a plain ταφεύς in Sophocles must be a bird, *pace* Jebb and the many who have followed him (e.g., Seaford, "Sophocles and the Mysteries," p. 321). At Soph. *OC* 582, Theseus is designated *tapheus* to Oedipus. See the sensible statement of C. M. Bowra, *Sophocles* (Oxford, 1944), p. 255: "we may assume that she does not wish the body to be treated in this impious way."

52. A makeshift burial outside the walls is in agreement with what visitors were shown at Mycenae in Pausanias' time (2.16.7). He is discussing the identification of the royal graves, evidently those of Grave Circle A, and he adds, "but Clytemnestra and Aegisthus were buried at some distance from the fortified wall, for they were deemed unworthy to lie inside where Agamemnon and those who had been killed with him were buried."

53. See Schadewaldt, *Hellas und Hesperien* 2:12, who sees Orestes as a kind of Fortinbras, an agent of purification who will finish the cleansing work of revenge.

54. Clytemnestra understood this process as mechanical and important only to herself; wiping her victim's blood on his head (447) and turning daimonic anger back upon enemies (635–36) were *luteria* in her way of thinking. With Electra's broader sense of household and communal cleansing compare Aesch. *Cho.* 819–20, where the chorus anticipates a ritual chant praising the new prosperity of the house as a δωμάτων λυτήριον.

55. There is a cursory analysis of this debate in T. B. L. Webster, *Introduction to Sophocles* (Oxford, 1936), p. 149, but Webster does not recognize the distinction made between Clytemnestra's misdefined revenge and its opposite, a just retaliation in accordance with a *nomos* of return. For G. Perotta, *Sofocle* (Milan, 1935), p. 341, the scene is meant to prove the nonintegration of Electra's character and is "la scena meno felice della tragedia."

Iphigeneia, she says, but she does not pretend to have been a secondary avenger compelled by a duty toward her child. Instead she argues from her own honor, claiming that the sacrifice of her child was a gratuitous outrage offered to herself. In her mind, the event was roughly parallel to the taking of Briseis in *Odyssey* 1: it deprived her of a creature who was her possession, a part of her panoply, and so demanded retaliation. (To support this claim, she has to argue that Agamemnon had no real rights in his daughter: "his part was only in the sowing, mine was in the pain of bearing," 532–33.) Agamemnon took this possession of hers when he might have taken someone else's, and worst of all he harmed her, his wife, in order to gratify another, since the sacrifice was intended to benefit Menelaus. "When, just to please his brother, he killed someone who belonged to me, did it not follow that he should pay me a penalty?" (537–38).

Electra's answer to that question is No, but in her response she nonetheless sketches the classic rationale of revenge. She assumes, exactly as Clytemnestra has done, that a homicide can be justifiable, that a correctly made vengeance falls into this category, and that such vengeance does not entail punishment. The killing of Agamemnon, however, was not such a deed because Clytemnestra is mistaken about what she calls its gratuitous provocation. The taking of Iphigeneia did not touch Clytemnestra's honor because it was not an act of wanton *hybris*, not intended as an insult, indeed not directed toward her at all. Nor was it done freely and for personal reasons but instead under duress and after protestation, in order to satisfy Artemis (563–76). Consequently, even if there had been a wish to accommodate Menelaus, the *nomos* of personal retaliation[56] would not have been operative (577–79). It will be well, moreover, for Clytemnestra to remember the precise shape of that *nomos,* for should it be replaced by the general and unregulated exchange of crime for crime that she has advocated, then the queen herself will have to beware.[57] On those terms any Argive, indeed anyone at all, might well decide to kill one who had killed the king (580–83). At this point Electra has proved that Clytemnestra's act did not conform to the recognized structures of revenge, and in her closing remarks she goes on to prove that her mother's motives were likewise not those of a true avenger. Clytemnestra gives children to the man who helped

56. Bowra, *Sophocles*, pp. 215 ff., documents this *nomos* from Antiph. 1.3 where the duty of vengeance comes from gods and ancestors in the form of *nomoi,* and vengeance is an act of kindness to the one avenged (1.25); he also cites Pl. *Leg.* 9.871a, with its punishments for those who do not move to avenge a murdered kinsman.

57. It is generally said that Electra here "condemns herself out of her own mouth" (so Kells, ad 582 f.), but that is to fail to take the point of the argument. Electra has not claimed that "retributive killing is wrong"; rather she has said, "We agree that a well-designed retributive killing in return for genuine injury to honor is just; your killing, however, was ill-conceived and motivated by more than a desire for justice."

her kill her children's father (587–90)—that is hardly repayment offered to a daughter (591–92)! Her present shameless coupling denounces her pretended interest in her lost child, as does her maltreatment of her surviving children fathered by the man she murdered.

The exchange is not coherent because the two speakers are not legal theorists but angry women caught in a peculiar fictional situation. Indeed, interrupted by a threatening gesture from Clytemnestra (610),[58] it degenerates into antiphonal accusations of shamelessness (607–9, 615, 616, 622). Nevertheless there is embedded in this interlocking defense and accusation a basic statement that is clear and positive. To strike, even to kill, in answer to an unprovoked and injurious attack on one's own honor (or presumably that of a kinsman) may be justifiable. So both speakers assume. This is not, however, the same as responding at random with violence returned for any violence suffered. The retaliation must be suitable, and the avenger must have no ignoble motives, nor should he seek anything beyond his own return to the same position in the hierarchy of honors that he held before. If he acts within this definition, his crime will be just and not open to punishment. This Sophoclean debate, in other words, is founded on the same proposition that was established in the middle of the Aeschylean *Eumenides*, when the avenger Orestes was sent home to Argos. It reflects the Athenians' belief that a court like the Delphinion was necessary for the judgment of innocent crimes such as his, and it looks forward to the Aristotelian picture of an admirable anger at work.[59] Here in the second episode of *Electra* the heroine and Clytemnestra together define and clarify the age-old Hellenic principle of personal retaliation that will, thanks to an Apolline trick, determine the drama's uncomplicated close.

III

The Sophoclean *Electra* ends in success, a fact distressing to those who think that revenge tragedy must always condemn its own violence. Some call on Furies who are not here,[60] others report a play that is a deplorable failure,

---

58. There is a summary of opinion and bibliography on the disputed 610–11 in J. Bollack, "Δίκη dans Sophocle *El.* 610f.," *Rev. Et. Grec.* 101 (1988) 173–80. With Kamerbeek, Kells, et al., I believe that Clytemnestra's words at 612 show that it is her battle-rage and lack of concern for *dike* (as exhibited during Electra's final insults) that the chorus refers to at 610–11. The subject of ξύνεστι is either the woman breathing *menos* (in which case one understands μένει) or the *menos* itself, in an expression like that at Aesch. *Sept.* 671.

59. Sophocles' *Electra* was translated into French in 1537 by Lazare de Baif, and this debate was probably influential in the distinction made by French scholars of that time between Italianate revenge, i.e., villainous and self-advancing, and Apolline revenge (see above, chap. 1, n. 39).

60. See Winnington-Ingram, "The *Electra* of Sophocles," pp. 20–27, who admits that "Sophocles neither asserts nor denies that Orestes was pursued by Furies" but insists that he

a piece about a coward who is urged by a madwoman to commit a disgusting crime that ought to be punished but isn't.[61] Nevertheless anyone who looks squarely at this text will find a unified drama wherein the quality of high tragedy is threatened only by a strong promise of imminent order.[62] Presumably some ritual of cleansing must now be observed,[63] but the historic pollution of the house will be dispersed when the corpses are carried out. No continuing chain of retaliations is predicted, nor do hideous supernatural punishments threaten, because in this extraordinary case the vengeance replica is like the original in design but opposite to it in spirit. The play ends with a brother and sister who have "issued into freedom by way of today's effort," according to the final choral words (1508–10).[64]

Sophocles has taken his elaborated fiction from the complex later traditions about Orestes' revenge, but he has nonetheless maintained the patriarchal ethos of the *Odyssey* version[65] by placing two adroit checks upon the

---

"deliberately indicates it as a possibility inherent in the system of justice he has successfully applied (1505 ff.)." I would argue, on the contrary, that all the references to Erinyes within the play suggest that these powers are appeased by the present revenge; e.g., 1387–88, which fulfills 112; 1418–21, which refers back to 111. A. Machin, *Cohérence et continuité dans le théâtre de Sophocle* (Quebec, 1981), p. 236, will have it both ways: the Erinyes are excluded by the poet but are nonetheless inevitable.

61. The unpunished success of the revenge is sometimes termed "an exercise in dramatic irony" indulged in by a poet who is warning his fellow citizens against callous fanatics, here represented by Orestes and the Tutor; so Kells, *Electra*, pp. 11–12. Yet other critics invent extra-textual psychic punishments, e.g., Kamerbeek, who is certain that "Electra pays for her triumph and her heroic faithfulness by the harm to her soul inherent in that very faithfulness and in such a triumph" (*The Plays of Sophocles*, vol. 5, *The Electra* [Leiden, 1974], p. 20); cf. G. Ronnet, *Sophocle* (Paris, 1969), p. 214, who is equally certain that Orestes is doomed to suffer anguish and remorse.

62. The later life of Orestes was in legend one of effective political power; having added the throne of Sparta to that of Argos when Menelaus died, he ruled for a long time (some said sixty-six years); he died, either at age 70 or age 90 (Asclepiades, cited by schol. Eur. *Or.* 1645) and left the throne to his son Tisamenos, who, when driven out by the returning Heraclidae (Paus. 2.18.6), became the first king of the Achaeans (Polyb. 2.41.4). Orestes had a tomb in Tegea (Paus. 8.54.4), and when his bones were returned to Sparta, they brought victory with them (Hdt. 1.67–68; Paus. 3.11.10).

63. Many places claimed to be the site of Orestes' cleansing; Pausanias mentions Troezene (2.31.4–8), Gythion (3.22.1), Keryneia (7.25.4), and Arcadia (8.5.3; 34.1–4; 44.2), but cities in Asia Minor and Magna Graecia also made the claim. As with the vase-painting purification scenes (see M. Bock, "Orestes in Delphi," *A&A* 50 [1935] 493) some stories contained pursuing furies, some did not.

64. Contrast this with the *eleutheria* of Chrysothemis, which was a freedom to offer obedience to tyrants (339–40).

65. See Davidson, "Homer and Sophocles' *Electra*," p. 71. This was the quality that Jebb lamented and tried to explain away as a deliberate amoral archaism; it is also the quality that those who believe in Sophoclean irony take to be a façade behind which an entirely different play is being staged. For an early example of this now-fashionable school see J. T. Sheppard, "Electra," *CR* 41 (1927) 2 ff., and cf. Kells, *Electra*.

overwhelming horror of the matricide. First, the mother-killing is presented as exclusively Apollo's affair, a project brought in from outside and achieved by way of a fictitious Pythian exploit and an empty Delphic urn. And second, the shock of the enacted matricide is cushioned by the preliminary scene of reunion, so that the tabu crime seems to follow as much from grief and love as it does from anger and vindictiveness.[66] As a result the spectator is encouraged to suppose with Electra that normalcy and piety are about to return to Argos. He knows the traditions about Orestes' long life, future rule, and inheriting son, and he might almost fall into an antitragic complacency were it not for a pair of strong Sophoclean antidotes. When this order-bringing action is finished, two unquenchable sources of unease yet remain to supply a continuing flow of dread so that, for all its successful regularity, the play still terrifies any mortal to the depths of his being. These two are the heroine herself and the god in whose program she finally enlists.

Boundaries and definitions have been irrevocably dissolved in the central figure of Electra. She is not depraved—for a depraved Electra one must turn to Hofmannsthal—but she is a reification of paradox and disorder. Her dramatist brings her on as an avenger, though she was never meant to play that role, and he makes her almost ridiculous: a tattered, haggard outcast, an upstart, a shameless and noisy woman who tries to be a man, a living creature whose affinities are all with the dead. That much we see, and meanwhile the poet's language shows her as a hybrid being, a bird-woman tomb-watcher who moans like a nightingale or cries like a parent-feeding stork. Men who have goals move like charioteers along a measured course, but she, the embodiment of a vital but futile will, swoops and soars in flights that lead nowhere. And meanwhile at a deeper level this unruly but also inactive principal is rendered both chilling and absurd by means of an ancient pun,[67] according to which A-lektra signifies the woman who hasn't been taken to bed (as at 962). The surface effect is to hold the heroine up to mundane scorn, but through her name Sophocles brings this uncouched daughter of a much-couched mother into contact with a power that is beyond nature. He tells us that there is an Erinys who attacks illicit beds (those that are *alektra* and *anympha*, 489–94; cf. 275–76),[68] and he empha-

---

66. This is precisely opposite to the opinion of C. Segal, "The *Electra* of Sophocles," *TAPA* 97 (1966) 473–545, who sees any love in this play as feeding on hatred.

67. Attributed to Xanthus, the predecessor of Stesichorus, by Aelian (*VH* 4.26 = 700 *PMG*). The natural inference is that, already in Xanthus' *Oresteia*, Electra played a part in the revenge.

68. The sequence χαλκόπους Ἐρινύς. / ἄλεκτρ' at 491–92 responds to εἶσιν ἁ πρόμαντις / Δίκα at 475–76, so that the ear initially hears *alektra* as an Erinys-name. As the song continues, however, the word is syntactically attached to the sexual "contests" of polluted coupling (the ἁμιλλήματα being "unbedded and unbrided" in the sense of unsanctioned) against which the Erinys will move.

sizes Electra's likeness to that demon by making his Alektra also *anympheutos,* unwed (165), and *ateknos,* childless (164), like the Furies of Aeschylus (*Eum.* 1034).[69] Electra's anger, in scenes with Clytemnestra the adulteress, thus seems to swell with something more than mere human passion. In addition, the poet renders this loud, self-chosen, androgynous spinster-demon truly monstrous by giving her a horrid power of generation. For years she has been breeding with her own soul, the chorus says, and giving birth to inner wars (218). Now she is the mother of a brood of new disasters, incestuously fathered by the elder ones (235). And then at last, with all these perverse and disturbing poetic notions trailing about her, Electra is brought to her meeting with her brother where she, the unwed fury who teems with destructive progeny, is seen to bring forth a brother avenger from a Delphic womb. With this momentary illusion she (like the Nurse in *Choephori*) robs the Clytemnestra-victim of her maternity, but she does so with a grief and desolation so intense that it is never quite dissipated, even though it is a false response created by a Delphic lie.

Absurd, monstrous, uncanny, useless, defined by what she is not, and manipulated by divine falsehood, this courageous princess who measures heroic humanity is herself a glimpse of chaos. Her marginality inspires enduring intimations of terror, and these are not put to rest but rather encouraged by Apollo, the god of regularity. In one sense he is the Apollo of tradition, a revenge sponsor who exonerates and cleanses, somehow taking the pollution even of this unnatural crime into his own mysterious purity. His urn brought the reasoning will of Orestes into contact with his sister's passionate impulse. And that same urn made it clear that, whereas the killing of Aegisthus was a thing both avengers desired, the killing of their mother was imposed upon them from outside. So, within the fiction, Apollo ameliorates, but at the same time, because this staged deed has been given something like a philosopher's analysis, the conclusion that its Delphic sponsor finally suggests is doubly and abysmally disturbing. On occasion and with divine help a mortal evidently *can* mix rectitude with remembering passion in an untainted approach to a physical act. And evidently also, should such a case occur—should a mortal actually bring an impulse both pure and efficient into the moment of performance—the same divine power will invest his deed with the taint of inevitable crime. For all its recovery of order, then, the *Electra* leaves its audience with the simple conviction that no human achievement will ever be perfectly clean.

---

69. Though these παῖδες ἄπαιδες are not so much childless as children no mother would want. One aspect of the normalcy to which Electra would return by way of revenge is marriage and childbearing: so she reminds Chrysothemis that if Aegisthus is not punished, she will grow old ἄλεκτρα . . . ἀνυμέναιά τε (962).

CHAPTER SIX

Women Doing Men's Work

Euripides' Children of Heracles *and* Hecuba

Somewhere in *The Ordeal of Richard Feverel,* Lady Blandish says, "A woman has no honor; she has only her . . ." As far as one can make out, this was also the ordinary opinion in classical Greece, for there the woman of fiction, at any rate, had only one sort of reputation, and it pertained to her sexual uses. Chastity was the *kleos* of Penelope, a lustful tendency the *dyskleia* that Phaedra feared.[1] A woman was not covered, like a man, by a carapace of outward status that could permit no dent. If injury was done to her in her one area of concern (as to the sister of Harmodius), it would be actively resented not by herself but by the men around her, for her public definition mattered only among them.[2] And if she herself were guilty of a sexual misdeed, her action would affect her husband's honor[3] and would put her life in his hands,[4] but he might use her as before if he chose. Diminution of consequence for a man meant humiliation within a peer group,[5] but it could be reversed; for a woman it meant repudiation by male nonpeers, and it was

---

1. Phaedra's meditation, at Eur. *Hipp.* 391–430, is perhaps the highest expression of this way of thinking; her concern is for the honor of husband and sons (420–21), and for that of her father's house (719); it is upon these that her sexual ill-fame would reflect.

2. Apollo, for example (with Artemis, it's true), traveled through Greece to take revenge upon all who had despised Leto during her pregnancy (Paus. 8.53.1).

3. Nauplius designed a revenge in which he repaid the Greeks for the death of his son by inciting their wives to adultery; in each case the honor of the kin-group was damaged (Apollod. *Epit.* 6.8.9).

4. So, at Apollod. *Epit.* 7.38 ff., when Penelope is seduced by Amphinomos, Odysseus kills her.

5. The female kin/companion group could be critical of style, judging from Sappho, but it was not thought of as enforcing an ethical standard. In fiction at any rate, the gynaikeion mixed women of family with lesser women and slaves and did not shun or exercise nemesis.

irremediable. On the other hand virtue in a male had to be actively expressed in the open, while the indoor maintenance of silence and modesty was a woman's finest deed (Eur. *Heracl.* 476–77). Consequently the violent but admirable restoration of personal weight which men achieved in the classic act of revenge was beyond the horizon of ordinary female existence. The woman who attempted it would be by definition an unwomanly, unnatural creature, her act an indecent error.[6] The unforgettable (and non-Greek) exception is of course the wife of Candaules (Hdt. 1.8–13), the reputation of whose "dot dot dot" was insulted by the man to whom it belonged, her husband. She "resolved to have her revenge" (Hdt. 1.11), and an artful one it was as the killer hid behind the very door from which he had spied. Nevertheless, even this enterprising barbarian woman struck back only by the hand of a male proxy who at once became her new lord.[7]

There were many Hellenic stories about retaliating women, oversensual wives who, like Stheneboea, resented a failure of sexual tribute as fiercely as Ajax did the denial of Achilles' arms,[8] or mothers like Ino, jealous for their sons' prerogatives.[9] There were hundreds of tales of female intrigue,[10] from which came the subplots for a number of dramas,[11] but these are cases of villainy, not of vengeance, because their destructive women worked in self-defense or for material advantage, not for an ideal restitution of honor.

6. So, in the tale of the women of Lemnos, retaliation upon husbands for sexual slights led first to the establishment of an Amazonian community, then to the reconquest of the women by other masculine masters.

7. The papyrus fragment thought by some to represent a Gyges tragedy (*P Oxy.* 2382) carries a speech of the queen describing the moment in which she understood the injury being done to her by her husband. Majority opinion now makes the text Hellenistic, its genre either drama or rhetorical exercise; see A. Lesky, "Das hellenistische Gyges-Drama," *Hermes* 81 (1953) 1–10; I. Cazzaniga, "Testi," *PP* 32 (1953) 381–98, and note H. Lloyd-Jones, "Problems of Early Greek Tragedy," in *Greek Epic, Lyric, and Tragedy* (Oxford, 1990), p. 234 nn. 20–26, reversing his earlier assignment of the fragment to Phrynichus.

8. Lys. 1.15 records the story of a woman whose adulterous lover ceased to visit her; she felt herself to be wronged, and had her slave betray him to the husband of his more recent mistress.

9. Ino, future goddess, had left her children to run off with a troop of Bacchantes, and her husband had married a second wife; returning unrecognized, she was taken in as governess (shades of *East Lynne*), and was able to foil a gynaikeion intrigue so as to ensure the death of her rival's children rather than her own; see T. B. L. Webster, *The Tragedies of Euripides* (London, 1967), pp. 98–101.

10. Hippodameia, in some stories, persuaded Atreus and Thyestes to kill Chrysippus, Axioche's son; Pelops then killed her and sent the two brothers into exile with his curse (Hyg. *Fab.* 85).

11. For example, the Sophoclean *Phrixos*, wherein Ino persuaded her husband to sacrifice the children of Nephele. Hermione's plot against Andromache and her baby is another example: essentially an attempt to remove an obstacle, not to restore honor because of an injury received (Eur. *Andr.*).

Even the Aeschylean Clytemnestra was proposed as no more than half an avenger, being in her other half a treacherous woman who acted from motives of lust, greed, and self-advancement. What appeared to be revenge was in truth an action of divine punishment, and this the dramatist made plain by employing the victim, Agamemnon, as his principal, by entangling a wife's criminal adultery with Thyestes' curse, and by wrapping the monarch's assassination in heaven's distaste for men guilty of sacrilege and mass destruction.

As long as there were male defenders of the household to which she belonged, even a fictional woman could have no vocation as an avenger. If, however, no such male existed (unthinkable outside of fiction) or if, as in the case of Candaules, the male who ought to defend the house was himself the enemy who injured it, the result was a potentially tragic situation. In circumstances like these, an imaginary woman might, like Sophocles' Electra, attempt to respond as a surrogate male, but her successful deed would be internally contradictory because, as one who brought female violence out of the gynaikeion, she would undermine the very household that she sought to defend. It was natural, moreover, that stories about such women should run to excess and confusion. Provocation had to be truly outrageous, flagrant, and cruel—the maiming of a sister, perhaps—to engender a masculine resolve in a feminine mind. At the same time means had to be more than usually cunning if a mere woman were to strike effectively, and in consequence magical operations[12] and secondary agents[13] made their appearance. And finally, since the avenger herself was acting against nature, tales of feminine revenge attracted motifs such as cannibalism, child-murder, incest, and human sacrifice to provide a suitable setting for a woman who took a man's role. Disempowered by physical weakness, disqualified by traditional passivity, and defined as a person with no honor of her own, a woman avenger necessarily brought disorder into any tale of punitive repayment.[14] In consequence, a successful female revenge performed in the outside male world promised to make splendid tragedy.[15]

---

12. Althaia's brand or curse is perhaps most notorious (*Il.* 9.527 ff.; Bacchyl. 5.136–44); Molione, mother of the twins, put a curse on every citizen of Elis in return for their refusal to avenge her sons—a curse that effectively kept them away from the Isthmian Games (Paus. 5.2.2–3).

13 In later stories such agents might be female; so Polyxo avenged the death of her son, killed at Troy, by sending slave women to seize Helen as she bathed and string her up to a tree (Paus. 3.19.10).

14. The female avenger was almost by definition a figure for the World Upside Down and a version of another favorite carnival notion, the Revenge of the Animals; see N. Z. Davis, "Women on Top," in *The Reversible World*, ed. B. Babcock (Ithaca, 1978), pp. 147–90.

15. For an opposite view, see S. Saïd, "La tragédie de la vengeance," in *La vengeance*, vol. 4, ed. R. Verdier (Paris, 1981), p. 71: "et des tragédies comme les *Heraclides, Hecube* ou *Ion*, qui

I

There are two Euripidean plays in which the masculine avengers designated by custom are absent or incapacitated, so that women must do their work: *Children of Heracles* and *Hecuba*. In the first of these the situation is something like that of Beaumont and Fletcher's *Maid's Tragedy,* for here as there the masculine world is so hampered by its own pompous civility that it cannot rid itself of an egregious evil, and consequently a woman has to do the job.[16] Which may be why the play is so little discussed, why it is usually reported laconically as a mixed action, probably incomplete and certainly unsatisfactory. Only the final revenge section has attracted much notice, and that negative, as indignant critics discover there a crazed old lady who performs an action both repulsive and illegal and thereby betrays the noble masculine city that has befriended her.[17] I would argue, on the contrary, that Alcmena is proposed as a justice-bearing avenger after the pattern of her hero son, and that this strange piece is a whole and successful Fourth Play meant, like *Alcestis,* to end a day of tragedy.[18]

The overt action of *Children of Heracles* shows a group of helpless suppliants pursued by Argive brutes but successfully defended, after one of them has offered herself as a sacrifice, by the men of Athens. On another level the play treats a conflict between a nice legalism concerning captives, this seen as masculine, and a rough justice that can only be achieved by a woman. Above all, however, this is a Heracles play. Its dominant event is the hero's

---

font de la vengeance une affaire de femmes . . . sont autant de demystifications de la gloire du vengeur."

16. Another Renaissance parallel occurs in *Revenge of Bussy D'Ambois* when Charlotte, tired of Clermont's shilly-shally, says, "I would once / Strip off my shame with my attire, and trie / If a poore woman votist of revenge / Would not performe It with a president / to all you bungling, foggy-spirited men" (3.2.165–69).

17. Alcmena has been described as "a wretch, mad with fear and blind to the world beyond her narrow insensible self, reacting with silly excitement to any outside occurrence" (G. Zuntz, *The Political Plays of Euripides* [Manchester, 1955], p. 37). Compare J. W. Fitton, "The *Suppliant Women* and the *Children of Heracles* of Euripides," *Hermes* 89 (1961) 430–61, esp. 456–57, who speaks of "a quite inhuman spirit of revenge"; see also T. B. L. Webster, *The Tragedies of Euripides* (London, 1967), p. 105, where Alcmena is reported as "crazed by triumph"; P. Burian, "Euripides' *Heracleidae,*" *C Phil.* 72 (1976) 1–21, esp. 16–17, where the end is said to be marked by "brutality . . . brutality." More recently, T. M. Faulkner, "The Wrath of Alkmene," in *Old Age in Greek and Latin Literature,* ed. T. M. Faulkner and J. de Luce (Albany, N.Y., 1989), p. 114, reports that "Alkmene's stark and brutal behavior effectively subverts the values and sympathies the play has worked to establish," while D. C. Pozzi concludes that Alcmena is shown as "an avenging Fury" ("Hero and Antagonist in the Last Scene of Euripides' *Heraclidae,*" *Helios* 20 [1993] 33).

18. As was suggested long ago by F. Paley, *Euripides,* vol. 1 (London, 1858), p. 323.

first epiphany,[19] which coincides with a revenge taken upon his erstwhile earthly tormentor, and it is this display of Heracles' divinity that has determined the play's curious locale. Marathon, where the action takes place, is tactically speaking an impossible position for fighting off an Argive invader, but it is exactly the right spot for restoring Heracles' earthly honor and revealing his sure place among the Olympians.[20] Here at Marathon he was first worshiped as a god (Paus. 1.15.4); here his games were held (Arist. *Ath. Pol.* 54.7; cf. Pind. *Ol.* 9.88 ff., 13.110, *Pyth.* 8.79),[21] and here he had one of his most famous sanctuaries.[22] What is more, everyone knew that in 490 B.C. the Athenians had camped in his Marathon *temenos* (Hdt. 6.108, 116) and that Heracles had helped them against the Persians[23]—as was only proper since, for every man present on the field, the hero had received a father's libation at the haircutting ceremony that made a boy an ephebe.[24]

Three tragic principals gather at this appropriate spot, all closely related to Heracles: his nephew and erstwhile companion, Iolaus; his mother, Alcmena; and his daughter, Macaria.[25] Of these, the girl is everything she ought to be, but the other two do not recommend themselves as proper agents of tragic action, for Iolaus is a feeble grandfather figure[26] while Alcmena is a dowager crone. They are far too old and shambling to be heroic, and their age is emphasized by the constant company of little boys, for here, as in no other drama that survives, there are children in the playing area from beginning to end. What is more, everyone in this Heraclid group is dressed in a peculiar costume, for they all wear the shaggy wool-tufted

19. Note the formal choral announcement at 910–12: ἔστιν ἐν οὐρανῷ βεβακώς.

20. See J. Wilkins, "The Young of Athens: Religion and Society in *Herakleidai* of Euripides," *CQ* 40 (1990) 329–39; also P. Holt, "The End of the *Trachiniae*," *JHS* 109 (1989) 69–80, esp. 70–71; N. Robertson, *Festivals and Legends*, *Phoenix* Suppl. 31 (Toronto, 1992), pp. 52–53.

21. Cf. *IG* 1³.3; Dem. 19.86; and see P. J. Rhodes, ad Arist. *Ath. Pol.* 54.7.

22. On the location of the sanctuary and the regulations for the games, see E. Vanderpool, "The Deme of Marathon and the Heracleion," *AJArch.* 70 (1966) 319–23.

23. Along with Theseus and the hero, Marathon, as shown in a painting in the Stoa Poikile (Paus. 1.15.3; 33.4).

24. Hesychius s.v. οἰνιστήρια; Ath. 11.494; see S. Woodford, "Cults of Heracles in Attica," in *Studies Presented to G. M. A. Hanfmann,* ed. D. Mitten (Mainz, 1971), pp. 211–25. With Hermes, Heracles was the protector of ephebes and as such was honored in the gymnasia (Paus. 1.19.3, Cynosarges); see C. Pélékidis, *Histoire de l'éphébie attique* (Paris, 1962), p. 259. He was also among the powers named in the ephebic oath (Tod 2.204).

25. Iolaus and Alcmena had altars with those of Heracles at both Cynosarges and Porthmos; see W. S. Ferguson, "The Salaminioi of Heptaphylai," *Hesp.* 7 (1938) 1–74. Macaria (whose name is not used in the play) may possibly have been commemorated in a ritual at the Heracleion of the *genos* of the Mesogaioi; see *IG* 2².1247 and Farnell's comments, *Greek Hero Cults* (Oxford, 1921), p. 166.

26. This by poetic fiat since, if myth were history, Iolaus son of Iphicles would not need to be any older than are the sons of Heracles.

wreaths and carry the special branches that mark the suppliant. As a result the audience can never forget that these people are Zeus' consecrated guests (112)[27] and that anyone who insults them is guilty of a religious crime (72, 107–8; cf. 264). Unless they seek sanctuary because they are in some sense guilty or in error,[28] suppliants tend to be too pure and too plainly pitiable to carry an entire tragic action, yet these figures are identified not only as innocent but also as the helpless and persecuted relatives of a son of Zeus. They are noble and irreproachable, which suggests that this will be no ordinary tragedy.

In keeping with this list of consecrated characters, the scene shows a temple-front with a spacious altar before it, dedicated to Zeus Agoraios. And the first thing the spectator sees—after the aged Iolaus and a troop of little boys have rushed in to take possession of the altar steps[29]—is an attack upon all these untouchably sacred things. A villainous herald from Argos, the representative of its tyrant Eurystheus, strides in and does what no one else is seen to do in surviving tragedy: he makes a direct grab at the chief suppliant and knocks off his wreath. The altar that these people touch belongs to the god who above all others makes suppliants his own, but this particular herald and his master believe that weaker men should revere those who are more powerful (25), and indeed, as the Athenian king soon puts it, they think they are stronger than god (258). They have already made sanctuary meaningless in city after city (17, 25), and unless they are stopped, the divine institution of suppliancy will be dead, and with it the freedom of every Greek state except Argos (198, 244–45, 286–87; cf. 868, 113). In the present moment it is the integrity of free Attic soil that the Argive tyrant threatens (62, 113, 198, 244, 287, 957), for if he is allowed to have his way, the Athenian state will perish and, what is worse, an earthly rival will have triumphed over the now divine Heracles. Violating sanctuary is not as sensational a crime as cannibalism, but nevertheless this Eurystheus is plainly an enemy of culture after the Cyclops pattern.

There is no moral or ethical ambiguity here, and the familiar suppliant format emphasizes one's sense that the old man and the children are too plainly in the right, the herald almost a caricature of violence.[30] Since this

---

27. Compare Eur. *Supp.* 32 and *Ion* 1285, where the suppliant is the god's possession.

28. As, for example, the Aeschylean Danaids are guilty of resisting nature, custom, and (unwittingly) the will of Zeus.

29. An early Lucanian column krater, ca. 400 B.C. (*LIMC* vol. 6.2, p. 45) shows a white-haired Iolaus sitting on the altar with two boys; a pelike from the same group depicts him as standing on the altar while two boys hold on to his clothing, a third sits, and a fourth puts his foot on the altar.

30. As Fitton remarks ("*Suppliant Women,*" p. 450), Copreus' "hand is the hand of Hybris." It is a χεὶρ βίαιος (102, 106), and the notions of *hybris* and *bia* extend also to Eurystheus; see 18, 924, 947–48 for *hybris*, and note the extreme density of *bia* words used in the first half of

is Attica, the spectator knows that champions will come, that the weak will be protected as the infamous villain is foiled,[31] and indeed these exact events follow rapidly, beginning with the arrival of a pair of Attic kings. It is just at this point, however, that Euripides gives his happy national legend the twist that will reveal a fundamental human dilemma. The problem is compressed into one swift gesture. The herald Copreus (whose name means Dung Carrier)[32] is caught in the worst of religious crimes, taking what belongs to the gods (*hierosulia*), and in direct defiance of the local rulers, he threatens to continue with his sacrilege (267). Incensed by such barbaric effrontery (131), the Athenian king raises his scepter to strike (270), but then he stands frozen in his mere intention. The punishment cannot be completed, though the crime is flagrant and the king is on his own turf, because a sacrosanct herald cannot be touched (271, 273).[33] This baffled act of justice predicts what is to come, for very soon the same civilized Attic legalism will offer a paradoxical protection to the tyrant who has sent this outrageous agent. Demophon's paralysis thus invests a pat situation with a serious tension by showing that, even in righteous contest, the man of scruples may be crippled by the very order that he wants to defend.

Another version of the same paradox is developed in the next episode, then given a kind of resolution by way of a female. The city of Athens has decided, instead of striking the herald, to go to war with his master. However, just as the army is about to march against Argos in a burst of patriotism and piety, Kore calls for a sacrifice. She demands the daughter of a nobleman, and the Athenians in consequence are paralyzed, just as their king had been with the herald. They want to strike the invading tyrant, so as to protect the Heraclids and the institution of sanctuary (and they also want to help Athena stand up to Hera, 349–50), but at this price their deepest

---

the play to describe the Eurystheus-Copreus mode of action (13, 18, 64, 71, 79, 97, 102, 112, 127, 221, 225, 243, 254, 286, 361). That this association was traditional is shown by the reference to the *hybris* of Eurystheus at Xen. *Hell.* 6.5.47.

31. The protection of the Heraclid suppliants was already a part of Athenian self-praise in the first half of the fifth century, cf. their speech claiming precedence at Plataea (Hdt. 9.27). The scholiast at Ar. *Plut.* 385 reports a painting by Apollodorus from the end of the fifth century showing Alcmena and the Heraclids at the altar.

32. No one uses this name inside the play, but it is used in the list of characters and mentioned in the hypothesis; see Wilamowitz, *Kl. Schr.*, vol. 1 (Berlin, 1935), p. 62. Copreus was already a notorious rogue in epic times (*Il.* 15.638–39), and Wilamowitz notes that this man named "Dreckle" is, along with the "jammerliche feigling Eurystheus," a frankly burlesque figure (*Herakles*, vol. 1 [Berlin, 1933], p. 52).

33. Philostratus, however, knew a story in which Copreus was not only struck but killed; it was an *aition* for the traditional black *chlamys* of the ephebe which was worn until the second century A.D. (*VS* 550).

blood-loyalty forbids action. Zeus will be angry, Kore will be disappointed, and Heracles' family will probably be stoned to death as Eleutheria disappears from Greece, but nevertheless no father wants to put his girl to death. Nor is this the kind of state in which a man could be forced into such an action (423). The generous campaign collapses, and for a moment, instead of civic pride, there is only shame, despair, and fear around this Marathonian altar (449–50, 473). Then the deadlock is neatly broken by the opening of the temple doors. The audience has known that a group of female suppliants was in possession of the cella, and now it sees one of them step out. With her woolly wreath and sacred branch she seems almost a cult curiosity, a priestess of Zeus,[34] but she is in fact Macaria, the eldest daughter of Heracles, and she cuts through the masculine predicament with three plain words: "I am ready to die" (ἐγὼ . . . θνῄσκειν ἑτοίμη, 501–2). She asks to die among women, she gives her blessing to her brothers, and having received a promise of elaborate pomps (568–69), she moves away, hoping for perfect oblivion (595–96). And indeed she gets her wish, for she is never mentioned again in this play, though her courage saves the lives of her relatives and the reputation of Athens, while it also empowers those who will defeat the enemy of Heracles.[35]

The figure of Macaria temporarily transforms a suppliant action into one of willing sacrifice, and it also claims for this female principal a moral glamour superior to that of either suppliant or king. Though it is actually only halfway to its close, the tragedy thus seems to want only a battle report to confirm a final woman-wrought safety for the remaining Heraclids, but Euripides has much more in mind. He means to stage yet a third version of the masculine dilemma of righteous inhibition, and he prepares for this final display with several extraordinary events. First there is a frankly funny scene in which an aide arrives with a report from Heracles' oldest son, the absent Hyllus. He brings the news that more allies have joined the Athenians, and Iolaus greets him joyfully, but the fresh loud voice of the newcomer penetrates into the temple and once more its doors open to show, not a calm young girl this time, but an exceedingly excited old lady.[36] She is Alcmena, and she is under the impression that she must personally fight off one more evil emissary from their enemy, Eurystheus (647–48). She totters

34. She is shown on the Lucanian krater (n. 29, above), sitting beside the altar and holding a small cult figure of Zeus. A. Greifenhagen, *Ein frühlukanischer Kolonettenkrater,* Winkelmannsprogramm 123 (Berlin, 1969), 15–16, identified this figure as Alcmena, but she is distinctively young, in contrast to the white-haired Iolaus.

35. Macaria is almost as badly treated in tradition, though later writers know a spring in the Marathonian plain associated with her name (was there a local tale of transformation?); see Strabo 8.377; Paus. 1.32.6; Plut. *Pel.* 21.

36. The contrast between the two entrances is noted by Faulkner, "Wrath of Alcmene," p. 117.

out full of antique rage and ready to use her weak body as a shield for her aged colleague (649–53). "Touch him, and you can boast that you beat up two old people!" she screams at the man her grandson has sent to reassure her.[37] Of course her mistake is soon corrected,[38] but more foolishness follows. With further allies assured, the coming battle has a prosperous look, and old Iolaus is so excited that he forgets his suppliant status.[39] He too will fight! Hyllus' man makes fun of him, telling him he is feeble and ridiculous, but he demands that votive armor be brought out of the temple for him.[40] He can't lift it. He can hardly lift his own foot (726–28, 735), but he is led away boasting of his youthful exploits, the picture of bellicose senility. "I'll smite the enemy!" he quavers, and the slave who props him up finishes, ". . . if we can make it to the field. That's what worries me!" (738–39).[41]

The old man does get to the field, and a messenger speech reports the events that occur there. Iolaus commands a chariot to chase the retreating enemy king, and as he races along he makes a prayer to Zeus and Hebe. He asks for one day of revived youth, so that he can have vengeance on his enemies (ἀποτείσθαι δίκην / ἐχθρούς, 852–53; cf. 882, 887, 971, 1025). And at once two stars appear over his team; a cloud hides his chariot, out of

---

37. Burian, "Euripides' *Heracleidae*," p. 11, reluctantly admits that Alcmena's entrance is "at least partly comic in its effect"; Zuntz, *Political Plays*, p. 36, describes Alcmena as "like a chicken in a thunderstorm"; and Faulkner, "Wrath of Alcmene," p. 119, speaks of the "near comic confusion" that results. B. Seidensticker, *Palintonos Harmonia*, Hypomnemata, 72 (Göttingen, 1982), pp. 90–100, discusses the comic elements in the rest of the scene and concludes that they are here, to the detriment of the play, because Euripides could not resist a bit of crowd-pleasing farce (p. 100 n. 2). Which is to say that Euripides had no self control. The scene as a whole, and its function in the play, should be compared with that of Heracles' drunkenness in Eur. *Alc.* (737–860), for there too a character moves from laughable behavior to an unreasonable but heroic resolve.

38. Her recognition of her mistake has the wonderful suavity of the old sailor's greeting to the Helen he had just reported as translated; each says ὦ χαῖρε as offhandedly as possible (*Heracl.* 660; cf. *Hel.* 616).

39. There is even a parody of the formal raising of the suppliant when the servant says ἔπαιρε σεαυτόν at 635; cf. Eur. *Andr.* 717. At 603 Iolaus was resting, probably on the altar step, but during the ode that celebrates Macaria's death he seems to fall to an almost prone position. Lesky believed that this change of posture was proof that a messenger speech recounting the killing of the victim has been lost, but this argument is based on the indemonstrable assumption that no actor may move during a choral ode: "It is to be hoped that no one will wish to assume that Iolaus fell to the ground during the song of the Chorus" ("On the 'Heraclidae' of Euripides," *YCIS* 25 [1977] 23). That however is exactly what 619 suggests; see J. Wilkins, *Euripides, Heraclidae* (Oxford, 1993), ad loc.

40. There is obvious *meiosis* in this parody of the heroic arming of the warrior; cf. Eur. *Rhes.* 99–130.

41. As Paley remarked (ad loc.), Iolaus had to be made old, in preparation for the miracle of rejuvenation, but he did not have to be made absurd; "the language of the servant is evidently banter, which was not necessary for this purpose."

which he drives in an instant, transformed into a young and powerful warrior. With no difficulty he snatches the Argive tyrant from his car, binds him, and brings him back as the finest piece of spoils ever taken (862–63). All this is told to Alcmena as she maintains her suppliant posture and her guard over the children, and her response is a recognition. The two stars are Heracles and Hebe, and they prove that her son has truly entered the Olympian family. The Heraclids have been verified as the children of a god; she is established as the mother of a god, and Zeus has proved to be more gracious than she had supposed (869–72). But does this mean that they will all be free again, able to return to their paternal homes and cults (876–77)? The report that Eurystheus is still alive gives her pause (879–82), but the messenger is quick to reassure. Iolaus pays her the special compliment of sending the captured tyrant to her, living, so that she may have the avenger's pleasure of watching as her enemy makes his repayment (ὥς νιν ὀφθαλμοῖς ἴδοις . . . ζῶν ἐς σὸν ἐλθεῖν ὄμμα καὶ δοῦναι δίκην, 883, 887). This news is so good that it wins from the ancient woman a tacit promise of emancipation for the slave who brought it (788–89; cf. 890, where Alcmena must respond with a positive gesture).

The following scene contains the vengeance proper, and it begins with the entrance of the victim, Eurystheus. It is important to remember that this was a figure familiar from vase painting where, from early black-figure through the red-figure pieces of the fifth century, he had many representations but only one pose. Eurystheus was always seen with his head just sticking out of a giant pithos, his fingers waving in abject fear as an angry Heracles approached.[42] No one could possibly forget that he was the king who hid in a pot, and many would also remember that this same ignoble head had, in local legend, been chopped off and sent to Alcmena, either by Iolaus or by Hyllus, so that she could gouge its eyes out.[43] Such is the infamous coward who is now dragged by his chains into Euripides' play, the same king who, as Dung Carrier's master, authorized the opening attack on the suppliants at Zeus' altar. Battle defeat has publicly punished his political and religious misdeeds, and Greece is once more free to honor suppliants. There remain, however, the tortures he once inflicted on Heracles, and also his

---

42. The series is easily appreciated at *LIMC* s.v. "Eurystheus," to which the red-figure hydria from Cerveteri (*CVA* Louvre 9.viii and ix) and the red-figure cup (*ARV* 62.83) might be added. The remarkable consistency of image is noted by F. Brommer as continuing "zwar von den frühesten uns bekannten Bildern von der Mitte des 6. Jahrhunderts v. Chr. an bis in die römische Zeit" (*Herakles* [Münster and Cologne, 1953], p. 19).

43. At Pind. *Pyth.* 9.78–82, Iolaus figures the noble use of *kairos* as he beheads Eurystheus, but there is no mention of Alcmena; Apollod. *Bibl.* 2.8.1. reports Hyllus as sending the head for eye-gouging; cf. Ant. Lib. *Met.* 33. Note also that there was a place on the Marathonian plain called Eurystheus' Head (Paus. 1.32.6).

recent acts of sordid violence against an old man, an older woman, and a cluster of defenseless boys and girls. And so, while his masculine conquerors make a dedication to the Zeus of Trophies (937; cf. 867),[44] another member of the Heraclid family addresses these private crimes, a female whom the men have formally designated a surrogate avenger.

The world is clearly upside down when a tyrant who thought he was bigger than *dike* (933; cf. 924) is pulled about like a puppet, to give an old woman pleasure (939–40).[45] The tableau could have produced a geriatric Baiting of the Bully, but Euripides means to create a sensation that is intellectual, not visual, and he begins the subsequent scene of confrontation in a moderate key. There has been no difficulty of access for this appointed avenger, and consequently no need for intrigue; indeed the situation, with victim tidily delivered, is so anomalous that Alcmena does not at first show the proper avenger's delight in her position of power. She will not in any case put this man to death with her own hand, and so this meeting of an injured party with the cause of her injury at first resembles a royal sentencing ("Justice has seized you at last!" 941) rather than a genuine vengeance stroke. Alcmena reminds her victim of his two sets of crimes, against her son, and against herself and the children around her. He has attacked freedom and so must die in a slavish fashion (958), but she notes bitterly that even now it is he who will profit because, owing so much, he can only die once (958–60).[46] With this statement of the justice of the retaliation, she is about to order the execution when a blunt remark from the leader of the Athenian chorus interrupts, and once more a deadlock between natural justice and civic law is exposed.[47]

The punishment that Alcmena intends cannot be implemented, according to this nameless citizen, because in Attica there is a decree about battle

44. They set up a καλλίνικον, reminding us that Iolaus was hailed with Heracles in the traditional *tenella;* see testimonia at Archil. 324 W.

45. The reversal in their positions is neatly put at 944: κρατῇ γὰρ νῦν γε κοὐ κρατεῖς ἔτι.

46. Is this the germ of the later motif of the avenger's dissatisfaction with his work as not big enough, as seen in Seneca's Atreus and Shakespeare's Aaron (*Titus Andronicus* 5.1.141–44)?

47. This interruption is exactly parallel to that at 271, where the chorus leader stopped Demophon's chastisement of Copreus. The most reasonable distribution of lines 961–73 is that of Barnes, reproduced in Murray's text, which keeps the MS attributions to the choregus but gives the lines labeled "messenger" to Alcmena. To this arrangement Zuntz urged a number of objections, all fundamentally subjective; thus he found "staunch opposition" in the lines here given to the choregus, and argued that the same speaker could not later express the sympathy of 981–82, or comply with the killing, as the chorus does in its exit lines (*Political Plays,* pp. 37–38). Himself assigning the "staunch opposition" to Eurystheus' guard, he failed to explain why this resistance would come from a Heraclid follower and why such a one would urge it against the mother of Heracles, or how a conviction about local ways would have come to this foreigner. Zuntz also asserted that Alcmena could not address 967 to an Athenian, since it concerns Hyllus, but this is to assume that she is really seeking information. In fact her question is part of her rhetoric: "And did Hyllus ratify such a decree? (No, of course not; only Athenians did, so why should I be bound by it?)" The "opposition" of the man who interrupts has

captives providing that, once spared, an enemy may not afterward be put to death (966).[48] Here, then, is the stalemate of the offensive herald all over again but in a larger form, for Eurystheus is not simply the impious man who gave Copreus his orders: he is guilty of violent and unjust outrages (924–25) that threaten every Greek state and all Olympian religion. His crimes demand a punishment more horrendous and more personal than the simple military defeat that has come thanks to the grace of Zeus (867, 869–70), and what old Iolaus begged for was the strength to take revenge upon the fleeing tyrant (852). Vengeance is what Heracles and Hebe sanctioned with their gift of miraculous youth.[49] Yet now, when gods and her kinsmen have delivered him into Alcmena's hands, the final punishment of this destroyer of religion and Hellenic custom is blocked by a secular law formulated by the civilized men of Athens. They have thought to do for captives what Zeus has done for heralds, giving them a special untouchable status, and in consequence the defeated tyrant is now personally safe, though flagrantly guilty, just as Copreus was in the first episode. "No one can kill this man," says the Athenian (972), and when Alcmena answers, "I can, and I claim to be someone," he threatens her with serious consequences. The city is paralyzed, much as it was when Kore made her demand, because once again the community can pursue the natural ends of justice only by "sacrificing" something of its own—a decree now, not a daughter—and this it refuses to do.

As before, the appearance of a willing victim saves the Athenians from abandoning an action that they know is right. This time, however, it is an ugly old villain, not a lovely young girl, who rescues everyone. Nor is his offer as spontaneous as Macaria's was. Eurystheus' immediate concern, on learning of his special untouchable status, is to influence his captors in his favor so that he might perhaps return to Argos. Consequently he makes a

---

been much exaggerated, for what he does is qualify. Alcmena's "don't they count it a fine thing to kill enemies?" is answered, "(yes,) but not one who has been taken alive" (965–66); her "isn't it a fine thing when a man is made to pay?" is answered, "(yes) but the man doesn't exist who can kill this one" (971–72).

48. When Alcmena asks what *nomos* prohibits the killing, the chorus-man answers that it is rather a decree of the local rulers: τοῖς τῆσδε χώρας προστάταισιν οὐ δοκεῖ (964; cf. 1019). The vaguely plural Hellenic *nomoi* that Eurystheus praises at 1010 apparently covered only those who have willingly surrendered on the battlefield when promised clemency; see Thuc. 3.66.2; 67.6; and cf. Diod. Sic. 13.23. This present captive certainly did not so surrender, for he was captured as he was running from the field by an Iolaus who did not intend any clemency at all, but rather that Alcmena should have the satisfaction of this particular killing. On the play's hierarchy of the various forms of custom and law, see A. P. Burnett, "Tribe and City, Custom and Decree," *C Phil.* 71 (1976) 4–26.

49. To the extent that Heracles and Hebe have entered into Iolaus in the miracle of rejuvenation, they have entered as well into his taking of Eurystheus and into his sending his captive to Alcmena; like Dionysus in *Cyclops*, they actively partake in the revenge.

fulsome speech in his own defense, with an eye to the chorus of locals. He took risks, he says, while persecuting Heracles according to Hera's orders, for it was dangerous to make such a man one's enemy, and as for his actions since, he was forced to attack babies because even with Heracles gone he would otherwise have had to live in fear of the enemy's cubs (991–1004).[50] He even presumes to praise the Athenians for their piety in making him safe (1012–13), and he of all men suggests that he be looked upon as a suppliant and a man of noble impulse.[51] He says more than he means, however, when he claims to be a "sophist of suffering," for it is the suffering of others that he has studied, and his presumptuous cleverness naturally increases Alcmena's hatred. She has already announced that this man is hers and no one can take him from her (976–80),[52] and now she is determined not to give him up. She must persuade the city to let her kill (1020), and it is her attempt to prove that her vengeance and the city's law may both be satisfied that provokes a solution—one that emanates all incongruously from Delphi.

Alcmena is defending her revenge rights with all the cunning she can find, and so she proposes that she might physically comply with local law by handing back the corpse of her victim to those "friends" among the Athenians who might wish to bury him (1022–25). She pretends that the city in this way might still honor its own decree, but there is no time for any choral reaction to this quibble because at the mention of burial Eurystheus' smug invulnerability explodes. He recognizes his own fate and shouts, "Kill me! I won't argue" (1026), because he has remembered a Delphic oracle that long ago announced his destined burial not in Argos but here in Attic soil.[53]

---

50. This speech has inspired sympathy, even enthusiasm among certain readers; Zuntz admired its "Realpolitik" and pitied the poor tyrant who only wanted to sleep without care (*Political Plays*, pp. 35 ff.); J. A. Spranger describes it as "a frank and manly statement" ("The Political Element," *CQ* 19 [1925] 122); even Burian judged it to be "brave, reasonable and composed" ("Euripides' *Heracleidae*," p. 17), and Pozzi ("Hero and Antagonist," p. 33) heard a "hero extolling another hero's accomplishments." See also M. Visser, "Worship Your Enemy," *Harv. Theol. Rev.* 75 (1982) 403–28, who says that with this speech Eurystheus "shows himself an honorable man" (413).

51. At 1015 Diggle marks τόν τε γενναῖον as corrupt, but the whole line seems suspect. J. Wilkins' summary of opinions discovers nothing that suggests real sense, reasonable or rhetorical; see *Euripides, Heraclidae* (Oxford, 1993), pp. 187–88. Some have supposed that at this point Eurystheus actually supplicates Alcmena, but this is not possible since he is bound throughout the scene.

52. Her practical indicative is in contrast to the choregus' theoretical optative at 972. The parody of her defiance at Ar. *Pax* 316 testifies to the emphasis with which this line was delivered.

53. Polyphemus likewise remembers an oracle at the very end of *Cyclops* (696), as does Polymestor at the end of *Hecuba* (1259–73). For the general pattern of a people who take an invading enemy as a cult hero, usually after having maltreated him in violation of sacred custom, see Visser, "Worship Your Enemy."

He had thought that Hera's protection would see him past any fate Apollo might intend, but now he accepts death on this spot as inevitable, and since they have spared him, he is even willing to instruct the Athenians in the advantages his tomb will bring. Indeed, the tyrant-bully who is about to be an enemy-hero is all complaisance, but for the moment his willingness to die only sharpens the horns of the city's dilemma. Eurystheus is ready to take his place in his balefully protective tomb,[54] but, as the chorus leader began by saying, no one can put him there.

Because of their own decree, Athenian men cannot provide themselves with the corpse that is destined to be their city's salvation, nor can any of their grateful masculine allies defy this local prohibition. And so at the end of Eurystheus' speech there is an awkward silence and a total lack of movement among the figures in the playing area. Then the spell is broken by an ancient foreign female not hampered by regulations made for men. "Why do you hesitate?" she asks (1045). "You have heard what he says. The salvation both of your city and of these suppliants depends on you, so why wait to kill this man? He himself has shown that this is the path of safety; as enemy, he must die" (1045–49). No one responds, and so she addresses her own servants: "Take him away—his killers ought to give him to the dogs" (εἶτα χρῆν κυσὶν / δοῦναι κτάνοντας, 1050–51).[55] Then, turning to Eurystheus, she has her last say: "You'll not live, don't think it, to drive me again from my country" (1050–52). The mother of Heracles is not only able but eager to supervise this destined killing, and the chorus accepts her agency, seeing it as a way to maintain both the ritual and the legal purity of the Attic rulers (1053–55).[56] And so, as the play ends, Heracles' old enemy, servant of Hera, tyrant of Argos, violator of sanctuaries, and bully of all Greece (but

54. His entombed anger will repel all Heraclid = Argive forces that may threaten in the future. The tomb was at the Scironian rocks (Paus. 1.44.10); in Thebes it was said that Eurystheus had been buried in a roadway, so that his remains would be constantly trampled and dishonored (schol. Pind. *Pyth.* 9.145a).

55. Following H. Erbse, who proposed χρῆν (*Ausgewählte Schriften zur klassische Philologie* [Berlin, 1979], p. 134 n. 15). This wish that the punishment could be worse is parallel to 960, the regret that the enemy can only be punished once. There may or may not be a few lines missing after 1052; if so, one might expect some further recognition from Alcmena of the Delphic prediction, though she has just referred to the coming "salvation" for the city (1045). Even with the text as it stands, however, it is clear that it is Eurystheus' death, not his corpse, that interests Alcmena; witness her proposed solution at 1022–24. For contrary opinions, see among others, Zuntz, *Political Plays*, pp. 46–52, and D. Bain, *Masters, Servants and Orders in Greek Tragedy* (Manchester, 1987), pp. 33–35, both of whom believe that Alcmena gives the order for dishonoring the body.

56. For the opposite opinion, see Wilkins, *Heraclidae*, p. 193, who asserts that a lacuna after 1052 is "certain" because "it is unbelievable that the chorus should acquiesce so readily in the death, let alone the non-burial of a prospective hero." Is it really unbelievable, when the last statement made by the chorus leader, in answer to Alcmena's "the deed is mine to do," was, "I readily agree that your quarrel with this man is a serious and pardonable affair" (δεινόν τι καὶ συγγνωστόν, 981–82)? That was said even before the revelation about the future usefulness of

also the man who hid in a pot) is surrounded by Heraclid servants and a chorus of Athenians. Encouraged by an angry old woman, they jostle him off stage, where he will be put to death as soon as he is out of sight. His remains will not be shown, like those of a standard vengeance victim; instead they will lie in Attic ground, unplaced,[57] but serving in their unrest as strong protection against invasion from the Peloponnese. And meanwhile the men of Attica will not have violated their own decree. The rule of law, like the right to asylum, survives, but only because a fierce old woman was not afraid to do the Heraclean work of brute revenge, and this harshly happy truth is reinforced by a final visual effect. The little boys who have clustered at the altar must also leave the playing area,[58] for they are free from fear and the city is free of responsibility for their further protection.[59] Each will take up his ritual branch, and their leafy procession will follow the group that follows Eurystheus. The children are on their way home, in company with their male relatives and their triumphant grandmother.

Such is the action of this short, sharp play. So much cleverness deployed by the poet, so little awe demanded from the audience, would seem to show that this is not a failed tragedy but instead a highly successful venture of another sort, and I would suggest that it was meant to cap a trilogy. Its length and its abrupt close are reminiscent of fourth play or satyr drama,[60] as are also certain characteristics of verbal style: colloquialisms, for example, and little literary jokes.[61] Here, as in *Alcestis,* there is a strong flavor of folktale as serious motifs of disorder, like abnormal sacrifice and attacks on what is sacred, combine with others that are inherently comic—an old lady who threatens a youth, a saucy servant,[62] and a tottering warrior who steals votive

Eurystheus' corpse. As to aquiescing in "non-burial," this the chorus plainly does not do; the spectator knows that Apollo and the city will see to it that the remains go into the fated tomb.

57. Apollo evidently forbade any ordinary cult honors (1040–41); the anger of the dead, thus unappeased, will offer a daimonic barrier to invasion.

58. And what of the girls in the temple? It would make a pleasing spectacle if the doors were to open for a third time so that they could join their brothers and the chorus in the final exit.

59. As long as there are suppliants, or even a suppliant bough at one of its altars, a community is in jeopardy, its religious life abnormal; this is why it was illegal at Athens to leave a suppliant bough in the Eleusinion during the Great Eleusinia (Andoc. 1.110). Note the careful removal of boughs at Soph. *OT* 142, and cf. Eur. *Supp.* 359, 39; Thuc. 1.133.

60. *Heracl.* has 1055 lines; Eur. *Alc.* has 1163; Eur. *Cyc.,* 705; Eur. *Rhes.,* 996.

61. At 166 Copreus calls Iolaus a "tomb of an old man," looking forward to New Comedy locutions like τυμβογέρων; see Zuntz, *Political Plays,* pp. 38–39 n. 3, for further examples, to which one might add Eurystheus' offhand πῶς οὖν at 1037. As for jokes, at 711 Iolaus absurdly alludes to Hector at *Il.* 6.490–92; at 952 Alcmena dismisses the Twelve Labors as a *makros mythos* too long to tell, and the chorus allows itself something of the same license at 771–72 with its Mother Athena.

62. For upstart servants as typical of Dionysus festivals, see schol. Dem. 22.68.

objects from a temple.[63] *Children of Heracles* also shows an almost allegorical manipulation of general concepts, as the heavenly wedding between Heracles and Youth finds its earthly reflection when Old Age grows young and strikes an enemy.[64] What is more, the emphasized motif of *eleutheria*,[65] along with the presence of children in a plot that gives them release and a return home, stamps this play as peculiarly Dionysiac and strongly reminiscent of plays like *Cyclops* and the Aeschylean *Isthmiastai*, wherein childish satyr bands are liberated from a monster. And finally, the vengeance of *Children of Heracles* is proposed as a rough but necessary step forward in man's social arrangements, much as the killing of Polyphemus is in *Cyclops*. Special to this play, however, is the extra touch of topsy-turvy disorder that accrues from the appearance of an old woman in the role of the fierce avenging champion.

II

A vengeance heroine superficially much like Alcmena is found in Euripides' *Hecuba*.[66] Like Heracles' mother, the Queen of Troy is old, but she nonetheless acts successfully in behalf of her house against a villain who is her son's enemy and a threat to culture. Furthermore her revenge is associated, like that of Alcmena, with the sacrifice of a girl who is close to her. Unlike Alcmena, however, Hecuba is always present, her response to the represented events always of central importance, her act of vengeance visibly accomplished and also reported. She is, in other words, the true principal of her play, an extraordinary creature who moves, saturated with grief, in a region outside ordinary human institutions. Her drama takes place not in Attica but in a temporary camp at the edge of a non-Greek continent, and it shows a moment just after the end of the great war, when victors released from both military and civil discipline have begun to slip back into anarchy. No friendly pair of star divinities looks down, no miracle of rejuvenation occurs among these paralyzed men who are no longer warriors or citizens, nor is there any place of safety open to these hopeless captive women who have neither husbands nor hearths. The whole mixed group does move in

63. Compare J. W. Fitton, "The *Suppliant Women* and the *Children of Herakles*," *Hermes* 89 (1961) 460, who speaks of a "world of pure fairy-tale," noting "cheeky slaves" and a "bringing in of the villain to be baited."

64. Rejuvenation of the old is among the blessings of Dionysus mentioned at Aristides 41.7; cf. Ar. *Ran.* 345 ff., and see E. R. Dodds, ad *Bacch.* 170–369. Here, in connection with a revenge that revives family honor, it is reminiscent also of the revival of Laertes in *Od.* 24.

65. Political freedom is the concern of Demophon (245, cf. 198; 287, and Alcmena at 957); Alcmena works for individual freedom (873–74); and the delivery of Eurystheus to the avenger brings emancipation to the slave (788–89, 890).

66. Much of what I have to say about *Hecuba* is now argued extensively and elegantly by J. Mossman, *Wild Justice: A Study of Euripides' Hecuba* (Oxford, 1995).

the end, the women toward slavery and the men toward home, but their release comes only after two acts of cruelty, one performed by the Greeks, the other by the captive women. A girl's throat is slashed, a man's eyes are gouged out before the departure is effected, and so a fundamental unease remains even after the entire cast has disappeared toward ships bound for Greece.

The scene of *Hecuba* is a savage strand, and the first figure to appear, the specter of a child horribly murdered,[67] tells of another specter who at this moment demands the killing of another child. Ghosts, not gods, are in control of this place where the men who have burned Troy sit baffled and rootless, kept from home by unfavorable winds. A few days ago these Greeks committed superlative crimes—bloody hands slashed at an ancient king who huddled on an altar (23–24)—and the continuing play occurs in the uncanny aftermath of that violence.[68] All these victors are polluted and there is no hope of purification, for there are no temples or altars in this unpeopled spot. The habits of religion have understandably lapsed and those of politics are decaying: these stranded men can remember how to go to an Assembly but not how to form an opinion, and so they are the tools of any leader whose rhetoric dazzles them.

The Greek army, however, is only half the population of this Thracian shore, for there is also a group of captives, so that to the community made up of men, Hellenes, conquerors, masters, and killers, a second is opposed, one containing women, Trojans, spoils of war, slaves, and makers of children. The women are rootless and without function like the men, but unlike them they are still close to a life of civic order. Their smoldering city is almost visible, and they can remember husbands and beds and small vanity mirrors (923–27).[69] They lost these things in common, on a single night,

---

67. If the audience knew the subject of the play beforehand, they were probably expecting to see the ghost of Achilles, known in connection with Polyxena from *Iliou Persis* (Procl. *Chrestomathia* 273 Severyns); he seems to have appeared in Sophocles' *Polyxena* (fr. 523 Radt). Polydorus' ghost is usually said to be modeled on that of Patroclus at *Il.* 23.62, because it is associated with a dream, but the phrase ἄκλαυτος ἄταφος (*Hec.* 30) is borrowed from Elpenor (*Od.* 11.54, cf. 72). This is the first surviving example of what J. A. Symonds called "the vulgar machinery of revenge and ghosts" (*John Webster and Cyril Tourneur,* Mermaid series [London and New York, 189–?], p. ix), but it should be noted that though he denounces his killer, Polydorus does not demand revenge.

68. Note Hecuba's phrase at 607: ἀκόλαστος ὄχλος ναυτική τ' ἀναρχία.

69. They remind themselves of these things in the song that precedes the entry of the vengeance victim, 905–51. In this lyric recreation, the destruction of their homes is commanded by the voices of Greeks who themselves only want to get home (930–32), while their marriages are destroyed by the nonmarriage of Paris and Helen which demolished all Troy (946–49). With their supplication of Artemis in the moment of danger compare Penelope at *Od.* 18.201–5, who likewise sees this goddess as one who may bring death as an escape from longing for a lost husband; cf. married women's cults of Artemis at Cyrene (*SEG* 72.3.12–13).

and because of their shared memory they have, in contrast to the men, a perfect solidarity among themselves. Hecuba is their leader, but she has no need to persuade them of anything because the women, who have no ambition, are as one in their simple need to remain themselves and survive. These truths about the women are not suggested by the prologue speaker, but as soon as he is gone they are visually announced by a tableau in which one woman crawls forward physically supported by a group of her kind— Hecuba coming out from her tent.

Power in this postvictory moment seems to be polarized, and the only communication between the two sectors of the camp comes in the form of commands issued from the men and received by the conquered women. The drama, however, is going to subvert this situation, and once the chorus has entered, its playing area is permanently filled with women, so that the lone male figures, when they appear, are always outnumbered and overshadowed. They will prove to be ethically dwarfed as well, and staged confirmation of a reversed power structure will come in a scene in which the men's king, Agamemnon, simply transfers his authority to the women's queen. This abdication will of course be no more than temporary—it will last just long enough for Hecuba to accomplish her revenge—but it will demonstrate a pair of truths about these confronted and strongly gendered communities. The Greek men, in the course of the long war, have almost forgotten what binds a mortal group together, but the women, though they are Trojans and captives, remember a fundamental social rule. They know that a return is always owed from one creature to another, whether for splendor or for viciousness, and in the course of this tragedy they help their Greek counterparts to relearn this great *nomos,* first as the law of gratitude and praise, then as the law of retaliation.

The first part of the play, the section in which Polyxena is sacrificed, analyzes the extent of the Greek regression. Yesterday a ghost of Achilles rose above his tomb, demanding the blood of a princess as his prize, and half of the army was ready to watch a girl's throat cut, while the other half resisted the proposal. There was an angry confusion in the Assembly, but then a demagogue appeared, the honey-tongued logic-chopper Odysseus, the darling of the people (131–32; cf. 256–57). He had no praise for Achilles and no reminders of that warrior's superb deeds,[70] but he did have a "policy" (331) based on a cynical sense of what would profit the military organization. Odysseus favored the sacrifice because only an army generous with rewards could recruit new soldiers and expect them to risk their lives (138, 313–20).[71] He meant to buy future exploits, in other words, not to repay

70. Contrast Pind. *Isth.* 8.63–66.

71. His speech is modeled after Achilles' response, in the Embassy; with *Hec.* 306–8 compare *Il.* 9.315–19.

those of the past, frankly arguing that, since Achilles seems to control the winds,[72] this so-called "prize" was in fact simply the going price for everyone's passage home (534–41).

Odysseus represents the disheartened opportunism now general among the Greeks, and his ethical state is explored when he comes to demand Polyxena as the ghost-hero's bribe. He comes among women already described as in touch with the superhuman and alive to one another's griefs, for Hecuba has been warned by a dream,[73] the chorus has hastened to share her pain, and Polyxena has heard of her own imminent slaughter with early-morning fatality, her mind more occupied with what her mother will suffer (197–215). This female ability to feel with and for one another, soon to be expressed in gestures exchanged between the mother and the girl (398, 400, 439–40),[74] isolates Odysseus in his inhumanity. According to

72. We do not know whether or not this is a tenet of the play; Polydorus says that Achilles has "held back" the Greeks (38) and demanded prizes and the sacrifice. In the appeasement ceremony as described by Talthybius, Neoptolemus makes no direct plea for wind but simply asks that the ships be "released" and that all may have a fair journey home (539–40). Agamemnon mentions the lack of favorable wind (900) as permitting Hecuba's vengeance, but in his mind it is a god who sends wind, and this would seem to be the accepted belief.

73. Wilamowitz questioned the authenticity of the dactylic lines in Hecuba's first speech (74–76, 90–91), and many editors have excised them, some removing 92–98 as well, thus doing away with the dream about Polyxena. The best summary of the whole question is that of H. Erbse, *Studien zum Prolog der euripideischen Tragödie* (Berlin and New York, 1984), pp. 48–54, who keeps both dactylic passages; for a defense of the Wilamowitz position, however, see J. M. Bremer, "Euripides' *Hecuba* 59–215," *Mnemos.* 24 (1971) 232–50. Erbse's interpretation seems reasonable: Hecuba reports a single symbolic dream about a fawn and a wolf (90–91), and a single apparently mute apparition (54). The dream she takes as a threat that refers to Polyxena (75) because she knows of Achilles' actual demand (92–94). The apparition she recognized at once as Polydorus, and from its conjunction with the dream (75) she assumes that it too has a fearful sense: φοβεράν (76) is predicative, "which I saw and recognized as fearful." Moderns tend to forget that according to ancient ways of interpretation, neither the dream nor the apparition was necessarily a promise of evil; this is why Hecuba wishes that she could consult Helenus (87). What she wants is to get rid of the combined vision (ὄψις, 72) that consists of dream and apparition; she casts it on the ground in a gesture much like spitting (70–72; cf. 1276) and her magical intention is reflected by the changed meter of the lines in which she describes what she would reject. (F. Castaldi, "Ad Euripide, Ecuba 74–75 e 90–91," *Rivista Indo-Greco-Italica* 12 [1928] 95, supposed that the dactyls were somehow prophetic.) Many believe that the apparition gave a message to Hecuba, presumably an account of his death, but there is no hint of this in her report, nor does she have any such information when the corpse is discovered. Others think that Polydorus appeared in a second dream that he himself controlled; thus R. Schlesier, "Die Backen des Hades," *Metis* 3 (1988) 11–35, speaks assuredly of "die Schau des Traums" which Hecuba will later interpret with the help of the "Rachegeist" of Polydorus. For G. Devereux the dream of the fawn is an expression of anxiety and a rare example of a vision of the "primal scene" from a parental point of view (!): the wolf is the male parent who makes a sexual attack upon Hecuba, the child between them being almost incidental (*Dreams in Greek Tragedy* [Oxford, 1976], pp. 259–312).

74. The closeness of the pair, like mother and nursing child, is further established by the choral phrase σῶν ἀπὸ μαστῶν (142), and by the simile that makes Hecuba ivy twining around

his own words he stands for the *psephos*,[75] the sort of law that a demagogue can elicit from a mob (219; cf. 196), and he also stands for the power of the strong over those who are weak (227). Hecuba knows that this is not a man with whom one argues, and so, remembering a lifetime of princely dealings, she moves instead to bind him in a positive obligation. Once he was her suppliant and she spared him; now she reverses the gesture, touching his hand and his beard (275, 286) and adding the argument from *charis:* let him now return the grace she had then granted him (276).[76] According to divine law he should respect an act of supplication, and according to the received rules of social intercourse he should render benefit for benefit, but Odysseus is not called Logic-chopper for nothing. Like Shylock and Portia rolled into one, he answers that what he once received from Hecuba was his life, and consequently what he owes back is her life, nothing less and nothing more. He will free her from slavery if she wishes (301), but he will see to it that her daughter is sacrificed. This dominant Greek male fears the appearance of ingratitude, and most particularly the bad effects that such an appearance might have in his martial world (315–16; cf. 138–40), but its actual practice bothers him not at all (254–57).

Odysseus and the Greeks have forgotten the true meaning of *charis,* but they do believe that Achilles must have his prize if they are ever to get home, and so, after a final incomplete embrace between mother and daughter (438–40), they take Polyxena to the hero's tomb. Officiants arrive, victim and implements are brought, and a rite that should change the wind's direction is begun. All this is recounted to Hecuba after the women have made their choral salute to the coming winds of slavery, but the story that Talthybius tells does not report a simple rite of placation. Something unexpected happened, and what the gathered army actually witnessed was a marvel that brought a change not so much in the weather as in themselves. It seems that when the self-appointed priest drew his golden sword, the victim—the equivalent of a beast[77]—spoke. She was a slave, but she proclaimed herself free by forbidding any hand to force her compliance. Then she gave unrestrained consent to the slaughter, and by granting to her killer a choice of

---

the tree that is her child (398). It is also notable that the chorus at 629–56 can move from their own sufferings to the sufferings they imagine Greek women know, with a leap of sympathy something like that of Stesichorus' Helen (209 *PMG*). There is, however, no indication that the poet wants us to recognize the "*nomos* of trust and openness" that figures so largely in the reading of M. Nussbaum, *The Fragility of Goodness* (Cambridge, 1986), pp. 397–421, esp. 406–9.

75. This is the *psephisma* that Aristotle warned against, the popular vote that overrides *nomos* (*Pol.* 1292a24)—here the *nomos* against human sacrifice.

76. Some deny that Hecuba actually supplicates, but her gesture is specified at 275, and his impious repudiation of it causes the choral exclamation at 332–33, with its reference to βία.

77. She has been figured as a doe (90–91), a filly (142), a young calf (205–6), and a calf (526).

easy spots for his blade,[78] she established her own psychic dominance. In effect Polyxena conferred his office upon the nonplussed priest (Achilles' son) and herself took command, reversing the inner dynamic of the rite by which the hero and his winds were to be appeased.[79] Her few words transformed the victim's passive agony into active decision, and what is more, they entirely changed the orientation of the ceremony, for according to Talthybius' report Polyxena—the intended means in an abnormal act of Achilles-worship—became herself the center of a rite of acclamation. She fell with her throat cut, but the watching Greeks saw her, the daughter of a vanquished king, as a kind of victor, and on the spot they invented a festival of praise for her.[80] Not one continued with the sacrificial acts, but all began to pile up garlands and gifts in recognition of the courage and nobility shown by this captive female beast-substitute. The need to return beauty for beauty had suddenly revived in them.

This is the sacrifice action that Euripides has coupled with Hecuba's revenge, and he makes sure that we understand it correctly before he goes on to the second part of his drama. Instruction comes when the mother offers a kind of funeral speech for her girl (585–603), translating the offerings of the army into her own garland of words. She asks what sort of education might produce such virtue, and when in answer she proposes the canons of beauty as the text for a training in nobility (602), we realize that Polyxena herself has fixed just such a canon for the Greeks.[81] They have been educated by her action, just as they might have been by a splendid deed recounted in an epic poem, and they have been moved to give it festive recognition. Their education, however, is not as yet complete, because the virtuous person must also be able to recognize and respond suitably to the opposite of what is fine, which Hecuba calls τὸ αἰσχρόν. In principle, to know the fair is to know the foul, but this is not yet the case with these dis-

78. By suggesting the alternative of her breast, she proposes that Neoptolemus kill her like a man, not like a beast, but he cuts her throat (563–67).

79. In Heywood's translation of Sen. *Troades* 1153–54: "Her corage moves eche one, and loe / a strange thing, monstrous like / that Pyrrhus even himself stoode still / for dread, and durst not strike." Polyxena's achievement can be measured by comparing this scene with the death depicted on a Tyrrhenian amphora in the British Museum where several men manipulate the girl's body as if it were an object (*JHS* 18 [1898] pl. xv = A. J. N. W. Prag, *The Oresteia: Iconographic and Narrative Traditions* [Chicago, 1985], pl. 62).

80. The scholiast at 574 notes, "leaves are cast upon the body as if she were a victor in the games; this was the homage given to victors"; cf. Pind. *Pyth.* 9.123–24. The Greeks even exhort one another with pseudo-insults, like playful members of a festival chorus (577–80).

81. Some critics report that Hecuba's speech brings her own moral degradation into ironic prominence; see, e.g., T. A. Tarkow, "Tragedy and Transformation," *Maia* 36 (1984) 135. Better would be to suppose a nonexplicit application to Agamemnon, whose education should have taught him to behave as an *esthlos* (844) but who cannot do what he admits would be fine, thus falling into behavior that is shameful.

placed and forgetful Greeks. They have, with Polyxena's help, remembered how to praise what is noble but not yet how to punish what is vile, and so in the second part of his play the poet makes his old Trojan queen show them the unbeautiful side of the rule of repayment.

Hecuba's deed of revenge returns the great outrage that was announced in the prologue by its victim's ghost. The youngest Priamid prince, a mere child, had been sent away to safety when the Greeks first came, and a treasure with him, so that if the city should fall, the royal line would still survive (4–15). It was a Thracian chieftain, Polymestor, who received the princeling, a man bound to Priam as his guest-friend (19, 26; cf. 82, 710, 774, 781, 793, 852, 890, 1216, 1244, 1247), but one who was unfortunately a villain (note 790, where he is described as ἀνοσιώτατος). The minute this "friend" heard of the Greek victory, he killed the boy and took the treasure, nor did he simply put his ward to death. He slashed and cut the body in a fashion so hideous that it cannot be named in Greek (714),[82] and after that he threw the corpse into the sea for fishes to eat (26). The recipient of Hecuba's vengeance is thus a triple enemy of culture, for he has broken the divine law of *xenia*,[83] dishonored the secular vows of contract (*enguesis*, which allowed the giving of brides and hostages),[84] and also defied the primary rule of all mankind, that of giving burial.[85]

82. For Thracians as killers of children, see Thucydides' account of the atrocities at Mycalessos (7.29), and for maiming the dead as supreme sacrilege, Hdt. 9.78–79 (Lampon's suggestion to Pausanias). Schlesier, "Die Backen des Hades," p. 18 n. 21, is certain that the corpse was castrated, its heart cut out, etc., in some imagined rite of the Thracian Dionysus, but there is no support for these notions in the play, and certainly no suggestion that the maiming of the boy was done for ritual reasons.

83. Killing a *xenos* (ξενοκτονεῖν, 1247) was classed with incest, cannibalism, and abusing a father, as characteristic of savage times; Aeschin. 3.224; Isoc. 5.122. Diod. Sic. 20.70.3–4 tells of Agathocles who murdered a *xenos*, then later, on the same day of the same month, lost both his army and his sons to allies of the murdered man; the historian sees in this that the god, like a good lawgiver, exacted a double punishment, "for when he had unjustly slain one friend he was deprived of two sons."

84. This is the notion behind the difficult expression τὸ ὑπέγγυον at 1027–28, where the chorus, evidently thinking of physical pledge-markers, says of Polymestor's coming punishment, "pledges made to gods and to justice don't collapse," i.e., they stand, and must be redeemed in one way or another. The formal promise to return a person or object under agreed circumstances was one of this society's plainest expressions of its basic Law of Return, of which revenge was another; see L. Gernet, *Droit et institutions en Grèce antique* (Paris, 1968), pp. 45–46, 108.

85. Note the play's emphasis on burial: the ghost of the prologue appears because he wants burial; the anomalous burial planned for Polyxena is the mechanical cause of the discovery of his body, and so of the final double burial. All of which is underlined by the fact that, strictly speaking, this sacrificial victim ought not to be buried; having been dedicated to a hero, Polyxena's remains are tainted, but presumably some special form might be observed, as in the case of the remnants of the ram dedicated to Pelops at Olympia (Paus. 5.13.2–3).

By poetic justice it is this last crime that now betrays Polymestor into Hecuba's hands, for the underworld gods cause little Polydorus' mangled but recognizable body to wash up almost at his mother's feet. When it is brought onstage (by a woman who links the two halves of the play together, since she was sent to get water for Polyxena's funeral) it is wrapped, and so the audience shares directly in the horrified discovery that opens this action of revenge. It is as if the inaugural crime were reenacted as the condition of the corpse is revealed, and though Hecuba's first cries are of grief, a spirit of vengeance, an *alastor,* speaks from the child's wounds to teach her (and the spectator) another sort of response (685–87). By the hideousness of what he has done, Hecuba can recognize the man who must have killed her son, and as soon as she knows her enemy she is ready to act. Justice demands punishment, for Polymestor has pitilessly carved the flesh of a boy he held in trust (715–20), and this means that Hecuba must take her dead husband's place. She stands by the corpse of her son, like the household-head at a kinsman's tomb, and she makes the formal denunciation: "The killer is my own guest-friend, the Thracian cavalry chief!" (710).

This juridical opening sets the tone for Hecuba's strangely formal and public act of revenge. She does not look for a private ally and make a secret intrigue but instead turns directly to Agamemnon, supervisor of the morning's sacrifice but also the supreme local authority.[86] She tells him that it is a ruler's duty, owed to gods and to the community, to act for her as avenger (790); he must punish her son's killer because this murderer has destroyed what was under sacred protection (803–4). The killing of Polydorus was an act of impious and greedy savagery; if it goes unrequited, such savagery will prevail. She makes her claim on the basis of the universal *nomos* of return (798–805); on the basis of the particular *charis* of Aphrodite, received by Agamemnon from Cassandra (834–35);[87] and finally on the basis of those accepted Hellenic virtues according to which a man of noble nature will always support what is just and suppress the doers of evil (844–45). "Lend an avenging hand to this extinct old woman" is the summation of Hecuba's

---

86. She also turns to him as a slave who properly asks her master to act for her; see R. Meridor, "The Function of Polymestor's Crime," *Eranos* 81 (1983) 13–20. Critics often complain that revengers act as if there were no constituted authorities, but when Hecuba turns to Agamemnon she is then condemned for lack of pride; thus D. J. Conacher, "Euripides' *Hecuba,*" *AJPhil.* 82 (1961) 23, accuses her of "grovelling before her city's enemies."

87. Critical reaction to this argument is particularly obtuse; Conacher, "*Hecuba,*" speaks of "bought favors and calculated returns of whores and pimps," and also of "pandering" to enemies "with her daughter's honor"; G. H. Gellie, "Hecuba and Tragedy," *Antichthon* 14 (1980) 35 n. 9, complains of the "tastelessness" and "vulgarity" of this plea, and Tarkow, "Tragedy and Transformation," p. 132, reports that Hecuba tries to "capitalize" on Cassandra. The argument from the return due for receipt of erotic *charis* is, however, standard; see for example Pelops, in Pind. *Ol.* 1. 75, and Tecmessa, at Soph. *Aj.* 520–24.

plea, but it is only superficially effective. Agamemnon pities her, and he admits that punishment of this criminal would be right and for the common good (902). If it were up to him, he would certainly do everything Hecuba asks (861–62), but unfortunately he is impotent, crippled by his unpopularity with the army. The men would not allow him to proceed against Polymestor, for they have named the Thracian villain "friend" because he is strong, while the dead child, being weak and a Trojan, will be called "enemy" (858).

Such is Agamemnon's confession, and it is followed by a power reversal something like the one that occurred earlier at the sacrifice, as Hecuba suddenly moves to dominant position. Agamemnon is the slave of mob opinion (864) but she, like her daughter, has never been enslaved; she even promises with searing disdain to liberate this victorious king from his fear of people beneath him (869). She had asked him to stand in for the missing male head of her house, but when this scene is done it is she who is to act, not only as father, for Priam, but also as ruler, for Agamemnon. Herself the vengeance agent that he would like to be (882; cf 852–53), she is to punish in the king's stead, shielding him from all responsibility (872–75). About this delegation of power the king does have one hollow doubt—he wonders whether Hecuba will be able to attack an enemy, female and friendless as she is! (876–79)—but he gives her license to proceed against a criminal now formally judged guilty and marked as open game, to be killed with impunity.[88] Thus empowered, Hecuba at once makes this royal judge her accomplice by issuing a few sharp commands (889, 985; cf. 870); in particular he is to solve the problem of access by giving one of her women a safe-conduct through the lines, so that the unwitting Polymestor may be brought to the place of his death (889–90). The Greek commander is also to hold up the funeral of Polyxena so that when the vengeance is finished, Hecuba can bury both of her children in a single ceremony (895).

Hecuba's revenge is thus formally sanctioned by the only authority that this desolate place can boast of, and this preliminary license from the Greek king is complemented by a subsequent "judicial" review. After the loss of his sons and his eyes, Polymestor comes like a raging Fury to demand Hecuba's blood, but an Agamemnon-mediator intercedes and the revenge is given a retrospective review. In the fashion of Athena in the *Eumenides* (1109, cf. Aesch. *Eum.* 397; 1130, cf. *Eum.* 436), Agamemnon fixes procedure and hears the complaint of the pursuer, though also like that goddess he strongly favors the defendant. Polymestor claims that he was attacked unjustly and

---

88. In Attic law, Polymestor's parallel is the man who plots against the state, or illegally returns from exile; the decree of Demophantus, 410/409 B.C., explicitly made the killer of such a one ὅσιος καὶ εὐαγής; cf. Andoc. 1.96–98; Antiph. 8.68.2.

that he himself was innocent of crime since his intention in killing his Trojan ward was to serve his Greek friends, knowing that the murder of a child can be a gracious action when there is profit in it (1175; cf. 1243). He does not, however, have the magic rhetoric of an Odysseus, nor is the army as demoralized now as it was earlier in the day, and when the Greeks won't hear his plea, Agamemnon formally announces that the ugly injuries done to this plaintiff by Hecuba are in right accordance with his own ugly crime (1250–51).

Certainly the Agamemnon who here sits as judge has been presented as a decadent and devalued leader, and Polymestor reminds him (and the audience) of the wife and the axe and the bath that wait for him at home (1277, 1279, 1281). Nevertheless he is the one authority that the present situation can provide, and under him the local community gives formal approval to what Hecuba has done. What is more, her revenge is taken under the public aegis when the Greeks add exile to the vengeful retaliation already suffered (1284–85). Inspired by the old woman's act of violence, the Hellenes thus reestablish a rudimentary criminal process, much as they earlier revived a rite of praise, inspired by Polyxena's act of noble submission, and so the reeducation of the desocialized Greeks makes a second advance. From one captive female they have learned to respond to what is fine, from another to repay what is shamefully done (1248), and it is time for them to go back to Greece. Burials are ordered for the two Trojan children, the sacrificed and the avenged; the wind freshens (1290), and everyone moves toward the shore. The elemental opposition has ended and some, though not all, of this company will reach home, where some, though not all, will rejoice.

III

I have been describing the function of Hecuba's violence in the double tragic plot and particularly in the balancing action of vengeance, but what about its quality? The structure of the *Hecuba* seems, like the final trial and the ultimate favoring wind, to announce the harsh primordial rightness of what the ancient queen has done,[89] but critics of our own time are almost unanimous in insisting that this cannot be what the poet meant. He must, they believe, denounce the blinding of Polymestor and the killing of his sons because this is a deed horrendous in its cruelty. They themselves are morally repelled by what Hecuba does, and so must her poet have been.[90]

---

89. See the discussion of R. Meridor, "Hecuba's Revenge," *AJPhil.* 79 (1978) 28–35.

90. Perhaps the most moderate is K. Reckford, "Concepts of Demoralization," in *Directions in Euripidean Criticism,* ed. P. Burian (Durham, N.C., 1985), 112–28. He states plainly, "I have substituted a modern 'we' for the ancient audience" (p. 123), and concludes, "We cannot help conniving at this victory. . . . Yet it is also a terrible defeat for Hecuba and for nobility. . . . she can only imitate her tormentors" (p. 118). But what cause have we to suppose that the fifth-

Consequently the play must be taken to mean the opposite of what it shows, for the revenge—being a manifest atrocity—cannot really resolve a frozen stage situation, permit a Hellenic return from a barbaric place, and stimulate a revival of Greek institutions. Hecuba in particular, though she may appear to move not only as Priam's surrogate but also as a temporary replacement for the Greek commander, must be recognized as a disintegrating creature who descends from her proper female condition (that of being "soft and womanly" in grief) into an abyss of bestiality.[91] From which decline the poet finally must want us to draw the post-Platonic conclusion that anger always works a degeneration of the soul.[92]

Proof that Euripides' Hecuba is proposed as "loathsome," even as a "fiend incarnate," is usually found in two aspects of her action against Polymestor: its cunning and its cruelty. Cunning, however, belongs generically to the vengeance deed. Only if his deviousness is cowardly or innately despicable will the tragic avenger be lowered by it, and in the scene of deceit that Euripides has made for Hecuba he plainly asks us to despise, not this avenger, but the greedy enemy who is caught in a golden snare (1002, 1009).[93] Polymestor himself eagerly pulls his sons into the killing place, looking for gain and reassured by the proleptically grim statement that there are only women within (1017–18). The whole episode is reminiscent of the trapping of the wily fox in an animal fable, and as the predator is taken in by the lesser beast who has lost her young, the audience can only feel a simple satisfaction.

Hecuba's subsequent cruelty, on the other hand, is thrust into our faces by the extended and horrendous miming of its physical results. The actual attack as usual takes place offstage, with only the standard cries ("Oh me, I am blinded!" and "Oh me, once again, my children are slaughtered!" 1035,

---

century audience would have seen this as a "defeat"? Nussbaum, *Fragility*, pp. 397–421, assumes that the play is addressed to an audience that values "openness" and rejects "non-relation" and "isolation," but these evaluations cannot be located in the texts of Attic tragedy.

91. See, e.g., J. W. Fitton, "The *Suppliant Women* and the *Heraclidae*," *Hermes* 89 (1961) 430–61: Hecuba becomes "a slavering animal" (p. 456), "a tortured soul becoming evil in the struggle against evil" (p. 457). Euripides has presumably beaten Chrysippus to the notion that grief can cause moral deterioration (*SVF* 3:237).

92. The play has not always been read in this way; see the account of its reception in the Renaissance by M. Heath, "Jure principem locum tenet': Euripides' *Hecuba*," *BICS* 34 (1987) 40–68, who reports of the sixteenth century, "I do not know, in fact, of any adverse judgment of Hecuba's vengeance in this period" (p. 47). One might compare the prayer of Shakespeare's Titus to "the self-same gods that arm'd the Queen of Troy / with opportunity of sharp revenge / upon the Thracian tyrant in his tent" (*Titus Andronicus* 1.1.136).

93. Polymestor attempts smug conscious ironies that are in fact self-condemning, as when he says that the stolen Priamid wealth is "treasured up" in his house (995, 997), or that Polydorus "longs to pay Hecuba a visit" (993); Hecuba responds with the avenger's irony: "Once you have done what is necessary, you will go back with your boys to where you have left my son" (1021–22).

1037) to indicate the event. After this, however, the spectacle goes far beyond the horror of the usual display of a fallen victim lying in his own blood.[94] First Hecuba comes out of the tent in the midst of a troop of women, some of whom hold up the corpses of Polymestor's sons. Then the Thracian himself crawls through the opening (the same from which Hecuba crawled at the beginning of the play), sightless like Cyclops, and cursing. His mask proves what has been done to him, but his voice tells it too as he howls at the sun to restore his gouged-out eyes (1067–68). Nevertheless, it is not pain but vindictive fury that is now translated into a turmoil of action, as a double complement of dodging Trojan females (chorus plus those who have come from the tent) are pursued through the playing space by a snarling male who moves on all fours.[95] Polymestor must in some sense be dancing beast-fashion with these women whom he cannot see, for he is singing of how he wants to gobble their flesh and crunch their bones (1071–72).[96] He clutches at invisible female bodies, denouncing them as his destroyers and calling for male reinforcements, then finally sinks into what is, by tragic convention, a womanish wish for magical escape,[97] from which he is roused by Agamemnon's voice.[98] As soon as he understands that Hecuba is actually present, his cannibal rage revives and he demands to be told just where she is, so that he can tear her apart and smear himself with her gore (1128). "My hand," he says in epic style,[99] "hungers to do her violence" (1128), and his illustrative gesture is so explicit that it shocks even a king debauched by ten years of war. "Hold there!" shouts Agamemnon, and this exclamation puts an end to the direct scenic representation of what Hecuba has done to the killer of her son.

It is usually assumed that the poet's intention, with this scene, can only have been to create pity for such suffering and loathing for the woman who inflicted it—which would be undeniable if we knew that the cruel imposi-

94. On the breaches of convention in this scene, see W. G. Arnott, "Off-stage Cries and the Choral Presence," *Antichthon* 16 (1982) 35–43, esp. 41.

95. The obvious parallel with the final scene of Eur. *Cyc.* has often been noted, but not the fact that this human Thracian is shown to be much more grotesque and savage than the fairy-tale monster. I cannot see why the similarity of these scenes should indicate any particular chronological relationship between the two plays, but D. F. Sutton, *The Greek Satyr Play* (Meisenheim, 1980), p. 115, argues that Polymestor must be "modelled on Polyphemus"; cf. R. Seaford, "The Date of Euripides' *Cyclops*," *JHS* 102 (1982) 161.

96. A cannibalistic lust for violence is a standard characteristic of the tyrant; e.g., Alc. 29.23, 70.7 Voigt.

97. This is the convention that is parodied by the effeminate Phrygian slave at Eur. *Or.* 1376–79; see W. S. Barrett, *Euripides, Hippolytus* (Oxford, 1964), ad 732–34.

98. The effect of Polymestor's anguish is not enhanced by Agamemnon's conscious entering reference to Echo (1111); see schol. Ar. *Thesm.* 1059 for this as a Euripidean mannerism, and cf. fr. 118 *TGF.*

99. Compare those Homeric weapons that long to glut themselves on enemy flesh; e.g., *Il.* 11.574; 15.317; 21.70, 168.

tion of extreme physical agony would in this theater inevitably create such emotions. In fact, however, we have no such information about Athenian sensibilities. Myths of revenge had always contained acts that were inhumane: Zethus and Amphion, for example, avenged their mother by tying Dirce to a wild bull (Paus. 9.17.3–7), and Heracles, to get revenge on Nereus, killed twelve of his innocent sons. What is more, actual punishments could be just as cruel. The Athenian general who took Sestus early in the fifth century found there a man who, like Polymestor, had tampered with what was sacred, and this criminal, by Athenian orders, was nailed to a board and made to watch as his sons' eyes were put out, after which the boys were stoned to death (Hdt. 9.116 ff.).[100] It would appear that gouging out the eyes was an accepted sentence, along with cutting out the tongue or lopping off a hand, in cases like that of Polymestor, where a sacred trust had been violated. The adulterer, a man who had tampered with what was given to another, was in some places blinded,[101] as was one who had custody of a Delphic tablet, if he opened it and looked inside.[102] By these standards this staged punishment of a Thracian *xenos* who had stolen the treasure and mutilated the child given to him in trust would not seem intolerably harsh.[103]

Since physical cruelty was not categorically reprehensible in Athenian eyes, Hecuba's action would not in and of itself bring about a revolution in audience response. A poet would have to use special dramaturgical means if he wanted his spectators suddenly to loathe the previously sympathetic queen and feel pity for her treacherous victim. He would, in particular, deploy his chorus so as to direct the desired reversal of sentiment. Here, however, the chorus that greets the maimed and howling Thracian shows no least tendency toward infectious pity. Having heard the first part of the injured man's complaint, its leader remarks sententiously, "You suffer unbearably; yes! because shameful actions are returned in fearful ways" (1085–86). Then, after listening to his full tale of butchered boys and blinded eyes, the same woman suggests that a man in his situation might try suicide (1107–8). This inner audience is of course made up of Trojan women,

---

100. Meridor, "Polymestor's Crime," pp. 13–20, suggests this as the source that inspired Euripides with the details of Hecuba's revenge.

101. For Locris, in cases of interference with something entrusted under *enguesis*, Ael. *VH* 13.23; see R. Hirzel, *Die Talion, Philol.* Suppl. 11 (Leipzig 1907–10), 422 n. 92. Aeschylus, however, makes Apollo class blinding with castration as punishments proper to Erinyes in their barbarity (*Eum.* 186).

102. Zen. 6.11; *Paroemiogr.* 1.164.

103. Cf. Erbse, *Studien zum Prolog*, p. 57: "ich möchte vermuten, dass das Publikum des 5. vorchrist. Jdt. Hekabes Erfolg bewondert, ja ihre Triumph (1258) bebilligt hat." It should be remembered also that the Athenian public was accustomed to the infliction of public tortures as part of the legal process; see G. Thür, *Beweisfuhrung von den Schwurgerichtshofen Athens: Die Proklesis zur Basanos* (Vienna, 1977), pp. 183–87.

devoted to Hecuba, but a poet who meant to elicit a charitable view from those in the theater would not have made them set such an example.[104]

Perhaps the actor who played Polymestor used tricks of gesture to make himself pitiable as well as horrible, but if this had been his chief aim, the poet would surely have made use of the children's bodies, a dependable source of tears. They would have been put into Polymestor's hands; he would have been given a paternal lament, and an irresistible sympathy would have invaded the audience. Euripides, on the contrary, has turned his back on such effects. He lets the small corpses become lost somewhere among the women,[105] and the few lines that the maimed man has about their fate are strewn with words that inevitably bring Polymestor's own victim horribly to mind. So, of their mutilation, he uses the same verb of carving out portions which had described what he himself had done to the corpse of his ward (διαμοιρᾶσαι, 1077; cf. 716). When he imagines their exposure, the word ἐκβολή revives his own casting of a small body out into the sea (1079; cf. 699, 781). And most damning of all, when he wishes to be the "guardian" of his sons' bodies, his words are a reminder of the office he himself had betrayed, in respect to Priam's son (1084; cf. 772). Such a speech inspires awe in a listener, as he wonders at the close response of punishment to crime, but it is manifestly not designed to engender pity. As for the rest of Polymestor's lines, they are filled not with grief but with rage and a hatred that becomes a longing for the taste of human flesh—emotions that are understandable, but not conducive to sympathy.[106]

Polymestor's suffering is thus actually depicted as a howling beastlike fury that offers a kind of preview of things to come on the Senecan stage, its grotesque ugliness working to keep the spectator from taking this witnessed pain into himself as his own.[107] And it is only after this preparation that the audience learns just how such repulsive agony was inflicted. This information, indeed, is given extreme emphasis by a structural oddity, for Euripides arranges that an unparalleled report of the revenge shall be made by the victim himself. Polymestor formally describes what happened when he makes his plaintiff's accusation against Hecuba in the *ad hoc* trial (1145–82), and

104. Cf. E. Hall, *Inventing the Barbarian* (Oxford, 1989), p. 126, who notes that Pontic barbarians were expected to be brutish and bestial (Arist. *Eth. Nic.* 7.1148b19–24) and sees in this scene a display of "the wild barbarian character at its most uncontrolled."

105. The poet is careless of these small corpses, and we only know that they are visible by the suffixes at 1118 and 1255; Hecuba promises at 1051 that they will be shown, but we never know where they are.

106. G. M. A. Grube made the distinction when he remarked: "our feeling is one of horror rather than pity" (*The Dramas of Euripides* [London, 1941], p. 227).

107. I have been arguing that Polymestor is not presented in such a way as to ask for audience sympathy; I trust it is plain, however, that I am in entire disagreement with Gellie, who writes that at Polymestor's blinded entrance "our faces relax into grins" ("Hecuba and Tragedy," p. 35).

surely here if anywhere the Trojan queen should be rendered hateful, if that were the poet's purpose. And indeed Polymestor sets himself to prove exactly what contemporary critics take to be self-evident, that this revenge was an atrocity. Nevertheless, when it is studied, his testimony proves something else entirely.

Even in his fury Polymestor, eyewitness until his eyes were taken, establishes two neutralizing facts. First, he shows that the damage done to him was a close reflection of his own original crime. And second, he testifies that this cruelty was not the work of a single rancorous Hecuba; rather, it was a female community that destroyed him and his sons. Polymestor begins by describing how he, the false host who killed his friend's child, was taken in and enfolded by a false hospitality—seated, cosseted, relieved of outer clothing and staff. Some of his hostesses fussed over his little sons, separating them from him; then he was unexpectedly held, the children were pierced with knives, and he was blinded so that the vision of their death should be his last. In his words the event becomes a compressed replica of his own reception and murder of a child-guest, a repayment that leaves him in a condition parallel to that of Hecuba, the slashed remains of his only heirs forever marked in his memory. This is a design that satisfies Priamid honor, but Polymestor's narrative shows it to have been the immediate work not of the Trojan queen but of a group of like-minded females. He remembers a "plenitude of women" (1167) and many indistinguishable hands (1158, 1159), as if he and the boys had been struck by the many indistinguishable stones of a public lapidation, and all moved, he says, without a word of command (1158–59). Hecuba led him in, but by his own unimpeachable account she took no effective part in the violence; she will assume responsibility for it after the fact,[108] but the physical deeds were not hers. In sum, then, what Hecuba has done as surrogate Priamid avenger is denounce her enemy, trap him, and bring him to this place, after which she has watched somewhat as a citizen of fifth- or fourth-century Athens might watch, while a communal punishment was given to her kinsman's killer (Dem. 23.69).

As Polymestor's accusing voice describes it, this scene of women's violence is dreamlike and filled with generalized terror. It happens in a dark, entirely female place, a close interior with flexible walls, and one is reminded of the similarly confused and crowded womb-scene in the *Theogony* (154–82), when Ge took revenge on Ouranos. There, the divine male who wouldn't let his children come to life was allowed to enter, then deprived of the power of engendering by a freshly invented knife. Here, the false Thracian who killed the children of others is likewise tricked into entry, then surprised in what seemed a place of safety by the sudden gleam of a hidden

---

108. Her ἔκτεινα, at 1046, repeated 1051, evidently means "I had them killed"; cf., e.g., Pl. *Ap.* 39c4.

blade (1161). This man is deprived of his sons, not his parts, but the taking of the lances and the cutting of the two manikins (as well as the common symbolism of blinding) dimly suggest some fearsome womb-wrought loss of masculinity. Reported in this way, the events that occurred inside Hecuba's tent take on a mythic aspect, their primitive ugliness demanding awe and dread, but not the banality of censure. Indeed, this account supplies no focus for any feeling of indignation on the listeners' part, because the agents who kill and blind have neither faces nor names. They have only their gender, and in the end Polymestor launches his accusation not against Hecuba but against the whole race of women. Let his denunciation stand as the sum of all former misogyny he says(1178–80), making a special bow to Aeschylus in proof of his character as a philhellene. It is women who have destroyed him, the friend of the Greeks, for "Neither land nor sea breeds such a race of monsters as is womankind" (1181–82; cf. Aesch. *Cho.* 585 ff.).[109]

IV

In sum, Euripides does not ask his audience to repudiate Hecuba's revenge as an inadmissible atrocity. Polymestor has been presented throughout as a greedy and grotesque barbarian, a savage who feeds on others' civility, and in these final scenes his punishment is displayed as an ugly but exact communal return upon him. Within the community this accurate retaliation is preliminary to the *nomos* of burial, and it is followed in the natural world by a revival of favoring winds. The punishment of Polymestor indeed avoids a satyresque quality only because its agent is an aged, grieving female, and because its companion action is the destruction of Polyxena. Where the ghost of a hero can move a Greek army to sacrifice a captive girl, no one will be brought to excessive complacence by watching an old barbarian lady as she punishes a guilty criminal. There is moreover one future fact—one for which Hecuba cares nothing (1274) but one that makes her vengeful justice uncanny and strange.

Hecuba's final fate is fixed at what is literally the last moment of the play. With just thirty lines still to be spoken, a familiar Euripidean device causes the blind and furious Polymestor suddenly to remember an oracle.[110] He has heard prophecies from a Thracian seer and he spitefully repeats them, so that Cassandra's name sounds out at the very end of the drama and the waiting axe of Clytemnestra hovers over its liberating departure (1275,

---

109. This unexpected penchant for literary allusion works, like his taste for gore, to distance Polymestor from his audience; cf. 961, with its reference to Alc. 335 Voigt.

110. Like Eurystheus, at the end of *Heracl.*, or Polyphemus, at the close of *Cyc.*

1279). By such means a unique stage event is attached to the body of myth and sometimes also to the present nontheatrical day, and so it is in this case. On the surface, Polymestor only wants to reduce Hecuba's victory—she is triumphant now, says her victim, but where will that triumph be when the water closes over her, as the prophet has told him it will (1259, 1261)? In explanation, he sketches the shape of her end. She is to be taken aboard Odysseus' ship, but as they set out for Greece she will of her own accord climb the mast (1263) and fall or leap into the water (1261), becoming a dog with fiery eyes (1265).[111] She will die there in the sea (1271, ἐνθάδε in 1270 looks back to 1259), and she will have a tomb called *kynos sema*, the Dog's Grave-Marker, which will serve as a signpost for sailors (1273).[112] There is no talk of a cult or a rite, but Hecuba is to have a monument that survives into what the audience knows as today.

This bit of prophecy excited Ovid's imagination. His Hecuba—a woman who drove furious fingers into the despoiled sockets of Polymestor's eyes— took the form of a demon dog and was shown howling, biting at stones thrown after her, and running forever across the Thracian plain (*Met.* 13.561–65).[113] Ovid's lines have in turn excited critics of the Attic play, causing them to report with satisfaction that the viciousness of the Trojan queen is made manifest when Euripides finally transforms her into a "howling bitch" or a "baying" "pariah dog."[114] This change is said to be "savagely appropriate" to her own "invulnerable bestiality," marking her not just with "shame and monstrosity" but as a "fiend incarnate."[115] And it is further taken as licensing the critic to hunt for early signs of this "bestiality" and to

111. She is to climb the mast with "her own foot" (1263), which no dog could be imagined as doing, so the actual transformation must be proposed as occurring either in the moment of the jump or in the water.

112. On this prophecy and its meaning for the play, see A. P. Burnett, "Hekabe the Dog," *Arethusa* 27 (1994) 151–62; to the bibliography found there, add C. Mainoldi, *L'image du loup et du chien dans la Grèce ancienne* (Paris, 1984), esp. pp. 143–86; B. S. Ridgway, "The Man and Dog Stelai," *JDAI* 86 (1971) 60–79; N. J. Zaganiaris, "Sacrifices de chiens," *Platon* 27 (1975) 322–29; S. Lonsdale, "Attitude towards Animals," *G&R* 26 (1979) 149–52. On dog burials, see H. A. Thompson, "Excavations," *Hesp.* 20 (1951) 52, dog with beef bone; L. P. Day, "Dog Burials in the Greek World," *AJArch.* 88 (1984) 21–32, early Iron Age to Geometric; see also Mossman, *Wild Justice*, pp. 194–201.

113. Ovid's gods, however, conclude that Hecuba did not deserve such an end (*Met.* 13.573–75).

114. For "howling bitch," see Reckford, "Concepts of Demoralization," pp. 118, 123; for "baying," Conacher, "Euripides' *Hecuba*," p. 9; "pariah dog," L. Matthaei, *Studies in Greek Tragedy* (Cambridge, 1918), p. 156.

115. For "savagely appropriate," M. Vickers, *Towards Tragedy* (London, 1973), p. 83; "invulnerable bestiality," Nussbaum, *Fragility*, p. 416; "shame and monstrosity," C. Segal, "Golden Armor," *AJPhil.* 111 (1990) 309; "fiend incarnate," G. Kirkwood, "Hecuba and Nomos," *TAPA* 78 (1947) 61.

watch as the grieving mother of the morning degenerates into the vicious beast of the day's end. Nevertheless, in spite of all this strong twentieth-century language, it is plain that the Hecuba of Euripides—she of Poly-mestor's words—will never run or howl or show the world any other sign of bestiality, because she will never live as a dog: she will only die and be buried in her canine form. Ovid's hellhound must be driven out of Euripides' tragedy so that we can look directly at the bizarre final revelation that the dramatist has actually provided—a momentary dog-transformation, the animal hidden (1261) in the waves of the sea, then buried where its grave can serve as a landmark for voyagers.[116]

To begin with, it is important to note that this briefest of metamorphoses was probably a Euripidean invention.[117] There were many viable fictions about the Trojan queen's final days, but nothing in known myth or legend even suggested, much less imposed, a dog upon an account of her fate. Everyone agreed that she never got to Greece, but Helenus could appear and lead her off into the Chersonese; Apollo, who had once been her lover, might translate her into Lydia; or she could enact her final defiance of the Greeks who had enslaved her by drowning herself from Odysseus' ship.[118] These were all attractive possibilities, but Euripides, instead of choosing one, produced an incongruous combination. He took the suicide, interrupted its realism with a fairy-tale transformation, and then at once did away with his newly created Hecuba-dog by drowning it! There had to be a purpose in this surreal manoeuvre, and it is to be found in the end result, for Polymestor's puzzling revelation becomes significant in every detail when it is read backward. The place in which the poet means to deposit his heroine demands a dog.

Hecuba will drown in canine form, then move at once (in the next word, θανοῦσα· τύμβῳ, 1271) into her eponymous tomb, for in this tale the grave is the goal. And once she has been positioned at Kynossema, the minimal dog-transformation declares itself for what it is, the poet's etymological trick for putting her there. Indeed, an artful interruption postpones and emphasizes the point: "The name of your tomb will be . . ." / "You don't mean it

116. With this brief underwater existence in animal form one might compare the case of Asteria, who threw herself into the sea to escape Zeus and was momentarily transformed into a quail before becoming the island of Delos (Apollod. *Bibl.* 1.21 p. 11), though this story was probably influenced by the passage under discussion.

117. This is denied by T. Stephanopoulos, *Umgestaltung des Mythos* (Athens, 1980), pp. 82–83, but there is no trace of its previous existence. There is an anonymous lyric fragment (965 *PMG*) attached by Dio Chrysostom to Hecuba, but it does not use her name, nor is its date necessarily pre-Euripidean.

118. Helenus, Dares Phrygius 42; Apollo, Stesichorus 198 *PMG;* Ibyc. 295 *PMG;* suicide, Nic. ap. schol. 3 at *Hec.* 1265.

will be called after my changed form?" / ". . . tomb of the wretched dog" (κυνὸς ταλαίνης σῆμα, 1271–73).[119] Only as a dog could she become the resident *daimon* at this famous landmark, but what was it about this place that made it worth the price of a canine transformation? Obviously, if she lay on the northern shore of the Hellespont, the Trojan queen would have a tomb that watched and balanced the opposite Achilles monument, where Polyxena had been sacrificed,[120] but if that were the poet's only purpose it could have been achieved at a place with a less arresting name. What special significance would Hecuba gain from her burial in the Tomb of the Dog?

Kynossema is a rough promontory jutting out from the Thracian shore of the Hellespont so as to create a narrow passage that takes a hidden turn. Whether entering or leaving, a ship risked disaster there, and the danger was increased by the powerful current running down from the Bosporus. In daylight the difficulty ahead was recognizable by the doglike shape of the headland, but after nightfall there could be no safety unless the place were marked. Nowadays at Kilid Bahr there are two beacons mounted so as to be read from either direction, and probably bonfires and torches were lit on the same spots by grain merchants even in archaic times. Certainly there was a fire post here in the fifth century, for just before the battle of 411 B.C. the Athenians at Sestos received signals telling them that the Peloponnesian fleet had entered the Propontis (Thuc. 8.102.1), and these could only have been relayed by a fire watch on Kynossema's heights. Here then is the clue to the transformation, for the Hecuba-dog so swiftly drowned and entombed has only one characteristic, the "torch glances" that Polymestor insists upon (πύρσ' ἔχουσα δέργματα, 1265). These are not just eyes inflamed with rage, for the adjective πυρσός (chosen over the more common πυρρός) indicates explicitly a signal or a beacon fire (cf. Eur. *Rhes.* 97; *Hel.* 1126; Hdt. 7.183; 9.3). The metaphoric emblem that closes the play is thus not Hecuba as an enraged beast, but Hecuba as a flagrant landmark that saves ships and their crews.[121]

The geographical Dog's Tomb marked a point where a ship's course had to be changed, and so it was literally a *tekmar* for sailors (1273). In a larger sense it was a natural threat transmuted into a warning, its baleful beneficence concentrated in its fire signs, and this was evidently the aspect of the

---

119. The term ἐπῳδός, in 1272, perhaps hints at spells or charms used by sailors looking for a safe course up or down the Hellespont.

120. So Quint. Smyrn. 3.739–41; on general sense of σῆμα as an enduring monument marked by a burial mound, see G. Nagy, *The Best of the Achaeans* (Baltimore, 1979), pp. 340–43.

121. It is the opinion of J. Gregory, *Euripides and the Instruction of the Athenians* (Ann Arbor, 1991), pp. 110–12, that Euripides somehow also meant this tomb as a warning to all future imperialists (?).

place that attracted Euripides. Hecuba had, doglike, borne many children, defended her house, and done the work of a fury, but above all she had dreamed the torch that was to burn Troy.[122] She is called "the dog of fire-bearing Hekate" in another Euripidean play (fr. 959 *TGF*), and now, like that torch-bearing goddess, she is to guard a gateway, taking the last of the Trojan fire as her implement. On this stage she has seen the Greek host more or less safely through its loss of ethical direction, and in the same way she will continue to take both Greeks and barbarians through a difficult passage. Her savage response to a savage outrage marked the place where mythic Greeks had to change course, for, like Kynossema, revenge is a danger that shows the way.

122. For the Paris torch, see Pind. *Pae.* 8.10–14; Eur. *Tro.* 922; schol. Eur. *Andr.* 293; Apollod. *Bibl.* 3.12.5; Hyg. *Fab.* 91, 249.

CHAPTER SEVEN

Child-Killing Mothers

Sophocles' Tereus

Alcmena and Hecuba fulfilled the male vocation of revenge in the absence of son and husband, but nevertheless each attacked like a lioness in (delayed) defense of her young, so that it was paradoxically mother-love that made surrogate males of them. As old women miscast in an active male role, they brought irregularity to the revenges they performed, but neither of their retaliations could have stood alone as the single praxis of a tragedy because both were not only crudely just but also emotionally easy to perform. Of course the two heroines were physically weak and debilitated, but each responded to instinct and felt herself to be on unassailable ethical ground. The truly disturbing tragedy of female revenge would have to show a woman caught like Orestes between two equally fierce imperatives and forced to oppose the strongest part of her own nature as she followed the socially imposed rule of retaliation. Maternal love—the impulse that moved Alcmena and Hecuba to unsex themselves and behave like men—was often posited as the strongest of human passions.[1] Therefore, if a dramatist could bring to the stage a heroine who not only worked a revenge but did so in defiance of her own maternity, then chaos would truly attack the innate stability of the vengeance plot.

The killing of a boy child[2] by its mother was the ultimate act of Dionysi-

---

1. Paternal love, by contrast, might rank no more than second (after love of honor) judging from the mythic Oedipus, who cursed his sons in angry retaliation for slights (*Thebais* 2 *EGF*).

2. The male child was the most valuable to mother as well as to father, since through him she perfected herself as mother of the heir. Discussion of female infanticide in the Greek world is inconclusive, but it is clear at any rate that the death of a female child was of lesser significance; see summary in R. Oldenziel, "The Historiography of Infanticide in Antiquity," in *Sexual Asymmetry*, ed. J. Blok and P. Mason (Amsterdam, 1987), pp. 87–107.

ac disorder,[3] but what, short of the god's madness, could make a woman perform this crime?[4] This was a question that had a practical as well as a theoretical interest because in early Greece, though all children belonged to their fathers, nurseries were under a separate and effectively feminine rule. When the time came, sons would be handed over to the world of men, but as babies and while they were little boys, their safety depended upon the mood of the women's apartments. Small male children were thus in a sense hostages of the household truce, and the paternal apprehension that resulted was explored in many popular stories about vicious women who attacked children. One favorite set banalized the nightmare of the destroying mother by introducing motifs of accident and villainy, producing women like Themisto[5] who brought punishment upon themselves by clumsily killing their own children when they meant to do away with those of a rival. This model was reassuring because it suggested that women's schemes, though dangerous, were fundamentally inept, and also because it tended to leave the true heirs of the house alive. And yet it begged the essential mythic question: Was it possible that a woman could with knowledge and intention kill a son she had borne to her husband?

The answer was affirmative, but it achieved its classic form[6] in a tale that is a consummate example of how storytelling works to assuage anxiety. The

3. Late antiquity told stories of child sacrifices offered to Dionysus Omadius on Tenedos (Porph. *Abst.* 2.55) and at Potniae (Paus. 9.8.2), and the child-killing Minyads supplied the aetiology for the Agriona at Orchomenos (Plut. *Mor.* 299E–300A). That any female child-killing could be referred to this Dionysiac model is clear from Nonnus, *Dion.* 44.265, where the knife that Procne used to kill Itys is said to have been buried by the Erinyes under the tree where Agave was to kill Pentheus.

4. The crime was not unknown in the real world, judging by Plato's discussion (*Leg.* 9.868c–d) of appropriate punishments for fathers or mothers who killed children in anger; these were the same as for killers of husbands or wives, brothers or sisters, in anger, and consisted of exile for three years, then prohibition of all contact with the household of the victim. A child who killed a parent, on the other hand, was guilty of *hierosulia* and was to be put to death. Antiphon (6.4; cf. 5.87) says that if a father kill a child, there may be neither prosecution nor revenge.

5. Hyg. *Fab.* 1, 4; Nonnus, *Dion.* 9.302–21; see chap. 6, n. 9. Creusa, in Eur. *Ion,* is a version of this figure, a woman who would (in ignorance) kill her own child in revenge upon a mate who has deserted her. The Aedon of the Boeotian and Asia Minor legends is another; moved by envy, she meant to murder Niobe's eldest son but mistakenly killed her own Itylus instead (schol. *Od.* 19.518; Hes. fr. 312 M-W; Paus. 9.5.9); see J. E. Harrison, "Itys and Aedon," *JHS* 8 (1887) 439–45.

6. The second major myth of son-killing by a mother was that of Althaia, but since this fiction (like that of Oedipus) allowed for killing from a distance, through curse or brand, the triumph of the vengeance passion over maternity was not so sharply drawn. On the development of this myth, see J. March, *The Creative Poet* (London, 1987), pp. 29–46; J. Bremmer, "La plasticité du mythe," in *Métamorphoses du mythe* (Geneva, 1988), pp. 37–56. Althaia's vengeance may or may not have been central to the Euripidean *Meleager* (apparently it was to Accius' tragedy of the same name, for there Althaia engaged in an inner debate like that of Medea (frs.

pan-Hellenic tale of Procne[7] took the most frightening creature a man could imagine—the son-killing mother—and wrapped her in song, so that as nightingale she became a figure of melody and grief.[8] Her child-killing rage was transposed into a lyric melancholy and then sent into exile among the members of another species, thus leaving the masculine auditor of this darkest of tales with his sense of safety mysteriously enhanced. In fact the legend eventually became positively reassuring, as storytellers directly addressed its priamel of female motives and produced a daughter's devotion to her father as the one emotion that might prove stronger than love of husband, stronger even than love of child.[9] Revenge provided the fictional structure: Procne killed her boy, yes, but she did this terrible thing in order to restore the honor of her paternal house, in retaliation against a husband who had broken faith with her father. And since, in most versions, the father who excited Procne's loyalty was a Greek, while the husband whose son she killed was a barbarian, the consumer of folktale found that his worst fear had been magically dissipated. The horror could in all mythic logic occur, yes—but only in the ultimate service of right Hellenic ways.

Nevertheless, as mythic cipher, Procne was like Orestes because she stood countercommanded by two immutable laws, and so, in spite of the awkward

---

443–47 *TRF*). Stesichorus' Althaia may also have argued within herself over the claims of sons and brothers; see R. Garner, "Stesichorus' Althaia: *P. Oxy.* 3876," *ZPE* 100 (1994) 26.

7. The legend of the child-killing wife of Tereus was generally said to belong either to Daulis, in Phocis (Thuc. 2.29.3; Strabo 9.423), or to Megara. The name Tereus suggested that of a Thracian tribe, and Thucydides supposed that in Tereus' time Phocis had been occupied by Thracians. Pausanias (1.41.8) was shown a tomb of Tereus in Megara, and he supposed that the Megarians had borrowed the story from the region around Chaeronea. (A late version connected with Miletus appears at Ant. Lib. *Met.* 11.) Homer, however, makes Penelope tell the companion story of the daughter of Pandareus, wife of Zethus, who killed her son Itylus unwittingly and mourns forever as the nightingale (*Od.* 19.518–23). She, as Aedon, was painted with a sister named Chelidon in the act of killing the boy in a late seventh- or early-sixth-century metope from Aetolian Thermon; see H. G. G. Payne, "On the Thermon Metopes," *BSA* 27 (1925–26) 124–26; M. Robertson, *La peinture grecque* (Geneva, 1959), p. 50. Meanwhile Hesiod calls the sister swallow "daughter of Pandion" (*Op.* 568), as does Sappho (fr. 135 LP). See M. Mayer, "Mythistorica," *Hermes* 27 (1892) 481–515; O. Schroeder, "Πρόκνη," *Hermes* 61 (1926) 423–36.

8. Hom *Od.* 19.518–23; Hes. fr. 312 M-W; Paus. 9.5.9. The nightingale's song was characterized as full of yearning (ἰμερόφωνος, Sappho fr. 136 LP); plaintive (πάνδυρτος, Soph. *El.* 1077); highly polytonal (πολυχορδότατος, Eur. *Rhes.* 550); most melodic (ἀοιδότατος, Eur. *Hel.* 1109). At Ar. *Av.* 212, Itys is πολύδακρυς. The story of Harpalyce belongs with the Procne tales, as shown by her bird transformation: she, raped by her father the Arcadian king Clymenos, killed their child and served it to him; he then hanged himself and she became a bird called *chalakis* (Parth. *Amat. Narr.* 13; Hyg. *Fab.* 292, 246, 255; Nonnus, *Dion.* 12.71 ff.)

9. In a parallel priamel, Sappho stated the feared alternative by capping love of parents, husband, and child with erotic love, though in the softened case of Helen in which the child was merely abandoned and was merely a daughter (16 Voigt).

birdification—the *apornithosis* that brought the legend to its feathered close—Sophocles made a play about her. This tragedy, called *Tereus* after the husband who was the enemy and indirect victim of its violence, is known only from fragments, and one's first task in discussing it is to try to forget the gorgeous horrors attached to the tale in book 6 of the *Metamorphoses*. Ovid must have known the Sophoclean piece, but his narrative, with its panoramic stretches of time and place, certainly does not reflect the shape of an Attic tragedy,[10] as is demonstrated when scholars take it as blueprint for imaginary plays.[11] There are, however, a few trustworthy indications of the Sophoclean treatment in a hypothesis (*P Oxy.* 3013 = *TrGF* 4, p. 435),[12] in a more tenuous Byzantine summary (Tzetzes ad Hes. *Op.* 568), and in the handful of commonplace fragments that have been preserved. In addition, vase paintings offer one or two vividly concrete details that may have their origin in the fifth-century play. This is slight evidence indeed, but nevertheless, with an awareness of how Attic stage conventions worked, one can draw a few conclusions about this Sophoclean tragedy of female child-killing revenge.

First, it is evident that in the *Tereus* Sophocles used the West Greek and Attic version of the nightingale legend, making Procne the daughter of the Attic king, Pandion, and pairing her with a sister, Philomela, in the killing of a boy called Itys. Procne had been taken into the wilds by her Thracian husband, Tereus, and when she asked that her sister might be brought to her for a visit, he agreed. He went again to Athens, took Philomela as sister-guest in trust from the king, then raped and maimed her on the journey

10. Ovid's sources will have included, in addition to the Sophoclean play, a *Tereus* by another fifth-century poet, Philocles (*TrGF* 1, 24T6b), and also the dramas of Livius Andronicus and Accius. See B. Otis, *Ovid as an Epic Poet* (Cambridge, 1966), pp. 377–81; F. Bömer, *P. Ovidius Naso, Metamorphosen VI–VII* (Heidelberg, 1976), pp. 117–18; H. Hofman, "Ausgesprochene und unausgesprochene," *Acta Classica* 14 (1971) 97 ff. Note the conclusion of Otis on the Ovidian version: "the masterly dramatic narrative seems to be entirely his own" (p. 410).

11. E.g., W. Calder, "Sophocles' *Tereus,*" *Thracia* 2 (1974) 87–91; A. Kiso, *The Lost Sophocles* (New York, 1984), pp. 51–86; D. F. Sutton, *The Lost Sophocles* (New York and London, 1984), pp. 127–32; N. C. Hourmouziades, "Sophocles' *Tereus,*" in *Studies in Honor of T. B. L. Webster,* vol. 2, ed. J. Betts, H. Hooker, and J. Green (Bristol, 1987), pp. 134–42; G. Dobrov, "The Tragic and the Comic Tereus," *AJPhil.* 114 (1993) 189–234. Calder supposes an action containing a time lapse of one year; the others assume a praxis of one day's duration which includes confrontation between Procne and Tereus, discovery of an imprisoned Philomela, her active rescue by a disguised Procne, recognition and intrigue which may be complicated by an attempted rescue for Itys—all this preceding the climax of killing, banquet, pursuit, and divine announcement of transformations.

12. The digest is entitled *Tereus* and refers almost certainly to the Sophoclean tragedy, though no poet is named; see P. Parsons, *P Oxy.* 42 (1974) 46 ff.; M. Haslam, "The Authenticity of Euripides, *Phoenissae* 1–2," *GRBS* 16 (1975) 150 n. 3; 154 n. 20; 172 n. 79; T. Gelzer, "Sophokles' *Tereus,*" *Jahresbericht der Schweizerischen Geisteswiss. Gesell.*, 1976, pp. 183–92.

back to Thrace. Once returned, he reported the girl as dead.[13] That was the background situation. The fragments suggest that the play proper began with a lament by Procne, grieving over her sister's death and her own isolation and looking back (like Deianeira) to girlhood as the only happy time in a woman's life (frs. 583–84 *TrGF*). She seems to have been answered by a friendly servant or perhaps a sympathetic chorus (fr. 585).[14] Next there seems to have been a scene in which Tereus, on his way out (probably to hunt, since he was a Thracian), repeated his lies about Philomela and urged his wife to accept her present situation (swearing falsely by the Thracian Helios? fr. 582). Then someone—a bribed servant or guard? (587)—brought a gift to Procne from an unknown source: Philomela's "speaking" robe. The bit of weaving will have worked like a messenger speech, as Procne made her half-joyful, half-uncomprehending interpretation of images that told her that her sister had been attacked but was alive and near. The servant was evidently sent back to bring the weaver of the web, preparing for a third episode containing the recognition and the formation of the scheme of revenge—an intrigue which may have been inspired by the inopportune entrance of little Itys. Procne's words and Philomela's gestures probably made it clear that the villain was to be presented with his dead son in the unrecognized form of a meal, since audience knowledge of this point would be necessary for the fullest exploitation of the scenes to follow. With the plan made, the sisters will have led the child into the palace,[15] where a swift offstage killing would inspire a choral song to cover the time of cooking. Then Tereus must have entered, returning to the palace from some outdoor place, to be met by Procne, come out to waylay him with summons to a ceremonious and solitary meal. This very particular invitation had to separate the lord from his followers, and in choreography it will have been something like the parallel scene from *Agamemnon*, though here it is the pleasures of table

13. Neither the hypothesis nor Tzetzes suggests local imprisonment for Philomela; she simply arrives, as if she had been left for dead along the way. The Ovidian complications surrounding the imprisoned Philomela and her liberation could not have been staged within the Attic conventions, for nowhere does a female principal go out to perform a secular project and return, at the end of a choral ode, with project complete, as is required by the reconstructions of Calder, Kiso, Sutton, Dobrov, et al. This anomalous sequence would also mean either that the recognition took place offstage or that it was postponed until the already reunited sisters returned to the playing area, neither of which is conceivable as theater.

14. Nothing in the fragments determines the sex of the chorus (usually reported as male because of their philosophical tone), but if at the end of the play the two women must run out of the palace, through the dancers, and up one of the parodoi, their maneuver is much easier to imagine if these dancers are women.

15. On the Louvre cup by Macron, ca. 480 (Louvre G 147.1, *EAA* s.v. "Filomela," 836), Philomela is moving rapidly, holding the child, while a gesticulating Procne follows, a sword hanging from her sash.

that are offered. The vengeance itself—the presentation of the stew, its consumption, and the revelation of its ingredients—will have been reported by a domestic witness, presumably a woman, since the false celebration must have excluded all men but Tereus.[16] She told of a feast held in the presence of an unknown veiled woman,[17] and of the horrid revelation engineered most probably, as in the Thyestes case, by a show of the boy's severed head.[18] Evidently this servant concluded by remarking sententiously that the two women had invented a cure worse even than the husband's crimes (589 *TrGF*),[19] which means that Procne had denounced Tereus and revealed the identity of Philomela, even as she disclosed the nature of the feast. In the final scene, Procne and Philomela

16. It is possible that this bogus ceremony pretended to honor Dionysus, but, however that may be, it will have been like the bogus funeral in Eur. *Hel.* or the bogus purifications of Eur. *IT,* an exceptional rite explained as dictated by the heroine's native customs. Because of the Bacchic masquerade in Ovid's tale, it is almost always assumed that the action of Soph. *Tereus* took place during a festival of the Thracian Dionysus (e.g., S. Luria, "Miszellen," *Hermes* 64 [1929] 496; Dobrov, "Tragic and Comic Tereus," pp. 200 n. 29; 205). F. G. Welcker, *Die griechischen Tragödien,* vol. 1 (Bonn, 1839), p. 381, even claimed a phrase from Conon (*FGrH* 26 F 1 xxxi) as a *Tereus* fragment on the grounds that it contained the presumably Bacchic word *thriambos,* but the attribution is not generally accepted (see the objections of A. Brinkmann, "Lückenbüsser," *Rh. Mus.* 64 [1909] 479). There is in fact no hint of Bacchism in the fragments, the hypothesis, Tzetzes' account, or the vase paintings, *pace* L. Koenen, "Tereus in den Vögeln," in *Studien zur Textgeschichte und Textkritik,* ed. H. Dahlmann and R. Merkelbach (Cologne, 1959), p. 84 n. 1, who erroneously reports that M. Bieber, "Tereus," *MDAI(A)* 50 (1925) 11–18, identified the scene on the Dresden sherd as Dionysiac. (Koenen is persuaded that, in the sherd's representation, fold lines descending from Tereus' belt represent a Bacchic wool tuft.) Even A. Cazzaniga has to admit that the trieteric celebrations that appear in Ovid cannot be postulated for Sophocles; see *La saga di Itis,* vol. 1 (Milan, 1950), p. 52. The Ovidian masquerade probably came from Accius (fr. 4 *TRF*) or perhaps from Verg. *Aen.* 7.573; its employment renders unnecessary Procne's description of the banquet as a paternal rite (*Met.* 6.648), giving that detail the look of a fossil from an older source.

17. Philomela appears veiled on a Paestan fragment which shows the emergence of Tereus from the banquet hall; see Bieber, "Tereus," Taf. 2; also A. D. Trendall, *Paestan Pottery* (London, 1936), p. 88. In order not to give the purpose of the false feast away too soon, she would have to be disguised.

18. A very late reflection of this messenger speech may be found on a sarcophagus from Intercisa (Bieber, "Tereus," Abb. 1), where Tereus has knocked over a table (like Thyestes with his curse?) and seized his sword; an arm and the head of Itys fly through the air, one sister stands at center excitedly accusing (has she thrown the head?), while the other runs away, her figure balancing that of Tereus.

19. It is often said that fr. 589 *TrGF* expresses the tragedy's condemnation of the sisters' deeds, but it seems rather to be a simple closing commonplace: "Anyone in misfortune who angrily applies a medicine worse than the sickness is a doctor who does not understand suffering." The verb for what the women were doing, ἠμύναντο, often associated with revenge, is explicitly mild and unaggressive, and the speaker's disapproval is merely pragmatic: the sisters have made things worse for themselves. Meanwhile, the audience may be expected to understand that a tragic principal (like Epicurus) is not ashamed to use cures harsher than the illness he treats (fr. 278 Usener = Themistius in Arist. *Ph.* 6.1).

must have burst forth (like Hecuba and her women from the tent), and an enraged Tereus (like Polymestor) will have pursued them, carrying an axe or perhaps a bone from the stew, if we can trust a vase painter's version.[20] The women fled up one of the gangways and their victim was about to follow when a god[21] interrupted. Whoever this divinity was, he/she announced (but not with the words of fr. 581 *TrGF*)[22] that the sisters were out of his reach, changed in this moment into nightingale and swallow, and that Tereus too would be transformed, to spend the rest of time as the crested dung-nesting Hoopoe.[23]

This minimal outline of the *Tereus* action reveals the essential dramaturgical difficulty that its poet had to face. How could an audience of parents be asked to watch first a representation (albeit offstage) of the killing of Itys by his mother and aunt, and then a miraculous release for the two blood-stained women and also for the man who was the cause of their crime? And how could that release be rescued from its dangerously comic feathers? Sophocles must have been powerfully attracted, to risk the naive horror and too wondrous resolution of this tale, and something of his engagement as well as a hint of his technique can be extracted from the hypothesis written for his play. First of all he set against the ugliness of the child-slaughter, as provocation and response, two acts of equivalent ugliness: the cutting of the rape victim's tongue (ἐγλωσσοτόμησε τὴν παῖδα, *P Oxy*. 3013.19), and the

20. On the Dresden sherd from Paestum, see Bieber, "Tereus," and Trendall, *Pottery*, p. 88.

21. Welcker, *Tragödien* 1:383–84, named Hermes; Calder, *"Tereus,"* p. 88, named a Thracian Ares, which seems excessively unlikely. Given her cult association with Procne, Athena would seem to be a possibility, but at any rate this is a message of rescue and pacification, whoever speaks it.

22. This fragment was attributed to Aeschylus by Aristotle (followed by Wilamowitz, *Aischylos: Interpretationen* [Berlin, 1914], p. 283), to Sophocles by Welcker (generally accepted). It does not seem worthy of either poet in sense or style; see J. van Leeuwen, *Aristophanis Aves* (Leiden, 1902) ad *Av*. 264, where it is suggested that this is the work of an inferior poet, possibly Philocles. The lines create a mood almost comic, with their heavily emphasized pun (ἔποψ, ἐπόπτης, line 1), their frivolous echo of the notion of decorated fabric (πεποικίλωκε, line 2), and their gross, almost Senecan reference to the belly of Tereus (line 6).

23. Tereus seems to have begun his legendary life as the human version of the aggressive hawk as contrasted, in popular imagery, with the shrinking nightingale (e.g., Hes. *Op*. 202–12, see West ad loc.; Aesch. *Supp*. 62). Aristophanes gives the impression that it was Sophocles who altered his bird form to that of the aggressive, crested hoopoe (*epops*, overseer); at any rate the comic Tereus blames his particular form on the poet (τοιαῦτα μέντοι Σοφοκλέης λυμαίνεται / ἐν ταῖς τραγῳδίαισιν ἐμέ, Ar. *Av*. 101–2). Sophocles will not, however, have brought a bird-man on stage, *pace* Dobrov, "Tragic and Comic Tereus," pp. 196–97; the Aristophanic creature is funny because he is the visible embodiment of the tragic poet's (risible) words. In later times the hoopoe was notorious for his filthy habits (Ael. *NA* 3.26; Plin. *HN* 10.29); see D'Arcy Thompson, *A Glossary of Greek Birds* (Oxford, 1926), pp. 54–57; R. Drew Griffith, "The Hoopoe's Name," *Quaderni Urbinati di Cultura Classica* 55 (1987) 59–63. Not all versions of the Procne tale included a transformation for Tereus; in the Megarian telling, he killed himself because he could not catch the women, who had fled to Athens (Paus. 1.41.9).

final cannibal feast (ὁ δὲ τὴν βορὰν ἀγνοῶν ἔφαγεν, *P Oxy.* 3013.29–30). It must be remembered that these two events, so familiar to us from Ovid, were, if not Sophoclean inventions, at least floating motifs that a storyteller or dramatist was free to take up or ignore.[24] It is clear, moreover, that Sophocles made central use of these elective atrocities, and his tragic purposes in doing so are not hard to recognize. With the maiming of Philomela, the immediate effect is both to intensify and to generalize the savagery that already marked the Thracian Tereus of folktale, making him almost a caricature of the canonical vengeance victim. The rape by itself was an outrage against the father who had trustingly given first one daughter and then another into this man's keeping, as the hypothesis notes when it says that Tereus deflowered his ward, "not caring about his pledged faith" (*P Oxy.* 3013.16).[25] Sophocles, however, has pushed his villain into a superabundance of outrage, the purpose of which was well appreciated by Pausanias. Tereus follows the rape—which was in itself "contrary to Hellenic custom," as the Traveler unnecessarily remarks—with mutilation of the girl's body, "thus drawing the women into the necessity of retaliation" (Paus. 1.5.4). With the cutting of the girl's tongue the Sophoclean Tereus gives his work of dishonor a permanent external mark, while he also attacks the entire girl, not just the part of her for which a father is responsible. This second act of violation thus fixes Tereus not just as a barbarian opposed to Greek ways but as an enemy to the whole human race—one who not only dismantles Greek marriage, breaks oaths, and insults an Attic king, but also represents mating itself as a barren cutting of female flesh.[26] And this means that the place where he rules, the Thrace where Procne will take her revenge, is a place where men are far worse than beasts.[27]

Tereus' knife-wrought horror evidently gave shape to the large design of the Sophoclean revenge, since it called for an answering use of a knife upon innocent flesh in the retaliation, and also for an answering use of the vil-

24. West, ad Hes. *Op.* 568, seems to assume that the swallow-sister had always been thought of as maimed ("to the Greeks she was Philomela with tongue cut out"), but note Aesch. *Ag.* 1050–51, where to speak χελιδόνος δίκην is to use a barbarian language, not to be unable to speak. The motif is missing in the versions of Hyginus (*Fab.* 189) and Apollodorus (3.14.8).

25. The agreement, with exchange of oaths (πιστά, 16) will have been like that between Oedipus and Theseus at the end of Soph. *OC* 1632–34 and 1637, when Theseus is sworn into taking solemn charge of Antigone and Ismene. Thracians, according to one proverb, do not understand oaths; barbarians, according to another, are not satisfied with one wife (Achilles Tatius 5.5.2).

26. *Suda,* s.v. "Chelidon" lists the bird-name of Philomela as a slang term for female sexual parts, presumably because both were "cut" and had no "tongue."

27. In later thinking this action also marked Tereus as a tyrant: all are without speech under a tyrant (Ant. Lib. *Met.* 11).

lain's tongue in the tasting of his punishment. The poet's most profession-al use of the severed tongue, however, is found in the ingenious inner plot where Philomela's speechlessness first stops retaliation by blocking any dis-closure of the initial outrage,[28] then releases it in a scene-sequence one longs to see played—first the "reading" of the woven gift,[29] then the pitying, passionate reunion of an articulate sister with one who makes only animal sounds. (Aside from the two voices and the necessity for extreme gestures there will have been the spectacle, for surely Philomela had a special mask that made her clipped tongue somehow visible, like Lavinia's bloody stumps.) After which will have come a unique scene of plotting in which an unspeakable crime is urged by a crime victim who cannot speak. Such were the superb scenic effects made possible by the shorn tongue and the woven denunciation, but Sophocles made another more subtle use of them in his implied definition of the women who would soon, behind the scenes, carve up a little boy and feed him to his father.

The tongue was presumably a woman's most dangerous part, her one powerful member. Think of Hesiod on the subject of Pandora's voice, which collaborated with her falsehood, her wily arguments, and her thievish char-acter (*Op.* 78–80). Think of Electra's tongue, honed to be an instrument of harm (Soph. *El.*), and Iphigeneia's that had to be forcibly stopped from cursing (Aesch. *Ag.* 235–38).[30] Tereus evidently supposed that, raped and with her tongue cut out, Philomela would be rendered impotent, would be castrated as far as a woman could be. She would be without the ability to tes-tify even in private, and she would also be robbed of her sex (i.e., her poten-tial of maternity) since, as a deformed creature, she could never be married. The Sophoclean Tereus had, however, forgotten one important fact which was that Philomela, like Pandora and all other women, was doubly equipped. As a man had sword as well as penis, so a woman had shuttle as well as tongue, and this implement—the gift of Athena Ergane (Hes. *Op.* 63–64)[31]—allowed her to work, to make, and so to communicate. The Greek shuttle was likened to a bird because it flew, because it sang, and

28. Here and in Eur. *Hec.* are found the first appearances of the later vengeance twist, the initial crime that has been hidden and must be discovered by the avenger in the course of the drama; cf., e.g., *Spanish Tragedy, Hamlet.*

29. The notion that the reading of a text can bring its author to the reader (found at Pl. *Phdr.* 228) is here given scenic form. For the identification of web with text, cf. *Anth. Pal.* 9.372, where the cicada caught in a spider's web figures the song captive in the text, to be liberated by a singer's voice.

30. One might add Sappho's which, powerless, proves that she is near death (31 Voigt).

31. Hes. *Op.* 63–64; according to local tradition it was Procne who brought the first statue of Athena Ergane to Daulis (Paus. 10.4.8). For the conventional opposition of shuttle to weapons, cf. Eur. *Mel.* fr. 522 *TGF.*

because in the house of an industrious woman it marked the dawn.[32] And so the Sophoclean Philomela, the girl who would become a swallow, used this musical tool as an alternate tongue and wove her recent history into a fabric (δι' ὕφους ἐμήνυσε, *P Oxy.* 1303.23) or, as Shakespeare had it, "in a tedious sampler sewed her mind" (*Titus Andronicus* 2.4.38). She made a web that was both text (γράμματα, schol. Ar. *Av.* 212.6) and song (ἡ τῆς κερκίδος φωνή, Arist. *Poet.* 1454b)[33] and got it into Procne's hands, where it spoke like a messenger about a lost sister, a criminal husband, and a father's ruined honor.[34] All of which means that the violent female revenge treated in the *Tereus* was made to grow directly from a denunciation which, as the work of her shuttle, represented the best and most "Athenian" side of this unfortunate Attic princess.[35] What is more, it expressed the aspect of women that in the best cases rendered these Pandora-like creatures valuable as wives—their potential for chaste[36] and silent work. Other tragedies have dealt with women who used woven stuffs to destroy manifestly virtuous heroes, but in the Sophoclean *Tereus* this peculiarly feminine skill denounced a villain whose crimes would otherwise have been hidden. Indeed, Philomela's visual representation of truth worked much like a play-

---

32. At *Anth. Pal.* 6.160, Telesilla dedicates her shuttle: one that with the swallow in the morning sings to Athena, whose own shuttle is a halcyon (cf. Ar. *Ran.* 1315–16, where halcyons are weaving a song). A similar dedication in 6.247 is of κερκίδας ὀρθολάλοισι χελίδοσιν εἰκελοφώνους; cf. 6.174.

33. For the "song" of the shuttle, cf. Soph. fr. 804 *TrGF;* Eur. fr. 523 *TGF.* Aristotle characteristically classifies Philomela's bit of weaving among the less good recognition tokens because it is manufactured instead of being congenital (like a birthmark). One wonders if he had seen the play performed. More generally on the "weaving" of texts, see J. Scheid and J. Svenbro, *Le métier de Zeus* (Paris, 1994), pp. 119–62.

34. It is not clear whether Philomela's threads are supposed to have made pictures or letters (as at Apollod. *Bibl.* 3.14.8), nor does it matter. This combined denunciation and recognition token is unique in surviving tragedy; closest to it is the prepared letter that triggers recognition in Eur. *IT* 725 ff., which is coupled with a remembered bit of tapestry as official token (814 ff.). Somewhat similar is the piece of writing that makes a false denunciation at Eur. *Hipp.* 856 ff. The satyrs of Sophocles' *Amphiaraos* danced out the alphabet (fr. 121 *TrGF*), but we don't know why.

35. Compare the funerary praise of a woman as *ergatis* (C. W. Clairmont, *Gravestone and Epigram* [Mainz, 1970], no. 49, p. 126). P. Brulé, *La fille d'Athènes* (Paris, 1987), p. 343, reports this as accounting for 8 percent of such praise, a figure that defies verification.

36. At *Anth. Pal.* 6.47, Bitto, about to turn prostitute, dedicates the shuttle of her respectable life to Athena; at 6.285 the future prostitute burns her weaving implements because she will no longer be "slave to her shuttle"; cf. 288. The wedge-shaped shuttle was so closely associated with femininity that it could stand for female parts at Ar. *Av.* 831: what sort of city has both a goddess who wears armor and a Cleisthenes with a *kerkis?* (The straight version of this world-upside-down trope is found at Eur. fr. 522 *TGF.*) The shuttle that Philomela used against Tereus thus represented both of her injured parts.

within-the-play, for it was a bit of *poiesis* that inspired its special spectator with a new emotion.

The maiming of Philomela thus paradoxically resulted in a work of art around which Sophocles made his tragedy of *Tereus,* but what of the cannibal feast?[37] Procne's legendary choice of father's honor even over son's life will have been visually conveyed in the moment that she and her sister laid hands on the boy and pushed him off stage. A minimal revenge would demand further only that the body should be shown to Tereus, so that he could recognize it, suffer, and know who had in this grisly way repaid his breach of faith. And meanwhile what would seem to be a maximum of horror would be achieved in the report of the act of killing, as the painter of the Munich kylix so well understood when he pointed the maternal sword directly into the throat of a squirming Itys.[38] Sophocles could have made a *Tereus* play without the nauseous meal; it is a motif of choice,[39] which means that it must have been the source of important tragic effects. But what effects exactly? When he put Itys on his father's table, did their poet, as many believe, label Procne and Philomela as a pair of fiendish monsters and the female equivalents of Seneca's Atreus?

As far as we know, cannibalism in fifth-century Athens was more strongly associated with the avenger's hunger for violence than with a possible mode of punishment. Homer had made his Hecuba long to devour Achilles' liver (*Il.* 24.212), while Achilles had wished to chop the meat from Hector's bones and eat it raw (*Il.* 22.346, an urge that Richard the Third shared, except that he wanted his enemy's heart "panting hot with salt").[40] In the *Tereus,* by contrast, the meal is not enjoyed in fantasy by the avenger but

37. W. Burkert believes that the cannibalism of the *Tereus* represents the original element of a myth that reflected a Dionysian Agriona rite and described "unspeakable night-time rituals" that included the eating of human flesh (*Homo Necans* [Berkeley, 1972], pp. 179–85). He supposes a mythic model parallel to that of the Minyads: women overdevoted to hearth and Hera are maddened and driven into an opposite overdevotion to Dionysus that ends in bird transformations. It must be noted, however, that in the Sophoclean version the killing and eating of Itys is a specifically indoor daytime domestic event which includes cooking; furthermore, the household art of weaving, instead of being exaggerated and set over against this activity, signals its beginning. Burkert's interpretation must overlook the fact that Procne's mythic cipher, the nightingale, is consistently associated with grief and song (e.g., Aesch. *Supp.* 64; *Ag.* 1144–45; Soph. *El.* 148–49; *Aj.* 627–30; Eur. *HF* 1021; *Hec.* 337; *Hel.* 1110, etc.), not with madness or cannibalism. The nightingale was messenger of spring (Sappho 135 Voigt) and Zeus' messenger (Soph. *El.* 150); she was also an emblem for sister-love and for the healing need to work (Pl. *Phd.* 85a)—a most un-Dionysiac significance.

38. *ARV* 1:456; Harrison, "Itys and Aedon," fig. 1.

39. The cannibal meal had already been associated with the tale, as witness Hes. fr. 312 M-W, but it was not necessary to the mechanics of this plot.

40. At *Anth. Pal.* 9.519.3–4, Alcaeus of Messene longs to drink Philip's brains from his skull.

forced in actuality upon his victim, and it is not enemy flesh that is eaten but that of the dearest of friends. According to this design, the victim's repayment is a gory parody of triumph and pleasure, a source of invincible uncleanness, and the worst conceivable human experience.[41] (The most notorious expression of the gods' hatred of such an action came in the tale of Tydeus, who lost his chance at immortality by devouring Melanippus' brains.) The tyrant was a figurative cannibal (Alc. 70.7, 129.23 Voigt), while monsters such as the Cyclopes and the Laestrygonians, distant peoples like the Scythians and the Massagetae (Hdt. 4.34; 1.216),[42] were thought to be actual man-eaters. Consequently, on the most obvious level, when the sisters force Tereus to swallow human flesh they make him act like what he is, a wild man from the outer regions.[43] More specifically the meal is appropriate to one guilty of incest,[44] because eating human meat stands to acceptable dining much as raping your sister-in-law does to acceptable mating: cannibalism is a kind of dietary incest.[45] The consumption of a son, moreover, has a terrible suitability in the case of Tereus, the oath-breaker and author of sexual violence, because with this action he destroys himself and his progeny, eating up his chance to have grandsons. He, the cutter of Philomela's tongue, performs a kind of self-castration by devouring what would have given him futurity.[46] And finally, with this feast Procne gives

---

41. So, at Callim. fr. 530, there is the request that an enemy should take part in a cannibal feast; similarly in Near Eastern treaty curses he who breaks faith is to eat the flesh of his son or daughter.

42. On the Scythians, see too Strabo 4.5.2; Plin. *HN* 7.2. Herodotus reports cannibalism also among the Anthropophagoi (1.18.106), the Essedonians (4.26), the Kalati (3.38), and the Padei (3.99). The cannibal meal, used as a test of the immortals (as in the Tantalos story), is a separate motif and one that evidently could bear a comic treatment if it is true that the feast of Lycaon was the subject of the Aeschylean satyr play, *Leon;* see Sutton, *Lost Sophocles,* pp. 23–24.

43. Hades of course was the ultimate cannibal (Soph. *El.* 543). Pausanias finds Tereus distinguished at Daulis as the first inventor of "pollution at table" (10.4.8), this being the same place that knew Procne as the bringer of Athena, but there is no way to gauge how early or late this polarization entered the story.

44. At Pl. *Resp.* 9.571c–d, incest, rape, and parricide are the savage appetites of the soul given free rein in sleep and in the tyrant's behavior, which is also a form of eating one's children (10.619b–c). Strabo describes the Irish as man-eaters and incestuous; see M. Detienne, *Dionysos Slain* (Baltimore, 1979), pp. 58–59. For other cultures, see D. Labley, "Incest and Cannibalism," *Journal of Polynesian Society* 85 (1976) 171–79, and more generally, P. Brown and D. Tuzin, eds., *The Ethnography of Cannibalism* (Washington, D.C., 1983).

45. The connection between sibling in-law incest and cannibalism is found again in Atreus' vengeance on Thyestes (as at Aesch. *Ag.* 1191–93) which was well known to Attic theatergoers. Plato (*Leg.* 838c) speaks of the many tragedies of Thyestes staged, and we know of at least eight with this title, including one by Sophocles, though it seems to have dealt with the exile's postbanquet Sikyonian meeting with his unrecognized daughter, Pelopeia.

46. The suggestion is deepened if Itys was decapitated and his head used in the identification. Ovid's Procne considers an actual castration as a means of revenge (*Met.* 6.616).

back to her faithless husband the product of her own misplaced faith, returning her son to his source.

We cannot know exactly what points of justice the Sophoclean heroines saw in their vengeance design, for these will have been brought out in the half-spoken, half-mimed scene in which they took their decision. Nevertheless one effect of the cannibal meal is certain, and it will have been crucial to the play's close. A Tereus punished only by the murder of his son would have rushed from the palace as a man like us—a knife-wielding incestuous rapist but a human being all the same, and one whose visible anger and grief would be available to our understanding, perhaps even to our pity. And on the other hand, as a more or less ordinary man who had been deprived of a son in repayment for savagery and broken faith, this justly punished vengeance victim would have been of no interest to the daimonic world. Too close to us, too far from the gods, such a figure could hardly have been the object of a major miracle of transformation. The Sophoclean Tereus, by contrast—as a man who has just dined on his son's flesh—has a colossal negative stature when he bursts out of the palace.[47] He provokes disgust and revulsion in the audience, but also awe, because of his incomparable internal pollution. And at the same time he compels the attention of the gods because he has broken a primary tabu sanctioned by Zeus (Hes. *Op.* 276–78). A creature so unclean cannot be dealt with by men, and so, while the women are transformed that they may escape his rage, he is exiled from the human species because he is beyond purification.

It was Procne, however, who was the principal of this tragedy, a woman who not only killed her son but used his corpse in this unspeakably ugly outrage. Both the killing and the cooking must have been organized by the sister who could speak and who was mistress of the household, and according to every literary and graphic witness it was Procne who actually attacked the boy. Finally, it will have been she who played the scene in which the royal victim was inveigled with promises of pomps and solemnities into the place of revenge. This entire responsibility for son-killing and cannibal feast has caused the few critics who write about her to assume that Procne was proposed as the surpassingly hideous principal of a tragedy that repudiated her.[48] The poet, they say, has proved that the vengeance wish, once harbored, is so virulent a poison that it can deprave even an Attic princess, rendering her more savage than a Thracian brute.

47. Contrast the Polymestor of Eur. *Hec.*, who is not to be the subject of any miracle: he is labeled as a savage by his wish to be a cannibal, but he is not permitted the exalted aberration of the actual practice.

48. See, e.g., Dobrov, "Tragic and Comic Tereus," p. 213. The twentieth-century response is much like that of John Bereblock, who in 1566 watched a production at Oxford of a play called *Progne:* "It is wonderful how she longed to seek vengeance for the blood of her sister. She goes about therefore to avenge wrongs with wrongs, and injuries with injuries; nor is it at all

This presumed condemnation of revenge—the same that is supposed to inhere in the Euripidean *Hecuba*—is a simple impossibility. No drama played at the city festival could have used the daughters of Pandion to represent depravity for the plain reason that Procne and Philomela were the heroine sponsors of the Pandionid tribe, roughly one-tenth of the watching audience. What is more, it was precisely this Thracian exploit that caused the two princesses to be cherished, as we know from a funeral speech attributed to Demosthenes (60.28). Members of their tribe went off courageously to war, ready to risk all, according to the orator, "because they held before themselves the example of Procne and Philomela, the daughters of Pandion, and remembered how they avenged themselves upon Tereus because of the outrage he had offered them. Pandionids hold that life is not worth living if they cannot show a spirit that is akin to these women's spirit, when an outrage is given to Greece." The speaker, indeed, is ready to compare the two sisters' punishment of Tereus to the self-sacrifice of the Hyacinthides, to Acamas' exploits at Troy, and to Theseus' establishment of *isagoria* among his fellow citizens (60.28). Pandion, moreover, was the only eponymous hero to be honored not just in his own tribe but in an all-city festival, the Pandia,[49] and Procne shared in this general regard. Sometime in the late 430s a more-than-life-sized statue was put up so that the whole of Athens could admire her as she strode along at the northeast corner of the Parthenon, little Itys clinging to her knee.[50] She was a princess who had spent what was dearer than life itself, her son, in order to harm her father's and the city's enemy.

The revenge deed of Sophocles' *Tereus,* a contest play roughly contemporary with Procne's statue,[51] must have been intended and understood as one in which Athenians struck back against foreign injury. In it a not unsympathetic female principal will have been forced to deny her own nature in obedience to a patriarchal imperative stronger even than that of the womb.[52] This does not, however, mean that the poet must have romanti-

---

reverent to add crimes to crimes already committed. . . . And that play was a notable portrayal of mankind in its evil deeds, and was for the spectators, as it were, a clear moral of all those who indulge too much either in love or wrath" (trans. W. Y. Durand, *"Palaemon and Arcyte, Progne,"* *PMLA* 20 (1905) 502–28, esp. 515–16).

49. E. Kearns, *The Heroes of Attica, BICS* Suppl. 57 (London, 1989), p. 81; for his cult as tribal hero, ibid., 191–92. On the glory of the Pandionids, see J. E. Harrison, *Mythology and Monuments* (London, 1890), p. lxxxviii.

50. G. P. Stevens, "The Northeast Corner," *Hesp.* 15 (1946) 10–11; H. Knell, *BSA* Suppl. 3 (1966) 89–92; M. Robertson, *A History of Greek Art* (Cambridge, 1975), p. 286.

51. It is usually dated ca. 430; it must be pre-414 (Ar. *Av.*).

52. This is why the Sophoclean Ajax says that Procne may regard Itys' death as honorable, whereas his own mother will be ashamed of his (Soph. *Aj.* 627–30). The same attitude is reflected in Euripides' phrase about Procne's "slaughter-sacrifice to the Muses" (*HF* 1021–22), though its overt meaning is simply that she provided a subject for song.

cized or softened his heroine, nor does he seem to have delivered a crowd-pleasing patriotic message.[53] The play's remnants suggest rather that in it Sophocles represented an inner transformation, in its way as strange as the final birdification, as a passive, isolated, Deianeira-like wife was changed into an indignant daughter of Pandion. And whereas it was a god who worked the feathered metamorphosis, the active forces in this psychic change were pity for the suffering of a royal sister, and anger at the betrayal of a father. These other-centered emotions proved to be stronger even than mother love, and according to Sophocles' showing they were also detached and pure because they were inspired by a work of art. Procne's revenge impulse was excited by a sister's dishonor and pain,[54] as these were represented in a tapestry that was both spectacle and song.

53. Such a message may have been delicately suggested by Philomela's part in the reprisal, however, since it figures the triumph of the arts of Athens, as represented by weaving (of the "speaking robe," and by extension of Athena's peplos), over aggressive savagery.

54. In that a kin-recognition inaugurates new passions that respond to the sufferings of another, and a consequent resolve built upon these, Procne will have been similar to the Sophoclean Orestes.

CHAPTER EIGHT

Connubial Revenge

Euripides' Medea

I

When Medea, the other great avenging maternal child-killer,[1] is placed beside Procne, there seems at first to be a perfect ethical opposition between the two. Medea is the barbarian this time, while her tortured husband is a Greek hero, and there is no question of defending a father's honor in the case of the woman from Colchis. Nor does Medea avenge a sister; instead she responds in primary fashion to an injury she herself has received. That injury, moreover, is one that we today do not take very seriously. Jason hasn't raped and he hasn't maimed; he has simply repudiated one wife and taken another, and so to us Medea seems to have answered an everyday misdemeanor with a stupendous act of unnatural cruelty. She has not even been moved by the true avenger's indignation, it would seem, but only by a sordid sexual spite, and so on superficial view her tragedy appears to be no tragedy at all but a melodrama meant to display the dangers that breed in flamboyant foreign females.[2]

---

1. It was Euripides who fixed this function upon Medea, choosing to give her the crime of infanticide and to label it as revenge. Whether or not Neophron had already made her the knowing killer of her children (for a recent argument for his priority, see A. Michclini, "Neophron and Euripides' *Medea* 1056–80," *TAPA* 119 [1989] 115–35), tradition offered at least three other versions of the children's death: accidental, during immortalization process (Eumelus, *Corinthiaca* 3A *EGF* = Paus. 2.3.10 ff.), used by Carcinus in a tragedy of the end of the fifth century (Arist. *Rh.* 1400b); killed by Corinthians (Paus. 2.3.6–7; Diod. Sic. 4.54.7; Apollod. *Bibl.* 1.9.28; schol. Eur. *Med.* 264, as found in Parmeniscus and Creophilus); killed as sacrificial victims, to end famine (schol. Pind. *Ol.* 13.74).

2. See, e.g., R. Just, *Women in Athenian Law and Life* (London, 1989), p. 276: the "message" is that "with women and the passions one is still playing with fire."

Certainly that is the way Jason looks at the event. He accuses his wife of being, like all women, interested only in bed (570–71). Baffled lust gives her an angry itch, he says (568, cf. 555), and most scholars agree.[3] Follow them and you find a heroine who kills her children in a fit of jealousy. She is an oriental witch, a psychopath, or a woman crazed by injustice,[4] but nevertheless she engineers a complex program of slaughter that ends in the intentional killing of her own two sons. She appears, moreover, in a drama with an aberrant and redundant structure, because while she moves ever in one direction and at a tremendous pace, she performs three separate scenes of decision, all reaching the same infanticidal conclusion, though the chorus reacts each time in an entirely new way (once with a horrified attempt to dissuade, once with consolatory wisdom, and once as if it had never before heard of such a decision). Finally, this usual twentieth-century reading shows its hard-grained and repetitious child-killer flying off incongruously in a heavenly chariot, leaving her audience filled with pity for her devastated husband. Such is the *Medea* one is ordinarily asked to read, a play variously summed up as a poetic excursion into perverse sensationalism, a study in abnormal psychology, a threatening lesson to males whose dominance may create such female monsters, or an ironic denunciation of violence as it is glamorized in myth.[5] There has been an increasing recognition of the heroic elements in Medea's character,[6] but nevertheless almost all critics agree that the Euripidean child-killer, like the Senecan, is proposed as an embodiment of

3. E.g., B. Gentili, "Il 'letto insaziato' de Medea," *SCO* 21 (1972) 60–72, who argues that the play's language of honor and justice is merely a reflection of the commonplaces of erotic poetry and that Medea herself is afflicted by a kind of erotic incontinence. For a quick summary of views, see G. Gellie, "The Character of Medea," *BICS* 35 (1988) 15–22.

4. E.g., K. Reckford, "Medea's First Exit," *TAPA* 99 (1968) 329–59, where the play represents "the corruption of a human being" who becomes "a witch totally lacking in human feeling" (p. 333).

5. E.g., H. D. Voigtländer, "Spätere Überarbeitung," *Philol.* 101 (1957) 220, who sees Medea as a satanic barbarian combination of cleverness and passion; for B. Knox, "The *Medea* of Euripides," *YClS* 25 (1977) 193–225 = *Word and Action* (Baltimore, 1980), pp. 295–322, Medea represents "the unspeakable violence of the oppressed and betrayed"; P. Pucci, *The Violence of Pity* (Ithaca, 1980), p. 158, asserts that "there is no doubt that she has exercised her will to sacrifice herself in view of redeeming herself from subjection" but also that the Sun chariot "symbolizes the purely rhetorical, contrived, mythical quality of her success"; S. Saïd, "La tragédie de la vengeance," in *La vengeance,* vol. 4, ed. R. Verdier (Paris, 1981), p. 71, reports the play's intention in this way: "c'est bien plutôt pour dénoncer d'imposture un langage qui pare de beaux noms une réalité sanguinaire"; cf. H. Foley, "Medea's Divided Self," *Cl. Ant.* 8 (1989) 87, who believes that the play's purpose is to illustrate "the problematic nature of this archaic heroism."

6. Led by Knox, "The *Medea* of Euripides." See also E. B. Bongie, "Heroic Elements," *TAPA* 107 (1977) 25–56; cf. R. Rehm, "Medea and the λόγος of the Heroic," *Eranos* 87 (1989) 97–115, whose heroine is finally possessed by the male heroic values she had attempted to replace with a female *logos*.

extreme sexual passion, her anger an example of Baudelaire's "fureur des cœurs mûrs par l'amour ulcérés."[7] I want now to propose the opposite—a reading of *Medea* as a carefully designed, truly Attic tragedy, its forward motion checked in a minor *peripeteia*, its passions complex and changeable, its chorus relevant, and its finale strictly appropriate. The principal, by this reading, is not a jealous woman but a unique female avenger ruled by a masculine impulse to recover a personal honor of her own. She is a heroine exploited, like Clytemnestra, by extrahuman powers, but, unlike Agamemnon's queen, she is countercommanded by her insurgent female self, so that her finished deed demands horror and consternation from its audience, but strong pity as well for her who must accomplish it.

Now to the play. Whether they are sympathetic, obscurely disgruntled, or openly hostile, critics agree that Medea is jealous, Medea is mad,[8] and that the dramatic action is not so much tragic as melodramatic.[9] And yet, if you listen to Medea herself, you hear only of motives neither sexual nor insane. She locates the injury that angers her not in the part of herself that is couched but in her hand (496), the hand on which Jason's broken oath of alliance was sworn. She never suggests that Jason should be punished as a womanizer: a husband who strays should be viewed with disdain—so Aegeus suggests, and Medea agrees (699–700). Nor does she show the prurient curiosity that invests sexual jealousy; she has no interest in the princess (which is one reason why we do not know that unfortunate young woman's name).[10] Even Clytemnestra is given a few nasty words about Cassandra, but for Medea the other wife is simply one of three corpses that she dreams of creating (375). The new marriage is hateful

7. Two traditional figures seem to have blocked modern understanding of Medea: that of the *abbandonata* (e.g., Donna Elvira) and that of the lusty would-be adulteress (e.g., Stheneboea or Potiphar's wife). Medea has none of the sexual nostalgia of the first of these, nor does she suffer the disclosure and punishment that come to the second (she cannot, since the love refused her is licit instead of illicit), but many readers try to make her conform to one or the other of these types. A further source of misunderstanding is Seneca's Medea, who does have some of the characteristics of the *abbandonata*, for she would still join Jason in a common exile (Sen. *Med.* 273), and her love for him undermines her anguished anger in the first inner debate (137 ff., cf. chorus at 849 ff.).

8. As proof that Medea was intended as a demon of jealousy, the name "Oistros," given to the chariot driver on the Apuleian volute krater from Canosa (*LIMC* s.v. "Medeia," 29), is sometimes cited. It is possible that the painter's source (probably a fourth-century tragedy, certainly not Euripides, since only one child is killed) meant the name to suggest female mating madness (cf. Eur. *Hipp.* 1300), but more probably it described the quality of the punishment that Medea inflicted (cf. Eur. *Or.* 791; *IT* 1456).

9. The most frequently used text instructs its readers, largely students, that they are to respond with "incredulity and horror"; see D. L. Page, *Euripides, Medea* (Oxford, 1971), p. xiv.

10. Only once does she give her rival a sexual aspect; at the end of the first confrontation with Jason she suggests, as a final insult, that he must (like a cowardly Paris) be eager to get back to bed (623).

not for the pleasures it presumably brings to Jason but because it is linked to a new power alliance for him, illegitimacy for his sons, and exile for her (399–400).[11]

"Bed" matters to Medea not for reasons of pleasure (as Jason somewhat fatuously asserts) but because her bed once gave her status and definition by making her the mistress of a household. She had been wife of Jason,[12] mother of the *genos* of Jason, reigning woman in the *oikos* of Jason, by virtue of her marriage bed, and he, by formally leaving it, has outraged and erased these three selves. Her identity is destroyed, her honor canceled,[13] and the only definition left to her comes from exclusion. *Phygas,* "exile," is the term by which the man who fathered her children would now hear her designated (273; cf. 74–75, and note Aegeus' astonishment at 707). In return, she now defines Jason as a shameless (472) traitor (489; cf. 17) who returns ill-treatment for benefaction, and for his own advantage (591–92) treacherously (587) betrays the bed where his children were made. The point is not that he enjoys another woman but that he gratuitously makes himself the enemy of what was his house (and so her status) by entering an alternate kin-group, wherein he will make new sons who demolish the legitimacy of hers (cf. his admission at 563).

That is Medea's version of why she is angry, but her denunciation stretches further, making Jason not just her enemy and the enemy of the house but the enemy of society as well. In the play's first moment we are told that Medea "howls about oaths and invokes the great faith of the right-hand pledge" (21–22), and this nexus of notions—oath, good faith, right hand— is the standard under which she actually goes to war.[14] It is Jason the perjurer, a man who so scorned the gods that he purposely betrayed his oath (161, 209, 492–95, 995, 1392),[15] who moves Medea to the extremes of her

---

11. In her rejected plan of revenge Medea enters the palace and goes to the bed of Jason (380), but there is no syllable to suggest that this is anything but the logical extension of the hypothesis under examination: Suppose I work alone and with direct violence, gain access at night when all are unarmed, etc.

12. D. M. MacDowell, *The Law in Classical Athens* (London, 1978), pp. 67 and 87, argues that Medea would not have been considered legally married by a fifth-century Athenian audience, but she is certainly so considered within the play by herself, the Nurse, and the chorus.

13. She is "deprived of honor" (ἠτιμασμένη, 20, cf. 33, 1354) and she says ὑβρίζομαι πρὸς ἀνδρός (255–56).

14. On the importance of Jason's oath, see also B. Vickers, *Towards Greek Tragedy* (London, 1973), pp. 283–86.

15. Cf. 755, where the perjurer is guilty of *dyssebeia*. At Pl. *Leg.* 885b, a man who commits sacrilege either doesn't believe in gods, holds that they don't care about affairs on earth, or thinks that he can outwit them. The last of these seems to be the case with Jason, for he still thinks there are some gods who might favor him (1373); cf. Psalm 10.13, "Why is it that the wicked one has disrespected God? He has said in his heart: 'You will not require an accounting.'"

rage.[16] And it is likewise this crime of perjury, attaching to the outrages she has suffered, that brings her response into conformity with the other revenges of Attic tragedy, as Jason's own self-curse joins Medea as a kind of avenger's daimonic companion.[17] By the same token, however, it robs her of freedom in the pursuit of her purpose because, by the will of Zeus Defender of Oaths (169–70), the perjured man stands necessarily doomed as to house and children.[18] Within the broad boundaries of this utter destruction, Medea can create a disaster of a particular design, but she cannot fail, and she cannot leave the work half done.

II

Jason is not just an opportunist who uses women. Rather, the play proposes him as a (somewhat seedy) exemplar of that Hesiodic perjurer who was the key to the dissolution of human society. Like his epic forebear at the end of the Age of Iron, he takes advantage of persons stronger than himself by using crooked arguments and swearing false oaths (Hes. *Op.* 193–94). Like the man of bad faith in that final time, he is associated with the disappearance of *philia* within families (*Med.* 77; cf. *Op.* 180–84) as he plans to make bastards of Medea's sons. And all this he does to advance himself in the world, like that final oath-breaker (*Op.* 192). We know that the Hesiodic passage was a commonplace because it is closely reproduced in the Theognidea (1137–42, where the irreverence of the oath-breaker is emphasized), and Euripides here causes the chorus of his *Medea* to make the epic allusion directly. After Medea's first promise of some kind of revenge, they sing of a world in which nature is reversed and justice stands on its head, where dishonor comes when honor had been promised, and all because men make treacherous plans and Pistis, good faith sponsored by the gods, no longer holds (*Med.* 410–45). When, in summation, they announce that "the sweet reciprocity of oaths (ὅρκων χάρις) has flown from Greece, with Aidos, into the upper air" (*Med.* 439–40), they clinch the identification of Jason with

16. Page, *Medea,* p. xix, instructed students to see this rage as a barbarian's "childish surprise at falsehoods and broken promises."

17. A. Rivier hints at this when he says that the appearance of the chariot was proof that "le crime n'était point de ceux que la nature de l'homme suffit à expliquer, qu'il fallait une energie, une force de haine et de détermination plus qu'humaine, une connivence avec les puissances de destruction qui, dans la nature et la vie, représentaient pour les Grecs la face obscure du divin" ("L'élément démonique chez Euripide," in *Euripide,* Entretiens Hardt, 6 [Geneva, 1958], pp. 45–72, esp. 68).

18. D. Kovacs, "Zeus in Euripides' *Medea,*" *AJPhil.* 114 (1993) 45–70, attempts to show that Zeus is directly concerned and is using Medea to impose a divine punishment (because of Creon's initial rejection of Medea's supplication?). There is, however, no indication in the play that Zeus does anything other than observe and rejoice at the independent performance of the oath-demon.

the perjurer whose Hesiodic misdeeds cause the sweetness of Oath-Keeping (εὐόρκου χάρις), Justice, and Uprightness to depart from men, along with Aidos and Nemesis (Hes. *Op.* 190–91, 199–200).[19] Small and despicable though he is, a falsely swearing man can cause the disintegration of an entire community.[20]

Jason the oath-breaker thus has a certain similarity to Tereus, to Eurystheus, even to the Cyclops; he threatens the armature of the social order, because in Greek thinking both cosmos and society are guaranteed by irrevocable oaths. In Homer's heaven the gods divided powers and places, confirmed agreements, and settled quarrels by oath,[21] and for Empedocles the eternal fluctuation from one to many and back to one was sealed by "broad oaths" taken between Neikos and Philotes.[22] In earthly reflection of these arrangements, Hellenic culture began when Chiron showed men "oaths and offerings and the arrangement of Olympus," while at Athens order commenced when Bouzyges taught men to back up common decency with oath and curse.[23] The ideal city rested upon the oaths men took to observe justice (Soph. *Ant.* 369);[24] at Ithaca Athena confirmed the reestablishment of order

19. In the Theognidean version Sophrosyne and the Charites retire to heaven in company with Pistis, 1137–38; cf. Eur. *Med.* 731. Compare old Oedipus' picture of social decline (Soph. *OC* 610–11): "Earth's strength gives out, the body gives out, Good Faith dies and Faithlessness is rampant." Thucydides produces a secular version when describing the general depravity of communities that had suffered revolution (3.83): "And there was nothing to resolve this distrust—no powerful word, no oath carrying fear. Instead, when men felt they were strong, they simply took precautions against injury rather than placing their faith anywhere, for they thought any real security was beyond hope." Cf. Pl. *Leg.* 949a–b, where justice is undermined by men who use oath and self-curse simply to influence a jury.

20. Compare the secular fourth-century words of Demosthenes that equate oath-breaking and swearing of false oaths with the most impure forms of irreverence such as eating the Hecate meats or the pigs' testicles thrown out in cleansing rites (54.39–40).

21. E.g., *Il.* 15.36; 19.108, 127; 20.313; cf. Pind. *Ol.* 7.65; *Pae.* 6.112. According to Cassandra there is a general oath-based agreement among the gods that sons shall avenge fathers (Aesch. *Ag.* 1290, a line obelized by Fraenkel), and at Aesch. *Cho.* 126, Clytemnestra's Furies are bound into their sodality by oath.

22. 30 DK; cf. 115 DK, where the eternal decree in Ananke's possession is likewise oath-sealed.

23. Chiron, *Titanomachia* 6, *EGF*; Bouzyges, Append. prov. 1.61 in *Paroemiogr.*, cited *CAF* 2:561. Even among Aesop's cynical animals there was a belief in oaths, and though other forms of deceit were admired, oath-breaking was seen as dangerous. In tale 50 a woodcutter tries to catch a fox by breaking his oath, and the fox gloats that the god of oaths will get him in return. On oaths in general, see K. Latte, "Meineid," in *Kl. Schr.* (Munich, 1968), pp. 367 ff.; J. Plescia, *The Oath and Perjury* (Tallahassee, 1970).

24. At Sparta all the citizens were bound by oath to keep the laws of Lycurgus in his absence (Plut. *Mor.* 239F; *Vit. Lyc.* 57D). In the cities of Crete there was an annual oath of new citizens promising loyalty; see R. E. Willetts, *Cretan Cults and Festivals* (London and New York, 1962), p. 107.

by introducing "faithful oath-agreements" (*Od.* 24.483), and actual colonies were sent out according to oath-based regulations.[25] The Delphic Amphictyony, the Athenian empire, and all other external alliances were held together by oaths,[26] while within the separate cities rulers, like soldiers, were oath-bound,[27] so that the broken oath became one of the characteristics of the standard tyrant.[28] The fourth-century orator Lycurgus could assume absolute agreement when he said, "The power that keeps our democracy together is the oath" (*Leoc.* 79).[29] Asylum was given, exiles brought back, parties and factions formed, kinship confirmed,[30] all according to oath, while business was carried on in the same way, the very weights and measures being fixed by oath.[31] Physicians took the Hippocratic oath;[32] at Olympia athletes and judges were oath-bound to fair play and fair training (Paus. 5.24.9) and everywhere supervisors of holy places—brotherhoods of priests, even the fourteen ancient priestesses of Dionysus at Athens—took oaths to observe

25. E.g., Locris, ML 20.45–46p; cf. the danced oath-taking ceremony at Cyrene, *SEG* 9.3.

26. Amphictyony, Aeschin. 3.110; empire, Tod 1.66.41. The Oath of Plataea (Tod 2.204), whether genuine or not, likewise embodies the Greek sense that Hellenic society depended upon the oath-bound agreement. On authenticity, see P. Siewert, *Der Eid von Plataiai* (Munich, 1972); Meiggs, *AE,* p. 504; W. R. Connor, *Theopompus and Fifth-Century Athens* (Cambridge, Mass., 1968), pp. 78–83.

27. Athenian archons, Arist. *Ath. Pol.* 55.5; cf. Pl. *Cri.* 119d, where the kings of Atlantis renew their oaths, swearing to give judgments according to laws of Poseidon. Athenian ephebes swore by wheat, barley, vines, olives, and fig trees as well as by the gods (Tod 2.204); see P. Siewert, "The Ephebic Oath," *JHS* 97 (1977) 102 ff. At Hdt. 3.11, mercenaries bind themselves together by drinking a mixture of wine, water, and the blood of a sacrificial victim; cf. Xen. *An.* 2.5.5–7. A particular crisis could inspire a particular oath, as that among the several groups at Thermopylae (Hdt. 7.132.2).

28. Eur. fr. 286 *TGF.* Philip of Macedon was the consummate oath-breaker according to Pausanias (8.7.5).

29. In 410 B.C. a decree of Demophantus required all Athenians to take an oath against tyrants (Andoc. 1.96–98); see H. Yunis, *A New Creed* (Göttingen, 1985), pp. 43–44 and nn. 10, 11, 12. Regular oaths opened each day of political and judicial work at Athens; boule, Xen. *Mem.* 1.1.19; Lycurg. *Leoc.* 31; boule and ecclesia, Dem. 19.70–71; areopagus, Dem. 23.67; 47.71; Antiphon 5.11; Din. *Demosth.* 46; Heliastic courts, Dem. 24.151; Palladion, at end of trial, Aeschin. 2.87. Less frequent oaths could establish innocence (e.g., Andoc. 1.126–27; cf. *Il.* 19.258–65; 23.553; Aesch. *Eum.* 29; Soph. *OT* 644–45; Eur. *Hipp.* 1025 ff.) or bring pardon to a convicted killer. See S. Todd, *Nomos* (Cambridge, 1990), p. 35; E. C. Mirhady, "The Oath-Challenge in Athens," *CQ* 41 (1991) 78–83. In general, see W. Hoffman, *De Jurandi upud Athenienses Formulis* (Darmstadt, 1886).

30. Exiles, Andoc. 1.90; 105; 107. For oaths of qualification for deme, phratry, or *genos*, see *IG* 2².1237; Dem. 43.13–14; 57.61; Isaeus 7.28; 8.19; Arist. *Ath. Pol.* 42.1. At Dem. 39.40 a (mother's) oath establishes the legitimacy of children; see L. Gernet, *Droit et société* (Paris, 1955), p. 66 n. 3, and 110–11; Todd, *Nomos,* p. 35.

31. Tod 1.67.12; cf. Stob. *Flor.* 44.22 for oaths in commercial contracts.

32. F. Muller, "Der hippokratische νόμος (und ὅρκος)," *Hermes* 75 (1940) 93–105.

their religious duties.[33] Finally, mystic initiates had secrecy imposed upon them by special oaths taken in the names of their own deities.[34]

Oaths were the cement of order, yet their breach carried no secular penalty because giving one's word was a religious, not a juridical, act.[35] The cosmos depended upon men's good faith, without which any oath was written in ashes, as a proverb had it.[36] The man who upheld his oath, the man who was *euorkos,* would have a long line of descendants according to common belief,[37] and Pindar held that reverence for oaths, *euorkia,* was potentially man's saving virtue, the practice of which meant a pleasant afterlife (*Ol.* 2.60).[38] Hypothetical rewards, however, were not what maintained the mysterious authority of the Hellenic oath. The entire system ran on dread, on *phobos,* and the source of this dread was the ritualized sacrilege and the conditional self-curse built into every solemn oath. Touching an oath object[39] that was ordinarily untouchable—an altar, a part of someone's body, the blood or entrails of a slaughtered beast[40]—each party

33. *IG* 2².1175.20–24. See D. Whitehead, *Demes of Attica* (Princeton, 1986), chap. 4, n. 130.

34. *PSI* 1162; 1290; *Syll.*³ 2.401–11, no. 736, Andanian mysteries. Cf. R. Merkelbach, "Der Eid der Isismysten," *ZPE* 1 (1967) 55–73, esp. 72–73. According to Near Eastern beliefs oaths could be used against afflicting demons; see T. Abusch, "An Early Form of Witchcraft Ritual," in *Lingering over Words: Studies . . . Moran* (Atlanta, 1990), pp. 1 ff. This belief is reflected at Aesch. *Ag.* 1570, where Clytemnestra thinks to use oaths to evict the Pleisthenid demon from the house.

35. See Todd, *Nomos,* p. 36; there was, however, a fine for one found guilty of giving false trial testimony (Dem. 29.16). On the other hand, a curse could serve as the religious enforcement of public law, as recorded in the stele from Teos (Tod 1.23).

36. Philonides, *Incert.* 1 (LSJ s.v. τέφρα); women's oaths were said to be written in water. See Pl. *Leg.* 948b3, on the degeneracy of oaths in the fourth century.

37. Hes. *Op.* 285; cf. Pl. *Resp.* 2.363c–d. At Eur. *Med.* 995, *euorkos* is explicitly what Jason is not.

38. Cf. Xen. *Symp.* 4.49; Ar. *Plut.* 61–105.

39. So in informal asseverations one "touched earth" in token of good faith; e.g., Bacchyl. 5.42; 8.119. See E. Benveniste, "L'expression du serment dans la Grèce ancienne," *Rev. Hist. Rel.* 134 (1948) 81–94, where the fundamental meaning of ὀμνύναι ὅρκον is found to be the same as the Homeric ὅρκον ἑλέσθαι, i.e., to seize hold of a sacralizing object. On the continuing discussion of the etymology of *horkos,* see N. Rollant, "'Ορκος et sa famille," in Université de Nice, Centre de recherches comparatives sur les langues de la Méditerranée ancienne, *Document* no. 4 (1979), pp. 214–304. On touching a forbidden object, see J. Plescia, *Oath and Perjury,* p. 11: "this amounted to attaching the oath to a sacrilege the pardon for which could not be obtained except by fulfilling the oath at all costs."

40. Altar: *IG* 2/3². 1237.76; cf. Thuc. 5.50.1; Arist. *Ath. Pol.* 55.5 mentions the stone where oaths were taken at Athens; this was probably a primitive altar with ancient *horkia* or *tomia* buried beneath; see P. Stengel, "Zu den gr. Schwüropfern," *Hermes* 49 (1914) 94. The remains of animals used in oath rituals had to be specially disposed of (*Il.* 19.267; Paus. 5.24.10; schol. Ar. *Pax* 717; Plut. *Phoc.* 1; *Mor.* 523C; *Suda,* s.v. χόλικες). This dangerous sacredness could also attach to implements; see Eur. *Supp.* 1205–7, where Athena prescribes special treatment for the knife used in the treaty sacrifices. Body part: Zeus' head, *Il.* 15.36; cf. Sappho 44A; the per-

dedicated himself to total destruction should he (intentionally or uninten-tionally)[41] not keep faith. The formulae hardly varied: the oath-taker asked for utter ruin, *exoleia*, to be visited upon self, children, house, and race,[42] or, in careless phraseology, he "pledged his children" (Dem. 54.23; 29.54).[43] In addition, possessions such as flocks could be dedicated to destruction, and famine, plague, or monstrous births might be particularly requested as its means,[44] but these were mere embellishments. In the same way, the words of the oath might be accompanied by gestures of sympathetic magic, like the pouring of wine at the truce in *Iliad* 3, the melting of a wax giant by those on their way to Cyrene,[45] or the throwing of an iron bar into the sea when the Phocaeans left home (Hdt. 1.165).[46] Such extra magical pressures were appropriate but not required, because the words in themselves meant that, should the speaker not "remain steadfast,"[47] a demon whose specialty

son of Eriphyle, Pind. *Nem.* 9.16; heads of Demeter and Praxidike, Paus. 8.15; 9.33; genitals, *Gen.* 24.2, 9; 46.26; 47.29; *Exod.* 1.5; *Num.* 5.21. Sacrificial victims: Dem. 23.67 (Areopagus oath); Aesch. *Sept.* 42 ff.; Hdt. 6.68.1; Aeschin. 1.114. W. Burkert, *Greek Religion* (Cambridge, Mass., 1985), p. 253, supposes that sacrificial victims were regularly trampled in Athenian pub-lic oaths, though parties were merely said to stand "in the presence of" the victims (ἐπὶ τῶν τομίων) as one might "in the presence of" witnesses (ἐπὶ μαρτύρων). Burkert is following Stengel, "Schwüropfern," pp. 90–100, where texts are interpreted so as to make the oath-sacrifice as aberrant as possible, with victims maimed or castrated.

41. Arist. fr. 148 Rose makes a distinction between the perjurer who willingly gives false oaths, then knowingly breaks them, and the simple oath-breaker, but this was a sophisticated attitude; see Latte, "Meineid," pp. 367–75, esp. 373.

42. [Dem.] 59.10; cf. Dem. 54.40–41; Antiph. 5.11; Lys. 12.10; Lycurg. *Leoc.* 79; compare the parodies at Ar. *Ran.* 586–88; *Eq.* 765 ff. When the oath-taker asked for the standard pun-ishment for *dyssebeia*, should he break the oath (as Aegeus does, Eur. *Med.* 755), this was called swearing ὡς νόμιμον. One of the reasons that women's oaths were not much respected is that, having neither house nor heirs, the self-curse could threaten only their own persons; see Just, *Women in Athenian Law and Life*, pp. 33–39. On women's characteristic oath deities, see D. Bain, "Female Speech in Menander," *Antichthon* 18 (1984) 24–42.

43. This is parodied at Eur. *Cyc.* 269, where Silenus asks the destruction of the satyrs, and it was later forbidden at Alexandria (*PHal.* 1 Z.217).

44. See the oath of the Amphictyons (Aeschin. 3.110 f.) or the Ephebic oath (Tod 2.204.39 ff. For biblical parallels, see D. R. Hillers, *Treaty Curses and the Old Testament Prophets*, Biblica et Orientalia, 16 (Rome, 1964), pp. 68–69.

45. ML 5.46–49. On the genuineness of this oath see A. J. Graham, "Authenticity," *JHS* 80 (1960) 94–111; L. Jeffrey, "The Pact of the First Settlers," *Hist.* 10 (1961) 139–47. For sympa-thetic oath-rites in general, see C. Faraone, "Molten Wax, Spilt Wine and Mutilated Animals," *JHS* 113 (1993) 60–80.

46. Compare Arist. *Ath. Pol.* 23.5 for the same gesture of permanence at the formation of the Delian league; for Near Eastern parallels, see H. Jacobson, "The Oath of the Delian League," *Philol.* 119 (1975) 256 ff. Cf. also schol. Soph. *Ant.* 264; Callim. *Aet.* 388–89, for prac-tices in which iron was simply grasped, that its permanence might enter into the oath.

47. To keep an oath was μένειν, as at ML 5.46, 49; Tod 1.39.11; cf. Eur. *Andr.* 999–1000, and note *Med.* 753–54.

was pursuit, torture, and eventual extermination would come into being. This punitive agent might be called Erinys, or Ara, or Horkos, or Oistros, or Alastor,[48] but whatever its name, the anguish that it worked was the greatest known to man (Hes. *Theog.* 231–32; cf. *Op.* 219–22, 803–4). Implacable and invulnerable to any countermagic—it could not be bound since it had neither hands nor feet[49]—the oath demon would root out all trace of a man who had sworn falsely, pursuing him, if necessary, even into Hades (Hdt. 6.86), and destroying his house and hereditary line as well.[50] It could attack directly, but it could also have the work done by a human curse-bearer termed *araios* or *araia*[51] who might be willing or unwilling.[52] And finally this demon, malign as it was, had Olympian sponsors, because any well-made oath was taken in the presence of various invoked gods who would serve as its overseers.[53] These might be many or few, and they usually included local powers, but Zeus, Ge, and Helios were favorites everywhere because they were universal and all-seeing forces.[54]

48. Erinys: *Il.* 9.453–57; 19.259–60; Alc. 129 Voigt. Ara: Soph. *El.* 111; *OT* 418. Horkos: Hes. *Op.* 219; 282; Soph. *OC* 1767; Arrian (156 F 94 *FGrH*) reports a river in Bithynia called Horkos because it would seize and drown a perjurer. Oistros: Poll. 4.142, cf. the Apuleian krater cited above, n. 8. Alastor: Aesch. *Ag.* 1501; Eur. *Phoen.* 1556; cf. *Med.* 1059. In Sicily the demon was double, a pair of brothers called Palikoi who had a sanctuary on the slopes of Etna (Diod. Sic. 11.89.5; Strabo 6.2.9).

49. It could not be crippled by an act like *maschalismos*. A simpler notion is expressed at Soph. *El.* 489, where the demon is *polypous* and *polycheir* because of its swiftness and striking power. Xenophon says that there is no refuge to which an oath-breaker could run (*Anab.* 2.5.5–7), and Demosthenes, more succinctly of the perjured juryman, "he won't escape the gods" (19.239).

50. The mechanical, magical quality of the punishment inspired stories in later times about men who had tricked the oath demon; e.g., the Locrians, who swore, "as long as we walk this earth with these heads on our shoulders," having shoes full of sand and false heads (Polyb. 12.6a-3; Polyaenus 6.22).

51. As at Soph. *Trach.* 1202; Eur. *IT* 778, and note *Med.* 608.

52. Aeschylus makes Orestes into a generalized oath demon who from his grave will work inescapable disasters upon all perjurers (*Eum.* 762 ff.). The term ἀραῖος can also be used of one under a curse, as at Soph. *OT* 644.

53. In the words of E. Benveniste, swearing an oath meant "devoting oneself in advance to divine vengeance" (*Indo-European Language and Society* [London, 1973], p. 442); that vengeance was imaged in the statue of Zeus Horkios at Olympia, showing the god with a thunderbolt in each hand (Paus. 5.24.9–11). Oaths were often taken in temples or at shrines or altars; a law requiring an oath might specify the place and the divinities, but many cities and sodalities had their customary *theoi horkioi*. Local gods were especially favored, and one could simply swear by "the god of this place" (*RE* s.v. "Eid").

54. See West ad Hes. *Op.* 249 and 267, for Vedic parallels, and in general, H. Usener, "Dreiheit," *Rh. Mus.* 58 (1903) 330. Chthonic divinities were also favorites for obvious reasons (e.g., Clytemnestra at Aesch. *Ag.* 1406); at Athens, Heliasts swore by Zeus, Poseidon, and Demeter (Dem. 24.149–51). Solon's oath-watching Three Gods were three aspects of Zeus (Hikesios, Katharsios, and Exakester) according to Pollux (8.143), but Hesychius reports that some took them to be Zeus, Athena, and Apollo (s.v. τρεῖς θεοί). At Pind. *Pyth.* 4.166, Peleus and Jason

Now consider the oath and the "right-hand pledge" that Medea howls about (21–22).[55] Ordinarily a bridegroom promised his bride's father, with or without formal oaths, that he would maintain the daughter as fairly as she was given, and would honor her as the mother of his legitimate children.[56] Jason, however, was the enemy of his bride's father, which meant that Medea had to play parent to herself, binding her husband to his future duties as Aetes would have done.[57] The "wedding" at Colchis, a sexual alliance sponsored by Aphrodite, was thus a union of Greek and Barbarian formed in a cultural limbo,[58] an agreement made directly between a male and a female who dealt with each other as equals.[59] We do not know what promises Medea demanded,[60] but we do know what the chorus supposes, for they sing their own mild curse on Jason for having broken faith (659–62). According to them, the marriage that he entered upon meant not just living together (1000) and having the same friends and enemies, but also the peaceable coupling (641–42) of partners who

swear by Zeus, as ancestor of both; the mystic swore by his special Creator (Merkelbach, "Der Eid der Isismysten"), and the Pythagorean by "him who gave our soul the *tetrakys*" (Plut. *Mor.* 877A = Diels, *Dox. Graec.* 282).

55. Page, ad loc., supposes that Medea shouts, "Horkoi!" as if she were summoning curse-demons.

56. Archil. 173 W seems to suggest an accompanying *xenia* ritual with table. Cf. Theoc. *Id.* 22.147–48, where Lynceus claims that the father of the Leucippides has given the girls to him and Idas, so that their marriage is γάμος ἐν ὅρκῳ. At Men. *Pk.* 1010, the father says, ταύτην / γνησίων / παίδων ἐπ' ἀρότῳ σοι δίδωμι; see Gomme-Sandbach ad loc. for the same formula in other plays, and cf. Dem. 59.52.

57. There was a tradition that Heracles had acted as *kyrios* for Medea (Diod. Sic. 4.54.7). For other associations with Heracles, see below, n. 130.

58. On the chest of Cypselus, in the second level, Jason stood with an enthroned Medea bride in the presence of Aphrodite (Paus. 5.17.2–18.3); see W. von Massow, *MDAI(A)* 41 (1916), pl. 10, for a reconstruction. Note that Pindar, at *Ol.* 13.74, lists Medea's giving of herself, without her father's sanction, as one of the glories of Corinth, Aphrodite's city. Jason's pledge was the "wild" version of the *enguesis* that was the necessary guarantee of the legitimacy of children in fifth-century Athens (though cohabitation would establish a woman as a wife); see E. J. Bickerman, "La conception du mariage à Athènes," *Bull. Ist. Dir. Rom.* 78 (1975) 1–28.

59. This is how gods might marry, and in later times at least the Medea-Jason union was thought of as a kind of *hieros gamos,* their wedding cave honored as a sacred place (Ap. Rhod. 4.1153). As between equals, the agreement also has an everyday parallel in promises exchanged by men, in love or in friendship pacts; so at Eur. *Or.* 1086, Pylades curses himself with an unquiet death, should he betray Orestes; this kind of oath is parodied at Ar. *Eq.* 765 ff. Pl. *Symp.* 183a speaks of the oaths by which the *erastes* wins the *eromenos,* adding at 183b that these are the only oaths that can be broken without divine punishment.

60. Later writers assumed an oath-bound promise to marry and to continue a common life until death; e.g., Diod. Sic. 4.46.4. At Ap. Rhod. 4.1084–85 Jason swears great oaths to keep Medea in his house as his lawful wife.

gave each other honor and opened each to the other the "inner doors of a clean heart-mind" (660–61).[61] These terms suggest those of a treaty in which Jason and Medea, like two sovereign states, summoned Theoi Horkoi and swore to a mutual friendship that would be faithful and undeceiving, to endure forever.[62] From the parties themselves we gather that Jason had promised to be a "faithful husband" (511), to treat Medea as the best of friends (449–50, that is, planning good things for her, 566–67, 595–97), perhaps even to make her "blessed among Greek women" (509), in return for her taking his enemies as her own, even when they were her own kin (506–8).[63] Now he has broken his oaths (like the chorus, Medea uses a phrase reminiscent of Hesiod, ὅρκων δὲ φρούδη πίστις, 492), harming his friends unjustly (470) with behavior that is unfaithful, deceitful, and anything but simple (566–67, 595–97). Other passages make it clear that these oaths were sworn in the presence of at least three Olympian powers, Zeus Guardian of Mortal Oaths, Themis (Dike), and Helios,[64] their curse upon self, children, and household clinched with a gesture that involved Medea's right hand (21–22). And when she holds up that right hand (496) as visible proof that Jason has broken faith, it is plain that she is not referring to a simple handclasp, as seen at the top of

61. Put in everyday language, this is close to the good marriage envisioned in reverse by Isocrates (3.40), when husbands κοινωνίαν ποιησάμενοι παντὸς τοῦ βίου are careful not to give pain to the wife who does not cause them pain.

62. Compare promises of a φιλότης that would be πιστή and ἄδολος forever (ἀείδιον), exchanged between Sybaris and the Serdaioi, 550–525 B.C.? (ML 10). Athens and Samos, in 439–438 B.C., bound themselves to speak and plan fair things each for the other, to be faithful, undeceitful, and simple, each party being just, neither party to do or to receive harm (ML 56.21–22). Cf. Athens and Rhegium, 433–432 B.C. (ML 63.11–15); Athens and Leontini, 433–432 B.C. (ML 64.21–25). Compare also the offer of Croesus, when courting Sparta, to be φίλος . . . καὶ σύμμαχος ἄνευ τε δόλου καὶ ἀπάτης (Hdt. 1.69.1–3).

63. Medea presents herself as one who promised salvation and delivered it (476–82); she also presents herself as a wife who valued her husband over father and brother (483) and made her husband's enemies her own (486). S. Schein, "Philia in Euripides' *Medea,*" in *Cabinet of the Muses,* ed. M. Griffith and D. Mastronarde (Atlanta, 1990), pp. 57–73, argues that Medea is shown as one who cannot make the distinction between friend and enemy, but what she says is that she has no friends because she took her husband's enemies as her own, and these happened to be her only natural friends (9–15, 508). He has now destroyed the oath-bound *philia* between the two of them (77, 84), and by doing so destroys Medea's only other "friends," the children.

64. Cf. 160, 169; at 209, Medea was brought to Greece by Zeus' Themis Horkia; at 764, Medea cries out to Zeus, Zeus' Dike, and Helios, when it appears that the broken oath may be punished. Artemis is named at 160, either because she also (with Aphrodite?) was among the witnessing gods or because she is the divinity to whom a woman cries out when she suffers. A third-century funerary stele in the Getty collection carries a curse upon anyone who might damage it, with Artemis Medeias appointed as its divine executor; see A. Oikonomides, "Artemis Medeia," *ZPE* 45 (1982) 115–17.

a treaty stele,[65] for she says that her knees, too, were used by the cowardly perjurer (496–98). It is thus no commonplace gesture of mutual disar-
mament that she refers to,[66] but a complex of sacred gestures in which
Jason, having succeeded as a suppliant,[67] became party to an oath-bound
marriage promise.[68] Medea's hand (forbidden as belonging to a young
girl)[69] was retained as the oath object, the *horkion,* on which he swore to
use her as his legitimate wife.[70] Medea's right hand was thus the location
of the continuing magical force of the oath's contingent curse, the "objet
dépositaire" that contained a promise of demonic destruction for
the oath-breaker, his children, and his house.[71] In Medea's language there
is an oath-faith witnessed by the gods and belonging to her right hand
(δεξιᾶς πίστιν μεγίστην, 21–23). When the oath is broken, that hand carries the contingent curse, the curse that Medea would activate with her

65. See, for example, the handclasp of Hera and Athena that decorates the stele recording the treaty between Athens and Samos of 404 B.C. (*IG* 1³.127).

66. Aeschin. 3.224, τὴν δεξιὰν ἐνέβαλες ἄνδρα φίλον καὶ ξένον ποιούμενος; at Eur. *IA*
58–60, all the suitors of Helen seal their agreement with handshakes; cf. Soph. *Trach.* 1181, the
oath of Hyllus; *Il.* 4.158, the battlefield truce; Xen. *Hell.* 4.1.31. Note, however, that the handshake does not necessarily imply an oath (Soph. *Phil.* 811–12). See J. Taillardat, "Φιλότης
πίστις et Foedus," *Rev. Et. Grec.* 95 (1982) 1–12; G. Herman, *Ritualised Friendship* (Cambridge,
1987), pp. 50–53; also G. Neumann, *Gesten und Gebärden in der gr. Kunst* (Berlin, 1965), pp.
49–71. Achilles says that there can be no oaths between men and animals (*Il.* 22.262 ff.), but
St. Francis persuaded a wolf to signal his good faith by offering his right paw to the right hand
of the saint (*Fioretti* 21).

67. For the hand in suppliancy, see, e.g., Eur. *Heracl.* 307; *IT* 1068–69, and the little joke
at Alcman 3.79–81 *PMG* = 26.79–81 Calame.

68. There is no evidence to show that a groom-to-father handshake was customary at the
end of an Athenian *enguesis;* see A. R. W. Harrison, *The Law of Athens* (Oxford, 1968), pp. 5–6.
Orestes, however, giving the absent Electra to Pylades, has him swear by his (Orestes') right
hand that he will not "betray" her couch (Eur. *IT* 700, 716–17).

69. Men did not ordinarily touch the female hand (though Heracles and Athena do clasp
hands on a black-figure amphora in the Vatican; see Neumann, *Gesten,* fig. 25, p. 54); as rapists
or bridegrooms they took a woman by her wrist. The rare male/female handclasps on fifth-
century funeral reliefs symbolize greeting or departure (cf. Alcestis with the servants, Eur. *Alc.*
193); see G. Davies, "The Significance of the Handshake Motif," *AJArch.* 89 (1985) 627–40. In
Hellenistic and Roman art male/female handclasps are more common, and at Ap. Rhod.
1.842 Jason marks his agreement with Hypsipyle by taking her hand.

70. At Eur. *Hel.* 835, Helen swears by Menelaus' head that she will die if he does, and he
asks her to confirm the oath by touching his right hand. Cf. Eur. *IA* 471, where Menelaus asks
Agamemnon for his hand, then swears that he speaks from the heart, in effect asking that this
hand should destroy him if he is insincere. On this kind of gesture, see D. Cohen, "Horkia and
Horkos in the *Iliad,*" *RIDA* 27 (1980) 55 n. 20.

71. Benveniste, "L'expression du serment," pp. 86–90; cf. *Indo-European Language and Society,* p. 486: "a material invested with baneful powers." That this hand will aid in killing both
dragon and Apsyrtos only makes it a more appropriate residence for the negative power of the
potential curse.

first consecutive words: "O children who stand under a curse, children of
a mother despised, may you be destroyed with your father, and let the
whole house crumble!" (112–14).[72]

The marriage scene that serves as a backdrop to today's action thus had
a certain resemblance to the staged encounter of Aegeus with Medea.[73] At
Colchis Jason had asked for salvation, as Aegeus asks for the perpetuation
of his line, and Medea had promised it, then as now exacting in return the
assurance of an unassailable refuge. Aegeus now swears by the gods that
Medea proposes (Helios prominent among them, 746) as Jason must have
done, and he dedicates himself, his children, and his house to destruction
should he not remain within the terms of his oath (754–55),[74] as Jason will
also have done. The difference, however, is that the Athenian king is *euorkos*,
one who will have a long line of descendants, so that his staged oath-taking
demonstrates the right working of the sacred institution that is threatened
by Jason's self-promoting transgression. Indeed, it demonstrates more,
because the present faithfully sworn oath activates the punishment of the
perjurer, signaling to Medea that she may now begin upon the action that
will "dissolve the house of Jason" (794).

III

An ordinary victim of perjury—an Aesopian beast, a slave, or a mortal not
worth singing about—would call the oath deities, activate the curse, and
then wait. A state whose treaty had been violated, however, would retaliate
with a perfect sense of justice—as would a city against domestic criminals,[75]

72. The children are κατάρατοι, the objects of a curse, like Oedipus at *OT* 1345. The term
ἐπάρατος covers persons or things protected by a curse (temple servants or sacred property),
while ἐπαρή signifies the force field of the curse; cf. the Thasian decree on informers, ML 83.5,
p. 253 (411–409 B.C.). Medea may also be compared to Alcaeus, when he calls on the erinys
of the conspirators' broken oath (129.13–14 Voigt).

73. In terms of standard revenge structure this is the recognition scene, and it works as
such scenes do to consolidate the tactical position of the avenger, while it adds to his humanity. Medea is unique, however, in that she does not share either the planning or the prosecution
of her intrigue with her ally.

74. His phrase is minimal but effective; he asks to suffer, if he should break his word, as do
those guilty of *dyssebeia* (755); one could also ask to suffer simply "according to *nomos*," with the
full self-curse implied, as is spelled out at Dem. 54.40; 57.22: ὡς νόμιμον, κατ' ἐξωλείας αὐτοῦ
καὶ γένους καὶ οἰκίας. The same extreme compression can be found in the formula εὐορκοῦντι
μὲν μοὶ εὖ εἴη, ἐφιορκοῦντι δὲ τὰ ἐναντία, as in the mystics' oath cited above, n. 34.

75. Cf. Dem. 19.70–71: "we leave the unknown criminal to the punishment consequent
upon his broken oaths, but him we know we prosecute." The Athenian state did not try to imitate the daimonic *exoleia*, but it did sometimes work the literal destruction of a criminal's
house; see W. R. Connor, "The Razing of the House," *TAPA* 15 (1985) 79 ff.

or a man betrayed by his sworn friend[76]—and this is what Medea does. Euripides thus gives his maternal child-killer a double definition: she is a woman whose honor is structured like that of a man, and also one who is directed by a nonhuman power. Her motives are thus serious and potentially tragic (as jealousy would not have been) but they are nonetheless hard for a dramatist to use because, with the curse at work, Medea's overdetermined crimes must enjoy an almost mechanical success. There is a risk that such a principal will seem to be a curse-fiend, not a mortal woman, and this, indeed, is what many critics find, after which they find themselves reading a melodrama instead of a tragedy. I would argue, on the contrary, that Euripides found in his Medea an entirely human counterforce, one almost strong enough to balk both honor and curse-demon, and that he gave this force a moment of ascendancy, just before the climax of his play. His heroine begins like another Clytemnestra, her passionate will in perfect agreement with the curse that uses her, but she is made to discover within her mortal gendered self another passion that resists the daimonic power. The curse carries the day as it must, but Medea nonetheless achieves what a fated mortal can—she determines the ethical color of her inescapable deed. When the task claims her, she slaughters her children, yes, but not as a mechanical agent, and not as an eager madwoman. This Medea paradoxically kills as mother, and also as a woman cornered, as any mortal may be, by past actions, time, and causality.

Medea knows that Jason must be the target of supernatural pursuit, and with her first intelligible words she calls on the gods for the destruction of the father, the sons who have been cursed, and the whole house (112–14). What is more, she tells Jason that she is "curse-carrier for his halls" (608).[77] The knowledge that her victim must be damned makes her expect success (764–65),[78] and yet she works hand in glove with the oath-curse through the first three episodes without recognizing her own collaboration. She arrives at the very deed that the daimonic world demands while listening to her own counsel and relying on her own powers. She is suited to her function by strength and temperament, certain of her superiority to all around her, and she has no intention of waiting for the possibly slow response from

---

76. See Herman, *Ritualised Friendship*, p. 126: "A man's whole moral personality was . . . at stake. Being left in the lurch was interpreted as an affront to honor, and if one party ignored his obligations, the other was not only freed of all obligations, but saw it as his own duty to punish the offender."

77. Compare 1259–60, where (with Page's reading) the chorus senses the presence of "an erinys who reports to an alastor" in the plan to kill the children; the degree to which they identify this force with, or separate it from, the woman Medea (1253) is unclear.

78. Compare Xen. *Anab.* 3.1.22, where the men are told that the gods will be on their side because they have kept their oaths while the enemies have broken theirs.

another world; she wants satisfaction now. She could simply kill and be killed, but her real desire is for a revenge designed like an epinician ode.[79] "Many are the roads," she says (376), and she means to choose the finest. The superlative revenge would let her look upon Jason in a condition like her own: living, but erased (as the curse demands) as the member of any future family. And above all there must be no enemies laughing at her in the end (404, 797, 1355, 1362). The ordinary plan needs only courage, but the superlative one demands trickery (δόλος, 391; cf. 783) and also a final refuge for the avenger. And so she wheedles twenty-four hours from the king and lets what she takes to be chance decide which of the two programs, the lesser or the greater, she will implement (389–90). When asylum appears in the form of Aegeus, she salutes herself as already *kallinikos* (765) and calls the oath divinities to enjoy her victory (764), but she still does not recognize herself as acting with or for the curse. She is Medea at the starting line, about to earn a superlative fame (810).[80]

In the opening episodes Medea has manipulated Creon, Jason, and Aegeus like a lion playing with mice (for her leonine quality, cf. 187, 1342, 1358). Her smooth success measures the strength of her anger (though no one of her antagonists is worthy of her), while it also reflects the perfect unanimity between her will and the curse that would use her hand. Now, however, at the moment of full opportunity, the agreement between the daimonic power and the woman begins to break down. The first hint of strain comes as Medea discusses her confirmed plans, her *bouleumata* (772; cf. 769), with the women of Corinth. The initial phases, the tricking of Jason and the despatch of poisoned wedding gifts, she relishes, but when she comes to that other "job that must be done" (ἔργον ἐργαστέον is what she calls it, 791), her tone shifts. If Jason's house and line are to be entirely dissolved (as her revenge and the curse demand), the children too must be killed. "I wail over it," Medea begins, and she speaks of the boys as "children / mine!" with the "mine" strongly enjambed (792–93). Even this angry lioness has a maternal instinct.

79. The vengeance/contest metaphor exists throughout: Medea sees the revenge as an ἀγὼν εὐψυχίας (403; cf. 366); the Nurse judges that no opponent will earn the *kallinikos* cry (45); Medea claims to be *kallinikos* over her enemies (767). Meanwhile there are agonistic touches in the suffering of the vanquished (1195) princess (*dromos*, 1181; *palaismata*, 1214). These serve as foil for the last appearance of the metaphor at 1245 (a line closely related to 403 by its urgent ἕρπε), when Medea urges herself toward the starting line of a race no longer seen as the way to a splendid reputation but instead as a long grievous course that will last her a lifetime (unless βαλβίς means "goal," in which case she moves toward a painful end to her life).

80. It is hard to understand how Saïd, "La tragédie de la vengeance," p. 70, can report that Medea's vengeance "est vécue comme une fatalité et une pure passivité."

The slight rift between avenger and mother, curse and curse-bearer, is focused in the hand that belongs to both in the scene that follows, that of Jason's beguilement. He is to be hoodwinked into taking part in the attack on his new bride (in vengeance terms, he will provide access to a well-defended surrogate victim), and to achieve this Medea has chosen a daring disguise—that of the humble and repentant little woman (892–93), a silly denigrator of her own sex (889–90) grateful for small masculine favors. She costumes her voice and manner, and Jason, for all his knowledge of her, is duped by his own fatuity. Meanwhile, however, Medea's hand—the hand on which this perjurer swore—has much to do.[81] It has been busy since early morning, first used like an actor's hand in the supplication of Creon (370), then addressed like a witness-object, even goaded, in the accusation of Jason (495). Now it has to project its strength into other instruments, for Medea means that the poisoned gifts should go from her hands (595) into those of the children (956), thence to those of the princess (1003), in order that finally the hands of Creon will touch them (1206). First, however, as a kind of proof of the beauty of her design, she means to make Jason repeat the very gesture on which this whole ugly retaliation is founded. The little boys, like herself long ago, are to make a "treaty" with him, their right hands joined to his (898–99). And this is where trouble comes, because in order to set the little tableau in motion, Medea must touch her sons as she presents them to their father. Her hand for the first time instead of actively dealing out effects, passively receives a sensation[82] and she gasps ("Oimoi!" 899). Then, pushing the children toward Jason, she mutters, "I begin to understand the pains that are hidden in this plan" (899–900). In a moment she is openly weeping (922), and since her tears will blend with her disguise she lets them flow, but they are nonetheless genuine (χλωρά, 922). They come, she says, from her woman's nature, because she gave birth to these boys (928). She means to use her sons as instruments in a murderous deception that will in the end take them as incidental victims, but in spite of her resolve, because she gave them the slightest touch, an insurgent pity has entered her mind (931).

The scene that follows the successful beguilement is marked by an entire absence of forward movement. Even behind the stage buildings nothing is

---

81. See S. Flory, "Medea's Right Hand," *TAPA* 108 (1978) 69–74, where the prominence of the hand is noted, though it is not seen as the sacralizing object of the oath-curse. I want to thank my student Chris Kirby, whose intense thought about Medea's hand helped me to formulate my own.

82. Wilamowitz believed that at 902 one of the children stretched out his arms to Medea, and that she seized him and kissed him; see "Excurse zu Euripides Medeia," *Hermes* 15 (1880) 496–97. I can see no indication of either of these gestures, but certainly she touches the children at this point; Wilamowitz supposes that she leads them, or even picks them up and passes them, to Jason.

happening because the initial phase of the revenge-violence is being played out in the royal palace on the other side of town, not in Jason's abandoned house. Here there is only Medea, to whom the Tutor and the boys come to say that the princess has accepted her gifts. Which is good news as far as it goes, but the intrigue can still go wrong: the drugs may be discovered or diverted to victims other than those intended[83]—there may be no corpses in the princess' chambers, or the poison may reach Jason himself, thus robbing her of the pleasure of prolonging his suffering as her own will be prolonged (as in Hyg. *Fab.* 25). Success or failure depends now on factors beyond Medea's control, and she who is accustomed to be at the center finds herself on the edge of the action and disengaged. With nothing to do, her vindictive passion relaxes its hold on her will, and when this happens, Medea's psyche falls into an unaccustomed state of loosened discipline, itself becoming the scene of an event, albeit an inner one. Pity, the emotion stimulated by the children's physicality, surges up again, and this time it openly challenges Medea's anger (and the allied curse-force) for command of this woman's mind and movements.[84]

What follows, the section of the play usually referred to as "Medea's monologue," has suffered every indignity that editorial brackets can inflict.[85] Though scholars have proposed cutting as many as forty of its sixty lines, the entire speech (except for 1062–63, which repeat 1240–41) will here be treated not simply as belonging to the play but as being the representation of its central event. First of all, the scene must be read for its stage directions because these indicate a system of visual signals meant to influence the spectator as he heard these lines. Until now, Medea has moved ceaselessly, but at the sight of the returned children she is said to stand stock-still (1005). She had earlier behaved like a woman of iron (264), but now, to the Tutor's manifest surprise (he draws in his breath, ἔα), she seems to collapse and melt (1005). She had entangled Creon, Aegeus, and Jason in a multiplicity of cunning words, but now speech is beyond her and she can only groan and groan again (1009). She had looked boldly into the eyes of tyrant and king, but now she cannot meet the glance of a domestic, and when she does lift her eyes they are

---

83. Like Creusa's poison in Eur. *Ion;* for the magic practice that strikes the wrong target as a standard fairy-tale motif, see A. H. Krappe, "La robe de Dejanire," *Rev. Et. Grec.* 52 (1939) 565–72; J. Fontenrose, "The Sorrows of Ino and Procne," *TAPA* 79 (1948) 125 ff.; S. P. Mills, "The Sorrows of Medea," *CP* 75 (1980) 289–96.

84. Note that Seneca places his close imitation of this monologue (*Med.* 893–958) after the coming of the messenger; his heroine is in command of the facts and in position to make a decision. She also has a strong ego that observes and supervises the debate.

85. See Appendix, Medea's Monologue, pp. 273–287 below, for a review of the complex debate over the text and a defense of the interpretation offered here.

drowned in tears (1012). The actor, in fine, is to signal an altered mental state even before he attacks the notorious lines that record the debate going on within Medea's mind.

The larger blocking of the scene is likewise implicit in the text. Medea has evidently gone well forward to watch for her emissaries, so that the Tutor comes upon her almost as soon as he is visible. They stand together long enough for the Tutor to suggest a likely disguise for Medea's sudden grief—she must mourn the coming separation (1017–18)—and then the old man and the children move on at her command, across the playing space and toward the house-door at the rear. Their backs are turned and they are already dedicated to the interior, so that Medea, looking after them, does not address listening and responding secondary players, but only three outlines. When they reach the door, however, the children turn and look back, smiling at their mother (1040–41). And they linger there through her more and more excited speech, marshaled toward the still unopened door by the Tutor when she tells them to go in (1053), but running out to her when, moving upstage, she reaches to touch them (1067–69). The door evidently opens but the Tutor waits until, at Medea's second command (1076), the children run back to him and all three exit. This leaves Medea still well forward and probably on her knees, since she will have sunk down to embrace the boys. These children, incidentally, are still young enough to enter the royal women's quarters and garner kisses there (1141–42); the youngest is able to walk, to understand instructions, and to carry a parcel, so he is perhaps three, his brother four or five years old.

Now to the Monologue itself. Because she is still formally in the presence of the Tutor, Medea begins her speech (1021) with calculated deceit, pretending that she means to go away while the children live on in Corinth. This time, however, the man she would fool is only a servant with his back turned, and the challenge is not sharp enough to distract her from the felt presence of the children. Her feigned regret overextends itself in an evocation of the delights the little boys' company would have brought (1032–35), then suddenly runs out of control, a real emotion instead of an imitation. And just at that moment the two little figures pause, glance back, and laugh (1040–41). She looks at their small bodies and sees the culmination of her perfect vengeance plan described now in palpable flesh. It is not just the abstract *genos* of Jason that she means to destroy but these immediate laughing children, and at this recognition rebellion breaks out in her mind.

Up to this point Medea's whole being has been flooded with a harshly confident daring or courage (αὐθαδία, 1028) that has its source in her heroic heart (καρδία, 1042). Under its unchallenged influence she has used her mind to develop her vengeance plans (βουλεύματα, 1044) and carry out their first phase, and until now it has dominated her speech. The children's aspect and gestures, however, provide a stimulus that brings another psychic tendency into Medea's spirit (her *thymos,* a vital, breathy, chest-located organ that can translate impulse into physical action),[86] crowding her Courage. This softer counterimpulse of maternity (called Cowardice, κάκη, 1051, when the vengeance thrust controls Medea's speech)[87] first whispers a half-simulated complaint against the plans of Courage (1028). Then, after the children have turned and smiled, it takes a stronger hold on Medea's tongue so that for the next few moments she speaks like a ventriloquist's dummy shared by two speakers, one harsh and one soft. Two impulses strive for control of her *thymos* and so of her speech, and their conflict is introduced by Medea's cry (αἰαῖ, 1042) at the enfeebling sensation caused by a recession of Courage. Briefly invested by the newcomer, Cowardice, she turns to the women of the chorus and gasps, "I could never do it. I will take the children with me—goodbye, revenge!" (1044). This lapse causes an outraged Courage to break in once more and scold Cowardice for introducing soft words into the mind (φρήν) that each of them would control (1052). "Am I to be laughed at for letting enemies go? It must be done!" (1049–51). Her spirit once again dominated by this assertive Courage, Medea orders the children out of sight as her restored daring proclaims the coming revenge (which is called simply χείρ, the work of the hand, 1055). With a slight accommodation to the mixed tendency of Medea's present mind, Courage even pretends that the killing will be a kind of sacrifice (1054), but maternal Cowardice is not appeased. It takes back Medea's voice and breaks in with, "No, my *thymos!* Don't *you* make that sacrifice! Spare the children—let them go!" (1056–57).[88] Implicitly admitting that escape with two small children is impossible, this softer voice urges, "Even if they aren't present, they will be a source of cheer because they live" (1058).[89]

86. R. B. Onians, *The Origins of European Thought* (Cambridge, 1987), pp. 93 ff. and the bibliography cited in Appendix, Medea's Monologue, p. 277 n. 17 below.

87. In Seneca's very similar version of this inner struggle (*Med.* 893–958) these two impulses are called, on the one side, *ira* (902, 916, etc.), *furor* (930), and *dolor* (907, 914, etc.), as belonging to her wifely self; and on the other side, *amor* (938, cf. 897), *pietas* (943–44), *pudor* (900), and *horror* (926), as belonging to her persona as mother; cf., e.g., 927–28: "ira discessit loco / materqua tota coniuge expulsa redit."

88. So, when Ion in retaliation would kill his mother, the Delphic priestess says μὴ σύ γε (Eur. *Ion* 1335), i.e., another might do it, but there is a particular reason (kinship) why you should not. Cf. also Thgn. 1031, likewise counseling *thymos* to relinquish retaliation.

89. Reading κεἰ μὴ μεθ' ἡμῶν ζῶντες εὐφρανοῦσί σε, as proposed by Hermann, and accepted by Pohlenz; see O. Regenbogen, "Randbemerkungen zur Medea," *Eranos* 48 (1950) 21 ff. Cowardice captures Medea's voice, but addresses a *thymos* wherein Courage still has the greater influence.

This is arrant foolishness, since children who took part in a plot against the throne will obviously not live on in Corinth, and it causes Courage to break in with an angry oath. "By all the destructive spirits of Hades, I will never hand my sons over to enemies who will maltreat them" (1059–61). And with that, the aggressive, honor-regarding impulse imposes what seems to be the last word, a clinching argument from necessity. "The thing is decided," says Courage, "there is no way out, because the crown already rests on the princess' head and the bride expires in her robes" (1064–66).

At this point, two-thirds of the way through the speech, the debate proper is over, leaving the revolt of maternal pity (defined as Cowardice) apparently suppressed, the victory of vengeance (defined as Courage) apparently assured. As a simultaneous report of an internal war coming direct from the battleground, the device of the two voices that issue from a torn spirit has been consummately theatrical. The ultimate power of the monologue, however, is owed to its strong epic overtones, for this projection in speech of an inner struggle likens Medea to familiar Homeric warriors. She has addressed her *thymos* and analyzed her situation much as Odysseus does in the *Iliad* (11.404–13; cf. Menelaus, 17.91–105; Agenor, 21.552–70; Hector, 22.99–130): retreat will be cowardly, attack will mean honor, therefore she must attack. This echo, however, only emphasizes the immeasurable difference between hers and a battlefield situation, since what Odysseus chooses as courageous is an act that supports friends, while her Courage calls for the killing of small sons. Indeed in ethos, though not in form, Medea's inner argument comes much closer to the famous conversation of Hector and Andromache, as a hero-Medea returns for an instant to a hearth within herself, there to hear a maternal voice begging that the young and helpless should be spared. Her courageous part, like Hector's, rejects such pleas and sends her back to "battle," but here again the epic doublet serves to identify Medea's special case. Like him, she would take a last farewell of the family members who will be destroyed, but she does not have the singleness and strength of the great Trojan prince. Full of heroic battle resolve, she calls the boys back from the palace door, and the result is psychic disaster.

Medea is no helmeted warrior. However strong her need for revenge, however forceful the push from the daimonic world, she is without armor against the poignant physical bliss of a child's softness and candor (1074). She touches small hands, kisses fresh mouths, and marvels at the structure of noble little heads (1071–72). Then in a fright she sends her sons scurrying into the house, for her avenger self cannot bear to look at them. It is unmanned and defeated by the suffering in store for it (1077), now all too real because sense stimuli arriving through eye and ear and hand have revived her pitying, cowardly maternity. The ideal of honor remains, and also the vocabulary, but the vengeance impulse can no longer command, and as she observes her inner collapse Medea concludes almost clinically:

καὶ μανθάνω μὲν οἷα δρᾶν μέλλω κακά,
  θυμὸς δὲ κρείσσων τῶν ἐμῶν βουλευμάτων,
ὅσπερ μεγίστων αἴτιος κακῶν βροτοῖς.

Certainly I understand that what I mean to do is cowardly,
but my impassioned will is stronger than my vengeance plans
—such is the cause of men's greatest sufferings.

(1078–80)

Medea had feared the laughter of enemies, but the laughter of her own children (1041, 1049) has brought her avenging self to this defeat. She had meant to use her violent hand against her sons, but having kissed their dear fists (1070), she cannot. She still sees vengeance as a splendid and heroic task, its loss a disaster, and she is ashamed of the softness that has invaded her, but she is helpless before it. She has decided nothing, and irresolution is the greatest of evils (1080), but in an overwhelming rush of weakness she has come to feel that she cannot complete the finest of revenges.[90] Her impulse to cherish the children and keep them from harm is stronger even than her impulse to restore her own honor by making Jason suffer.

Medea must have knelt to embrace the little boys, and when her speech ends she probably sinks to the ground, for she has arrived at perfect *amechania*.[91] The chorus had doubted that she could perform the final part of her intrigue (856–57), and she has now confirmed that doubt. "I could not do it," she has said of the child-killing (1044), but she has not discovered anything else that she might do. She is, perhaps for the first time in her life, without a plan. Her pleading maternal pity has babbled of taking the boys with her or leaving them here, but these are both impossible notions. If the poisons have done their work, and her reason suggests that they have, then her sons will now be killed on sight like herself, as accessories to murder. An adult might conceivably attempt an escape, but no pursued criminal could run in search of the necessary cart or ship (1022–23) with two small children tagging along, and she has sworn not to abandon them. In the next

---

90. See Appendix, pp. 273–281 below, for detailed discussion of the debate over the reading of 1079–80.

91. The *thymos* can be seized by *amechania*, as Odysseus' was when the Cyclops ate his shipmates and he was unable to resist (*Od.* 9.295).

few minutes, then, Medea can expect to be taken and stoned to death, along with her sons. That is where her emergent maternal pity has left her, and the chorus offers what bitter consolation it can find with a song about the inevitable griefs of parenthood (1081–1115).

For Medea the moment is comparable to Electra's perfect hopelessness as she embraced what she thought were her brother's ashes. For the spectator, however, the experience is opposite, for he who watches the Sophoclean play knows that a happy recognition and a swift resolution are just ahead, whereas he who watches Medea's collapse is filled with conflicting responses. He is relieved, for like the chorus, he wants Medea to spare the children, and yet he cannot rejoice because the present danger is intense, and also because (again like the chorus) he wants to see the perjurer punished. Probably he is familiar with stories in which the children were at this point killed by angry Corinthians—he may even know the old tale of their accidental death in the course of an immortalization process[92]—but nothing seems to point toward any such resolution in the present drama. Its action has concentrated entirely on Medea's revenge, and the Athenian theatergoer doesn't need Aristotle to tell him that the major deed of a tragedy cannot be well begun and then simply abandoned for lack of enthusiasm (cf. *Poet.* 53b). Medea's present immobility thus comes as a welcome drop in tension and an enriching shift in tone, but it is extremely unsatisfactory, and the dramatist does not prolong it. A breathless servant arrives to say that a strange and horrid event has occurred at the palace, and that Medea must save herself however she can. He has come shouting, "Run! Run!" and this brings Medea to her feet, but she doesn't move. When told that the princess and Creon have died from the poison, she cries, "Splendid!"—glad to have done at least this much harm. She insists on a full report, though angry Corinthians are presumably on their way, and what she learns (from one of the longest and most elaborate speeches to survive from the Attic stage) causes her to resume her role as heroine of a tragedy of revenge.

As the Servant delivers this messenger speech, players, chorus, and audience all watch an imaginary drama in which Medea has no visible part. At first almost baroque comedy, it shifts for a moment to ritual parody, then closes as an apocalyptic revelation of the instability of the human form. A figure of Vanity appears at the opening, a pouting princess made happy by golden gifts and her own looking glass, smiling, as this Euripidean common man says, "at the lifeless image of her flesh" (1162). The princess is throned like a bride,[93] surrounded by handmaids; then, having decked herself out,

92. See above, n. 1.

93. See H. Lohmann, "Das Motiv der Mors immatura," in *Kotinos: Festschrift E. Simon* (Mainz, 1992), pp. 103–13, esp. 110.

she moves into a stately dance (1164), but instead of wearing her ceremonial costume, it wears her. Now the rite places its dancer on a throne while an old woman, expecting the epiphany of some maddened god, gives the sacrificial cry (1172–73). The girl answers with an antiphonal call (ἀντίμολπος ὀλολυγῆς κωκυτός, 1176–77) and the women around her split into two sections that run away for help, ending this part of the ritual. What follows is the revelation, a nightmare vision in which the poisoned gifts destroy mortal life through a degradation of living matter that is far uglier than death. For a few moments the central abomination keeps the appearance of a lurching female, but then it slips into an appalling realm where known forms decompose and are confounded. Strands of hair become fire and mix with blood to blot out features (1186–87). Deadly clothing gnaws and chews the human wearer (1188–89), but the victim—the father now—clings to the fragile web as if he were the parasite vine and it the tree he chokes (1213–14). Flesh oozes as resin would from a pine trunk, leaving the skeleton bare (1200), and dissolving bodies tangle in a wrestling match that peels meat from the bone (1217). In the end, what had been a king and his daughter are become a promiscuously mixed heap of mortal decay (1220).

As she listens to this report, Medea at first recognizes her own design. She had poisoned the gifts (789) because she meant to dress this bride for a marriage with death. She had hoped to erase the new wife as Jason had erased the old, and to attack the wife's father so that no other man would ever give his daughter to this perjurer. As the narrative continues, however, she hears of effects too uncanny to have come from even the strongest of *pharmaka*,[94] and when the agonized princess melts like a waxen oath-figure it is plain that Medea's was not the only magic involved.[95] Something with the unearthly force of Styx water or the Hydra's gore has been at work,

94. Within this action Medea has done nothing beyond what a plain dealer in herbs and spells might do; like Deianeira, she has applied a substance to a piece of fabric, but the audience has not witnessed any major magical operation. Medea once swears by Hecate (395–97), but she does not call her force directly into the business at hand, as does the Medea of Soph. *Rizotomoi* (fr. 535 *TrGF*). Seneca's Medea, on the other hand, prays to Hecate for exactly the effects that occur here, and hears her response (*Med.* 833–43). See M. Schmidt, "Sorceresses," in *Pandora*, ed. E. Reeder (Princeton, 1995), pp. 57–61, esp. 59: "Medea is little more than a woman who is particularly apt at mixing poison."

95. In ordinary magical operations one might melt, burn, or mutilate a manikin, but one did not expect the victim's sufferings to be a literal version of these operations: "bind him" meant make him unable to move, "melt him" meant make him unable to resist, etc. Even in the Babylonian parallels wherein the Sun was asked to execute curses upon practitioners of witchcraft while petitioners burnt statues and then trampled them in water, the action was metaphoric: "May they come to an end in a trickle like water from a waterskin"; see Abusch, "Witchcraft Ritual," p. 3.

which is why Creon cried out from within the scene, "Oh my suffering child, which of the daimonic powers is it that dishonors you so, as he destroys you?" (1207–8). Medea knows, and the audience now remembers, that though the drugs were hers, the gifts that made them effective—the stuffs and the crown—were the heirlooms of Helios (954).[96] He was one of the gods who had witnessed Jason's oath, and he has been physically present in this hideously chaotic episode. Her recognition of the enormity of what has happened leaves Medea understandably speechless when the messenger finishes, and there is a moment of dead silence. Then the voice of the chorus leader breaks the stillness, saying reflectively: "It would seem that some power (ὁ δαίμων) has loaded Jason with great suffering today, and with justice" (1231). After which Medea announces her conclusion, which is absolute and economical. "Friends," she says, "it is now decreed that I should kill the boys at once, then leave the country. Any waste of time will mean giving them a rougher hand than mine for their execution" (1236–39).

In a sense the messenger's speech has done for Medea what Pylades' few words did for Orestes in the Aeschylean play,[97] for it has reminded her of her otherworldly allies. What is more, the palace horror has shown her the nature of the power that inhabits her hand: it is fierce and undeniable, and the punishment begun under its guidance enforces its own completion because the terms of the curse are not yet fulfilled. Jason has not been destroyed, and there is now no chance of an attack on him; he has been deprived of future Corinthian sons, but his house will disappear at his eventual death only if these present children are removed. That is what the standard oath-curse demands, and meanwhile Medea is cornered by the results of her now partially successful scheme, because the complicity of the little boys makes their public slaughter certain. She has no choice but to return to the letter of her plan, but she does so in a totally altered mode. She must ask her heart now to arm itself against the pity that had earlier captured her spirit because pity, at this point, would keep her from doing what a larger tenderness commands. She urges her wretched hand (ὦ τάλαινα χεὶρ ἐμή, 1244)

---

96. The fiery diadem is the doublet of Helios' ray-spiked crown, the attribute by which he was recognized on Attic pottery. For golden diadems found in burials in later cults of Helios, see J. G. Szilagyi, "Some Problems of Greek Gold Diadems," *Acta Antiqua Academiae Scientiarum Hungaricae* 5 (1957) 45–93.

97. The Messenger's function is also like that of the ghost of Apsyrtus in Seneca's play (958–66), though he only affirms the turn back to vengeance that Medea has already expressed with the wish that she had as many children as Niobe, that she might kill them all (954–56).

back to a task that is now necessary to its human, as well as to its daimonic, proprietor. To do what is necessary now, she must be both mother and not mother, and so she commands herself to forget for an instant
that she bore these children so that she may give them the better of the
two alternative deaths that are their only future (1246–48). Better her
hand should do it than that of some enraged Corinthian (1239). "Afterward you may grieve," she reminds herself. "Though you kill them, they
were born to be your own dear ones" (1249–50).[98] She has made her
decision, and the chorus, sensing the presence of a gory erinys that
serves an alastor (1260), cries out to Earth and Sunlight to stop her
bloody hand (1253–54).[99]

As crude physical motion, the killing that Medea will now perform is
exactly the same as the killing she had resolved upon when she hailed herself as victor in an *agon* of vengeance (765, 792). Here at the climax of the
play, however, a true speech of decision gives her deed a new definition
and an entirely altered quality (1235–50). She still uses an athletic
metaphor, but instead of anticipating the fall of an opponent in a contest
of courage (403), she treats what she has to do as a long and miserable
race that will last her lifetime (1245, where ἕρπε echoes 403). And
it is significant that as she brings herself to commit her act of violence, Medea utters no single word either of hatred or of retaliation. Jason
is never mentioned because the child-slaughter that she will now accomplish has no reference to him but is reoriented so as to become a rescue
instead of a revenge. In effect she will triumph over him, and in the end
she will rejoice in that triumph, but the poet has scrupulously banished any expectation of such victory from the phrases with which Medea
urges her hand to take up the sword. It is once more her reason that commands, but not as it did in the early scenes when the most excellent
vengeance was its aim. Her thought is exercised for the children: how they
may have the least deplorable death. It is not Medea the avenger who now
chooses to kill; it is Medea the woman of misfortune, as she says in her last
statement as an earthbound mortal: Δυστυχὴς δ' ἐγὼ γυνή (1250; cf.
928). In this persona she enters the palace and at once takes a sword to
the boys.

---

98. See Appendix, p. 284 n. 45. Throughout this speech Medea is doing the opposite of
what the Nurse described at 103 ff. There she roused her *kardia* to anger, whereas here, though
she would evict pity, she asks for an act of violence based entirely upon reason, one that will be
as nearly as possible dispassionate. On 103 ff., see J. E. Harry, "Medea's Waxing Wrath," *AJPhil.*
51 (1930) 372–77.

99. They also call her hand αὐτοκτόνος (1254): one that itself kills, that kills its own, that
kills itself (cf. Aesch. *Ag.* 1635; *Sept.* 805, cf. 681, 734).

Medea's voice is next heard from the airborne chariot of Helios which evidently picked her up in the instant that the children breathed their last. From this superior position she speaks in an altered voice, as Vengeance Achieved and Curse-Demon Satisfied. When she killed the little boys, she killed the source of her tenderness, the one stimulus that could bring soft arguments into her mind, and so what remains of her in the exodus is once more in angry harmony with the force that uses her. At some future time she will grieve (1249), but in this moment she feels only hatred and triumph as, like Hecuba, she boasts to her victim's face about what she has done. "Call me beast or monster or what you will," she says. "I have wounded you to the heart as you did me" (1358–60). And from the ground Jason testifies to the completion of his self-curse when he groans, "I shall get no profit from my new marriage" (a fitting lament for the princess!) "and I am deprived of the sons I had already engendered—I am destroyed!" (1348–50). He cannot see why this has happened and thinks a mistake has been made in heaven, that the gods have carelessly sent upon him a destructive daimon meant for Medea (1333).[100] The wiser audience, however, knows that this daimon is the *alastor* whom Medea serves (cf. 1260) and that in striking Jason it has struck where it meant to strike. When Medea laments the children, as destroyed by a father's moral sickness (νόσος, 1364; at 471–72 she called it ἀναίδεια, greatest of such sicknesses), Jason objects that it was not his right hand that struck them. No, but it was his *hybris*, she answers, the new marriage that broke faith and outraged the old (1366); the hand that killed is the hand he touched when, promising faith, he laid a curse upon himself and these sons of his. The gods know, she says, the origin of this "bane," using the word proper to miseries that follow on a broken oath (πημονή, 1372, 1398).[101]

In this ultimate confrontation Medea's "finest" vengeance is achieved. She has inflicted a lasting psychic suffering, in place of quick death or mere fugitive physical pain, and she has watched as her victim begins to understand what has been done to him. From her point of view, she has

---

100. Jason says τὸν σὸν ἀλάστορ᾽ at 1333, though strictly speaking, ὁ σὸς ἀλάστωρ means "the *alastor* that you called into being by speaking a curse"; cf. Soph. *OC* 788. The schol. at Eur. *Phoen.* 1556 suggests "*alastor* sent against you" (citing also *Phoen.* 1593–94) as an alternative, which proves that this second sense was conceivable. Euripides here exploits the ambiguity of the phrase, making Jason intend its least obvious sense, so that the audience, taking it strictly, will correct him: "Ah no! Not hers, but the destruction you called down on yourself!"

101. Horkos is a πῆμα to perjurers (Hes. *Op.* 804); he punishes through the verb πημαίνειν (*Theog.* 232), which can also mean to violate an oath (*Il.* 3.298–99); consequently πημοναί were the sufferings one asked for in a self-curse (Soph. *Trach.* 1189; Quint. Smyrn. 13.379). At *Med.* 1185 and 1368, πῆμα has its less restricted meaning.

forced Jason to look upon his own crime,[102] and she repeats her essential accusation against him, calling him "false to his oath" (ψευδόρκος, 1392). She herself, instead of standing among dead enemies, is surrounded by the corpses of those who were most dear to her, but she has the satisfaction of knowing that they were also dear to this man who lightly dissolved the union that defined them as his. He asks to bury them, he would at any rate give them a final kiss, but it is in her denial of these privileges that her return upon him is finally perfect and complete.[103] It forces from him an unconscious ratification of his initial curse of destruction—the wish that he had never engendered these sons that she has killed (1413–14). To give him a part in their funeral would have been to let him reenter the household and the *genos* which have been utterly destroyed by the *exoleia* he asked for. And meanwhile they, the unfathered offspring of a marriage that was unmade, will be safe forever, protected from their enemies by the patron goddess of marriage,[104] and honored in a perpetual festival that centers around legitimate Corinthian children. This knowledge evidently came to Medea with the coming of the golden car, and she announces it like a divinity from her hovering machine.[105] Her hand is her own again, and the burial of her sons in the temenos of Hera Akraia will be its final work: τῇδε θάψω χερί (1378).[106]

102. So at Pl. *Leg.* 9.872b, the slave who has killed a free man is made to look upon his victim's tomb while he is whipped to death.

103. It is appropriate to remind oneself that in parallel tales of vengeance by child-murder the ultimate punishment came through a cannibal meal; e.g., Tereus, Thyestes, Harpalyce (Hyg. *Fab.* 93), Harpagus (Hdt. 1.119).

104. Medea was associated with Hera in a tale that told how she, like Thetis, pleased that goddess by resisting the advances of Zeus (schol. Pind. *Ol.* 13.74).

105. She is evidently alone with the children's bodies in a chariot that drives itself (like that of Oceanus in [Aesch.] *PV*); it was supposed to be of gold, and the work of Hephaestus (Mimnermus, fr. 12 W).

106. The audience presumably knew of rites for a Corinthian Hera Akraia which took the killing of Medea's children as their *aition;* exactly where and how these rites were observed, however, was for them of no importance. Spectators need not have known of the annual sequestration of fourteen children and the sacrifice of a black goat (whether this was in fact ritual procedure in 431 B.C. is moreover not certain; see W. Burkert, "Greek Tragedy and Sacrificial Ritual," *GRBS* 7 [1966] 87–121). Nor would they need to have sensed this as the fossil of an initiation ceremony, as proposed by A. Brelich, "I figli di Medea," *SMSR* 80 (1959) 213 ff.; *Paides e Parthenoi*, vol. 1 (Rome, 1969), pp. 355 ff. The significance of Medea's announcement remains the same, whether one pictures a temple at Perachora or a tomb in the city near the spring of Glauke. On the conflict between the commentators and Pausanias (who states explicitly that in his time the old rites were no longer observed), see F. M. Dunn, "Pausanias on the Tomb of Medea's Children," *Mnemos.* 48 (1995) 348–49; "Euripides and the Rites of Hera Akraia," *GRBS* (forthcoming).

IV

Medea disappears in the chariot, a conveyance that Aristotle deplored, as everyone knows.[107] Many moderns feel that in kindness to the poet it should be overlooked, but there it is, hanging above the scene building at tremendous dramaturgical risk—"Souvent au plus beau char le contrepoids résiste / Un dieu pend à corde et crie au machiniste," as La Fontaine wrote of a much more confidently mechanized theater.[108] The magic car serves immediately as a "fortress" against the violent hands of Jason and the Corinthians (1320, 1322). It is also a means of escape for Medea, and as such it supplies a balancing mythic emblem to the flying gold-fleeced ram that once rescued Phrixus and Helle and so inaugurated the great adventure of the Argo. Moreover, as blatant spectacle it provides an overwhelming cap to the unseen slaughter of the boys. This has just been represented by a double off-stage cry, a terrified exchange between the two victims that was subsumed into a short choral song (1271–92)[109] in which the child-killing was swiftly restated in a sublimated mythic form.[110] The intolerable maternal crime has, in other words, been given the smoothest scenic imitation that a poet could contrive, and now the chariot completes this manoeuvre by blocking any reconstruction of the unseen horror with an immediately visible miracle. Above all and most obviously, however, the chariot brings the supernat-

---

107. On the use of the chariot mechanism in Attic tragedy, see D. Mastronarde, "Actors on High," *Cl. Ant.* 9 (1990) 247–94.

108. "Sur l'opera," in *Œuvres complètes*, vol. 2 (Paris, 1958), p. 617.

109. It seems probable that there was only one such exchange, that at 1271–72. In no other case is there active communication between the victims inside and those who wait without (as here at 1276/1277); no other victim cries out "Please help!" to a questioning chorus. Elsewhere outsiders can hear the voice from behind scenes, but the victim does not hear those outside (though lines may be broken between the two locations, as at Eur. *El.* 1409–11, 1415–16). Since this is the only case in which two victims are dispatched, one might expect irregularity, but this lyric dialogue between chorus and one of the victims is highly suspect. It seems likely that an unparalleled exchange between the children has been duplicated at 1277–78, where the chorus is addressed and the gladiatorial ἀρκύων ξίφοι are employed; these lines are missing in the Strasbourg papyrus, as are the corresponding 1288–89, where Ino unaccountably has two children.

110. There is no other case in which the cries of vengeance victims are incorporated into a strophic structure (and so given a musical accompaniment), though at Eur. *HF* 887–905 the cries are part of a nonstrophic song. The strophe's representation of a (curse-driven) Medea in the act of killing, cries included, is overlaid by the antistrophe's image of a Hera-driven Ino leaping into the sea (1284–89) in the symbolic deed that transformed the Cadmaean Bacchic child-killer into a divinity. For Gilbert Murray, however, the effect was somewhat different: "That death-cry is no longer a shriek heard in the next room. It is the echo of many cries of children from the beginning of the world" (*Euripides and His Age* [London and New York, 1965], p. 242).

ural directly into the playing area. Because the action has grown out of the breaking of an oath, and because that oath was witnessed by invoked divinities, the gods have been closely interested in all that has happened today—so the mortal characters have told us, and so now the flying chariot proves. Medea had called on her grandfather, Helios, to witness her revenge (764), and he had supplied the instruments of its first phase, the golden crown and the robe that reduced Jason's allies to a tangle of bone and melted flesh. The chorus had later asked Helios to interfere, to stop the killing of children sprung from his golden seed (1252–54), but instead he has sent a radiant contrivance that seems to confirm the crime's accomplishment. In this chariot his granddaughter now transports his great-grandsons to a place of safety and perpetual honor.[111]

Though he was especially associated with Corinth and the Near East,[112] Helios was everywhere treated as a god from the Other Time. He was the folktale sire of Amaltheia or Aix, the goat-nurse of Zeus, and the original race of men were supposed to have worshiped him (Pl. *Cra.* 397c).[113] He was the essential creative force, with Ge the first parent, so that he could be called "progenitor of the gods and father of all" (Soph. fr. 752 *TrGF*);[114] at Olympia he shared an altar with Kronos (*Etym. Magn.* s.v. "Elis"). Because he was the source of sight and blindness, he controlled knowledge,[115] and he was guardian of justice and oaths because nothing escaped him.[116] Helios could bear witness to hidden wrongs and denounce secret criminals,[117] and consequently the fear of his testimony could keep men from

111. In another version Medea flies off to a temenos of Helios near the sea (Diod. Sic. 4.46.2).

112. So at Ar. *Pax* 406 ff. Helios and Selene are plotting to bring barbarians into Greece because barbarians give them cult honors.

113. For evidence of Mycenaean cult, see Nilsson, *NMR*, pp. 412–14, Abb. 55, 158; Wilamowitz, *Glaube der Hellenen*, vol. 1 (Berlin, 1931), p. 115. See W. Fauth, *Helios Megistos* (Leiden, 1995), pp. xvii-xxviii, who argues that Orphics honored Helios as a god of pre-Olympian cult. In Orphic thought Helios sat beside Phanes as partner of the demiurge (Procl. *In Ti.* 40b = iii 131.30D, p. 216 Kern); see M. West, *The Orphic Poems* (Oxford, 1983), p. 214 n. 126.

114. Wilamowitz assumed that this statement reflected theology, not actual belief (*Glaube*, p. 254 n. 4), and he compared the Menander fr. cited by Clem. Al. *Protr.* 6.59 P:ʽΉλιε, σὲ γὰρ δεῖ προσκυνεῖν πρῶτον θεῶν, / δι' ὅν θεωρεῖν ἔστι τοὺς ἄλλους θεούς. We know at any rate that the Sophoclean speaker identified this as the belief of "wise men." Cf. Soph. fr. 535 *TrGF*, where Helios is called δεσπότης. Other appellations were Time's Father (*Hymn. Orph.* 8.10.12 Kern); Parent and Overseer of All (Aesch. *Cho.* 985–86); Eye of Dike (Soph. fr. 12P; *Hymn. Orph.* 7.13 Kern); Megas Daimon among both men and gods (Ar. *Nub.* 573–74).

115. Hes. fr. 148 M-W; Soph. *OC* 868–70; Eur. *Hec.* 1068–69; cf. Pind. *Pae.* 9.4.

116. As witness and guardian of oaths, e.g., *Il.* 3.277–80; *Hom. Hymn Dem.* 26, 62; Ap. Rhod. 4.229; Helios is πιστοφύλαξ at *Hymn. Orph.* 7.17.

117. Hom. *Od.* 8.302; *Il.* 3.277–80; *Hom. Hymn Dem.* 26, 62, 69 ff.; Ap. Rhod. 4.229. See K. J. Dover, "ʽΉλιος κῆρυξ," in *Greek and the Greeks* (Oxford, 1987), pp. 186 ff.

crime (Dem. 19.267). The chorus of the *Oedipus Tyrannus,* calling him "captain of the gods" (*promos, OT* 660),[118] swears by him as a power who will punish, if they break faith, and this is the belief that dictated later inscriptions on graves of murdered men: "Helios, avenge him!"[119] And finally, in connection with Medea, it may be noted that some mythographers gave Helios a daughter, Ichnaia, who (like Themis or Nemesis) could track down doers of wrong.[120]

In Attica the presence of Helios was most strongly felt in popular practices and extra-city celebrations.[121] Thus a priest belonging to Helios took his place with a priestess of Athena and a priest of Poseidon in the procession of the Skira,[122] and he was honored (with the Horae) in ancient children's begging rites at the Pyanopsia and Thargelia.[123] Most significant, however, was his position in the persisting pre-city cults of ancestors, for there Helios was generator and father of the wind-daimon Tritopatores who, as the source of familial seed, were worshiped by each phratry and called upon at marriages as guarantors of legitimate sons and grandsons.[124] It was thus ultimately because of Helios that each man

118. Cf. Ar. *Nub.* 571–74, where he is called upon (in prominent last position, after Zeus, Poseidon, and Aither) as "*megas daimon* among both men and gods." For Heraclitus he was subordinate to Dike and the Erinyes (fr. 94 DK). Helios could cure and purify (Hes. fr. 148 M-W; Bacchyl. 11.101; Pind. *Ol.* 7.58 and schol.; Eur. *Hec.* 1068–69), and so he could also blight and punish (Eur. *Phoen.* 1–5).

119. Ἥλιε, ἐκδίκησον. See F. Cumont, "Il Sole vindice dei delitti," *Atti della Pontificia Accademia Romana di Archeologia,* ser. 3, *Memorie,* 1 (1923) 65–80; D. M. Pippidi, "Tibi commendo," *RSA* 6–7 (1976–77) 37–44; D. Jordan, "An Appeal to the Sun for Vengeance," *BCH* 103 (1979) 521–25. Compare Oedipus in his vengeful curse upon Creon (Soph. *OC* 869), and chorus at Soph. *El.* 824–26, who look to thunderbolts of Zeus and chariot of Helios for revenge.

120. Lycoph. *Alex.* 129 and schol.

121. Note the large painted double disk found in an Agora well. The work of a follower of Brygo, it shows Helios emerging from the waves and was evidently an important dedication; see L. Talcott, "Vases and Kalos Names," *Hesp.* 5 (1936) 333–35.

122. Lysimachus, *FGrH* 366 F3; schol. Ar. *Eq.* 729; Harp. s.v. "Skiron"; Deubner, *Attische Feste,* p. 48. For fourth-century inscriptions recording cult honors, see Nilsson *GGR* 2:315 n. 7.

123. Pyanopsia, schol. Ar. *Eq.* 729; *Plut.* 1054. Thargelia, Porph. *Abst.* 2.7 (cf. Ath. 14.565a), but Deubner, *Attische Feste,* p. 192, finds the association with Thargelia dubious.

124. For their temenos in the Ceramicus, *IG* 1².842, 870; cf. 2².2615; and for cult at Marathon, 2².1358b30 ff., 51 ff.; see I. T. Hill, *The Ancient City of Athens* (Cambridge, Mass., 1953), p. 22, fig. 6 and p. 216; further, schol. *Il.* 8.39; Arist. fr. 415 = Poll. 3.17. According to Phanodemus, cited in *Suda* s.v. "Tritopatores," Athenians prayed to these powers ὑπὲρ γενέσεως παίδων; they are sons of Helios and Ge, according to Philochorus, and the *goneis* of mankind (cf. *Med.* 1255, the choral prayer to Ge and Helios, in which Medea's sons are said to have come from the γονή of Helios); see S. Eitrem, "Die Labyaden und die Buzyga," *Eranos* 20 (1921) 97–99, for offerings from phratries at the Apatouria. Jane Harrison equated the Tritopatores with the Anakes, whose priest had a throne in the Theater of Dionysus (*Mythology and Monuments* [London, 1890], pp. 162–63). There may have been a connection with Hecate: the temenos of the Tritopatores in the Cerameicus (*ΠΑΕ,* 1910, pp. 102–4) is

had his place in family and tribe as his father's son, and so took part in the city's ceremonies. Sitting in the Theater of Dionysus (where in Roman times at any rate the priestess of Helios had a special place),[125] Athenians had seen Orpheus punished for revealing that Helios and Apollo were one and the greatest god of all.[126] They had heard Cassandra beg Helios for vengeance (Aesch. *Ag.* 1323–26), heard old Oedipus name Helios executor of his vengeful curse against Creon (Soph. *OC* 869),[127] and listened as the chorus of the Sophoclean *Electra* named the car of Helios, along with the thunderbolts of Zeus, as instruments of right revenge (824–26).

At the end of the *Medea*, then, Euripides' audience will have seen the play's principal propelled toward their city in the chariot[128] of a primordial, paternal, and punitive god,[129] a fearsome power who guaranteed patriarchal seed, the firmness of oaths, and the inevitability of vengeance. Like Nemesis in the Hesiodic parable, Medea was flying away from a society corrupted by a perjurer who denied his own sons' legitimacy. And like the Erinyes, she was about to find a place in the city of Harmony (832) because she had been in service to an oath's curse-demon (1260). Before she reached Athens, however, Medea would stop at a sanctuary of Hera, there to deposit her freight of child corpses and let the goddess' hospitality rinse the kin-gore from her hands. The boys, the great-grandchildren of Helios, would be honored as heroes in Corinth under Hera's protection, while Medea, his granddaughter, would be delivered by his car to Athena's city. There she was to stay, a

---

neighbor to that of Hecate (*RE* s.v. "Tritopatores," 2777), and at Samos women sacrificed at the crossroads while men honored the Tritopatores with a fire ceremony (Eitrem, "Die Labyaden").

125. *IG* 3:1.313; Φιλίστωρ 3 (1862) 460; *RE* s.v. "Helios," 66.

126. Aesch. *Bassarai* frs. 82–84 *Supp. Aesch.*; cf. Eur. *Phaethon* 224–25. See West, "Tragica VI," *BICS* 80 (1983) 63–67; *Orphic Poems*, pp. 12–13.

127. Helios is prominent among the divinities of the revenge curses cited by H. S. Versnel, "Beyond Cursing," in *Magika Hiera*, ed. C. Faraone and D. Obbink (Oxford, 1991), pp. 70–71.

128. It may be that Helios was depicted driving his chariot in one of the Parthenon metopes, but the piece is so weathered that no certain identification can be made; see *LIMC* s.v. "Helios" no. 30.

129. Just at this time Athens was peculiarly aware of the sun because of Meton's observation of the solstice on June 27 of the previous year, but what effect this would have had on the ordinary man's view of Medea's chariot is anybody's guess (Ar. *Av.* 995–1011 and schol. 997; Phrynicus, frs. 21–22 *CAF*; Diod. Sic. 12.36.3; cf. 2.47.6; Philochorus, fr. 99 *FHG* 1.100; Plut. *Nic.* 13; *Alc.* 17; Ael. *VH* 13.12). The fact that Meton was caricatured on the comic stage does not tell us whether his calculations were thought to have enhanced or diminished the sun's divinity. E. Heitsch, "Drei Helioshymnen," *Hermes* 88 (1960) 139–58, supposed that the Homeric Hymn to Helios was composed at this time, expressive of a conservative reaction against newfangled notions.

terrifying agent of primitive justice, until Athens was refounded in its milder modern form by Theseus.[130]

130. It is usually assumed that Euripides expected his audience to foresee an attack on Theseus by a Medea who had become the wife of Aegeus, as is recounted by Diod. Sic. 4.54 (cf. Apollod. *Epit.* 1; Ov. *Met.* 7.404–24; Plut. *Thes.* 12; *Myth. Vat.* 1.1.48). Because this later story has a double action ("wie Euripides es liebt"), it was appropriated by Wilamowitz as the content of the Euripidean *Aegeus* (*Griechische Tragödien*, vol. 3 [Berlin, 1910], pp. 175–77; *Sitz.* Berlin, 1925, p. 234 n. 3), which play has been thought to precede *Medea*. There is, however, nothing in the fragments from *Aegeus* to prove even that Medea was among its characters, nor is there any indication of a date as early as 431. It should be remembered that Herodotus knew a story in which Medea, with a surviving son, merely stopped in Athens on her way to the Medes (7.62), while Diodorus found a report that sent her from Corinth to Thebes, where she cured Heracles of madness and restored his children to life (see M. Schmidt, "Medea und Herakles," in *Studien zur Mythologie und Vasenmalerei*, ed. E. Bohr and W. Martini [Mainz, 1986], pp. 169–174). Vase paintings moreover give evidence of versions of the tale of Theseus' return in which Aithra, not Medea, has a central role. An amphora from the British Museum by the Oinanthe Painter (*LIMC* s.v. "Aithra," 1.46) shows Aithra presenting Theseus to Aegeus; other vases seem to show an attack on Aithra by Theseus (*LIMC* s.v. "Aithra," 1.25; see Beazley, *Paralipomena*, pp. 512–13); a cup from Bologna by the Codrus Painter, ca. 440–430, shows Theseus, Aegeus, Phorbas, Aithra, and Medea associated in what seems to be perfect amity (*LIMC* s.v. "Aithra," 1.48; see C. Robert, *Archaeologische Hermeneutik* [Berlin, 1919], pp. 145–47; Preller-Robert 2.1, p. 144 n. 8). Certainly Medea appears in scenes of the bull of Marathon from the 430s (see B. B. Shefton, "Medea at Marathon," *AJArch.* 60 [1956] 159 ff.; V. Zinserling-Paul, "Medea in der antiken Kunst," *Klio* 61 [1979] 401–36), but nothing suggests that the attempted poisoning by Medea was at this time a necessary part of Theseus legend.

CHAPTER NINE

The Women's Quarters

Euripides' Electra

I

At the close of the fifth century, two decades of external war and internal conflict had worked a change in Athenian ways of thinking. In particular, the multiplication of political gangs and the related outbreak of murder and retaliation within the city had given an altered aspect to fictional deeds of revenge. Even at mid-century men had still felt concern over the possibly softening effects of too much civilization, and celebrations meant to perpetuate wild virtues were important in the civic calendar. Athenians had still gathered in the theater to share in a subversive nostalgia for alternate forms of association, whether as warriors or as hunters, and to borrow a sense of individual potential from heroes who were insubordinate even to the gods. After Syracuse, however, Attic citizens, like others in time of civil war, were, in Thucydides' phrase, inventing "ever more ingenious attacks and revenges ever more grotesque" (3.82.3). Civic disorder was actual, and consequently the deed of violent self-assertion began to lose its poetic attractions. Retaliation had become an everyday fact and a source of commonplace fear,[1] as men grown all too wild threatened the actual secular order. In these new circumstances, enormous crimes could no longer serve, even in fiction, as atavistic assertions of mortal vitality.[2] The traditional matter of

---

1. Thucydides' description of cities in throes of civil war will suit Athens in this period; see W. Burkert, "Die Absurdität der Gewalt und das Ende der Tragödie," *A&A* 20 (1974) 97–109.
2. G. Herman, "How Violent was Athenian Society?" in *Ritual, Finance, Politics,* ed. R. Osborne and S. Hornblower (Oxford, 1994), pp. 99–117, describes the coexistence of two codes, a "primitive" one that valued retaliation, and a "civilized" one "according to which retal-

tragedy was too common to be splendid, and revenge tragedy, in particular, faced a new system of problems, because its central deed, instead of being too orderly and too close to justice for the Dionysiac purpose, was now too banal in its evident disruptiveness. It might evoke a simple sordid fear, but not awe, and meanwhile it might also, like comedy, rouse a kind of satisfied envy among those who dreamed of disabling their own enemies. These dangers are met in different ways in the last of the Attic vengeance plays to survive, Euripides' two treatments of the great Atreid revenge.[3] The *Electra* and the *Orestes* represent a genre that knows it has lost its footing; they question the tragic mode but also the changed society that it no longer suits, and they interest themselves in psychology, as the older plays (whose characters were ruled by individual honor and the exigencies of fate) had not done.

The *Electra* is often treated as a botched job, a sensational piece in which a traditional plot interferes with a wonderfully modern portrait of a woman who is sexually deprived.[4] There are some who would read it as a serious denunciation of the "indecency" of all revenge, and a protest against its glamorization in Greek myth and legend.[5] And finally there are those who see the play as absurdist, an attempt to find a form that might reflect the new "gangster morality" of the end of the century.[6] It will be argued here that this play offers, not a portrait of a pathological human being, but the

iation was a crime and failure to retaliate a virtue" (p. 109). This description is more applicable to the fourth than to the fifth century, and exaggerates the opposition, since the second code did not deny the value of striking back but merely shifted the locale of retaliation into the law courts.

3. *Orestes* was produced in 408 B.C.; *Electra* is generally placed between 420 and 410 B.C.; see A. M. Devine and L. Stephens, "A New Aspect of the Evolution of the Trimeter," *TAPA* 111 (1981) 43–64, esp. 47–49. There is much argument over the temporal relation of this *Electra* to the Sophoclean, on the futility of which see W. Steidle, *Studien zum antiken Drama* (Munich, 1968), p. 82.

4. "A deft and damning portrait of a matricidal woman in action" (D. Conacher, *Euripidean Drama* [Toronto, 1967], p. 203). If Electra speaks of hypothetical suicide—the only feasible plan, should Orestes be taken in the first part of the revenge (755; cf. 687, 696–98)—this is Euripides' indication of the "depressive side of her hysterical character" (G. Arnott, "Euripides and the Unexpected," *G&R* 20 [1973] 49–64, esp. 51 n. 1). B. Knox described an Electra who acts from "paranoiac jealous hatred" (*Word and Action* [Baltimore, 1979], p. 254). A summary of opinion and bibliography can be found in J. R. Porter, "Tiptoeing through the Corpses," *TAPA* 31 (1990) 255–81.

5. S. Saïd, "La tragédie de la vengeance," in *La vengeance*, vol. 4, ed. R. Verdier (Paris, 1987), p. 71.

6. J. Kamerbeek, *The Plays of Sophocles*, vol. 5, *The Electra* (Leiden, 1974), p. 8: "the tragedy of the absurd." A. Michelini notes deliberate confusions of genre in a play that aims at ambiguity and discontinuity; see *Euripides and the Tragic Tradition* (Madison, 1987), pp. 181–230. M. Heath, *The Poetics of Greek Tragedy* (Stanford, Calif., 1987), pp. 71–80, describes *Electra* as melodrama decorated with ingenuity and paradox.

representation of a heroic human action in its decadence. Taking advantage of a story that provides two assassins and two avengers, Euripides has split the return of blood for blood so as to bring the classic act of patriarchal revenge into contact with a deed of visceral resentment. The first of these has some of the grotesque simplicity of the *Cyclops,* the second is a vengeance from the gynaikeion, and the two join in a final hybrid achievement that is simultaneously archaic and all too contemporary. Here, says this play, is a solemn and god-inspired crime, as such a crime would be were it committed today—a debased deed but still a bit of chaos grander than mere political disorder.

The *Electra* is charged with an unnerving atmosphere somewhere between the splendid uncanniness of the old tragic stage and the banal fearsomeness of actuality, and the fact that this is neither a conventional vengeance play nor a realist alternative is expressed at the outset in the stage topography. The drama is located in a nontragic spot that is neither magnificent nor sordid, neither city nor country, neither mythic nor actual. This place is on the boundary between Argos and non-Argos, where there is a habitation that is something between palace and hut, and the action is carried out by creatures who are neither noble nor base, exemplified by the first to appear, a man of good family who digs in the ground, a husband who does not sleep with his wife. As might be expected, this place on the edge is negatively ordinary and secular; except for the usual small table for offerings at the cottage door,[7] nothing suggests the existence of any divinity—no statue, shrine, or tomb is to be seen, nor does any report of a dream create a sense that Hades and the dead are near. In the *Electra*'s opening scenes Delphi is mentioned only as a place of "the god's mysterious cults" (87), and Orestes will later describe Apollo as a power that spreads ignorance in the world (971), a tormenting demon that might be confused with an *alastor* (979). As for local cult practices, we learn as the play progresses that these are in such a state of dysfunction that a murderous usurping tyrant can offer a sacrifice to the Nymphs in gratitude for his success. Finally, it is not just this chosen physical locale that announces an alienation from the conventions that ordinarily lend grandeur to stage revenge. The timing likewise announces the same avoidance of any heightening effects, for this play's "today" is described as not the day of a great festival that is to be celebrated, not here but nearby, and by a group among whom the play's principal does not take her place. Hera, the goddess of marriage, is imminent but elsewhere because in this playing area marriage means either the palace-copulation of a pair of adulterous assassins or the rustic noncoupling of a princess with a laborer.

---

7. This might be a conical *agyieus* stone; cf. schol. Ar. *Vesp.* 875; Eur. *Phoen.* 61, and see P. Arnott, *Greek Scenic Conventions* (Oxford, 1962), p. 45.

For the marginal world of this nongeneric tragedy the poet has contrived various baroque and self-conscious scenic effects. His Electra does not sit on the palace steps in splendid rags, but she is like Sophocles' heroine in that she resists her enemies by overplaying her role and proclaiming her suffering through conspicuous costume and gesture (58).[8] She has hacked off her hair[9] and dressed herself like a peasant's wife, and she insists on doing unnecessary physical work; she puts down her humble water jar only so that she can indulge in the full gestures of lament. Then, when she is in the middle of a lyric reconstruction of Agamemnon's death, complete with the traditional bath and bloody axe, a chorus of young women dressed to the nines and wearing golden jewelry interrupts her. The consequent ill-matched grouping of happy girls soon to be brides with a single desperate woman who is both married and unmarried occupies the stage through the rest of the action, and it will soon transform itself into something inconceivable, a female *komos* that gives out the triumphant Olympic cry when two men enter carrying a dead body.[10] After which these girls who are dressed for Hera take part in an almost farcical bit of business as this first corpse is hastily bundled behind the scenery because she who is to be the second has just come into view. This suspenseful anomaly is then absorbed by an exaggerated parody of a god-come-to-visit tableau, as a splendid carriage like that of Agamemnon[11] draws up before a lowly hut, and a wondrous female steps out. She is given "hospitality," but she is recognized as one whose powers are betrayal and death, and her reception brings blessedness neither to host

8. Until the arrival of Orestes this is her only mode of revenge, but modern critics are almost personally offended—e.g., M. O'Brien, who calls her "the most ostentatious martyr in Greek tragedy" ("Orestes and the Gorgon," *AJPhil.* 85 [1964] 13–19, esp. 28). Contrast the more sympathetic judgment of Michelini, *Euripides*, pp. 189–91.

9. If Thomas Love Peacock was right in identifying chopped hair as a sign of chastity, then this shorn Electra will face the celestially coiffed Clytemnestra as sexual purity contrasted with criminal sexuality; see "Electra's Hair," *AJPhil.* 116 (1995) 319.

10. A. Henrichs, "Why Should I Dance?" *Arion* 3.1 (1994–95) 89, speaks of Electra's "refusal to perform the victory dance for Orestes," but it is rather a division of labor; the chorus sings, "You attend to the crowns while we do the dancing" (873–75). The bloodied killers are crowned like victors, thus reversing Clytemnestra's failure to receive Agamemnon with crowns (163). Since the crowns come from the house, they would seem to be the same festal wreaths that the Old Tutor brought, and they raise an interesting problem: Are they still on the young men's heads when the three killers come out with the corpse of Clytemnestra? If not, when were they removed? If so, are they kept to the end (is a "victor" Orestes chased away by demons?) or thrown down in the final moments (perhaps at 1196, when Orestes refers to his head)?

11. It might actually be Agamemnon's property; note 320 where chariots are explicitly mentioned among the royal effects now in Aegisthus' murder-tainted hands. For this scene's allusion to the arrival at Aesch. *Ag.* 810 ff., which in turn imitated the arrival of a god, see S. Brown, "A Contextual Analysis of Tragic Metre: The Anapest," in *Ancient and Modern: Essays . . . Else,* ed. J. D'Arms and J. Eadie (Ann Arbor, 1977), p. 75.

nor to guest.[12] And to cap his collection of visual dissonances, Euripides provides a double show of supernatural effects at the close—radiant Dioscuri who hover in the machine, black demons with arms like snakes who swarm on the ground (1342).[13]

Meanwhile the players of the *Electra* enjoy a new sort of psychic interchange that commands a language not quite like that of other tragedy. These stage figures are seemingly more responsive to one another than those of other Attic plays, and being more ordinary they court an easier response from the audience. When, for example, Electra does not at first recognize a man she knows quite well, the messenger sent to tell of Aegisthus' death, she apologizes and explains, with an informal self-familiarity, that she was momentarily distracted by her fears (767). A similar sensitivity to wholly nontragic states of mind causes Aegisthus to foresee a possible travel anxiety in the men he has invited to dinner, and he reminds them that they need only get up a bit earlier to be just as far on their journey by tomorrow night. (This is the kind of remark that has endeared him, a hardened assassin, to critics of our own time.) Or again Clytemnestra can dismiss her grand chariot as if she were any society lady making calls: "Pick me up when you think I shall be finished here" (1136). The tragic tone is lowered by this awareness of the mundane, and so it is also by more naturalistic speech. A typically leveling note is struck early on when Electra's farmer husband urges his wife to hospitality, in the presence of their elegant guests, by saying, "We've grub [βορά, 425; cf. 429] enough for a day. . . . It takes about the same to fill a rich man's belly as it would if he were poor" (430–31).[14] Even the principals use colloquialisms[15] and a slightly relaxed

---

12. N. G. L. Hammond argues from the lack of a deictic in 995 that there were two chariots, but this conclusion is far from convincing; see "Spectacle and Parody," *GRBS* 25 (1984) 375 n. 6. F. Zeitlin, "The Argive Festival of Hera," *TAPA* 101 (1970) 645–69, would see this arrival as a representation of the priestess of Hera on her way to the celebration of a *hieros gamos* at the Heraia, though the choral greeting (994–95) suggests rather the arrival of a divinity, and there is no reference to the sacred white oxen.

13. Of these Erinyes Denniston (*Euripides, Electra* [Oxford, 1939]) says, ad 1342, "It is unlikely that they were made visible to the spectators"; cf. H. Weil, ad loc., "le spectateur ne les voyait pas." Nevertheless, these beings are referred to as present (κύνας τάσδε), and they can only be banished by some imported principle of "taste."

14. Using ἐμπίμπλημι as neither Aeschylus nor Sophocles did, but in common with Aristophanes; see C. Amati, "Sull'uso della lingua familiare in Euripide," *Stud. Ital.* 9 (1901) 125–48, esp. 142.

15. Note "rest stop" (καταλύσεις, 393), "that's your business" (σὸν ἔργον, 668), "I'm no expert" (τρίβων γὰρ οὐκ εἴμ', 1127), "what's the matter?" (τί χρῆμα; 831), and something almost like "OK" on receiving a command (ἰδού, 566). Other examples of ordinary or comic speech from principals appear at 113, 261, 285, 413, 596, 618, 751, 907, 909, 910, 959, 1033, 1078; from the mouths of lesser characters at 439, 606, 657, 831, 840, 842. The density is not as great as in *Helen* and *Orestes*, however; see Amati, "Lingua familiare," and also P. T. Stevens,

syntax,[16] so that at moments this seems to be an Aristophanic tragedy in which players wear rags and call out, "Where's the garlic got to?" (Ar. *Ran.* 987).

This contrived discordance between a sometimes emphatically ordinary stage-world and a tragic plot is restated in the design of the *Electra.* As in the Sophoclean play, the presence of two avengers here permits a double portrayal of the act of vengeance, and this time the two are kept as far apart as the story will allow. The ethical color of an avenger and his deed are necessarily determined by the intrigue, and here there are two markedly separate plans made, so that the brother and sister in effect perform two separate crimes. One of these is open-air and entirely masculine, as two men trick an Aegisthus who stands among his supporters into inviting his own death. The other is enclosed and as nearly as possible exclusively feminine, as one woman draws another with promises of an intimate household rite into a birthing space that is to be the scene of a killing. Of course convention demands that Orestes shall be the actual killer of both victims, but this pair of heavily gendered deceptions allows Euripides to bring the timeworn Atreid legend closer to a wary *fin de siècle* audience.

The Euripidean solutions to the classic problems of the matricidal avenger—overdetermination and excessive horror—are direct and simple. Apollo is almost abolished as counselor by means of human doubt (like Hamlet, Orestes is not sure of the quality of the nonhuman voice he has heard, 979), while Orestes is almost excused from his matricide by the thrust of his sister's eagerness (967–84). His own special work, the killing of Aegisthus, is accomplished in setting and circumstances that liken him to the boyish Harmodius,[17] and also to a satyr-drama hero. He has crept across a forbidden boundary to the very edge of enemy territory (96) because like his Aeschylean namesake he wants to take possession of his patrimony and enter the world of men, but this boy is peculiarly tentative and without direction.[18] He has come from the mysteries of an unnamed god, but he mentions no divine directive, and though he has saluted his father's grave, he does not name Agamemnon any more than he does Apollo. This Orestes

---

Colloquial Expressions in Euripides, Hermes Einzelschriften, 38 (Wiesbaden, 1976), pp. 64–65 and passim.

16. Asyndeton and direct speech not introduced by speaker, at 831, unless Wecklein was right to suspect a lost line; see Denniston, ad loc.

17. This parallel has been suggested by M. Lloyd, "Realism and Character in Euripides' *Electra*," *Phoenix* 40 (1986) 1–19, esp. 16.

18. He has sneaked in and is ready to flee if danger threatens, not because the poet condemns him as "unheroic" (so T. A. Tarkow, "The Scar of Orestes," *Rh. Mus.* 124 [1981] 143–55, esp. 147), but rather because this is the behavior of a youth in the process of becoming a man.

does not call himself an avenger, he has no plan, and he does not exhibit any emotion. For the moment he hopes only to discover his sister and through her to get information about conditions in Argos. He has come essentially to learn (101), and the immediate stage response to his arrival is a call for a rustic feast (413–14).

Orestes' first move is a bit of classically comic business as he bursts out of hiding and frightens Electra. He knows her but she does not know him, and this produces the familiar stage shriek, "Don't touch me!" from an ignorant party who will in a moment embrace this same objectionable person (223; cf., e.g., Eur. *Ion,* 517).[19] Disguised as his own ambassador (228), Orestes is welcomed with promise of food and ceremoniously taken into the fateful hut,[20] while his continuing anonymity produces a notorious recognition in the course of which the audience is asked to join the poet in chuckling at the absurdity of the Aeschylean way of staging these things. The key figure here is an Old Tutor, a figure of rustic plenty who struggles into the playing area loaded with a lamb, garlands, a flask of wine, and a large cheese (494–99), but nevertheless wiping his eyes on his sleeve (501–2).[21] He has found Orestes' offerings at Agamemnon's neglected tomb, and he falls into a dispute with Electra over the credibility of these as recognition tokens.[22] The resulting bit of satire is made the more piquant because the spectator who knows the fine points of tragic practice also knows that Orestes is just offstage, perhaps even listening. There is amusement when Electra's sense of the high style makes her declare, virtually in his presence, that no brother of hers would enter Argos secretly, just as there is when her common sense condemns the beloved tokens of the *Choephori*. A man's hair would be marked by rough lack of care (and how tactless to suggest comparison with

19. Compare the appearance of Menelaus, Eur. *Hel.* 541; of Hyllas' servant, Eur. *Heracl.* 646.

20. One effect of the set speech (367–400) in which Orestes approves the character of Electra's husband and accepts his invitation is to underline the importance of his entrance into the place where he will soon kill Clytemnestra; it is as if he entered upon his fate, and he says as much with his reference to Apollo at 399. S. Goldhill, "Rhetoric and Relevance," *GRBS* 27 (1986) 157–71, reads this speech (defending it as genuine) as ironic self-condemnation uttered by a "snobbish nobleman" who is himself spiritless and unmanly, but it can be more simply heard as coming from a boy on his first trip abroad, one conscious of playing the role of an adult ambassador.

21. "The comic effect of much of this is unmistakable" (Knox, *Word and Action*, p. 72).

22. E. Fraenkel, *Aeschylus, Agamemnon*, vol. 3 (Oxford, 1950), app. D, pp. 821–26, concluded that this scene, with its "cheap juggling" of the problem of what is persuasive, was the work of an interpolator. Expanding on arguments of H. Lloyd-Jones (*CQ* 55 [1961] 179), G. W. Bond defended the "obnoxious" (so T. G. Tucker, *The Choephori of Aeschylus* [Cambridge, 1901], p. lxxi) scene as genuine ("Euripides' Parody of Aeschylus," *Hermathena* 118 [1974] 1–14). More recently M. West has suggested that lines 418–44 were interpolated by the poet himself, just before performance ("Tragica IV," *BICS* 27 [1980] 17–18). There is a general sense that such "levity" is insulting to Aeschylus and beneath Euripides' proper tragic means.

hers when she hasn't got any!), a man's footprint would be bigger (but perhaps not than hers, since she is played by a man?),[23] and how could Orestes
still wear his baby clothes?[24]

Once these para-tragical effects are exhausted, Orestes is brought out for
the recognition proper, only to become the center of a bit of clowning as
the old man (does he still hold his cheese?) looks him up and down, squints
at him, walks round and round him, checking his person from every angle
(558–59, 561).[25] Among serious figures such conduct would be a provoca-
tive insult, but here the audience is asked to enjoy the tableau of an old
trickster who sniffs out the youngster—the unmasking of a youth who has
sneaked back into town by the old man who first stole him away. Electra
emphasizes the silliness by suggesting that the old man has gone mad
(567–68), but he points to a convenient scar that settles the question of
tokens while it also makes Orestes a childlike Odysseus,[26] himself a more
quick-witted Laertes.[27] The busy old fellow almost pushes the brother and
sister into each other's arms (576), and there they stay, in a long embrace,[28]
while the girls of the chorus salute the coming of this savior with a hyper-
Euripidean song of thanksgiving: "You have come! you have come! O, thou
long postponèd Day," etc. etc. (585–95).[29] The rustic reunion thus formally rounded off has been proposed as a kind of play-within-the-play, a slightly skewed quotation which the audience is to compare with other tragic
recognitions. It is to be enjoyed, not as a representation of mythic reality,

23. If there is an ambushed joke here, it will be parallel to Marston's jokes, in *Antonio's
Revenge*, about schoolboys in false beards.

24. I cannot understand how, according to Bond's suggestion ("Euripides' Parody," p. 11),
the tone of light parody in this scene works to "bring out the unpleasantness in Electra's character."

25. On Orestes' responding impertinence and the general lightness of this encounter, see
J. Diggle, *Euripidea* (Oxford, 1994), pp. 159–60.

26. The scar on Odysseus' thigh was proof of his passage into hunter status by way of wild
contest, κλεπτοσύνη, and an oath (*Od.* 19.396). Orestes' scar is a small-boy version of the
same, borne on his brow, gained as a child, at home in a girl's company, and playing with a gentle beast. The effect is thus most obviously to emphasize his youthful, pre-initiation status, but
some have argued that this small-time scar is typical of "strategies mobilized to disqualify
Orestes" by provoking a negative comparison with Odysseus; so B. Goff, "The Sign of the Fall,"
Cl. Ant. 10 (1991) 265; cf. Tarkow, "Scar of Orestes."

27. J. Dingel, "Der 24 Gesang der *Odysee* und die Elektra des Euripides," *Rh. Mus.* 112
(1969) 103–9, argues that the meeting of Odysseus and Laertes prefigures most tragic recognitions; his parallels between Electra and Laertes, however, seem rather strained.

28. Critics often find that the absence of an extended "recognition duet" shows that Electra and Orestes are portrayed as stiff and shallow, but the unusual duration of their embrace
contradicts this notion; see Steidle, *Studien zum antiken Drama*, pp. 77 ff. A "duet" would be
otiose because this recognition is to be restaged in reverse at the play's end.

29. With ἔμολες ἔμολες, ὤ, χρόνιος ἀμέρα (585) compare τις ἔμολεν ἔμολε δάκρυα
δάκρυσί μοι φέρων, Eur. *Hel.* 195; ἔλεος ἔλεος ἔμολε ματέρος, Eur. *Phoen.* 1286.

and certainly not as a reflection of real life, but as a witty imitation of what happens in the theater when tragedy quickly reverses mortal figures from ignorance to knowledge.

The same old man of good augury who arranged the recognition at once becomes the author of the intrigue now mounted against Aegisthus. The usurper has left the guarded city in order to make a sacrifice to the Nymphs, and this will allow Orestes to approach him, since a man who wants his prayers to succeed will pay proper honor to passing strangers and invite them to the ritual feast (621–37). The only deception necessary to these young avengers will be a failure to identify themselves by name and purpose, for the victim's own "piety" will allow access (as in the Sophoclean play, when Clytemnestra's "funeral" for her son permits the entrance of her killers). This, then, is a version of the perverted ceremony that is a standard motif of the vengeance plot, but moderns respond with outraged religiosity. They are sure that the ritual context of Aegisthus' murder necessarily labels Orestes' revenge, and revenge in general, as both sacrilegious and abominable.[30] Furthermore, they insist that its horror is intensified by a sympathetic portrayal of the victim as not only pious but gentlemanly and likable,[31] so that Orestes is here defined by his dramatist as a revolting creature who defies the laws of good breeding as well as those of religion.[32]

But what, after all, is the nature of Aegisthus' "piety," and what is the particular action in which he is engaged when Orestes attacks? He and his wife are carriers of uncleanness (ἀνόσιοι μιάστορες, 683; cf. 322). As murderers they are properly excluded from all sacred places, and particularly from any religious functions that once belonged to their victim, nor does the fact that this particular killer has for years practiced just such aggressive sacrilege in any way dilute the poison that must spread from such forbidden observances.[33] Moreover, in today's offering to the Nymphs, this tainted killer who sleeps with his victim's wife presumes to address the powers

30. Note, in contradiction, Parker, *Miasma*, p. 159: "Murder at a festival is not explicitly identified as *agos* in our sources." See further Lloyd, "Realism and Character," p. 16, who notes that a person in the act of sacrifice has no special invulnerability.

31. He is "courteous," "a perfect gentleman and a good host," according to O'Brien, "Orestes and the Gorgon," p. 27; "by no means unappealing" (C. Whitman, *Sophocles* [Cambridge, Mass., 1951], p. 157); "disconcertingly polite" (Porter, "Tiptoeing," p. 257).

32. P. Easterling, "Tragedy and Ritual," *Metis* 3 (1988) 101–9, is sure that the audience would be shocked at Orestes' unguestlike behavior; cf. Goldhill, "Rhetoric and Relevance," p. 163, who reports that Orestes kills Aegisthus "at a sacrifice after having been graciously accepted as a guest." For a more moderate view, see Lloyd, "Realism and Character," p. 16, and also the conclusion of M. Cropp, "*Heracles, Electra* and the *Odyssey*," in *Greek Tragedy and Its Legacy: Essays . . . Conacher,* ed. M. Cropp, E. Fantham, and S. E. Scully (Calgary, 1986), p. 195: "the killing of Aegisthus is never explicitly questioned in the play."

33. Pl. *Leg.* 865E; see L. Moulinier, *Le pur et l'impur* (Paris, 1952), pp. 81–82, 86–90.

immediately responsible for the health and cleanliness of the entire locality. The Nymphs are by definition the divinities most outraged by his impure presence because, as the clean water necessary to all life, they are virgins associated with springs, dew, and rainfall.[34] They supply lustral baths to all local brides, as well as the water that cleans away the blood of childbirth,[35] and they are solicited and gratefully thanked for the health and growth of legitimate children. It is to these limpid powers that a regicidal usurper now comes with the perverse prayer that they should protect the bloodstained riches of a pair of adulterous killers, and that they should furthermore reverse their appointed work as *kourotrophoi* and bring harm to the child who is the true ruler of the land (806–7; cf. 833). Aegisthus with knowing impiety prays for the death of his wife's son, while he unknowingly asks also for the destruction of one who is his guest, so it is no wonder that he reads divine displeasure in the innards that he examines (829). And yet this same man is described by sympathizing critics as "a respectably generous host, properly sacrificing to the Nymphs"![36]

With his prayer for his own prosperity and for Orestes' death (805–8),[37] Aegisthus makes a symbolic reenactment of the crime for which he must die, for he would ensure the perpetuity of the profits gained from Agamemnon's murder and would arrange the death of his victim's son. Aegisthus is also made to ratify his own punishment when he invites Orestes to stand close and take a weapon into his hands (815–18). What is more, the poet insists upon our noticing this, for his Aegisthus asks the unknown traveler to take a blade and prove the Thessalian boast of cutting well. What he wants is a display of butchery, but Euripides makes him employ a verb (ἀρταμεῖν, 816) that signifies murder to a knowing ear. Ironies both situational and verbal thus proclaim Aegisthus to be a proper victim of revenge,[38] but

---

34. Νύμφαι ὕδωρ, *Hymn. Orph.* fr. 160.1–3 Kern. Cf. for springs *Od.* 17.205–11; Porph. *De Ant. Nymph.* 14; for rain, Paus. 8.38.4; see F. G. Ballentine, "Some Phases of the Cult of the Nymphs," *TAPA* 15 (1904) 77–119.

35. Bridal baths, [Aesch.] *PV* 566; Ar. *Lys.* 378 and schol.; Thuc. 2.15; Poll. 3.43. Birth, Eur. *El.* 626; Ael. *VH* 10.21.

36. This murder is compared to that of Becket in Canterbury cathedral by W. G. Arnott, "Double the Vision," *G&R* 28 (1981) 179–82. Even Michelini speaks of "sympathetic circumstances in which the two villains come to die" (*Euripides,* pp. 210–11).

37. His phrase is τοὺς δ' ἐμοὺς ἐχθροὺς κακῶς (807); compare Clytemnestra's prayer at Soph. *El.* 648–54.

38. Note Orestes' use of the avenger's irony at 795: he accepts Aegisthus' invitation, "if it is right for strangers to share a sacrifice with men of the city," knowing himself to be the true man of the city, Aegisthus to be an outsider. It should be noted also that Orestes keeps himself strictly separate from all consecrated elements in this rite, refusing lustral water (792–93); he takes no part in the preliminaries (810–12) or in the slaughter of the victim, and at the last minute he demands a fresh implement so that his killing is not done with the ceremonial

these alone do not necessarily rule out the negative portrayal of Orestes that most critics find. The mere fact that he kills at a sacrifice cannot be taken as condemnation, and of course the use of a verbal disguise—Orestes and Pylades are "pilgrims to Olympia" (782)—is the normal ruse of the avenger. In this case, however, there are particular details which, we are told, are meant with their "gross specificity" to produce "a sickening alienation from revenge" and all such violence.[39] These details occur in the report brought by Orestes' servant, who tells how Aegisthus crouched over the ill-favored innards of his sacrifice, and how Orestes rose up on tiptoe behind him, then struck downward with the cleaver that had been given him, splitting his enemy's spine and causing the body to flail about in the convulsions of death (839–42). According to this enthusiastic witness, the men of Aegisthus' household shouted with joy when they saw who had done this rough work (855), and visible local girls who make up the chorus fall into raptures on hearing just how the tyrant fell (859 ff.). Nevertheless scholars of today are nauseated and sure that Euripides meant them to be so—disgusting physiological description, being unaesthetic, can be here only to inspire audience condemnation of this deed. The fact is, however, that this convulsive body (with its verb, ἀσπαίρειν) is a borrowing from Homer. Mention of Aegisthus' muscular spasm puts his killing in an epic category and asks each listener to remember how Adamas twitched like a captured bull when struck by the loyal Meriones (*Il.* 13.570–75), or how the hundreds shown to Hippocoön by Apollo struggled in their dying (*Il.* 10.521). Perhaps some few, alerted by the *Odyssey* echoes in the recognition scene, will also picture this present victim as twisting like the lustful maids hanged as part of Odysseus' grandiose revenge (*Od.* 22.473). Whatever the particular epic memory aroused, however, one thing is certain: this familiar convulsive motion cannot have been meant to suggest that the killing of Aegisthus was "accomplished in an unheroic fashion," nor will it have awakened a "heightened aversion" in an Attic spectator. Orestes can only gain in stature when his enemy dies with epic agonies.

II

Orestes' revenge is true to tragic models but strongly flavored with grotesque comedy, as in a satyr play. As soon as the killing is done, however,

---

cleaver (837); he wears no ritual costume but strips (820) like the butchers on the Ricci vase (for which see J.-L. Durand, "Bêtes grecques," in *La cuisine du sacrifice*, ed. J.-P. Vernant and M. Detienne [Paris, 1979], pp. 139–48 and pl. 1).

39. H. Foley, *Ritual Irony* (Ithaca, 1985), p. 44; cf. Tarkow, "Scar of Orestes," p. 144: "gruesome detail" marks the action as "unheroic." See further Porter, "Tiptoeing," p. 277, who assumes that "vivid use of detail serves to heighten the audience's aversion to the murder," and argues that Orestes is meant to suggest the *boutypos* at the Bouphonia (though that man notoriously uses an axe) and that this renders the scene the more "disturbing."

this young principal abandons his role. He displays the split corpse,[40] but he says only, "I have killed him" (893), without a word of denunciation or a mention of Agamemnon.[41] The honey-sweet pleasures of revenge—the triumph, the retrospective summation, and the insults offered to the enemy—are all handed over to Electra. Perhaps she would like to expose or impale the corpse (896–98)?[42] No, says Electra,[43] but she has been rehearsing some verbal insults (910–12), and she spits out a speech in which she tells this corpse that he was a girl-faced cuckold. She hates him because, as her father's killer, he made an orphan of her, but it is as tenant of her mother's bed that she despises him most. Consequently she does not review his Homeric crimes[44] but tells Aegisthus that he was a failure even as an adulterer. He has been the curled darling of many women, but his royal mate was no more chaste than himself, his children are not known as his (934–35), and people saw him not as ruler but merely as Clytemnestra's servant and stud (930–31). Using only her tongue, Electra tramples on the masculinity of the corpse at her feet (in what is often criticized as a gratuitous exercise in bad taste[45] or as proof that Electra is a sex-starved virago[46]). In doing so, she extends the reach of Orestes' patriarchal revenge, which now answers the insults of Aegisthus and the outrages of Clytemnestra as well as their father's death. At the same time, however, she is taking the part of avenger upon herself as she settles an additional score of her own by returning like for like—one bad marriage for another. Electra's farmer-husband has explained how Aegisthus and his wife, instead of killing Agamemnon's daughter, had given her to him so that any child she might bear would be crippled by its low status (25–30, 267–69). This was, in Electra's words, a "death-bringing marriage" (θανάσιμος γάμος, 247) because

40. The "head" of 856 belongs to the messenger's rhetoric: "He comes to show, not a Gorgon head, i.e., not a fairy-tale trophy, but the very Aegisthus whom you hate," which is to say, not a sight to turn you to stone, but a sight to make you rejoice. On the persistent notion of a decapitated Aegisthus, see D. Kovacs, "Where Is Aegisthus' Head?" *C Phil.* 82 (1987) 139–41.

41. He did, however, formally label his action as revenge while still on the spot (848–51).

42. As Menelaus would have done (*Od.* 3.254–61), and as her mother traditionally did, to the corpse of Agamemnon.

43. Like Pausanias, when urged by Lampon to maim fallen Persians after Plataea (Hdt. 9.78–79). Electra says that *aidos* would inhibit her from insulting the dead, but Orestes answers that their enmity against Aegisthus is not bound by battlefield conventions (905–6).

44. She covers them in a line and a half: "he, a war-dodger, killed the leader of the Greek armies" (916–17).

45. See J. de Romilly, *L'évolution du pathétique* (Paris, 1961), p. 24. It should be remembered that these are insults returned upon the man who danced about Agamemnon's tomb, hooting at the dead for having lost his wife and throne (326–31). Aegisthus' behavior was a perfect example of that encouragement of others to laugh at a victim, that crowing like a cock, which was, according to Dem. 54.8–9, typical of the author of *hybris*, and which, as such, cried out for revenge (Arist. *Rh.* 374a13–15; 1378b23–25).

46. See Conacher, *Euripidean Drama*, pp. 205, 207.

it killed her princely son by disallowing his conception, while it also killed her own gendered potential, which demanded mating with an equal.[47] Electra has denounced this womb-based persecution as a crime for which she will make Aegisthus pay (269), and now with her "funeral oration" she does so, with her balancing erasure of his children and his existence as a male. "You gave me a distorted marriage; now I give you back your own in a like state as I make public all its aberrations. You were no mate to a chaste wife, you were no dominant man, and you were no maker of fine children."

With Aegisthus' depravity as tenant of the palace brought forward as if it had been part cause of Orestes' vengeance, the archaic justice of that initial deed is contaminated by qualities more contemporary, more ordinary, more sympathetic perhaps, but also more suggestive of decay. And since this depravity was, by Electra's showing, shared with a dominant Clytemnestra, her speech also becomes the first move toward the play's second revenge, one that is by this play's showing something quite new—the primary feminine return of an injury that afflicted not honor but sexual status and that came from a female enemy. This second deed, the matricide, belongs essentially to Electra, and it is not, for all of Orestes' suppositions (974, 976, 978), performed for Agamemnon's sake. That much the poet makes plain in the few tense minutes that pass, after Clytemnestra has been sighted but before she makes her entrance. Electra has finished her formal triumph over Aegisthus, and the chorus has approved by saying, "Justice is done" (957–58). The next event scheduled is "mother's arrival" (961), but as the present victim is being bundled into the house, Electra calls out "Hold! there is something we must discuss" (962), because she sees the prematurely approaching chariot of the queen.[48] She would shore up her brother's resolve against a closer view, but at first Orestes is unmoved. "She falls splendidly into our net," he says (965), and she turns his meaning bitterly, "Splendidly indeed—just look at her dress and her car!" (966). The exchange so far is unusual for its sense of pressing time,[49] and it is played before an unusual bit of background business, as servants hastily pull a split corpse through the scene door. Nevertheless it is, up to this point, simply a

47. It was a double substitute for the simple murder of Electra that Aegisthus had first considered (27).

48. Lines have here been assigned in various ways by various editors for various subjective reasons, but the MSS provide a perfectly comprehensible exchange: Orestes directs his servants to take the body in and is about to go with them (959–61); Electra says, "Stop a moment" (962); Orestes looks for supporting troops from Mycenae (963); Electra, who knows the palace equipage, says, "No, it is my mother" (964); Orestes remarks that she is in good time (965), and Electra points to her hateful splendor (966), leaving Orestes to ask exactly what they are to do (967).

49. A lesser melodramatic suspense was created earlier by the slightly retarded arrival of the messenger, accompanied by Electra's anguished, "Where is the messenger?" (759).

slightly unconventional announcement of arrival, strongly flavored with the triumphant confidence of avengers whose plans are going well.[50] In any other play, however, the figure thus announced would now enter. Here and only here does the newcomer take so long that principals who stand between two crimes, one accomplished, one visibly taking shape, can play out a full scene of consideration and resolution. With their eyes upon her ever enlarging figure, brother and sister stand discussing whether or not to kill their mother, and the utter novelty of their situation is smartly exaggerated by explicit Aeschylean echoes. Like his well-known predecessor,[51] Orestes hesitates so that Electra must function as a Pylades (incidentally emphasizing the speechless presence of that figure), but where the old play resolved an instant of reluctance with three Delphic lines, Euripides in this melodramatic moment stages a twenty-line debate in which Apollo figures far from decisively. Clytemnestra is almost within hailing distance, and still the son who must be hidden lingers outside the hut, worrying over the infallibility of the Pythia. The question of whether matricide is imperative if commanded by a god is settled by the traditional patriarchal threat of the unavenged father (977–78, a loose reminder of Aesch. *Cho.* 924–25), but Orestes only goes on to another. Would a real god recommend trickery (983)? In answer, we expect the traditional reference to Clytemnestra's procedures, but Electra is more pragmatic. She reminds Orestes that he has already used a kind of ambush in killing Aegisthus, and this decides him. It is not because of Apollo and not because of Agamemnon that he will kill his mother, but simply because he is already launched on the doing of fearsome things (985–87). After all, this revenge upon his mother is sweet as well as bitter (988)—with these words he ducks into the house, only just in time to miss meeting Clytemnestra face to face.

Orestes is backstage during the crucial all-female scene of entrapment, for this matricide is a crime set in motion without any help from him. Electra has made her own plan,[52] and it has none of the haphazard, satyr-drama quality that marked the killing of Aegisthus. She does not seize an opportunity but makes one, using what was used against her, her gender, as con-

50. O. Taplin, *The Stagecraft of Aeschylus* (Oxford, 1977), p. 297, classifies this as a "long announcement," as if it were easily comparable to Eur. *Or.* 456–69, or Aesch. *Supp.* 710 ff.; M. Lloyd, *The Agon in Euripides* (Oxford, 1992), p. 58, follows Nevertheless, the upsurge and defeat of Orestes' reluctance that occurs here is a phenomenon unlike anything in these simple announcements.

51. Eur. *El.* 967, τί δῆτα δρῶμεν μητέρ'; ἢ φονεύσομεν; cf. Aesch. *Cho.* 899, Πυλάδη, τί δράσω; μητέρ' αἰδεσθῶ κτανεῖν.

52. As she announces at 647; note the stichomythic break at 651–52, marking the shift from the intrigue proposed by the Old Tutor to the one proposed by Electra; note also the separating emphasis of Electra's instructions: first set him on his way, then deliver the message that will inaugurate my scheme (664, 666).

text for a deceptive device—an imaginary baby that will bring Clytemnestra to this isolated place. Her design is a marvel of symmetry, since it was a non-son that the palace pair meant to give her, but nevertheless this trick out-rages sentimental critics. Electra, they say, viciously manipulates a false maternity while exploiting the real "maternal sentiments" of her mother, for they are sure that Clytemnestra's coming proves that there is some good in this explicitly rotten queen.[53] These observations provoke immediate doubt as being culture-bound, but they do at any rate call attention to the importance of this baby-bait. Obviously it reflects the injury Electra has suf-fered, but it must also suit the poet's ethical portrait of Clytemnestra. Why has he caused this ordinarily fearful woman (643) to leave the safety of her palace on hearing that her daughter has a son?

Clytemnestra has been told only that Electra gave birth, ten days since, to a male child (651–58). She has not been asked to come, but this informa-tion brings her at once to a house she has never visited before. What is more, Electra knew that it would. Her trick must play upon one of three responses expected from the queen: innate maternal solicitude,[54] fear of a grandson,[55] or conviction that this birth will increase her own safety. The first of these is at once ruled out when the poet makes his jeweled and flab-by queen congratulate herself on being fitted out (like a temple) with spoils from Troy, handsome slaves taken as "a small return, but splendid," for a lost daughter (1000–1003). That is not how a character meant to be softly motherly in affect is introduced, and this luxurious person's next move is to refuse her daughter's assisting hand, preferring that of a serving woman (1007). The second possible motive for Clytemnestra's swift arrival is like-wise negated as soon as she appears, for a grandmother who has come out of fear, intending to harm a potential avenger, should make her way to the child as quickly as possible, while ensuring a means of escape, once the small enemy has been taken care of. Instead of which the present Clytemnestra sinks into a lengthy exposé of her first husband's failures, as father and sexual partner, before she even thinks of going in to the baby, and she airily asks her driver to return whenever he chooses, making it clear that she is not in a hurry. She shows no sign of having any baleful plan or indeed of owning enough wit to make or even follow one. All she knows is

---

53. Even J. Mossman, who so well understands Hecuba, reports that Clytemnestra here "yields to a kindly impulse and is deceived by a trick which violates decency" (*Wild Justice* [Oxford, 1995], p. 187).

54. O'Brien, "Orestes and the Gorgon," p. 27: "motherly feeling"; cf. G. Ronnet, *Sophocle* (Paris, 1969), p. 210.

55. As proposed by M. Kubo, "The Norm of Myth," *Harv. Stud.* 71 (1966) 15–36, where Electra's fictitious child is compared to other folktale children of exiled mothers, such as Cypselus, Cyrus, Perseus, and Achilles, though none of these tales produces the motif of attack by a grandparent.

that long ago she was insulted by Agamemnon—somewhat when he took away her child, more sharply when he brought back a concubine (1030–34)—and that she made him pay with cuckoldry and death. She killed him for the most sordid of the reasons assigned by tradition, and she is proud of her crime. Indeed, her sense of present safety is so strong and her self-satisfaction so complete that she can comfortably admit that she always acts from self-interest (1114). She knows her own evil and preens herself upon it; it is a little tawdry, but serviceable. At times in the past she may have gone a bit far—perhaps she was a touch too cross with Agamemnon (1110)—but how good it is to have gained these imported luxuries!

This complacent Clytemnestra can only have come here because the message she received suggested, with its tenth-day timing, the presentation of Electra's son to his paternal kin-group,[56] a ceremony that will fix him forever in the status that she, Clytemnestra, intends for him. She wants to weep crocodile tears (658) over an ignominious creature who might as well never be given a name because he will be nobody, a laborer's boy, the son of Autourgos, and never the avenger of great Agamemnon. She is well satisfied that her daughter should have given birth all alone, without the aid even of a neighbor or friend (1129–31), and she is even ready to perform a sacrifice properly the work of a midwife. She is the last person who should take part in any ritual concerning the grandchild of the man she has murdered, but no matter! She exudes a sense of newfound security (as is fitting just before her fall), and like a Chrysothemis suggests that Electra will now wish to enjoy the benefits of collaboration with her stepfather and the palace party (1119). Nor does she make any attempt to hide her relief; she will go directly to Aegisthus, though she does not ordinarily appear in public, so that she can thank the Nymphs for this birth that will make her own illegitimate marriage almost secure (1134–35). She knows that the news will please her fellow assassin, and for this woman who has just explained that she slept with Agamemnon's enemy because she needed a confederate in his murder,[57] the poet has contrived a devilish exit line. She goes to her death saying, "One must always try to give pleasure, even to a husband!" (1138).

It will be this particular Clytemnestra whose throat is cut: a woman who is despicably ordinary as she enjoys the profits of an unspeakable crime. With a victim like this, vengeance must be likewise debased (though the dis-

56. The household *amphidromia* that recognized a child's legitimacy was usually held on the fifth day after birth, the presentation to the larger family on the tenth, when it was assumed that the child would live and the mother might be purified. The father played a central role in both ceremonies (Ar. *Av.* 494, 922; Dem. 39.22; 40.28; Isae. 3.30); see E. L. Samter, *Familienfeste* (Berlin, 1901), pp. 59–62; L. Deubner, "Die Gebrauche der Griechen nach der Geburt," *Rh. Mus.* 95 (1952) 374–77.

57. In her openly corrupt sexuality, this Clytemnestra looks forward to the Duke in *Revenger's Tragedy.*

appearance of a figure of sexual corruption is appropriate at a time when young girls are preparing for marriage). The poet's intention with Electra, however, is harder to appreciate. The scene of entrapment lets her play principal in the tragedy that bears her name, yet it makes her almost botch the deed she has planned. She has designed a neo-Aeschylean temptation in which a regal, chariot-brought figure will be drawn into the house by the treacherous promise of an intimate ceremony, only substituting baby for bath (note the shifting winds at 1147, a whispered reminder of those that blow throughout the *Agamemnon*). Consequently she should put on an emotional disguise and mimic hospitality while engaging in a version of the strewing of carpets—a display of enticements that will address her victim's weakness while it soothes suspicion. None of which Electra achieves, for it turns out that, though she has art enough to make an elegant intrigue, she has no talent for the seductive deception that it demands. She means to appear as an abject new mother in need of purification and reconciliation, but she almost drops her disguise when she confronts her maternal enemy. She ought to overflow with fraudulent womanly need, but this overcandid deceiver snarls like a kicked dog. She ought to suggest a resurgent daughterly love, but instead her every word betrays disgust and resentment until, at the end of her long speech, she finds herself almost openly threatening the very revenge that should be hidden in blandishments: "If blood will judge blood and answer with the same, then I and your boy Orestes will kill you in vengeance for our father" (1093–95). In spite of Clytemnestra's celestial self-satisfaction, what begins as a revenger's ensnarement threatens to become an open quarrel, and the scene, as it looses its conventional definition, develops a novel tension.

Speaking formally, one can say that the poet brings elements of a denunciation or "Gerechtszene" into the business of decoying a victim. Both functions are indispensable to a developed revenge action, but they do not lend themselves to easy mixture because the temptation asks the avenger to lie, while the denunciation demands perfect truth.[58] And it is just this contradiction that Euripides exploits when he causes the necessarily sly work of deception to be interrupted by open censure.[59] The near quarrel comes as a formal (though not psychological) surprise, and consequently it is as if nature had broken through theatrical convention to reveal unvarnished truths about each of the contestants.[60] The vengeance victim is not only a

58. "Um die Königen ins Haus zu locken, bedarf es das Agons nicht" (H. Strohm, *Euripides*, Zetemata, 15 [Munich, 1957], p. 14).

59. The open quarrel, coming where it should not, is a formal surprise for the spectator, as if the first Medea-Jason confrontation had been substituted for the second.

60. Rhetorically this debate is much like that of the Sophoclean *Electra*, but it is ethically entirely different because the Sophoclean daughter is in her mother's power and has no scheme against her, so that her anger, though dangerous to herself, need not be checked.

corrupt woman pleased with the profits of an extraordinary crime, but one eager to boast of having taken her husband's enemy to bed (1046–48). And at the same time her daughter is discovered as preparing, not the secondary and patriarchal vengeance that her brother imagines, but a primary return for injustices suffered by the avengers themselves (1086–93).[61] What Electra denounces is not her father's murder but its sequel, as she accuses her mother of having bribed her criminal lover with what should have been her children's heritage (1088–90). After which, according to these charges, Clytemnestra protected herself and her stolen situation by sending Orestes into exile and sentencing Electra to a death twice as hard as that of Iphigeneia (1091–93). Electra refers to her marriage and the interference with the fruit of her womb, but it is clear that she is also angry over the poverty she has known. Urging her mother into the trap, she says: "Enter this workingman's house, but do take care that its filth doesn't smudge your robe!" (1139–40). She continues, "You shall make what sacrifice you ought, to the daimonic powers," but after such a preface her avenger's irony seems to carry not simple confidence but a load of envious malice.[62] It is not really her father's killer but a mother whom she loathes that she sends inside to have her throat cut.[63] Here then is a new sort of vengeance, a retaliation built on resentment, a violence that looks to the improvement of worldly condition rather than to the restoration of honor, and that takes its most effective inspiration neither from Delphi nor from the underworld but from a jealous envy of those who have won what the avenger has lost. "She ejected me from the house in order to pleasure her husband, she bore him children who now make mere extras of Orestes and me" (61–63).

This disorderly temptation scene defines Electra's vengeance as sordidly misconceived (and in a womanized way like that of Ajax). Clytemnestra pays not for Agamemnon's death[64] but for the assassins' refusal to grant Electra

61. Compare her emphasis in her early "message" to Orestes: ten lines of how poorly she lives (304–13), nine lines of how richly Clytemnestra and Aegisthus live (314–22), nine lines of how Agamemnon's tomb is dishonored (324–31).

62. There is revenger's irony also at 1120 when Electra says, presumably of the living Aegisthus at the palace, actually of the corpse hidden in the hut: "He gets above himself; he has taken up residence in my house!"

63. The killing of Agamemnon is, however, musically mixed into Clytemnestra's death by a choral song that begins ἀμοιβαὶ κακῶν (1147–63) and revives the old murder so that Agamemnon's past death-cries sound (1151–52) just before we hear those of Clytemnestra (1165, 1167). Cf. 1189 where it is again the chorus who refer to Agamemnon.

64. Thus there is no consistent report of his death: at 9–10 he fell by Clytemnestra's scheme and Aegisthus' hand; at 763, 769, 869, 914–17, Aegisthus is killer; at 123, 160, 279, 1031, 1086, 1088, Clytemnestra strikes with the axe. Electra seems sometimes to manipulate her recollection in order to excite her own anger over her sufferings; see, e.g., 279, when she affirms that (like Hofmannsthal's heroine) she longs to hack her mother with the axe that killed her father.

a prize that was her due. She has not been given the marriage that should have crowned her royal girlhood, nor does Orestes inhabit the palace, though both conditions were rightfully theirs. These denials have caused genuine suffering, but, as part of a worldly scheme made by enemies, they are not examples of that unprovoked and arrogant attack on personal honor which calls for revenge. Indeed in Electra's case the audience knows that whatever a woman has of honor is still intact—this is the reason for the sensational detail of her persisting virginity. There was a plot against her womb, an attempt to control what it might contain, but this plot has failed because the adulterous assassins unwittingly handed Electra over to a good man who checked their scheme. As one untouched, Electra is still the potential mate of a nobleman, potential mother of a noble son, as the finale will prove. The marriage with Pylades is not, as troubled critics think, an undeserved reward for a murderous woman (and an unkind slight to her virtuous consort) but objective evidence that she has misconstrued the nature of her injuries.[65] All of which means that, where the Sophoclean Electra brought a pure and ungendered passion to her brother's Delphic revenge, this Electra adds error and feminine resentment to the old patriarchal revenge.

III

The compound deed of brother and sister is an example of vengeance corrupted, but it does not ask for simple condemnation. Instruction on how the sum of the two revenges should be viewed comes as the spectator's emotions are wrenched from horror to an endurable grief at the play's close. The ending, like all else in this *Electra,* follows the formal conventions of tragedy and respects the fictional details set by tradition, while yet producing unheard-of noveltics, and the most astonishing of these is a replay of the matricide. Usually the final display of a punished enemy is accompanied by a retrospective justification that marks the deed as finished, but here Orestes and Electra repeat, not their reasons, but the murder itself. As they bring their mother's body onstage, they are singing and dancing with the chorus, miming the victim's screams and grasping hands (1214–17), the blade that enters her throat (1221–23), and her last gurgling breath (1220). This audience, then, comes as close as any Attic audience ever will to watching a staged act of revenge, and in this case it is a mother-killing. Just as unique, though not so sensational, is the subsequent tableau of recognition destroyed, as two principals who have discovered their relationship and realized it in action now unyoke themselves (1323) because

---

65. It is also necessary that Orestes should recover his status as Electra's true *kyrios* by canceling the marriage that Aegisthus made and replacing it with another.

they recognize each other as borne by one mother to be killers, not brother and sister (1229). Earlier in this day their mutual discovery was marked by a long stage embrace, and so is their renunciation now as the two blood-stained siblings fall into each other's arms and wail, each as if for the other's death (1321–26).[66] Then they turn away and leave the stage separately by the two opposite exits.

Between these two tragic anomalies the machine has appeared in conventional fashion, bearing the Dioscuri, who are Clytemnestra's brothers and her proper avengers.[67] The twin gods interrupt the revival of the matricide and relieve the spectator of his too-close participation in it by shifting the viewpoint.[68] It appears that in heaven these same events rouse, not sensational horror, but a pity that stretches out to all humanity (1329–30).[69] The airborne pair moreover announce truths about cause and effect which transcend mere visible facts. First of all, the death of Clytemnestra was imposed by Apollo and it was just, though what Orestes had to do was not (1244).[70] (The death of Aegisthus is evidently of no interest to the dwellers on Olympus: he is to be buried by the locals, that's all, 1276.) Furthermore, from the standpoint of heaven, Orestes and Electra are seen to have committed the same crime, both forced to act by a combination of Moira, Ananke, Apollo, and an Ate that belongs to their paternal family (1301–5). Nevertheless their futures will differ. As Apollo's agent and his father's avenger, Orestes will follow his traditional course of exile and public cleansing (though there is no mention of a return to Delphi), and he will ultimately enjoy civil power in an Arcadian city that will bear his name (1273–75). He was commanded by a god and will be supported by that deity (1266), but not so Electra. She will have a noble husband and princely sons, as a daughter of Agamemnon should (1311–12), but Argos is no longer open to her, and she and her brother must endure a common fate of

---

66. The standard Euripidean recognition scene is marked by heavy use of vocatives, specific description of physical contact, and references to eyes and tears. These were missing in the actual recognition but are present now at the parting; note esp. 1321, cf. Eur. *Hel.* 634; 1322, cf. *IT* 851; note also 1325, 1332, 1339.

67. On the assignment of speeches at 1292–1300, see D. Kovacs, "Castor in Euripides' *Electra*," *CQ* 35 (1985) 310–14; because no other chorus speaks with a god in the machine, Kovacs gives 1292–93 to Orestes and 1295 to Electra, though perhaps these assignments should be reversed since Electra is technically less contaminated than Orestes.

68. There are those who hold that the audience is meant to refuse belief to what these divine figures say; see, e.g., J. M. Bremer, "Exit Electra," *Gymnasium* 98 (1991) 325–42, esp. 331: "Glaube es, wer kann."

69. The concept of pity has been given a brief gnomic expansion at 290–95; note also its primary place in the avengers' prayer (671–73).

70. Compare Orestes' own sense that what Apollo commanded was a justice that one could not see, but a suffering all too visible (1190).

absolute separation (1305). Her purification will be more perfunctory, but she will never quite cover the corpse of Clytemnestra, and she is left to deal as she may with the remembrance of having put her hand, unasked by god, to the sword that shed her mother's blood (1224–25). Worst of all, the dancing out of the matricide seems to promise that the same agonizing scene will be reenacted ceaselessly in her memory. For her, Euripides has evidently invented a new form of suffering that here touches the avenger for the first time,[71] the remorse that Emily Dickinson called "Memory awake . . . the Disease not even God can heal" ("Remorse," 744 Johnson).

Euripides' *Electra* contains intimations of a new sort of drama. Its situations tremble between bloodshed and farce, it teaches its audience to enjoy suspense for its own sake, and it introduces the notion of a purely psychological punishment for ill-considered violence. Above all it is unusually topical, for with its debased revenge it labels the factional street avengers of the close of the fifth century as womanish in their self-interest and their ignorance of honor. And yet in spite of these signs of a generic shift, two early choral odes give strong indications that this topical and discordant action is still proposed as tragedy. The song of Achilles' Shield (431–86) and the subsequent song of the Golden Lamb (698–746) are usually described as glimpses of a fairy-tale world, meant to intensify the sordidness of this "realist" drama, while this drama in turn denounces them as childish stuff.[72] In fact, however, the ultimate effect of this pair of early songs is to cast a mantle of hard mythic necessity over the unadmirable events that follow. Agamemnon, whom Clytemnestra destroyed, was according to these odes a man greater even than Achilles,[73] as well as an Atreid chosen by Zeus as king and part of the cosmic order. With such a victim, Clytemnestra's old crime is effectively enlarged,[74] and its punishment, though misguided and repellent in the doing, takes on an equivalent weight of seriousness when it is accomplished. There is an abysmal gap between the sung Clytemnestra,

71. Medea hints at it with her κἄπειτα θρήνει at 1249.

72. See, among others, V. Rosivach, "The 'Golden Lamb' Ode," *C Phil.* 73 (1978) 189–99; G. B. Walsh, "The First *Stasimon* of Euripides' *Electra*," *YClS* 25 (1979) 277–89. K. C. King, "The Force of Tradition: The Achilles Ode," *TAPA* 110 (1980) 195–212, argues that the ode somehow puts its hearers in the position of Hector, leading them through sympathy with him as victim into like sympathy with Clytemnestra, so that they finally grasp "the inhuman reality behind the seductive beaux gestes of romance" (198). The conventional icons and epithets of the shield's description have somehow exposed the Trojan legend as "obscene."

73. Achilles, at the close of the ode, serves only to exemplify the splendid valor of the host that Agamemnon commanded: "it was the lord of warriors such as this that you, daughter of Tyndareus, killed with your adultery" (479–81).

74. Indeed, by producing her where we expect Helen, the singers leave the impression that it was Clytemnestra's bed (481) that was responsible for all the Greeks who fell at Troy, an effect enhanced by addressing her simply as "daughter of Tyndareus" (480).

with her enormous destructiveness, and the visible queen who took a lover and killed her husband for bringing home a captive bedmate (1032–34, 1048), but it is exactly in this disparity that Euripides locates a new source of pity and terror. The Golden Lamb provides an emblem, for if an adulterer's[75] greedy theft of a small beast, albeit a golden one, can be written in the skies as a reversal of the cosmos,[76] then tragedy may follow suit. When sordid actions are depicted by its masks, its music, and its settled movements, the result will be a reorientation, but the altered order may still impress men with fear of the gods—the fear that Clytemnestra forgot (745–46). The powers above are more mysterious than ever if they can exercise their will through creatures such as these.

75. Thyestes is made parallel to Clytemnestra, his treasonable "secret couchings" (719–20) like her evil-minded "beds" (481).

76. Euripides tells of the settlement of two phenomena, sunrise and sunset, in east and west respectively, and of two climates, cold and moist / hot and dry, in north and south respectively. In this song, then, Zeus' interference in opposition to Thyestes and in behalf of Atreus was the same permanent cosmic change that is described by Plato, *Plt.* 12.269a. Similarly at Eur. *Or.* 1001–6, Electra tells how Eris fastened the sun's evening road into dawn's place.

CHAPTER TEN

Philanthropic Revenge

Euripides' Orestes

I

Those who want tragedy to show a reasonable sequence of serious events make heavy cuts in the Euripidean *Orestes*,[1] but lop off everything inconsequent or ridiculous, calling it "interpolators' deadwood," and this vast play becomes a bare stick. Others gladly accept aberrations seen as intentional in a play that studies the "moral madness and degradation" brought about by an "obsession with revenge." Some indeed believe that its Orestes is what our century calls a lunatic,[2] so that a crazy text is no more than a reflection of its crazed hero. The argument of these present pages, however, will not

---

1. Note the recent text of J. Diggle, *Euripidis Fabulae,* vol. 3 (Oxford, 1994); also the commentary of C. W. Willink, *Euripides, Orestes* (Oxford, 1986). See the critical summary of M. D. Reeve, "Interpolation in Greek Tragedy," part 1, *GRBS* 13 (1972) 247–65; part 2, ibid., pp. 451–74; part 3, ibid. 14 (1973) 145–71. Lines have been deleted in the name of symmetry, order, sense, seriousness, or simply because they are found to be "inartistic" or "unnecessary." So, e.g., A. S. F. Gow, asked of lines 706–7, "Does anyone admire?" and assuming a negative response got rid of them ("Notes," *CQ* 10 [1916] 81). Compare G. Seeck, "Rauch im Orestes des Euripides," *Hermes* 97 (1969) 8–22, who would remove every mention of firing the palace (1149–52, 1541–44, 1593–96, 1618–20) because such an action cannot be seen as logical. For a survey of disputed passages as of forty years ago, see W. Biehl, *Textprobleme in Euripides Orestes* (Göttingen, 1955).

2. So, e.g., C. Fuqua, "Studies in the Use of Myth," *Traditio* 32 (1976) 29–95, esp. 69; H. G. Mullens, "Meaning," *CQ* 34 (1940) 153–58, finds "a pathological study of criminality." Cf. H. D. F. Kitto, *Greek Tragedy* (London, 1939), pp. 349–54; H. Parry, "Euripides' *Orestes*," *TAPA* 3 100 (1969) 37–53. W. Burkert, "Die Absurdität der Gewalt und das Ende der Tragödie," *A&A* 20 (1974) 97–109, describes the piece more accurately as a protomodern melodrama of villainy and gangsterism. W. D. Smith, "Disease in Euripides' *Orestes*," *Hermes* 95 (1967) 291–307, reads a play in which disease is a "symbol of moral and intellectual disintegration."

follow either of these paths. It will assume that this extraordinary text is essentially valid, but will recognize in it neither a tragedy of psychic deterioration nor a replica of insanity. The *Orestes* here presented will be instead a parody that is stamped with a bitter comic intent.[3]

As a rule, the largest sign of literary parody is an ostentatious display of conventions, both structural and verbal. Parody demands an audience of collaborators and tips them off by posturing and pinning on labels; it treats the assumptions and mannerisms that define the parent genre to disrespectful emphasis and over-marked delineation. It also indulges in allusions, friendly or inimical, to well-known examples of that genre.[4] And in the case of a parody of Attic tragedy, moreover, a manipulation of structure and verbal style will automatically result in a distortion of character, since the *ethos* of a tragic personage always depends upon what he does. Caricature, impossible in a classic work, will thus be among the modes of parodic tragedy.

Parody often announces itself by jokes that take the rules of the target genre as their subject, thus detaching the onlooker's spirit from its own response and directing it toward the means by which that response is sought. In drama, such jokes invite the audience backstage with the fleas and the greasepaint, and this is exactly what Euripides does with a genre joke that is planted at the climax of his *Orestes*. Orestes, Pylades, and Electra are all on the roof threatening arson and assassination, and their enemy, Menelaus, challenges them from below. Only one of the three would-be avengers can speak, however, because the third speaking actor is at the moment preparing to be wafted in as Apollo. This is a familiar fact of tragic production, and the ensuing exchange, as Orestes and Menelaus shout back and forth, is all according to Hoyle. Then suddenly, defying all tragic propriety, the man on the ground turns to one of the necessarily silent figures above and howls, "And what about *you,* Pylades? Do you agree to this murder?" (1591). His words force an audience presumably concerned with blood and fire to think instead about a curious dramaturgical custom, to ask themselves if it is about to be violated, and to remember how in another play this same character did astonishingly open his mouth, after walking mum through seven-eighths of the piece. Menelaus has made a tear in the tissue of illusion, such as it was, and Orestes turns it into a gaping hole by answer-

---

3. Cf. L. Radermacher, "Über eine Scene des euripideische *Orestes*," *Rh. Mus.* 57 (1902) 278–84, who found "Travestierung der Charaktere" and concluded that this was a fourth play. The author of the second hypothesis reported that all the characters except Pylades were "low" and that many of the effects were "base" or "unworthy of tragedy" while the climax was "comic." Cf. also F. Zeitlin, "The Closet of Masks," *Ramus* 9 (1980) 69, who calls the play "the mimesis of a mimesis."

4. Willink, *Orestes*, p. lv, notes the prominence of such allusions but considers them a sign of the poet's desire to give his "audacious new play" a respectably traditional air.

ing for his friend, "He says 'yes' by keeping quiet. It's enough that I should talk" (1592). This "in-house" joke confirms the knowing spectator's assumption that he will very soon be hearing the third voice, and makes him wonder whose it will be—Helen's? Hermione's? that of a god? He thinks, in other words, about the performance of the play, not about the desperate situation it represents, and Pylades is meanwhile left in an uncomfortable fix—does he stand motionless as well as voiceless, or does he make gestures of lackeylike agreement? Either way, he is the focus of an extradramatic ridicule aimed at the conventions of the tragic stage.[5]

As tragic parody, the *Orestes* treats of destiny and man's potential in forms that ring hollow, then comes to a comic conclusion. Proper tragedy shows that a mortal, however noble, however magnificent his deeds, can always be destroyed from above, but this drama demonstrates the reverse. Here we are shown that a man, however bootless and distracted he may be, however disgusting his doings, may sometimes be rescued from his foolishness by an opposite exercise of divine power.[6] Needless to say, this does not mean that the play is in any sense jolly.[7] Its true subject is man's nature, which is discovered to be not merely grotesque and ridiculous but vicious, self-destroying, and defiant of those higher forces that are fitfully kind. Great Tantalus stands in the opening lines of this drama as ancestral cipher for the ungoverned, ungrateful, and unbelieving mortal who spoils his own blessedness,[8] but for his present purpose Euripides uses figures and events made on a lesser scale, so that the vast architecture of tragedy shall echo with emptiness. He opens, indeed, with a young killer who lies helpless on a cot, and he locates this man in a brief glitch in the inevitable unrolling of destiny. Everyone in the Attic audience knows that in the wake of the revenge-murder of Clytemnestra there was a twofold divine action in which Orestes was cleansed of ritual filth, at Delphi or somewhere else, then exonerated from social guilt, usually at Athens. He returned to the individual aristocratic status that was his, and meanwhile his innocent patriarchal

5. D. Mastronarde, *Contact and Discontinuity* (Berkeley, 1979), p. 94, would see him rather "as a symbol of the dumb bestiality of the behavior of the 'conspirators,'" though he also recognizes the poet's "delight in flaunting the unrealistic aspect of the convention." For F. Nisetich, the point is simply to "implant anticipation" of a proximate appearance ("The Silencing of Pylades," *AJPhil.* 107 [1986] 46–54).

6. Anyone judging by the standards of tragedy finds this ending at best "unsuitable for the characters as we have come to know them" (N. Greenberg, "Euripides' *Orestes*," *Harv. Stud.* 66 [1962] 157–92, esp. 157). Note the more sympathetic reading of Smith, "Disease," p. 307, who sees in the ending "what human love and wisdom should have achieved, but could not."

7. As B. Seidensticker remarks (*Palintonos Harmonia* [Göttingen, 1982], p. 101), it is comic but not "lustig."

8. The reference may be to the story told by the schol. at Pind. *Ol.* 1.57, according to which Tantalus (like some in this play who doubt the divinity of Apollo) called the sun a stone; see R. Scodel, "Tantalus and Anaxagoras," *Harv. Stud.* 88 (1984) 13–24.

crime (with Athena's help) called into being permanent communal procedures for trying cases of murder. But suppose, says Euripides, that mankind
had been left to itself in the aftermath of that crime? Suppose Orestes were
simply here, polluted, tearful, and mad, while his fellow citizens decided
what to do with him? What would he have done, and how would his community have dealt with his justice-bearing crime? This *Orestes* is going to
treat of a man who is (like most mortals) both guilty and innocent, both
mad and sane, as he ventures on a life led outside the gravitational force of
divine intention. And it will show not only a hero demythologized but also
a dramatist in like condition—one who deals with an aberrant fiction. All of
which will result in a new sort of suspense because the audience will be
deprived of its tragic certainties. What may such a principal do and not do?
Will the poet bring his unpredictable actions into final congruence with
beloved tradition, and if so, how?

For this play that apes a tragedy Euripides makes use of a double plot.
Half the action is retrospective—a depiction of the community as it tries to
assess the Delphic crime just committed and decide on a sentence for the
criminals. And the other half is immediate and forward-looking—a depiction of the young man who killed his mother, as he responds vindictively to
the treatment he gets at the hands of his peers. Such a twofold action could
have been proposed in genuine tragedy,[9] but in this case the large design is
undermined in its every part by results that do it no credit. A figure brought
on as a champion runs away, a great public appeal falls flat, and what is
planned as a quick and sinister revenge turns into carnival hurly-burly, with
crowds in exotic costumes pressing around two men who carry on like wild
animals but do no harm at all (1401, 1459). Even at the very end, when the
revengers' inadequacy has led to failure and then to an unprecedented
threat to burn down the set, the whole situation collapses. Torches are
smoothly snuffed out and the frantic disorder is quashed by a divine
announcement that the revels are now at an end.

These fruitless stage events are moreover all constructed of scene forms
that proclaim themselves as if by placard. First comes what promises to be
an action of last-minute Rescue, a salvation (70) labeled as "Our Only
Hope" by one of the principals (52), its champion identified on arrival by
another who cries out, "Save us! You have come in the nick of time!" (384).
Because they killed Clytemnestra, Orestes and Electra are threatened with
stoning by the Argive populace, but here is Menelaus, finally back from
Troy, entering with Agamemnon's name in his mouth (360). It is an almost
gnomic case of the unfortunate man who turns to his fortunate kin for aid

---

9. The structure is similar to that of Eur. *Hec.* with public decision in the first half and private act of vengeance in the second, though the *Orestes* sequence is tighter because the two
actions are causally connected.

(449–55), but things start off badly because this nephew is filthy[10] and unrecognized by his splendid and complacent uncle, so that the Savior flinches and cries out in horror—"Ye gods, what is this thing?" (385; compare Helen, at the sight of him some years earlier, Eur. *Hel.* 541). This fastidious Menelaus-champion shows a peculiarly practical interest in Argive politics (431–38; it turns out that he has his eye on the throne, 1058–59), and he is undeniably foppish (349, cf. 1532),[11] but nevertheless he has entered in the role of Rescuer. By the rules of story form he ought next to confront the monster-demos and defeat it; at the very least he should (like Orestes and Pylades in *Iphigeneia among the Taurians,* or like himself in *Helen*) support the threatened principal(s) in a tricky escape. Instead of which this Menelaus listens while Tyndareus insists that, though the normal punishment for killing is exile, these killers must be stoned to death. He continues to listen while Orestes offers a superlogical demonstration of his mother's guilt and so of his own innocence—"Sons only kill mothers who are unchaste: I call to witness, Telemachus: he didn't kill the chaste Penelope!" (588–90).[12] Menelaus stands between this pursuing plaintiff and the protesting pursued as if to judge their debate, but when it is over, instead of announcing his support for one side or the other, he skulks away behind a screen of ill-chosen similes. The *demos,* he says, being like a raging fire, should be controlled as if it were a horse—by giving it its head! or perhaps as a ship—by slackening the sheets (697–701)! He is a self-proclaimed aristocrat, exempt from the pressures of Nomos and Necessity (488), but once he has sensed the popular mood, he begins to preach the wisdom of tailoring one's actions to the power of whoever may be stronger (710–15). He is also a self-proclaimed sophist (710, 716), but he doesn't waste any of his

10. Even in this fix, he can't resist the overworked sophism, "My body may be destroyed but not my name" (390); on this form of expression, especially in *Helen,* see F. Solmsen, "*Onoma* and *pragma* in Euripides' *Helen,*" *CR* 48 (1934) 119–21; A. N. Pippin, "Euripides' *Helen,*" *C Phil.* 55 (1960) 152–54, and many more recent discussions of the play.

11. Menelaus, Helen, and their servants are all associated with oriental luxury (1426, 1467). In the eyes of Tyndareus the luxurious Menelaus is touched by barbaric moral infection (485), and W. Krieg, *De Euripidis Oreste* (diss. Halle, 1934), pp. 18–21, held that Euripides meant to show him and his wife as monsters of libidinous depravity.

12. Fraenkel called 588–90 "ridiculous" and therefore a "monstrous interpolation" (*Agamemnon,* vol. 3 [Oxford, 1950], p. 814 n. 3; cf. *Eranos* 44 [1946] 86 n. 1); the lines were likewise rejected by Page ("a frigid mythological parallel," *Actors' Interpolations* [Oxford, 1934], p. 33), and di Benedetto ("assai inopportuno," *Euripidis Orestes* [Florence, 1965], p. 120). In their defense, see M. S. Mirto, "Oreste Telemaco e una presunta interpolazione," *ASNP* 10 (1980) 384–402. An allusion to the Telemachus who was urged to be like Orestes is a comic anachronism suitable to parody. Likewise rejected as ridiculous and "crass" (Reeve, "Interpolation," part 3, p. 156) is 554, "Without a father there can never be a child," at which ancient audiences were said to have laughed (Eust. *Od.* 1498.58–59). However, with its comic allusion to Athena's speech at Aesch. *Eum.* 736–38, it functions well in a play that ridicules its own genre.

wise words on the Assembly that threatens to stone his nearest kinsman. In fact he doesn't go near that gathering, and his retreat from both ethical and tragical duty is plainly announced in Orestes' valedictory words: "He runs away . . . he is gone . . . I am betrayed[13] . . . he was our Safe Refuge!" (718–24). So much for the Cowardly Champion (784, cf. 754) and the inactive Rescue Action.[14]

In a quick switch the endangered principal decides to defend himself. He believes that his upper-class bearing will evoke pity from the Argive Assembly (783), and indeed he is allowed to make a speech before that group in which he shows that he is the savior of Hellenic society. If he had not killed Clytemnestra, her crimes would have become the norm, and all men would now everywhere face either murder or enslavement at the hands of the sex "bold enough for anything" (935–42). The *demos* is evidently spared the argument from Telemachus, but nevertheless the Messenger reports tersely: "He did not persuade the crowd, though they thought he was a fine talker" (943). Talthybius had already made the same kind of argument to the opposite end, holding that, without extreme punishment, parent-killing like that of Orestes would become customary among today's young people (892–94). He spoke for the party of the dead tyrant as did also a demagogue whose tongue had been bought, while an ordinary dirt farmer (920) urged that the man who murdered an adulteress ought to be crowned. In the entire debate, however, only one voice is reported as speaking for settled precedent and the Hellenic practice of exile (899–900), because law is not what is wanted by this democratic assembly. Obedient to the friends of Aegisthus, the people vote that Orestes and his sister must die before sundown, though they may kill themselves instead of being stoned. All of which is reported to Electra by a garrulous rustic twice ticketed as Messenger (850, 856) and one who savors his role. She asks him, "How are we to die?" (863–65), but he doesn't even open his report of the debate until he has favored her with a formal preface (866–83, cf. Eur. *Hel.* 1526–35; *Bacch.* 677–96), this decorated with comment on local antiquities (872–73) and a bit of lively but wholly unnecessary direct quotation featuring himself (875–78, cf. Eur. *IT* 267–68). When he has finally answered Electra's question, however, he defies the rules of stage-messengership with a businesslike exhortation: "Well, sharpen your blade or hang up a noose, because you've got to die!" (953–54). He even revives Cassandra's well-known pun for his exit line: Apollo has destroyed them with the verb that echoes his name,

---

13. Crying προδέδομαι at 722, Orestes exactly echoes the previous year's Philoctetes, when he learned that Neoptolemus would not help him escape from the Achaeans (Soph. *Phil.* 923). These are the only occurrences of this form in tragedy; see Willink, *Orestes*, p. xxxii, n. 34.

14. Arist. *Poet.* 1454a29 points to this Menelaus as an outstanding example of low behavior (πονηρία) that is quite unnecessary to the plot.

apolesen (955–56, cf. Aesch. *Ag.* 1080–82). So ends the action of Self-Defense, no more successfully (and no more nobly) than did the opening Rescue.

An Assembly meeting is occupation for a day, but nevertheless the sun has not gone down and there is time for a Revenge action[15] in which the poet almost sets fire to the tragic genre. For the formal beginning of this second movement one must look back to the play's opening, for the initial tableau does the work of the regulation scene between avenger and ally. Indeed, this powerful initial image of sisterly devotion leads one to suppose that Euripides, like Sophocles, intends to sweeten this present vengeance with fraternal love. Electra is the first creature to move on this stage, the embodiment of an affection that is directly shared with the audience as she rises from her place by her brother's cot and tiptoes forward to deliver her hushed prologue speech. She fiercely protects the sleeper from Helen and the chorus, and she bends close to learn if he still breathes, watching for the flutter of an eyelid (155).[16] Once he is awake she touches him again and again, lifting, lowering, stroking his hair from his face.[17] She uses her own body to block the wild contortions of his, and she lets him strike her when he takes her for part of his delusion.[18] This demonstration of physical tenderness goes beyond what has been seen in other plays,[19] and it coincides

15. The time sequence doesn't work in this play, as the poet admits; note 1215, where Pylades says that Hermione ought to be back soon, "for she's been gone long enough." Though she was told to hurry (125), her visit to her aunt's tomb takes as long as all the actions just witnessed put together: Orestes' madness, Menelaus' arrival, the debate with Tyndareus, the meeting of the Assembly, and the time spent traveling there and back.

16. The three tragic sleep scenes aside from this are Eur. *HF* 1031–85, Soph. *Phil.* 826–64, and Soph. *Trach.* 971–82, though the latter is played between two actors, not actor and chorus. There are strong formal likenesses between the two Euripidean scenes, in the motif of listening for breathing (*Or.* 155, *HF* 1057), and the extended series of imperatives addressed to the chorus, esp. μὴ κτυπεῖτε (*Or.* 141; *HF* 1047); see A. Dieterich, "Schlafscenen auf der attischen Bühne," *Rh. Mus.* 46 (1891) 25–46.

17. Physical contact is required at 113, 219, 223, 227, 231, 262, 268, 475, 671, 800, 1044, 1049, 1575.

18. There are parodic allusions in the onslaught of the madness; 238, cf. Aesch. *Cho.* 1026; 253, cf. Aesch. *Cho.* 1056; 259, cf. Aesch. *Cho.* 1051; 261, cf. Aesch. *Cho.* 1057–58; in connection with the bow, 272–74, cf. Aesch. *Eum.* 628, 190, 192; see also the pseudo-Aeschylean αἱματωπούς at 256, used already at Eur. *Andr.* 978. There are also dim echoes of the Aeschylean furies scene at 238 (cf. *Cho.* 1026) and 259 (cf. *Cho.* 1051, 1053). Note too the bathetic drop at 307–10, where, in answer to Orestes' suggestion that she rest, Electra protests, "Never! I live and die with you! Were you to die, what would I do?" etc., then finishes, "But if you say so, I'll have a nap." J. Diggle, *Euripidea* (Oxford, 1994), pp. 362–63, gives this passage serious attention but is unable to do away with its inconsistency of emotional style.

19. Euripides had written an equally physical scene for Phaedra's nurse (*Hipp.* 176–266), and more recently for Amphitryon, who fusses over the sleeping Heracles like a parent bird (*HF* 1039), but the prayer to Night at 174–81 suggests that we are meant to think of Soph. *Phil.* 827–32. This echo will be the more striking if Orestes' bow is visible, as suggested by the scho-

with a general vulnerability in these present stage figures, some of whom were once children in need of care; Tyndareus and Leda fondled little Orestes (460 ff.), and Hermione was brought up by Clytemnestra when Helen left home (109). There is even an early moment when the hero apologizes to his sister in a verbal gesture otherwise quite outside the spectrum of possible heroic behavior (281–82). All of which suggests that *philia,* the warm concern felt by one human being for another who is close, will prove to be central to the Euripidean picture of extramythic mankind.[20]

The first section of the play has dismissed an example of untrue *philia* in Menelaus, but in the very moment that he retreated up one exit channel, Pylades came running down the other clearly labeled as the True Friend. He was greeted as "sweet sight" and a "trustworthy man" more welcome than fine weather to a sailor (727–28), and in answer he called Orestes the dearest of all age-mates, friends, and relatives (732–33). This supreme comrade shared in the killing of Clytemnestra, and when he went off with Orestes to share in his self-defense, the two offered a second visual representation of love—Orestes supported by Pylades (800) as he was earlier by Electra (as Heracles is by Theseus, in the play about his criminal madness, and as Philoctetes is by Neoptolemus, when they descend to the shore). This departure has seemed to equate *philia* with good faith, common sense, hope, and a moderate scheme of action, but in the episode that begins the Revenge all these attributes disappear. Pylades' recent support in a reasonable (and ineffective) move is suddenly reversed to become leadership in a deed that is both unjust and desperate.

The scene of intrigue begins conventionally with an inverted Recognition, as Electra and Orestes (like their namesakes at the end of Euripides' *Electra*) mingle their grief at parting in the manner of other stage pairs who mime joy at reunion. Here are the same embraces, and the same slightly brusque gestures depicting a virile fear of softness,[21] all of which leads an experienced spectator to think that an act of vengeance must be in preparation. But how could that be, since Clytemnestra and Aegisthus have already been repaid and no new injury has occurred? The answer comes

liast at 268, who says that in later times actors liked to play the mad scene with an imaginary weapon. Modern editors, however, tend to reject an actual weapon; see the summary of opinion by Willink, ad 268–74. If the bow was a physical prop, it will have served as a visible sign of Apollo's sponsorship; moreover, if it remained where it was dropped at 277, it will have been an ironic witness to later statements of disbelief made on this stage. However, since Orestes' cot was somehow removed, the bow could have gone with it.

20. Many critics believe that it does; see, e.g., H. Erbse, "Zum 'Orestes' des Euripides," *Hermes* 103 (1975) 438–45; Greenberg, "*Orestes,*" pp. 157–92, studies the opposition between *philia* and *sophia*.

21. Embraces: ὦ φίλτατ' . . . ὦ στέρν' ἀδελφῆς, 1045–49; cf. Aesch. *Cho.* 235; Soph. *El.* 1224; Eur. *IT* 827; brusque gestures, 1022, cf. Soph. *El.* 1236.

from a Pylades who, by twice labeling himself "friend" (1095, 1096), makes Friendship the self-proclaimed sponsor of the ill-conceived, applause-seeking, and ultimately unsuccessful Revenge that he now proposes. What he urges in the name of *philia* is that by killing Aunt Helen they three can make the cowardly Menelaus "feel a bit of pain" (1105) while they themselves take a profit of general praise (1134–39).[22] Their chances are good, he says, because their uncle's wife is in the house, making free with family possessions and guarded only by barbarian slaves. They can enter her presence as suppliants, weapons hidden in their clothing, and ask her for pity. Then they can avenge the whole of Greece by killing her, which will furthermore wipe out their own former guilt, effacing the label "mother-killer" with the glorious title of "Helen-slayer" (1140–42). This new act of violence, then, is to be a practical and profitable substitute for the rituals of supplication, cleansing, and reintegration that ordinarily closed the Orestes tale.

Pylades is full of enthusiasm, but as he displays the attractions of his scheme, its divagations from tragic revenge are striking. Most blatant is his conception of the initial provocation. This is presumably to be primary revenge, a repayment (by way of a surrogate victim) by injured parties upon one who injured them, and yet no opening injury, no gratuitous act of personal outrage, has occurred. Nor do these agents ever express the avenger's characteristic passion, anger.[23] There is no denunciation, no indignant word, the single epithet attached to Menelaus being the commonplace "wicked," in passing (1213). Indeed, the only charge made against Menelaus in this scene is that he is indebted, for his wife, to Agamemnon's spear (1146–47).[24] The man has not gratuitously attacked Orestes' honor, he has simply failed to defend his nephew's person before the Assembly, and a hero does not take vengeance on a coward who has disappointed him.[25] Furthermore, Pylades makes it clear that this retort against Menelaus will perhaps create a mode of escape[26] and at any rate will bring glory,

22. Is there a parodic echo of Soph. *El.* 975–83? Electra there anticipated only secular celebrations, but Pylades sees all Greece transforming this new murder into a sacrifice (1137), from which Orestes as officiant will take his new title (1142).

23. Their focus is all on Helen, about whose death Orestes expresses the excited curiosity of a child playing a game: "How could we manage it? . . . How, since she has servants? . . . Explain how we should do it!" (1106, 1110, 1118).

24. Likewise earlier, in asking about the sentence of the Assembly, Electra calls him merely "coward" and "the man who betrayed my father" (1057, how exactly?). The emptiness of their passion is emphasized by Pylades' farcical exclamation, "Menelaus must not prosper, with your father, and you and your sister all dead, and your mother too—well, let's drop that" (1143–45).

25. Aristotle said that noble anger was incompatible with scorn (*Rh.* 1380a34; *Eth. Nic.* 1149b20). Compare Seneca's judgment: "The most despicable form of revenge is that taken against an unworthy author of offense" (*De Ira* 2.32.3).

26. Much discussion of the play assumes that self-preservation is proposed as, by definition, a more acceptable motive for killing than is revenge; see, e.g., A. Lesky, "Zum Orestes des

whereas a tragic revenger does not seek fame or any form of advancement but acts merely to restore the position among his peers that his enemy has damaged; he is careless even of survival once he has claimed his deed. Nor does a tragic revenger pretend that he moves magniloquently in the interest of some large group or principle; instead, he defends the honor of his own clan as economically as possible. And finally it is downright countertragic to say that, since the intended victim is totally defenseless, the work will be easy—"bloody slaughter done in tranquillity," as the chorus later puts it (1284–85; cf. Electra's similar oxymoron at 1349–50).

What Pylades offers as a friendship gift is a ready-made pseudovengeance that is both shabby and dishonorable, and Orestes is delighted. He had not thought of such a deed, but he is seduced by the sudden vision of happy notoriety and easy violence,[27] and accepting it he cries, "There is nothing better than a good friend!" (1155–57). The smirching of the notion of *philia,* however, has only begun, for Electra is now moved in her sisterly tenderness to add a surpassing touch of cruel and self-seeking opportunism to Pylades' scheme. Being a woman, she is more interested in survival than in the recovery of reputation, and she sees a way to use the killing of Helen as much for blackmail as for revenge. Why not seize Hermione, their foster sister (1184, cf. 64), threaten to kill her as they will have killed her mother, and in this way extract help from Menelaus in getting out of the country? With this grisly proposal for utilizing a cousin and lifelong comrade, Euripides gives the coup de grâce to the comforting idea that these people are moved by human affection, and he also marks the revenge as wholly off track.[28] A hostage is taken to force negotiation, and negotiation is a concept diametrically opposed to the thrust of vengeance. Electra's hard-boiled plan ignores honor and concentrates on advantage, but nevertheless a dazzled Orestes cries out in admiration: "Oh what a blessed bedmate for you, Pylades, to enjoy if you live and regret if you die!" (1207–8). His fearsome sister's "masculine mind in a female body" is to be his return gift to his dearest friend, a perfect expression of the bonds that hold these three together.

The complexity of this scheme, its several possible outcomes, its emphasis on survival, and above all the nonvengeful notion of forcing an "enemy"

Euripides," *Wien. Stud.* 53 (1935) 37–47, where the three would-be assassins are said to be heroic because their deed is aimed at escape from a seriously threatening situation. In the ethic of tragedy, however, self-preservation has no positive moral value and is dangerously close to the attachment to life, *philopsychia,* which could lead to cowardice and flight from danger, as at Tyrtaeus 10.18.

27. He is determined that at least one or two of Helen's retinue should be killed as extras (1126, 1129).

28. Those who take the play as serious drama discover in Electra one more case of the degenerative effects of revenge; see, e.g., Parry, "*Orestes,*" p. 347: "she is reduced at last to the type of cruel vindictive devil woman."

to become a "friend" all suggest that this intrigue is meant as a reflection of real-life factional politics. Pylades, the source of this staged plot of revenge, is extraordinarily like the man who wins highest praise in Thucydides' strife-torn cities by urging an outrageous action upon a comrade to whom no such thing had occurred (ὁ ἐπικελεύσας τὸν μὴ διανοούμενον, Thuc. 3.82.5). Indeed, Pylades shows all the misnamed "virtues" of the historian's man of faction—ardent impulsiveness in a policy of foolhardy boldness (3.82.4), a taste for enormity and ingenuity in reprisal (3.82.3), and no waste of time in thought or consideration (3.82.4–5). He is the comrade closer than kin, bound to his fellows by common crime,[29] and ready to enter on an action for which there is no cause (3.82.6; 8.73.3). He urges a sudden strike against an opponent whose trust will put her off guard (3.82.7), and outlines a trick that promises to be sweet. All of which infects his weaker companion, so that Orestes likewise repudiates hesitation and proclaims his readiness for whatever holds promise (1106). He literally "calls reckless audacity by the name of courageous friendship" (Thuc. 3.82.4, cf. Eur. Or. 1155), and like one of the conspirators in the revolutionary cities (Thuc. 3.82.7), he sees the new game of vengeance as a kind of contest of wits (admiring Electra's cleverness in the hostage scheme, 1180, 1204). And finally, all three take up their projected action not as a self-defining deed but as a step in what may be an advantageous negotiation (like men of faction hoping for profitable offers from opponents, Thuc. 3.82.7). Nowhere else has Euripides used the word *hetaireia*, but it appears twice in the scene in which the *Orestes* conspiracy is made (1072, 1079),[30] so that one is almost forced to hear a contemporary reference. This "Band of Three Friends," united in a self-promoting contest of retaliation (1190), joined by a password (1130) and a sign of safety (1190), is a stage version of one of the many political clubs that threatened Athens' inner peace in the last decade of the fifth century.

The scene of the intrigue ends with an allusive revengers' prayer that forces the audience to stand back and make odious comparisons.[31] The young people's tripartite plea follows the pattern of the invocations that

---

29. Burkert, "Absurdität," p. 107, likens the proposed killing of Helen to the initiatory crimes performed by members of political clubs, but these three are already so bound, having together accomplished the killing of Clytemnestra (767, 1074). As parallels, Burkert mentions the murders of Androcles and of Phrynichus, and the honors for the killers of the latter, voted in 409 B.C. (85 ML).

30. Elsewhere in tragedy only at Soph. *Aj.* 683. Note also *Or.* 804, which may reproduce an actual club jingle.

31. "Soll das Parodie sein? . . . es ist die ad absurdum geführte Entartung des heroischen und religiosen Erbes" (K. Reinhardt, *Tradition und Geist* [Göttingen, 1960], p. 252). Compare Kitto, *Greek Tragedy*, p. 353, who remarks that, placed beside the older prayer, this one "sounds positively blasphemous."

close the call upon the underworld in Aeschylus' *Choephori,* and so the hear-
er remembers these same three when they wrought a terrifying Aeschylean
vengeance made to Delphic specifications in the name of Agamemnon. The
present group, by contrast, is preparing a despicable act of spite, an attack
of their own inspiration, to be made upon a woman they dislike so that a
flabby kinsman may be forced to help them to a stronger position. Instead
of gathering close to the tomb of Agamemnon, these stand at an insignificant spot, gesticulating in a vacuum. Instead of offering, like their Aeschylean counterparts, to be the saviors of a father's honor (Aesch. *Cho.* 505–7,
if the lines are genuine), they blame their father: "We are your creditors, but
because of you we suffer! your brother betrays us!" (1226–28). Instead of
begging for Dike as their ally (Aesch. *Cho.* 497), they ask Agamemnon's
ghost to come as "collaborator," tactlessly choosing the term (συλλήπτωρ,
1230) that described Clytemnestra's demonic helper in the murder of her
husband (Aesch. *Ag.* 1507–8).[32] And where the earlier children of Agamemnon denounced the outrages of net and bath (Aesch. *Cho.* 491–92),
Orestes explains the provocation of this new revenge almost in nursery
terms: "Your brother deserted me, though I was in the right, so I want to kill
his wife!" (1228–30).[33]

In the scene that follows, the theatrically dangerous one in which a chorus stands and waits while the invisible avenger does his work, Euripides' parodic revenge becomes openly ridiculous. Electra tries to position the chorus
so that the women can prevent a discovery of what is going on inside the
palace. She wants the dancers to divide, half going toward one parodos and
half toward the other (1251–52), but the two lines evidently pull only a bit
apart, one group with heads turned sharply toward the country, the other
with faces toward town. Electra sees them as a single walleyed choral creature, but when she voices this dubious conceit by saying, "Now cast your
glance sidewise in both directions" (1261),[34] the women in both lines all
turn their heads from side to side in unison, singing, "Now this way, now that
way and back again, just as you command!" (1264–65). Which foolishness
Electra raises to bedlam level by commanding, "Roll your eyes, give the whole
panorama to your pupils as they peer out through your curls!" (1267–68).[35]
The women obediently toss their heads to such an extent that they befuddle

---

32. It also occurs at Antiph. *Tetralogiae* 2.3.10.

33. Willink, ad 1227–30, rejects these lines, adding to the usual arguments the assertion
that they are "pedestrian" and contain specific reference to revenge, which he thinks the conspirators should treat with "euphemistic reticence," because a request for help in saving oneself is more seemly.

34. In a dochmiac context she asks them to move the pupils of their eyes δόχμια (1261);
cf. the Phrygian's description of the wild-eyed assassins inside the palace (1457–58).

35. Choral reference to tossed hair is conventional; cf., e.g., Alcman 3.9 *PMG* = 26.9
Calame.

themselves, and one group breaks all stage rules by announcing the approach of a nonexistent peasant. Their error puts Electra into a panic, and the two choral branches then rival each other in *not* seeing anyone: "Not an Argive that moves on this side!" "Same over here, no crowd here!" (1279–80). A spectacle perhaps as silly was seen when the satyr chorus of Sophocles' *Ichneutae* was divided by Papa Silenus to rush this way and that, sniffing false trails (F314 *TrGF*), but the tragic stage provides no parallel.[36]

At last the expected cries come from behind the scene,[37] and in response, where her terse Sophoclean double calls out, "Strike again, if you have the strength!" (Soph. *El.* 1415), today's Electra produces a volume of redundantly feverish instructions: "Slay, slash, kill, thrust the double-edged double-jawed swords at the woman who abandoned her father, abandoned her husband, killed hundreds of Hellenes who fell by the spear . . . etc. etc.!" (1302–5). The chorus tells her to be quiet[38] (1311, a tragic first) because, though elsewhere the scene in which the enemy is dispatched is not interrupted, someone is coming. Happily the newcomer is Hermione, the extra victim essential to Electra's elaboration of their scheme, and Orestes swiftly draws her in to where she is to be bound, perhaps killed.[39] He doesn't take her, however, before she has a chance to remind the audience that she is close kin to this affectionate brother and sister (1329, cf. 1340). Nor does she go before Electra enjoys a bit of revenger's double speech; she might be Hecuba with the villainous Polymestor, except that this is an innocent girl, when she suggests that Hermione should "fall upon her so blessed mother" (1338) as she intercedes for her cousins. Other victims have been trapped by their own greed or lust or wish for power, but this one walks softly into the killing place moved by pity and hoping to "save" (1345) these unhappy kinsmen whom she cannot not recognize as murderers.[40]

36. Closest would be Eur. *Rhes.* 674–727, if that play represents tragedy; see A. P. Burnett, "*Rhesus:* Are Smiles Allowed?" in *Directions in Euripidean Criticism,* ed. P. Burian (Durham, N.C., 1985), pp. 13–51. The chorus of satyrs that waits through the *Cyclops* revenge is less risible than are these ladies.

37. This false death-cry has been prepared for by the earlier choral repetition of Clytemnestra's cry (827–30), which in a serious play would suggest that Clytemnestra was now being avenged (cf. Eur. *El.* 1151–52, where Agamemnon's death cry is made to sound out just before that of Clytemnestra).

38. A chorus may urge silence on itself, as at 140, but here the Electra who has just been singing must be the object of their reprimand.

39. Electra calls to the men within to seize this prey (1345–46), and as the text stands Orestes makes what Willink, ad 1347–48, calls a "weird jack-in-the-box appearance" to snatch her in. This breach of convention has been removed by di Benedetto, who gives Orestes' lines to Electra, and by Willink who brackets 1347–48 as "upsetting" and "silly." Orestes' next appearance, however, will be yet more unconventional, and if "silly" were cause for cutting, then the entire speech of the Phrygian would have to go.

40. Electra follows her for a quick costume-change if it is the second actor who will play the Phrygian.

Hermione is a human measure of how far these young Atreids have strayed from the ethos of classic vengeance, and as soon as she has disappeared Euripides makes a plain statement of comic intention. At this point in the action the audience expects the display of a victim, which in this case should mean the showing of an inconceivable object—the ugly corpse of a semi-immortal who was the world's most beautiful woman. In place of which there comes a blubbering, bounding[41] Phrygian who is quite alive though quivering with fear.[42] This creature is flamboyantly nonheroic,[43] being a barbarian[44] slave who is not only without courage but also without Greek as a mother tongue; indeed he is even without the anatomical equipment of manliness, as Orestes will rudely remark (1528) and as his falsetto voice confirms.[45] He is the only Singing Messenger known to the Attic stage,[46] and though he comes from second-millennium Troy he has an insider's knowledge of the latest fifth-century fashions in vocal performance. Rhyth-

41. The schol. at 1366 implies that in the original production the actor jumped down from the roof of the scene building, which might have been a spectacular allusion to the Watchman at the beginning of Aesch. *Ag.* Because lines 1366–68 refer to noises behind the palace door, they are usually assumed to be interpolated to cover for a later actor who did not want to make the leap; see Reeve, "Interpolation," part 1, pp. 263–64. A. M. Dale, on the other hand, argued in *Collected Papers* (Cambridge, 1969), pp. 126–27 and pp. 268–69, that the scholiast, "one of the chattery Byzantine kind," invented the leap from his own misunderstanding of 1371–72. If Euripides really meant to give his audience a surprise, however, it could be that the choral introduction was a trick (like Jason's command to have the bars withdrawn, at Eur. *Med.* 1314–16) intended to distract the spectator's eye and render the Phrygian's leap the more shocking; cf. O. Taplin, *Stagecraft of Aeschylus* (Oxford, 1977), p. 443.

42. More than one critic has suggested that the Phrygian should be removed as interpolation; see B. Gredley, "Is *Orestes* 1503–36 an Interpolation?" *GRBS* 9 (1968) 409–19; Reeve, "Interpolation," part 1, pp. 247–65. In his defense, Radermacher, "Über eine Scene," pp. 278–84, suggested that the Phrygian might have been made after the pattern of Heracles in *Busiris;* see also Seidensticker, *Palintonos Harmonia,* p. 111: "ein makaber lächerliche Karikatur des tragische Höhepunkts der Sophokleische *Elektra* und—noch deutlicher—der *Orestie.*"

43. A. W. Verrall saw this messenger scene as one that takes the tremendous poetic risk of daring an audience to laugh where it knows it must not; this is somehow the "supreme test and confirmation of gravity" (*Essays on Four Plays of Euripides* [Cambridge, 1905], p. 249). Reinhardt less paradoxically called it a "mannerist" bit of pure theater (*Tradition und Geist,* pp. 227 f.), and for analysis of its comic elements see A. P. Burnett, *Catastrophe Survived* (Oxford, 1971), pp. 217–19.

44. He is given this label five times, 1370, 1374, 1385, 1369, and 1430, where mention of βαρβάρυις νόμοισιν is intensified by the preliminary Φρυγίοις . . . Φρυγίοισιν νόμοις at 1426.

45. The *harmateion melos,* specified at 1584, was sung at a very high pitch; on the genuineness of this line, see O. Taplin, "Stage Instructions?" *PCPS* 203 (1977) 125; on the falsetto voice, Seidensticker, *Palintonos Harmonia,* p. 104 n. 19.

46. The charioteer of *Rhesus* enters singing but delivers his report in iambics (Eur. *Rhes.* 756–803). The Phrygian is also the only nonprincipal, and so nonaristocrat, to sing a tragic monody; furthermore, this is the longest monody and the only one interrupted by remarks from a chorus; see W. Barner, "Die Monodie," in *Die Bauformen der griechischen Tragödie,* ed. W. Jens (Munich, 1971), p. 282.

mically unsteady, highly colored, quickly changing, his aria[47] exemplifies the nonstrophic New Music that conservatives disliked as exotically immoral. What is more, this Phrygian is also knowing in the extremes of the high tragic art, and his monody is as devastating of that style, and especially of the composer's own tricks,[48] as is the song that Aeschylus sings in the *Frogs* (Ar. *Ran.* 1331 ff.). He is a Trojan houseboy, but he knows the entire vocabulary of theatrical grief, moaning "*ailinon, ailinon*"[49] with the *Agamemnon* chorus (1395, cf. Aesch. *Ag.* 121, 139, 159), "*ialemon ialemon*" with the Danaids (1390; cf. Aesch. *Supp.* 114, Eur. *Phoen.* 1034), "*Ilion Ilion*" with the women of Troy (1381, cf. Eur. *Tro.* 806). The effeminate sound of his voice is exploited in two-tone howls of "*ga-a ga-a*" and "*ai a-i*" reminiscent of the Egyptian-bred daughters of Danaus (1373–75, cf. Aesch. *Supp.* 890). He even indulges in the wish for impossible escape so familiar from choruses of Euripidean women: "Where shall I flee, friends? Shall I winged fly into the pale air, or to that Pontic land round which horned Oceanus twines embracing arms?" (1376–79). An auditor with sharp ears will note that, to describe the embrace of this quite gratuitous Oceanus, the Phrygian picks a word for which Euripides had a notorious weakness, as witness the Halcyons of Aristophanes' parody, who "twi-i-i-ine" their song (ἑλίσσων, 1379; cf. εἰειειειλίσσετε, Aesch. *Ran.* 1314, and the spinner-singer at 1358).

It is not merely costume, dance, and verbal style that mark this messenger as incompatible with serious tragedy. His message itself is an annihilating subversion of the genre. To begin with, it comes when the spectator wants a corpse, denied which he, like the chorus (1368), wants a clear and moving narrative of what is going on inside, but nothing of the sort is to be had from this melodious person. An initial self-portrait of fear is all very well, but when twenty-three lines of song have produced only a pseudo-Aeschylean babble about the presumed victim (δυσελένας δυσελένας . . . ἐρινύν, 1387, 1389; cf. Aesch. *Ag.* 688, 698, 745–46), the chorus testily suggests that the man might speak clearly and stick to facts (1393). With sixty more lines of "Asiatic speech such as barbarians use" (1396–97) the Phrygian manages to place a redoubled pair of Aeschylean lions (1401–2, cf. Aesch. *Cho.* 937–38)[50] in the palace, but still there is no hint of the outcome. Helen's servants, it seems, learnedly suspected a trick, "the nettiest of devices" (ἀρκυστάταν μηχανάν, 1421–22; cf. Aesch. *Ag.* 1116, *Cho.* 1000), but they were easily locked into closets and loose stalls. Here the impatient

47. Analyzed by Barner, "Die Monodie," pp. 293–97.

48. The Phrygian is fond not just of anaphora and anadiplosis but also of resolved repetitions like ἔβαλον ἔβαλον, 1414; cf. 1416, 1468, 1500.

49. The Phrygian answers a modern scholarly question by explaining that this cry is "what all barbarians say, *aiaï*, in their Asiatic way" when a king dies (1395–97).

50. Compare also Neoptolemus and Philoctetes (Soph. *Phil.* 1436).

chorus interrupts again to ask for a plain report (1451), and the next section of song finally carols forth the attack of a pair of friends now likened to
wild boars (1459), using such phrases as "each seized a sword and rolled his
eye, one one way, one another" (1457–58), and "in flight, with her foot she
lifted, she lifted her gold-sandaled footstep, but he advanced his Mycenaean
boot, thrusting fingers through her hair" (1467–71). Somehow the sword
does get to the victim's throat, but just at this moment the chorus thought-
lessly asks the whereabouts of all the Phrygians who should have been
defending their mistress (1473), and the account swerves. The slaves, it
seems, were noisy but not idle; "with cries and crowbars we broke the stables
and doors of the house, and beneath the roof we rushed about in all directions to give help" (1474–75). There are skirmishes, wounds, fallen bodies,
and comparisons with the fields of Troy before the singer gets back to the
moment of the poised sword, only to say that it failed of its mark. The arrival
of Hermione excited the two killers and they dropped Helen, to make a
combined Bacchic leap upon this fresh prey (1492).[51] Then, at last, after
125 lines of fashionable song and dance, the climax comes—or rather, it
goes, as the Phrygian, suddenly tired by all his heavy language, flatly concludes, "He did return to the murder of Zeus' girl, but she had gone out
of the room, out of the house, and wasn't to be seen" (like her disappear-
ing dream-figure at *Agamemnon* 425, or her invisible phantom at *Helen*
605–6).[52]

A Messenger Speech with loose ends is as great an anomaly as one that is
sung. There are reports of events that were clearly interrupted (as at Eur.
Ion 1122 ff.; *IT* 1333 ff.), but no other messenger leaves the act he tells of
neither done nor undone. "It may have been a potion, it may have been
magic, or she may have been carried off by a god, because whatever happened after that I don't know—I ran away" (1499; cf. Aesch. *Ag.* 248, on disappearance of Iphigeneia). Has Helen been found by now and been killed,
or has she not? The Phrygian doesn't know, the chorus doesn't know, nor
does the audience, and the poet prolongs this general doubt with a clear
intention to tease. The spectators have heard Helen cry out twice, exactly as
a dying victim should (1296, 1301), and the chorus has greeted her presumably accomplished death as a work of justice, a nemesis from the gods,
just as a chorus should (1362, perhaps with play on the tale that made
Nemesis her mother). What is more, the enthusiastic Phrygian, though he
wasn't there, has said that Hermione came in as her mother's gore flowed

51. This moment will have occurred just when Orestes turned to pull Hermione in at 1347,
and since the Phrygian was not an eyewitness to the attack on Helen (1452 and see Willink, ad
1425), slight discrepancies (as the double pounce) do not seem in themselves adequate
grounds for rejecting that earlier brief appearance.

52. Seidensticker, *Palintonos Harmonia*, p. 107, supposes that this long narrative might be
meant to suggest a Tale of Troy that ends with the disappearance of the Helen-*eidolon*.

to the ground (1491). Unhappily, he has also said that Helen disappeared before Orestes could strike, so whence this gore? His wondrous speech has created a doubt so uncomfortable that a glimpse of the divine Helen as a slashed corpse would be a positive comfort, even to the most traditionally minded member of the audience.

When instead of a gory display an empty-handed Orestes bursts out of the killing place, it seems that at any rate he will announce the accomplished deed (as at Soph. *El.* 1424 or Aesch. *Cho.* 972), but this avenger has neither success nor unsuccess to proclaim. He has, in fact, lost track of what he is or isn't doing, and has momentarily left the scene of his complete or incomplete crime to keep the Phrygian from giving a melodious alert. What he actually does, however, is insist that this kowtowing barbarian slave should reassure him about his current crime (as Pylades did in a similarly crucial moment, Aesch. *Cho.* 900–902). He wants the Phrygian to say, "Helen is justly killed" (1512), yet when the hyperbolic eunuch, swearing sincerity, shouts, "Most justly, were it with three blades!" (adding that he doesn't say this just to please, 1513–17), Orestes still lingers. He, the self-appointed avenger of all Hellas, amuses himself, first with threatening this crawling creature,[53] then with sparing him on the unexpected grounds of his "intelligence" (σύνεσις, 1524).[54] The encounter is much like the belaboring of one fool by another, and before it is over the notions of supplication, wisdom, justice, oath-taking, and gnomic truth have all been rendered senseless. This achieved, Orestes returns to whatever inept confusion the palace now holds, threatening an absent Menelaus with a pair of corpses, wife and child, if he will not negotiate (1536).[55]

The chorus once more imitates a chorus left outside during a vengeance killing—"What should we do? Should we alert the city?" (1539)—but just as they perceive torches being lit indoors, Menelaus arrives on the scene. He has somehow heard of his wife's strange disappearance but discounts it as "a ridiculous invention of the mother-killer" (in his unfortunate phrase, "a big laugh," 1560).[56] He believes his wife has been killed, and when he sees Orestes on the roof with the hostage Hermione, he asks, "Would you add

53. Burkert, "Absurdität," pp. 104–5, notes that the tableau of Orestes standing over the kneeling Phrygian will caricature the Albani relief recently set up in the Ceramicus to commemorate those who fell in the Peloponnesian War.

54. Orestes' discovery of *synesis* in the tired commonplace, "Even a slave rejoices in life" (1523), has a lowering effect on his own earlier use of the term at 396, which seems to mean not that he felt conscience or remorse but simply that he knew mother-killing was not considered a good thing to do; see H. Osborne, "Σύνεσις and Συνείδησις," *CR* 45 (1931) 8–10.

55. There may be an echo here of Eur. *Hec.* 45–46; cf. 66 and *Hec.* 279; 1280 and *Hec.* 748.

56. "The expression jars," according to Willink, ad loc., and he consequently rejects 1556–60, calling the lines "muddle-headed," though the Menelaus of this play has never been a clear thinker. Willink likewise rejects 1579–84, on the grounds that Orestes must believe that Helen is dead (?).

another act of slaughter to the slaughter of Helen?" (1579). "I would if I could," responds the baffled avenger, "if only the gods hadn't robbed me!" (1580). Aha, thinks the spectator, the Phrygian told the truth! But at once he notices that Menelaus still believes that Orestes is lying. The whole exchange has been designed to push the audience's desire for some sort of certainty almost to the breaking point, and the blocking has the same effect, for everything on this stage is wrong. Menelaus, as the ultimate Victim (like Jason), has come on as he should to suffer the Revenger's Triumph, but the young people on the roof, instead of flaunting a dead surrogate, show him a living girl, on whose life they would bargain. They misplaced their victim, and so they would change roles, becoming once again Andromedas open to rescue by this same unlikely champion. They will pay for escape with the life of Hermione, but if Menelaus refuses to bargain they have arranged a makeshift disaster, part holocaust and part exhibitionist murder—an extreme of stage destruction such as only the Zeus of *Prometheus* has until now contrived. Having botched their Revenge, knowing that their Escape is probably poisoned, they are ready to set fire to tragedy itself, not for any reason large or small but simply for the sensation. Their general aimlessness the poet makes perfectly plain by causing Orestes and Menelaus, at this scorching moment, to indulge in a tiff much like the hero's earlier exchange with the Phrygian—one that leaves both parties deprived of all dignity (1613–17).[57] This is the occasion on which Pylades' mutism is put into the spotlight, but he is not the only one who is made to look a fool. The would-be avenger is marked not by vindictive rage but by self-pity, and when Menelaus groans, "Wretched Helen!" Orestes whines, "Am I not wretched too?" (1613). Meanwhile the man who notoriously let others fight battles for him falls into the same pretentious bluster that made him the type of the miles gloriosus a few years earlier, in the *Helen*. He, the prince who would not face an Assembly of citizens, cries out to his undead wife, "Did I bring you back from Phrygia only to be slaughtered? . . . bring you back after my ten thousand martial toils!" (1614, 1615; cf. 689; cf. Eur. *Hel.* 593, 603, 621, 707, 1113).[58] Orestes interrupts, "You didn't toil for me!" and when Menelaus continues, "I suffered frightfully!" the other cruelly adds, "And all for nothing!" "You have me there," says Menelaus, and Orestes returns to his initial complaint against his uncle, "You can blame your own cowardice (for having lost your wife)" (1616–17).[59]

---

57. On this exchange, see T. Falkner, "Coming of Age in Argos," *CJ* 78 (1983) 289–300, esp. 297–98.

58. His lines are also a strong echo of Helen's to him at Eur. *Hel.* 777–78. Apollo's echo of his boast at 1662–63 suggests that in this world gods are capable of irony.

59. Usually Menelaus' ἔχεις με (1617) is taken to mean, "I surrender," i.e., "I agree to your terms and will try to help you." This would mean that Orestes' answering command to Electra to fire the palace is evidence of total raving madness; so Burkert, "Absurdität," p. 10; cf. M. Pohlenz, *Die griechische Tragödie,* 2d ed. (Göttingen, 1954), p. 419, who sees Orestes as suddenly

This can't go on, and the collapse of the dramatic structure is restated now as massive confusion in the playing area. Crowds of citizens rush in, creating one of the situations Orestes had foreseen (1533; compare Electra, at 1289–90), and from his high post he gives the signal for torching the palace.[60] At the same time Menelaus calls on the arriving Argives to open siege (1622), exhorting them to move against their three public enemies (1621–24).[61] There are shouts, rushing feet, and an instant of flame, but then, with a final example of mortal malfunction, the two commands are forgotten as all present stop and look up. The machine has swung a golden carriage out, and in it sits the missing Surrogate Victim accompanied by Apollo. The gods have reached the end of their patience, the mortals the end of their freedom, and the Delphic divinity demands an immediate cessation of hostilities, speaking first to Menelaus because at the moment he is the aggressor (1625).[62] With truce secured, Apollo goes on to impose marriages all around, not just that of Pylades and Electra but the union of Orestes and Hermione as well, and satisfactions fall from the air as if this were the close of an Aristophanic comedy. Even Menelaus is to get a new wife while keeping Helen's dowry (1638, 1662), and though he is not to

---

possessed by a vengeance-hunger stronger than his will to self-preservation. It was the seeming inconsequence of this answer that made Seeck athetize every reference to burning the palace ("Rauch im Orestes," pp. 9 ff.). It seems better to hear 1613–17 as referring to Helen throughout: at 1616 Orestes taunts Menelaus for having now lost what he suffered for at Troy; at 1617 Menelaus admits that the taunt hits home, and Orestes adds that he has only himself to blame for the loss of his wife. Somewhat similar is the conclusion of J. G. Griffith (review of Biehl and di Benedetto, *JHS*, 87 [1967] 146), who believes that Menelaus acknowledges Orestes' advantage (possession of Hermione) "but in no sense agrees to treat with the Argives."

60. The coming of the Argives at 1617 brings the exchange of split lines to an end because it reverses the power balance between the three hostage-holders on the roof and a Menelaus now backed by an armed (1622) population. This understanding is supported by the hypothesis (cf. *P Oxy.* 27.2455, fr. 4, col. IV, 32–33; J. Diggle, *ZPE* 77 [1989] 1–11), where Menelaus ἐπεβάλλετο τὰ βασίλεια πορθεῖν or ἤρξατο πορθεῖν but those on the roof give the command to fire. Mastronarde, *Contact*, p. 90, argues that such staging is "highly unlikely" because there are no parallels for a decision taken on the basis of an unannounced new perception, but neither are there parallels to a stage threat to ignite the scene buildings while cutting a girl's throat.

61. Reading the MS ἡμῶν in 1623, with di Benedetto ("Note critico-testuali," *Studi Classici e Orientali* 10 [1961] 153–54), but ζῶν for ζῆν in 1624, with Lloyd-Jones ("Euripidea," *CR* 7 [1957] 97–98): "By living, this man commits an act of violence against our city," which comes to, "Protect yourselves by killing the polluted and condemned creature."

62. Heracles, in the Soph. *Phil.* finale, had reversed the two principals' direction of departure in a similar interruption. Both gods stop a passage of excited split-line dialogue; both speak without warning or introduction, beginning with a negative command and vocative address (Μενέλαε, παῦσαι, 1625; μήπω . . . παῖ Ποίαντος, Soph. *Phil.* 1409–10), before identifying themselves. Both gods claim the sanction of Zeus (1634; cf. Soph. *Phil.* 1415), and both impose good things on the mortals turned aside from an erroneous purpose (in *Or.*, end of strife, secular power, marriage; in *Phil.*, end of pain, prizes and renown, companionship).

have the throne of Argos as he had hoped (1660), he is slated for worldly power, as are the avenging comrades, Clytemnestra's killers. The young people group themselves by twos, and Menelaus waves goodbye to Helen (1673) as she flies off to join Hera and Hebe in the sumptuous halls of the gods (1674), from which comfortable spot she will watch over the safety of sailors on the high seas (1690).[63] Here on earth there will be perpetual honors for lovely Peace (1683).

II

Until the moment that Helen is discovered on her way to her heavenly post, the spectator who watches *Orestes* is kept in a state of carefully manufactured confusion. The only thing this audience knows is that it has been promised a number of familiar theatrical pleasures, then given a pastiche of substitutes. Instead of an effective rescue-champion, there came a cowardly power-seeker who abandoned his young relatives. Instead of a tender sister and valorous friend, ready to die for the hero, two scheming figures appeared and offered the hero a bloody plan for survival, after which, instead of a slashed corpse, a dancing eunuch burst from behind the scenes. Something or nothing has occurred in the mysterious interior of the stage palace, but the spectator has been made to realize that there is no witness here in whom he can put faith, nor can he fall back on his educated sense of what may and may not happen in the Attic theater. The poet who could present him with the Phrygian as messenger is capable of anything—he could show the corpse of Zeus' daughter, or hide the living Helen in a wardrobe . . . or could he? The Helen problem forces the playgoer to speculate about the flexibility of myth and the license of tragedy, thus robbing him of his capacity for terror or pity. The reigning emotion, just before the coming of the chariot, is a blind and undirected excitement. Which is at once transformed into delight when the heavenly conveyance shows, for the miracle paradoxically makes the spectator feel that at last he has his feet on the ground. Here is a generic scene-type that comes when it should and holds its shape; its god speaks and behaves as a god,[64] its daughter of Zeus is confirmed as immortal (1635), and its men respond as they should. Watching from his bench the theatergoer laughs from relief because ignorance is at an end, and also because he knows now that it was all right to have laughed earlier. The stage has resumed the yoke of myth, its people

63. Mortal characters have blamed her for those killed at Troy, but Apollo (1639–42) explicitly confirms the explanation of the *Cypria*, according to which Helen was only a tool of the gods; cf. 79.

64. Apollo's appearance answers Orestes' words at 598–99: "what escape will there be for any man, if he who commanded me doesn't save me from death?"

that of their necessary unfreedom, and this submission to gods and genre has been likened to trading scorched human flesh for an epiphany—it is a substitution of beauty for distortions too long endured.

Purged of anxiety over the outcome, some at least of the *Orestes* audience will remember that this evasive Helen had, at the very beginning, hinted at a wry grace that might touch the ugliest events. She has just one appearance on the ground, when she comes out of the palace early in the morning. She means to ask Electra to carry offerings to her sister's grave, which gives her a formal likeness to the Aeschylean and Sophoclean Clytemnestras, but this daughter of Tyndareus would be grossly miscast as a woman of evil. She only wants to be well with the world, with her dead sister, but also with her niece and nephew, to whom she offers sympathy (90), knowing without being told that they were under Apollo's direction when they killed their mother (121, cf. 76). When as a grave offering she cuts a curl that won't be missed,[65] a sour Electra (and why not?—she has just been greeted as "Virgin of long standing," 72) is full of contempt. "O selfish human nature" she says under her breath, "you bane of men—but salvation too when rightly used" (127).[66] She speaks more truly than she knows, because in fact this self-regarding but good-natured woman will, with her daughter, be the salvation of them all. Her choice of which curl to cut should not distract us from the substance of the astonishing petition that she asks Hermione to carry with the offerings. Because she is a woman, Helen cannot give the killers the formal *aidesis* that Tyndareus refuses to grant,[67] but she can try to elicit indulgence from the dead, and so she sends her daughter to ask for general benevolence from Clytemnestra, not only toward Helen's family but also toward the son and daughter who have murdered her—"this wretched pair whom the god has destroyed" (120–21). Helen, for all her vanity, shows the same large pity for the avenger that was gravely voiced by Athena in the Aeschylean treatment of this tale.

Hermione is told to go to the grave and hurry back, and her exit, carrying liquid offerings and the skimped strand of hair, establishes Clytemnestra's tomb as standing just beyond the visible playing space. This means that during the first four-fifths of the play's action Helen's daughter is barely out of sight, her libations and her prayers providing a sustained though unperceived accompaniment to all that happens. Onstage Tyndareus refuses,

65. One thinks of Belinda's wish that she might have lost "Hairs less in sight, or any / Hairs but these!" (Pope, *Rape of the Lock* 4.175–76).

66. By *physis* Electra seems to mean what we call "instinct of self-preservation," which in Helen's case means preservation of her beauty. She evidently refers to a proverb about bad *physis* / good *physis* (like bad *eris* / good *eris*, or bad *aidos* / good *aidos*, etc.), but recent editors have suppressed its second member by bracketing 127 (di Benedetto, Willink).

67. In Attic law this could be granted (in cases of unintentional homicide) only by the kinsmen of the murdered, acting unanimously; see R. Stroud, *Drakon's Law on Homicide* (Berkeley, 1968), p. 50.

Menelaus betrays, the messenger reports that the assembly condemns, and the young people elaborate their plot, but offstage Helen's kindly intervention continues toward its successful conclusion. While her cousins discuss the murder of Helen and her own use as a hostage, Hermione is asking Clytemnestra to withdraw her anger, and it is a sign from the dead showing agreement to this plea that brings her back onstage precisely when she is wanted by the avengers (1315). An Electra who is aping grief and despair (1319–20) calls out, "Are you come from Clytemnestra's tomb?" and Hermione answers, "Yes, and I have gained her gracious favor!" (πρευμένεια, 1321–23; cf. 119).[68] She goes in to the killing place promising, "You are saved as far as in me lies" (1345), and her timely appearance does in fact save Orestes from committing an idiotic crime. Meanwhile, at another level, the placations of Hermione and Helen have a far-reaching result, for there is no further question of Furies—the phantoms seem to have dissolved, and no demonic pursuit is mentioned in Apollo's final forecast (1644–52).[69] When, after a year's secular cleansing in Arcadia, Orestes goes to Athens to be acquitted, it will be the transformed Three Mild Ones who meet him at his trial (1650).[70]

The epic Helen was used by the gods to draw many heroic men to their destruction (1639–42), but this bland lady has the opposite function. In heaven she will be a savior of seamen, throning beside her brothers (1637), and here on the earth represented by this stage she is the *symbolon* of the undeserved rescue that sometimes comes to senseless mortals. Not that she is recognized as such. It is characteristic of the benighted Orestes that he takes "Murder Helen!" as the password to orgies of perverted violence (1130), when in fact she is the key to peaceful safety. The same unseeing youth complains at the very beginning that Menelaus, in bringing Helen home, brings a great bane (247). As Orestes' misguided plot progresses, however, Helen rescues him first by slipping through his fingers in the moment of slaughter, then by flying past to interrupt the ultimate may-

---

68. This word and its associates can have a secular meaning (e.g., Aesch. *Ag.* 840), but it more frequently signifies the attitude requested, with prayer and libations, from gods or those in the underworld (as at Aesch. *Supp.* 210, 141; *Pers.* 219–20, 609–10; Eur. *Hec.* 538). Willink chides Hermione for her "naive confidence in the efficacy of the ritual," but nothing suggests that her confidence is misplaced. Clytemnestra's shade does not block the astounding grace that descends upon all for whom Hermione has prayed.

69. In this secular and up-to-date stage world a well-educated person (410) believes that demon apparitions are delusions, the symptoms of an illness that has either a physical (blood, 36, 199, 285) or a psychic (consciousness of association with fearsome things, 396) cause. A "sophist" like Menelaus does not want to believe in Furies as daimonic powers, but all the same he has a superstitious fear of speaking their name (409), and at 423 he refers to them as "goddesses." The chorus is more traditional (321–38), but they too are careful to call the powers they would supplicate by their euphemistic name, Eumenides.

70. The trial, like that of Ares, will be judged by the gods (1650), probably the Attic Twelve (cf. Dem. 23.74).

hem.[71] She has moreover sent her daughter among these criminally distracted people, and Hermione is plainly though unknowingly labeled as a pledge through whom salvation is to be gained (ἐς σωτηρίαν / ... ὅμηρον, 1188–89), and also as a healing cure (*pharmakon*, 1190). She is the play's one example of pure *philia*, for she acts only out of affection, and she is steadily associated with the notion of safety, "not for yourself but for us" as the unwitting Orestes truly says (σωτηρία, 1348; cf. 1345, 1188, 1203).[72] Through her, her cousins hope to extort escape-aid from a false Menelaus (1178, 1188, 1203); having lost that hope, these idiotic mortals are about to cut the throat of their one true friend, when an absolute rescue comes from Helen and Apollo. The final tableau thus stands as an enacted revelation, a *dromenon*, that shows a god who must force survival upon men so foolish that they would slaughter their own salvation.

III

The audience that laughed at the Phrygian because he was reprehensible will laugh at the celestial Helen of the final rescue because of her earlier frivolity. They will probably do the same when Apollo announces, "Now about that girl whose throat you are cutting—you are fated to marry her!" (1653–54). They certainly will laugh when the Happy Ending is labeled as such (1670) by an Orestes who says, "Watch how I don't butcher Hermione—I'm ready to couch her!" (1671–72). Nothing is sacred here, not because the poet is engaged in a banal attack on received religion but because this is a skeptical drama about skepticism. Its unbelieving characters disengage themselves from gods who are seen as troublesome and wrong,[73] and they likewise ignore the earthly customs that maintain the ritual cleanliness of their community.[74] Murderers go in and out of the house

71. This Helen who is to be situated ἐν αἰθέρος πτυχαῖς (1636) suggests the exonerated Egyptian Helen (Eur. *Hel.* 44, 605), as she did earlier in her sudden disappearance from the pseudo-Trojan exploits recounted by the Phrygian.

72. Of thirty occurrences in *Orestes* of words with this root, twelve are connected with the false savior, Menelaus; five with Hermione; four with Helen.

73. E.g., 419–20: Men.: Apollo doesn't protect you? Or.: He's waiting; that's what gods do. Mid-century critics took these expressions of damaged faith as simple reflections of the poet's opinion; e.g., C. M. Bowra, *Sophoclean Tragedy* (Oxford, 1944), p. 214, "Euripides puts the blame on established religion and on Apollo"; J. D. Denniston, *Euripides, Electra* (Oxford, 1939), pp. xxvi, xxii, "Apollo ... stands condemned" as a god "who has deceived an unhappy mortal and then left him in the lurch."

74. It has not occurred to Electra or to Orestes to look for purification at an altar or shrine; indeed, Orestes seems to feel that Apollo should have approached him with some sort of purification (597–98). When Menelaus asks if Orestes' hands have been purified, he speaks only of the secular form granted by a host who receives the polluted man at his hearth (429–30); such cleansing is ordinarily sought abroad, but Orestes complains that no such host has stepped forward among the citizens. By contrast, the chorus does at least songfully "supplicate" Clytemnestra's Furies (324).

of their victim without any thought of pollution (301), and the miasmatic Orestes has actually presided at his mother's funeral (404).[75]

Having reached an unprecedented peak of independence and secularity, the principals of the *Orestes* develop a new and fearful definition of justice and so of revenge—one that contradicts the whole tendency of earlier Hellenic thought. Anger was the passion appropriate to traditional revenge; by Rhadamanthine law the one who gave an injury had to receive a like injury, and on earth it was the sufferer who knew the punishment's right measure because his anger told him. Anger was the necessary fuel for a justice that looked to the injured party and saw to his restoration to his former status. But Euripides' secular and skeptical Orestes is not angry. His passionate condition is fixed at the opening as one of retrospective, defensive fear; then with sanity he arrives at self-justification and longs for comfort and good repute. Cross with Menelaus, he indulges in bloated talk about "enemies" who have contributed to his wretchedness (1160–66), but he embraces the notion of killing a friendly Helen out of infantile ambition. He will be the worthy son of a great commander father if he can only play out his spite against his uncle's wife (1167–71). As Apollo says in the end, Orestes "fabricates" a passion against Menelaus.

All of which might seem merely despicable, but Euripides has designed his Orestes to be an avenger who gives his vocation a monstrous form. Detached as he is from both fate and myth, he invents a sinister retaliatory violence that justifies itself not by anger, not by divine command, but by common advantage; it knows no limit because it claims to make society better. The weak and impressionable Orestes embodies the dangerous idea that crimes may be committed for the good of humanity, and the play's action shows how a man (or a group) may come to this notion. The early-morning Orestes weeps and looks to Apollo's bow for aid, but as soon as the delusions are gone he blames Apollo (285)[76] and turns exclusively to men. Without any sort of purification,[77] he would move into the civic territory of the commonplace, and so he repudiates everything that is not "real," his

75. The first stroke of madness came when Orestes was supervising the collection of bones from his mother's extinguished pyre. This gratuitous anomaly is forced on our attention by the short colloquy between Orestes and Menelaus in which the latter presumes to diagnose Orestes' fits of madness as mechanically caused and open to cure (399–411). On the prohibitions against association between killer and kin of victim, see R. Parker, *Miasma* (Oxford, 1983), pp. 124–25, who cites Pl. *Leg.* 868c–869a; Dem. 22.2.

76. He brings forth the god's command as the climax of the tactical speech by which he hopes to deflect Tyndareus' denunciation, arguing that the state has no jurisdiction over one whose act was divinely determined, and rising to the rhetorical reductio ad absurdum, "Convict *him* of impiety and put *him* to death!" (595). Fairly standard criticism of Apollo comes from Electra at 162, 194; from Menelaus, at 416.

77. Note the astonishing exchange at 1600–1605, where Orestes asserts that his blood taint is of no importance, that he, unlike Menelaus, is "pure at heart" and in a condition to rule Argos. (And at 1605 note the allusion to Aesch. *Eum.* 738.)

own guilt along with the god. He will be ordinary, and so he reshapes his matricidal remorse into boasts of public service, and invents a non-Apolline version of the Clytemnestra episode. And it is just here, in the process of banalizing his own myth, that this everyday Orestes makes himself into a monster. It was not, he now claims, as a servant of Delphi that he killed his mother, nor was it primarily as a supporter of the patriarchy. No, he did it in a new and dread capacity as a self-appointed sword-carrying arbiter of morals. He has a characteristic bit of logic at hand, much like his demonstration from Telemachus. What benefits society must be just: the killing of an adulterous husband-killer was certainly a social benefit: ergo, he was right to do it. "I destroyed her with full justice" (572).

Performance of mankind's most stringently forbidden deed has made this secular Orestes self-righteous, and once he has explained matricide as an act of public benefaction (565, 570–71, 932–34), similar projects naturally recommend themselves (1158–61).[78] Having said, "I was right to kill my mother because she was a threat to all Greek men," he sees that it must be more than right to attack other such women, where the connection is not so near. It is not that his Delphic crime has made him bestial (though he does look forward to killing a few extraneous slaves, 1128).[79] On the contrary, it has made him theoretical, and consequently insatiable: a cleaner Hellenic society demands the shedding of women's blood. (Note how he comforts the cringing Phrygian: "Fool, don't suppose that I would bother to cut your throat; you're not a woman!" 1527–28.)[80] Pylades speaks to this conviction when he predicts that they will win praise by shedding the blood of an "evil woman" (1139), and soon Orestes is heard shouting, "May I never tire of killing evil females" (1590), without noticing that his sword teases the throat of the play's single "good" human being. The erstwhile client of Apollo and son of Agamemnon has made his way into "real" life, and has there become a philanthropic avenger who loves his work and

78. The chorus sings the second stasimon (807–43) after having heard Orestes' sociological justification of the mother-murder, and I would argue that they attempt to reinstate the objective traditional view. In paraphrase, they say that the weight of past Atreid crimes (807–18) enforced the killing of a parent, which was a fine deed that was foul (τὸ καλὸν οὐ καλόν, 819–22); the doing of evil as if for good (τὸ δ' εὖ κακουργεῖν), on the other hand, is an elaborate impiety, the aberration of men whose thinking hearts don't work right (παράνοια, 823–24). Clytemnestra made the deed as ugly as she could for Orestes (825–30), and he, who dared as Agamemnon's son (838) to perform such a foul deed, is a creature to be pitied. Implicit is the parallel statement: had he actually performed the crime as he now describes it, pretending that it was intrinsically a good thing to do, he would not be open to pity. In singing of this other sort of crime, the one that pretends to advantageous purposes and whose agent is not pitiable, the chorus looks forward unknowingly to the attempt to kill Helen.

79. For the opposite opinion see, among many, P. N. Boulter, "The Theme of ἄγρια," *Phoenix* 16 (1962) 102–6.

80. In addition to displaying his own view of his vocation, Orestes is also preparing here for the comic cap, "nor are you exactly a man" (1528).

wants to go on forever. Nor is this madness; Orestes is explicitly a man free of delusions when he espouses the notion of murder as public policy.[81]

No previous tragic avenger that we know about has even pretended to justify his action with any such claims. Each thought that what he or she did was necessary according to a specific code that concerned only the honorific status of a particular individual or household. Some knew that their violence was necessary also to the working of divine will, but that knowledge was not grounds for any extension of range in the revenger's activity. And all were satisfied when repayment had been successfully taken. This final Euripidean Orestes, however, is not only less simple and less magnificent than his predecessors—he is dreadful in a way that they were not. His argument from public advantage makes him the evil twin of the man Plato imagined, one whose very errors must be called just, because they came from a soul directed by (mis)belief in the highest good (*Leg.* 864a). And with his program of reform through selective murder, he is a proleptic caricature of the stoical justice-bringer who refuses to waste his passion in the mental crime of anger. Like that man, he is outside the reach of any pitiable plea, nor would his crusade be closed off by satisfaction; he would stand ready to exterminate whole households should policy so dictate (*De Ira* 1.19.1). Because he confuses revenge with self-advancement, Orestes is also a prevision of the villainous avengers so common on the Renaissance stage, while his febrile weakness looks forward to excitable figures like Vindice, ready to snatch at any mode of retaliation.[82] This, the poet seems to say, is what our skeptical world has come to. Men like Orestes have forgotten their fathers and their gods, and so have lost touch with the inner principle of what they used to see as justice. The Attic courts still encompass the divinely sanctioned retaliatory anger of the injured (the anger of Ares, or of the Furies), but the idea of a community-oriented forward-looking justice is abroad,[83] inflammatory for lesser minds. One can only hope that a flying chariot is at hand, for the present populace—this audience now laughing at its own vices[84]—has grown too secular for tragedy and too small for revenge.

81. See R. Padel, *Whom the Gods Destroy* (Princeton, 1995), p. 36: "characters not said to be mad are sane as any others." We may call him "morally mad" or even "a psychopath," but with the early ejection of the phantom-furies the play announces that it deals with a principal who is in its terms sane.

82. In that he is a parodic figure he is also like Antonio in Marston's play.

83. Pl. *Prt.* 324a–b; in Stoic statement, Sen. *De Ira* 2.32.8.

84. Like the Roman audiences that Seneca described, *Ep.* 108.8–12.

Appendix: Medea's Monologue

The speech that stretches from Eur. *Med.* 1019 to 1080 is generally assumed to be deeply corrupt.[1] Particular objections to particular lines differ, but critics and editors all note a repetitiousness, as each of the two positions ("I must kill the children"/"I must not kill the children") is stated twice. And all likewise find that the final lines present extreme, if not insuperable, difficulties, for as the children disappear into the house Medea says:

καὶ μανθάνω μὲν οἷα δρᾶν μέλλω κακά,
θυμὸς δὲ κρείσσων τῶν ἐμῶν βουλευμάτων,
ὅσπερ μεγίστων αἴτιος κακῶν βροτοῖς.

(1078–80)

I understand that what I am going to do is bad (i.e., painful,
   base, cowardly, worthless, wicked)
but my *thymos* is stronger than my considered plans
—such is the cause of men's worst disasters.

Since there has been an inner conflict, and since 1079 announces that one psychic part of Medea (*thymos*) is stronger than the product of her considering mind (*bouleumata*), it looks as if these lines are reporting a decision taken between the two positions (must kill / must not kill). And since the *thymos* is the psychic part that turns emotion into impulse, while *bouleumata* are plans that issue from the mind, the statement seems at first glance to record a perverse victory won by a murderous anger over a loving reason that would spare. So it was confidently reported by Chrysippus (as quoted

---

1. There is a review of opinion in B. Seidensticker, "Euripides' *Medea* 1056–80," in *Cabinet of the Muses: Essays . . . Rosenmeyer,* ed. M. Griffith and D. Mastronarde (Berkeley, 1990), pp. 89–102.

by Galen 4.2.27 = 372 Kühn): "she understands how evil the acts are that she is about to perform, but her anger is stronger than her deliberations."[2] Nevertheless, within this particular scene, the contest has been framed in a reverse fashion: a passionate pitying desire to spare the children pitted against a considered program of vengeance. Consequently line 1079 seems on second glance to contradict Chrysippus as it reports a victory of maternal passion over deliberate vengeance intention. And since critics, scholars, and editors are almost to a man convinced that this cannot be Medea's conclusion (she must, they say, choose the pleasure of torturing Jason over the call of mother love),[3] they follow one of two courses. Either they cut this line—which generally leads to cutting others as well—or else they apply ingenious special interpretations to the final statement.[4]

Radical solutions to the Monologue's "inappropriate" conclusion (and to its seeming incoherence) range from athetizing, through emendation, to the suggestion that the final lines might simply reflect an irrepressible Euripidean irrelevance.[5] Many scholars delete not just the close but the last twenty-five lines of the speech, bringing it to an end with the statement, χεῖρα δ' οὐ διαφθερῶ (1055).[6] In this truncated form, an economical Monologue records one upsurgence of reluctance and one restatement of deter-

---

2. Cf. Clarius Eustratius, ad Arist. *Eth. Nic.* 6.85.6. For an attempt to defend the Stoic interpretation of these lines, see C. Gill, "Did Chrysippus Understand Medea?" *Phronesis* 28 (1983) 136–49.

3. H. Erbse, "Zum Abschiedsmonolog," *Archaiognosia* 2 (1981) 66–82, esp. 72.

4. The almost unanimous belief that the Monologue must end with a determination to kill is based on failure to understand what happens in the scene that follows, and also, one suspects, on the fragment of a like monologue from Neophron (fr. 2 *TrGF*). The speeches from the two poets are superficially much alike; Neophron's has not one but two apostrophes of the *thymos* (1 and 9) as well as a sputtering sequence of questions and commands addressed from one part of the self to another. It reads like a bad imitation of the Euripidean speech, though of course it could be the second-rate model that a better poet improved upon. Be that as it may, the Neophron monologue cannot be taken as a witness, either preliminary or after the fact, to Euripidean intention. In it the maternal impulse dominates the first four lines, to be interrupted by the vengeance impulse at line 5 (cf. Eur. *Med.* 1049); this latter voice, however, is not angry but self-righteous, not sharp but waffling, and it ends by begging the *thymos* not to betray itself. At this point there is deadlock, resolved by a decision which the speaker frigidly attributes to an attack of madness (11–12). For a review of arguments about the date of Neophron, see A. Michelini, "Neophron and Euripides' *Medea*," *TAPA* 119 (1989) 115–35.

5. H.-D. Voigtländer, "Spätere Überarbeitung" *Philol.* 101 (1957) 230, sees a sophistical touch added "in einer nicht ganz konsequenten Weise."

6. So the most recent Oxford editor, J. Diggle, *Euripidis Fabulae*, vol. 1 (Oxford, 1981), applauded by B. Gredley, "The Place and Time of Victory," *BICS* 34 (1987) 27–39. O. Zwierlein, "Die Tragik in den Medea-Dramen," *Literaturwissenschaftliches Jahrbuch* 19 (1978) 35, finds in the Monologue a conflict between Grief and Better Understanding that in his judgment has no place in the play. See also Th. Bergk, *Griechische Literaturgeschichte*, vol. 3 (Berlin, 1884), p. 512 n. 140; G. Jachmann, "Binneninterpolation II," *Gött. Nachr.*, 1936, p. 193 n. 1; M. D. Reeve,

mination. Others would begin cutting even earlier, at 1051, where the neces-sary "decision" has presumably been made, or—on the grounds that this is a "farewell scene" and consequently all that is not farewell is intrusive—at 1040.[7] (It has even been said that Medea is heroic and calm, and therefore all that is not calm must go.) Finally, among those who suspect major inter-polation, there are some who would keep the ultimate lines as genuine but make earlier excisions (1056–64) so as to remove the second intrusion of pity and the second assertion of implacability.[8] (It should be noted, incident-ally, that Bethe, while agreeing that the last third of the speech had to be cut from this scene, asserted that no one but Euripides could have com-posed the lines, which caused him to suppose that there was another Euripi-dean play on the same subject, from which the long intrusive passage came.)[9]

Another and eminent body of scholarly opinion abjures such major surgery and proposes to read the Monologue essentially as it stands in the manuscripts. If the final lines can somehow be made appropriate, the most egregious cause for suspicion disappears, since what is called repetitious incoherence may also be termed a poetic rendering of the speaker's emo-tion. There have been a few attempts at emending the penultimate line (1079), but the results are unsatisfactory. Stadtmüller long ago suggested writing καλῶν or σωφρόνων for ἐμῶν, so that Medea announces her *thymos* to be stronger than her "fine" or "sensible" plans (though no such have been proposed). Koechly wrote φρονημάτων for βουλευμάτων in the same line, and Erbse proposed μαθημάτων,[10] but gnomological citations show that βουλευμάτων stood in the ancient texts. A solution that demanded no revision was proposed by H. Diller,[11] who suggested that κρείσσων, instead

---

"Euripides, *Med.* 1021–1080," *CQ* 22 (1972) 51–61; B. Manuwald, "Der Mord an den Kindern," *Wien. Stud.* 17 (1983) 27–43.

7. U. Hübner, "Zum fünften Epeisodion der 'Medea' des Euripides," *Hermes* 112 (1984) 401–18, finds almost every line subsequent to 1039 unworthy of Euripides, whereas "ohne die Verse 1040–80 stellt Euripides' Medea als einheitlicher Charakter," one who comes to a clear decision for tragic action, in spite of her love for her children (415); cf. "Uneuripideisches," *Philol.* 128 (1984) 21–40; 129 (1985) 20–38. G. Müller, "Interpolationen in der *Medea*," *Stud. Ital.* 25 (1951) 65–82, supposes 1056–80 to be the work of a Platonic interpolator.

8. D. Kovacs, "On Medea's Great Monologue," *CQ* 36 (1986) 343–52, cuts 1056–64, which he scorns as "high fustian" (p. 348); H. Lloyd-Jones, "Euripides, *Medea* 1056–80," *WJA* 6a (1980) 51–59, suggests that 1059–63 may be work of a fourth-century producer (p. 56).

9. E. Bethe, *Medea-Probleme*, Ber. Sächs. Ges. Wiss., 70.1 (Leipzig, 1918), pp. 8–16; O. Regenbogen, "Randbemerkungen zur *Medea*," *Eranos* 48 (1950) 21 ff., asks who but Euripides could have written 1068–80.

10. Erbse, "Zum Abschiedsmonolog," who notes that the emendation had already been suggested by H. Stadtmüller, *Beiträge zur Textkritik der euripideischen Medea* (Heidelberg, 1876), p. 31 n. 1.

11. "Θυμὸς δὲ κρείσσων," *Hermes* 94 (1966) 267–73.

of meaning "is stronger than, is victorious over," might have the sense of "rules over" or "dictates": that is, "Passion is master of, author of my plans." Read this way, the penultimate line no longer reflects the push for pity evident in the preceding conflict but instead announces the power of a single angry resolve, and many have been pleased to hear it so.[12] The majority opinion, however, is with R. Kassel, who pointed out that the sense of κρείσσων on Medea's tongue has been established at 965, where she notes (with fine disdain for both Jason and his princess) that among mortals gold is stronger than, in contest wins out over, ten thousand persuasive words (κρείσσων μυρίων λόγων).[13] Moreover, as A. Dihle has shown,[14] the statement about *thymos* and *bouleumata* is obviously influenced by a common proverb-formula of the scissors/paper/stone sort. This can be seen at its simplest at Theognis 218, κρέσσων τοι σοφίη γίνεται ἀτροπίης, "Urbanity is more powerful than Stiffness,"[15] but the best parallel to the present line is Eur. *Telephus* fr. 718 *TGF*: ὥρα σε θυμοῦ κρείσσονα γνώμην ἔχειν, "See to it that Principle is stronger than Passionate Impulse with you."[16] Medea's phrase reflects a failure to comply with this rule, for she reports that *thymos* holds a position above *bouleumata* in a psychic power structure that rules her from within. The two are at odds, and *thymos* has the upper hand.

Those who do not choose to cut or emend the final lines or understand them as making *thymos* the author of vengeance plans attempt to evade the evident statement of 1079 (i.e., my passionate feelings, being stronger than my vengeance plans, have won out over them) by employing elaborate interpretation. In general, the method is to give *thymos* the late and restricted sense of "anger," while endowing the term *bouleumata* with loose and unexpected meanings. First, as to *thymos* and anger. Anger, in this play, is nine times called ὀργή (176, 456, 520, 615, 637, 870, 909, 1150, 1172) and seven times called χόλος (94, 99, 172, 590, 898, 1150, 1266), yet nevertheless it is assumed that just here the poet has chosen to call it *thymos*. Certainly this

12. E.g., W. Steidle, *Studien zum antiken Drama* (Munich, 1968), pp. 158–60; V. di Benedetto, *Euripide* (Turin, 1971), pp. 41 ff.; C. Casali, "Alcune osservazioni," *Atene e Roma* 30 (1985) 26 ff.; J. de Romilly, "*Patience mon Cœur*" (Paris, 1984), p. 101, "resolutions dictées par le thymos"; Michelini, "Neophron"; H. Foley, "Medea's Divided Self," *Cl. Ant.* 8 (1989) 71, "my heart determined on revenge is master over my revenge plans."

13. R. Kassel, "Kritische und exegetische Kleinigkeiten," *Rh. Mus.* 116 (1973) 103 n. 21. One might also point to *Med.* 122, where the Nurse says that living on a level with others is better than, wins out over (κρείσσον, cf. 126, where the verb is νικᾷ), ruling many; cf. 290.

14. *Euripides' Medea*, Sitz. Heidelberg, 1977, Abh. 5, p. 27.

15. Cf. Thgn. 631. This kind of saying, like the kindred priamel, often took a negative form, e.g., Eur. *Or.* 1155; οὐκ ἔστιν οὐδὲν κρεῖσσον ἢ φίλος σαφής, οὐ πλοῦτος, οὐ τυραννίς.

16. Many more statements reflect the same tendency to make hierarchies among psychic attributes, without being quite so close; cf., e.g., Eur. fr. 393 *TGF* γνώμης γὰρ οὐδὲν ἀρετὴ μονομένη.

term would convey the idea of anger in later centuries, but here in this drama Euripides has consistently exploited the broader psychic meanings found in Homer, Theognis, and Pindar. The archaic *thymos* was not one particular passion; it was instead a psychic executive chair that rival emotions strove to occupy because it gave out the commands that shaped bodily action.[17] In the language of the *Medea* the *thymos* can on occasion be occupied by anger, for Jason once claims to have evicted *orge* from the king's mind when he was *thymoumenos* (455; cf. the epithet *bathythumos* applied to *orge* at 176). Nevertheless it is more frequently taken over by other emotions: *thymos* is the place where erotic love strikes (8), and also where married chastity resides (639); occupied by parental feeling or perhaps by self-interest, it can lead a father to give his daughter away (310); and though it can be the residence of feminine bad temper (979, 1152), it can also be the instrument or concurrent element in a movement of passionate grief (106–8). Most instructive, however, are the choral speculations at 855–65. The women know that in theory a *thymos* could be occupied by the boldness and daring necessary to a mother who kills her children; such a mother, however, would have to seize on the attributes of a hero's spirit, so as to make for herself a heroic impulse to action, a τλάμων θυμός (865, cf. *Il.* 5.670, of Odysseus; Tyrtaeus 12.18 W, of the frontline warrior; Pind. *Pyth.* 1.48, of Hieron). If her *thymos* were thus rendered bold by the application of daring, it might direct her *phren* in its plans, and her strength and courage (χειρὶ . . . καρδία τε, 856–58) in their work, letting her look at the children without pity so as to seize this bloody task (861–62)—but such will not be Medea's way. "You won't be able to do it!" they say (862), and the positive half of their prediction, though unexpressed, is plain. She will look at the children, the deed will seem lamentable (860–61 in reverse), and instead of making for herself a bold warrior's *thymos* she will find herself with a spirit that pities and so leaves heart and hand incapable. The whole sense of this passage is that a *thymos* does not automatically contain anger, that an individual aids or inhibits conflicting emotions as they try to occupy this organ. Furthermore there is, within the scene of the Monologue, conclusive proof that for Medea the term *thymos* does not signify anger but rather the psychic seat from which any dominant passion commands. When she addresses her own *thymos* (1056), begging it to spare the children, she does not say, "Anger, have pity!" which would be absurd. Rather, following a strong poetic tradition, she tries to influence the part of herself that fuels action. "Don't, *thymos,* don't do what the revenge passion presses you to do!"

17. S. D. Sullivan, "How a Person Relates to θυμός in Homer," *Indo-Germ. Forsch.* 85 (1980) 138 ff.; "The Function of θυμός in Hesiod and the Greek Lyric Poets," *Glotta* 59 (1981) 147 ff.; cf. Dihle, *Medea,* pp. 26–27 and n. 17. See also A. P. Burnett, "Signals from the Unconscious," *C Phil.* 86 (1991) 275–78, and bibliography cited there.

(1056). In sum, the *thymos* that she says has won out over her *bouleumata* in 1079 cannot be understood simply as Vengeance Anger. It is a psychic organ containing whichever passion has captured it at the moment the line is uttered—either rage for revenge, or pity for the children.

But which? Anyone who holds that it is rage that controls Medea's *thymos* (or that *thymos* means anger) must go on to explain what the plans are that this rage overpowers. The action of the play so far has consisted of Medea's formulation of specific *bouleumata,* schemes ending in the killing of the children, and in this immediate scene her cowardly part has just dismissed those schemes with a heavy emphasis upon the word, which is voiced twice at line-end (1044, 1048). Earlier, too, the complex vengeance-intrigue that was to end with the death of the boys was called *bouleumata,* also at line-end and in quick repetition (769, 772).[18] Even Lesky reluctantly admitted that, after such usage, the designation of the opponent of what he took to be an angry *thymos* as *bouleumata* was neither an easy nor an obvious choice for a poet to make.[19] Nevertheless his understanding of *thymos* as Anger forced him to suppose that suddenly, in 1079, Euripides used *bouleumata* in an entirely new way: it here meant the speaker's recognition of a moral world-order which her intended deed would break.[20] She has not only been engaging in Stoic meditations without letting the audience know, but she has carelessly called her unexpressed philosophical conclusions "schemes"! These hypothetical newly-formed *bouleumata* that are paradoxically contrary to the vengeful schemes called by the same name[21] have by others been glossed as plans in the general interest of humanity,[22] "l'intelligence asso-ciée à l'amour maternel,"[23] "the counsels of her knowledge that killing the

18. In its other occurrences the word has always been attached to pragmatic, conscious, slightly sinister schemes. At 372 Medea refers to more general revenge schemes but not nec-essarily to the killing of the children; cf. 449. Elsewhere the word denotes Jason's schemes of advancement through his new alliance (886), and also the scheme for Medea's exile (270). Forms of βουλεύω have likewise referred to the making of the vengeance plan (37, 317, 893), or to the formulation of the wedding scheme (567, 874). Cf. Lloyd-Jones, "*Med.* 1056–80": "until now it (*bouleumata*) has always meant vengeance plan . . . this is a major reason for athetizing"; he himself, however, insists that here and only here the word is "colorless" (pp. 58–59).

19. A. Lesky, "Psychologie bei Euripides," in *Euripide,* Entretiens Hardt, 6 (Geneva, 1960), pp. 141 ff.

20. He calls it "das positive Vorzeichen der Einsicht in das, was der Ordnung der Welt entspricht. Jener Ordnung gegen die der θυμός in seinen Masslosigkeit aufsteht" ("Zum Prob-lematik des Psychologischen," *Gymnasium* 67 [1960] 18).

21. See Müller, "Interpolationen," where the "Verkehrung des Sprachgebrauches" is a rea-son for athetizing; also Manuwald, "Der Mord," p. 44.

22. E. Schlesinger explains them as "die Gedanken, die Erwägungen, die Planungen, die im Dienst verschiedener und sogar gegensätzlicher Funktionen des Seelenlebens stehen" ("Zu Euripides' *Medea,*" *Hermes* 94 [1966] 30).

23. A. Rivier, "L'élément démonique chez Euripide," in *Euripide,* Entretiens Hardt, 6 (Geneva, 1960), p. 62.

children would be evil,"[24] "calculations (caused by the awareness of what the murder of the children would mean),"[25] and so on. To all of which there is a double objection. First, *bouleumata* is not the right term for a general conviction or "Einsicht" (this would probably be called *gnome,* as in the *Telephos* fragment already cited), and it is certainly not the right term for a numerical calculation like that at 1047, where Medea reckons that there will be twice as much pain for her as for Jason if the children are killed. (This calculation, moreover, is set in direct contrast with the vengeance *bouleumata* of the next line.) And second, there is no indication anywhere that Medea has entertained any thought about humanity or world order, much less made these the subject of "considered examination." In the attempt to meet these objections, still others have suggested that Medea speaks of "plans" for the physical rescue of the children, or more loosely of calculations which "tried to avoid the harm revenge will cause to herself,"[26] but practical rescue schemes are no more present in the preceding lines than is moral speculation. The five words, "I will take the children with me" (1044), launched in the first open outbreak of pity and never repeated, could not possibly be termed a product of deliberation, and there is no further hint of any dream, much less of any plan for rescuing the boys.

The obvious sense of *bouleumata* as "vengeance plans" is refused only because these plans are set in opposition to a *thymos* which is presumed to be angry. One attempt to reconcile an angry *thymos* with the evident meaning of *bouleumata* was made by Meissner, who supposed that what now guides Medea is a lust for the children's blood, so that what she says at the end of the Monologue is, "my obsessive desire to kill my children is stronger even than my vengeance plans!"[27] This is Seneca's madwoman, not the prudent avenger of the Aegeus scene, and certainly not the divided woman of the immediately preceding scene; Meissner's suggestion does, however, serve as a reminder that *thymos* is the flexible term here and that it need not be dominated by a passion for revenge. In the speech just uttered, the immediate and explicit opponent of the vengeance plans has been maternal pity, labeled Cowardice, but as far as I know, only A. Dihle has been willing to suppose that this might be the passion now in possession of Medea's impulse-source.[28] And yet we know that the Euripidean *thymos* can entertain

24. Lloyd-Jones, "*Med.* 1056–80," p. 58; cf. Zwierlein, "Die Tragik," p. 35, where a major reason for athetizing 1054–80 is said to be that 1079 sets up an impossible conflict between Grief and Better Understanding.

25. Siedensticker, "*Medea* 1056–80," p. 96. W. W. Fortenbaugh, "On the Antecedents of Aristotle's Bipartite Psychology," *GRBS* 11 (1970) 237: "realization that total revenge is in the long run an evil for herself and her children."

26. Kovacs, "Medea's Great Monologue," p. 351.

27. B. Meissner, "Euripides' *Medea* 1236–50," *Hermes* 96 (1968) 155 ff. esp. 160.

28. Dihle, *Medea,* p. 27. Cf. his "Euripides' Medea und ihre Schwestern," *A&A* 22 (1976) 175–82.

hope (*Supp.* 480) and can be assailed by grief or pain (*Hipp.* 1114; fr. 1039 *TGF*). Furthermore, there is a relevant fragment from his *Erechtheus* (fr. 362.33–34 *TGF*) in which the king forgoes embraces because they might give him a cowardly resolve, a γυναικόφρων θυμός: he fears precisely the stimulus that softened Medea.[29] And finally Medea, in this very speech, has suggested to her own *thymos* that it would be rejoiced by knowledge that the children had survived (1058): she knows it to be an organ where love may have influence. All of which shows that, as Dihle argued, the final lines of Medea's speech could conceivably announce that her formulated plans for vengeance are overborne by a spirit now filled with maternal pity.

Dihle's suggestion was not taken as seriously as it deserved to be. Lloyd-Jones dismissed it as an unconvincing "subterfuge" that turns on a proven impossibility, since we know that "Medea has never seriously contemplated renouncing her revenge, for if she did so she would not be Medea."[30] To which one might answer that the Attic poet was not bound to create the Medea whom Seneca and others have taught us to expect. A more specific rebuttal of Dihle was undertaken by Zwierlein,[31] who made four objections, none of which really stands. First, that in this reading the command to the children, "Go!" once arises from revenge intention (1053) and once from pity (1076), though why this is objectionable he does not say. It is true that the words would be spoken harshly the first time, later imploringly, but in both cases they would have the same immediate sense: "Go, because the sight of you softens me." The second objection proffered is that Dihle's reading produces an absurdity in 1080, that is, the statement that "maternal feelings" are the cause of greatest evil to man. This absurdity, however, is a scholarly invention, for parallel commonplaces make it obvious that it is the victory of passion—any passion—over plan that Medea says is proverbially harmful (see below, p. 282). Zwierlein's third objection is that Ovidian monologues of a similar sort end with a decision to kill, which cannot be relevant (so does Seneca's version of this very passage). And finally he complains that the chorus subsequent to this scene is no more appropriate to a relaxation than it is to a reaffirmation of the vengeance resolve—a judgment that Zwierlein wisely does not attempt to elaborate. There is in fact no objective reason for refusing to consider Dihle's suggestion, and though it produces a Medea who hasn't the monolithic cruelty that many want to find in her, it deserves to be thought about further.

The first question to ask is whether or not a pitying *thymos* can fit into the immediate context. If such an impulse rules in 1079, then 1078 will mean

29. At *Il.* 15.35 Hera hopes that even the *thymos* of Zeus may lend itself to pity; at 11.394 pity works in the *thymos* of Achilles.

30. Lloyd-Jones, "*Med.* 1056–80," p. 59.

31. "Die Tragik," pp. 35–36.

not "I know how evil is the (killing) that I am about to do"[32] but rather "I know how cowardly is the (abandonment of vengeance) that I am about to make." This gives *kaka* its archaic sense of retreat from danger, or any like action typical of one who is not noble but base. Carrying this sense, it harmonizes with the play's usage of forms of *kakos* to designate one who is cowardly or lacking in honor (most commonly Jason, as at 84, 229, 452, 465, 586, 618, 699; of womankind, 264, 889). Here a craven surrender of vengeance called *kaka* will, moreover, be the work of the soft impulse that Medea has just termed ἡ ἐμὴ κάκη (1051), her reprehensible cowardice. (Compare 1246 where Medea, afraid that she will fall back into her maternal mood, admonishes herself, μὴ κακισθῇς.) But what about δρᾶν? Can this word refer to the negative relinquishing of the vengeance plan? In the present play the verb has been used of doing harm both positive and negative—killing (507–8), or abandoning a wife and generally behaving in an unjust manner (578, cf. 606)—and it has also signified giving a daughter in marriage (311), taking an oath (742), and offering hospitality (613). Beyond this it appears three times in the neutral formula of agreement where the sense is hardly more than "I take your meaning" (184, 927, 1019). In one of these cases, however, the agreed-upon action is explicitly negative, for when the chorus has been asked not to speak but to keep silent about Medea's plans, their leader answers, δράσω τάδ' (267). Furthermore, there is a passage from Sophocles which proves that the tragic δρᾶν can be used precisely for the abandonment of a plan. At *Antigone* 1099–107, the situation is much like that of the Monologue except that it is the chorus leader rather than an inner voice which urges Creon to give up the program of extreme punishment that he has begun upon. In the course of the exchange δρᾶν is used three times, always in the sense of undoing the action resolved upon (1099, 1106, 1107). One may also compare *Philoctetes* where, at 1241, δρᾶν refers to returning the bow (cf. 1245), at 1252 to *not* returning it.[33]

If lines 1078–79 mean, "I understand that giving up the vengeance program is cowardly, but my passionate heart (now filled with pity) is stronger than my plans," the statement will have been prepared in 1076–77 by the outburst that interrupts the maternal embrace: "Go! go! I cannot look at you longer, for I (as an avenger) am defeated (νικῶμαι, 1077) by unheroic pains and griefs." (Touching you, looking at you, pity returns and it comes over me that I cannot do it.) This is surely a possible sequence, but what about 1080, the line that caps the speech? It is the kind of sententious tag

---

32. Or, with Kovacs ("Medea's Great Monologue," p. 352), reading τολμήσω, "I know well what grief I shall endure."

33. See D. Mastronarde, *Contact and Discontinuity* (Berkeley, 1979), p. 123, who notes that δρᾶν, while it cannot mean "fare, suffer," may stand as a generalized substitute for a verb that specifies a particular sort of doing.

that Euripidean characters often employ, but it must make minimal sense. And with Dihle's understanding it does. Having reported that her vengeance program is disabled by pity, Medea closes with an ethical commonplace to express her ironic sense that a strong plan has been bested by passions that are a form of weakness. A system of old saws, based on the question, "What is the source of greatest suffering among men?" had produced answers like "Exile" or "Woman."[34] There were also more sophisticated responses in which a psychic source was found in Thoughtlessness, or Being without a Plan (ἀβουλία). Thus the Messenger in *Antigone* closes his report of the passionate confusion in which Haemon and Antigone died with the reflection, δείξας ἐν ἀνθρώποισι τὴν ἀβουλίαν / ὅσῳ μέγιστον ἀνδρὶ πρόσκειται κακόν (1242–43).[35] And since Thoughtlessness and Fecklessness appear when the *thymos* is allowed to dominate the *nous*,[36] the inherent logic of the commonplace shows that the passionate *thymos*, when stronger than consideration or good counsel, was the ultimate source of superlative suffering.[37] Of this axiom Medea (now hopeless and doomed) offers herself as a demonstration: her *thymos*, filled with pity, has defeated the considered vengeance-intrigue, and she is now in the midst of extreme griefs, without purpose and without means. *Aboulia* is a great cause of disaster, yes, but *aboulia* itself has a cause—it results when a brute emotional impulse wins out over *bouleumata*.

Problems with this understanding of the end of the Monologue arise not so much from the text as from the nearly unanimous scholarly assumption as to what Medea must be made to say. Critics assume (still under the influence of Snell)[38] that she will here announce a decision taken between two courses easily recognized by us as Right and Wrong, and also that she will knowingly choose Wrong, that is, vengeance. To which there attaches a pendant reverse hypothesis: were Medea to choose against vengeance, that would be a knowing choice of Right, on which she could only congratulate herself.[39] Consequently, her final line proves that she has indeed chosen Wrong (vengeance), for how could one say that the victory of a good impulse is typically a cause of pain for mankind? These have been the

34. Exile, Tyrtaeus, 3.4; woman, Semon. 72, 115.

35. Cf. Soph. *El.* 398, καλόν γε μέντοι μὴ 'ξ ἀβουλίας πεσεῖν; Pind. *Ol.* 10.41, where the power of Augeas is destroyed by *aboulia*.

36. So Thgn. 631, ᾧτινι μὴ θυμοῦ κρέσσων νόος, αἰὲν ἐν ἄταις / Κύρνε καὶ ἐν μεγάλαις κεῖται ἀμηχανίαις. Cf. Pind. *Isth.* 8.28, where those who are *sophrones* have "admonished" the *thymos*.

37. Cf. Eur. *Archelaus* fr. 257 *TGF*, with its reference to an overbold *thymos*: πολλοὺς δ' ὁ θυμὸς ὁ μέγας ὤλεσεν βροτῶν / ἥ τ' ἀξυνεσία, δυὸ κακὼ τοῖς χρωμένοις.

38. B. Snell, "Das frühste Zeugnis über Sokrates," *Philol.* 97 (1948) 126.

39. It is felt that, in such a case, she ought to have a line something like Odysseus' at Soph. *Aj.* 1357 (νικᾷ γὰρ ἀρετή με τῆς ἔχθρας πολύ), but for Medea "virtue" and hatred are in the same camp: hers is the unregenerate heroic ethic.

underlying assumptions of all the post-Stoic readings of this speech, and yet in actuality Euripides has not proposed Medea's choice between fulfilling her vengeance and sparing the children as one between Wrong and Right. As far as external labels go, he has made it a choice between Honor and Dishonor, or, according to Medea's own terms, between Courage (*authadia*, 1028, cf. the *eupsychia* of 403) and Cowardice (1051).

The Monologue has furthermore been designed so as to exclude from Medea's choice both rational thought and reasonable decision.[40] We are acquainted with Medea's reason, for we have seen it at work on the pros and cons of two different vengeance-intrigues in the long speech that followed Creon's exit (364–94). There reason considered; it counted probable results, and made contingent resolutions in cool and coherent language. In the present scene, by contrast, as soon as Medea stops producing deceitful speech for the ear of the Tutor (the shift is strongly marked at 1040), this reasonable aspect of Medea's mind falls silent as two sorts of passion speak. True, the vengeance passion fights to preserve the plan that reason has made, but it does so heatedly, threatening shame and making heroic protestations. And meanwhile maternal pity, true to its nature, is melodramatic ("Farewell, vengeance plans!" 1044, 1048), full of nonsignifying sounds (φεῦ φεῦ, αἰαῖ, ἆ ἆ) and pathetic apostrophes—yet this, for Snell and others, must be the style of Reason! The nearest thing to speech from the *nous* (the part of Medea that made the plans) is the argument from consummated event that appears quite suddenly at 1064–66, but this pragmatic voice is at once interrupted by maternal Cowardice (at the moment overpowered but not extinct), calling for the final embrace. And once the children have been touched, there is no reasoned choice; there is only an irresistible surge of emotion in response to external stimuli. Reason observes, as the body shows symptoms of physical weakness and the commanding spirit is taken over by pity; its habitual vocabulary and ethical stance are maintained, so that the abandonment of its plan is termed a cowardly act, but Reason has taken no real part because there has been no deliberated choice.[41]

Medea has not made a decision in the course of the Monologue; rather, she has suffered an emotional shift which has left her will unable to support an earlier resolve. There is no single moment when a revised plan is stated

40. This is another point of contrast between this and the Neophron version; there the maternal Medea, having recognized the error of treating friends as enemies, does call upon her *thymos* to formulate a reasonable program (2.1 *TGF*).

41. F. Solmsen, while arguing that Medea "persuades herself that the brutal plan must run its course," nevertheless sees that "Reason . . . has no power of its own" (*Intellectual Experiments of the Greek Enlightenment* [Princeton, 1975], p. 134). Cf. Reeve, "*Med.* 1021–1080," pp. 51 ff., where lines 1056–80 are condemned because of their patent unreason.

because there is no revised plan: the maternal emotion has murmured dubiously, "I'll take them (1045) / I'll leave them (1058),"[42] but the first is impossible, while the second would simply mean that the boys would be killed by angry Corinthians. This is why the vengeance emotion, joined by reason, was able to say, "The whole affair is achieved—there is no evasion" (1064), and with these words seem to win the debate.[43] The maternal impulse seems to be permanently bested at 1066, and admitting that the road of daring must be taken (1067), it asks only for the luxury of a farewell, one last moment of behaving like a mother. The need for revenge, what Medea calls her Courage, is in regained control as the defeated mother dedicates the boys to death (ἀλλ᾽ ἐκεῖ, 1073), but the onslaught of their physicality, their touch, their flesh, their warm breath, causes a terrible increase of maternal emotion.[44] Her *thymos* swells with weakness rather than with strength, and Medea knows that what she said a moment ago (1044) is true: she would not be able to do it. She cannot attack; she still holds that giving up the punishment of Jason is cowardly,[45] but the plans of Courage have lost out to this inner incapacity.[46]

The fact that the Monologue presents its fluctuating resolve as a series, spare/kill, spare/kill, has been urged as a reason either for cutting presumed interpolations or for reproaching the dramatist, but this same repetitive organization appears in the Homeric speeches that are clearly the

42. Reading Hermann's κεῖ μή at 1058, as accepted by Pohlenz; the line will contain a silent admission that the proposal to take them was a momentary dream (cf. Diller, "Θυμὸς δὲ κρείσσων," p. 273). The question of whether or not Medea could have taken the boys has been argued as if it were a matter of suitcases and timetables; e.g., Steidle, *Studien*, pp. 157 ff.; G. A. Seeck, "Euripides' *Medea* 1059–68," *GRBS* 9 (1968) 291 ff., whereas the one certainty is that Euripides has not asked us to consider this as a serious possibility. The Messenger will soon arrive, urging Medea to find a cart or ship with utmost speed, but even he doesn't mention the boys; an ordinary escape is not practicable even for one woman, let alone a woman with two small children, and Medea knows this.

43. On the line, see Kovacs, "Medea's Great Monologue," p. 347.

44. See R. Padel, *In and Out of Mind* (Princeton, 1991), p. 113, for reaction of *thymos* to sense stimuli; cf. Hdt. 7.39, where the *thymos*, in response to a pleasing sound, is said to fill the whole body with pleasure.

45. A strong parallel is provided by Hypermestra, whose *gnome* called her to be courageous and loyal and to kill, while *himeros* blunted her honor, enchanted her, and made her spare her enemy/friend, so that she chose to be cowardly rather than bloodstained ([Aesch.] *PV* 865–69).

46. At 1242–50 this disorganized psyche puts itself back together. Moved by outward necessity (1240), Medea's conscious self addresses her *kardia* (1242) as the location of courage; it sank down when pity took over (as at 1042), but now it must arm itself. After this the hand is given a motor command, "take the sword" (1244), and when it is not instantly obedient, the command is repeated. Just as, earlier, the murder was disguised as a sacrifice for a squeamish *thymos* (1053–54), so now it is likened to an athletic trial. What can only be the *thymos* is urged not to be overcome by cowardice (1245) as it was before, and the *nous* is warned not to supply the stimuli that might cause this: "Do not remember . . ." (1246–47).

model for this one. In the four inner monologues with address to *thymos* that occur in the *Iliad* (11.404–10; 17.91–105; 21.553–70; 22.98–130), the hero states his two alternatives in a first section, leaving them at deadlock; then he reconsiders the same alternatives,[47] arriving at a decision that is not announced in the speech but is externalized in the action that follows (except in Hector's case when his action reverses his decision). It is clear that Euripides had these speeches in mind as he composed Medea's Monologue. He cannot alert the listener, as the bard did, with a formulaic line (ὀχθήσας δ' ἄρα εἶπε πρὸς ὃν μεγαλήτορα θυμόν), but he does give certain signals which show that this is an epic-style inner debate (τί πάσχω; 1049, cf. *Il.* 11.404, *Od.* 5.465, τί πάθω; τῆς ἐμῆς κάκης, 1051, cf. *Od.* 5.299, ὤ μοι ἐγὼ δειλός). And the analysis of her mental process follows the pattern of the epic analyses. Her first alternative, like that of the warriors, is non-heroic and passive, and it is seen to have positive and negative aspects, for it will mean less pain for self (1047), while it allows laughter to enemies (1049). Her second alternative, like theirs, is to take a courageous but painful action, which will repay enemies and avoid dishonor but which, for Medea, involves making a "sacrifice" of the children. At this point there is deadlock, and where the warriors use the mind-shift formula, "Why does my *thymos* decide in this fashion?" (ἀλλὰ τί ἦ μοι ταῦτα φίλος διελέξατο θυμός; *Il.* 11.407; 17.97; 21.662; 22.122), Medea says, "No, my *thymos*, do not do that work!" (i.e., make that "sacrifice," μὴ δῆτα, θυμέ, μὴ σύ γ' ἐργάσῃ τάδε, 1056). Now the unheroic alternative is offered again with modification ("say the children are left behind," κεἰ μὴ μεθ' ἡμῶν, 1058), after which the heroic impulse is powerfully reasserted with an oath (1059), and given an added aspect, that of necessity (as Odysseus adds the aspect of reputation to his second alternative, *Il.* 11.409–10). At this point Medea is in the correct heroic position; she has not, like Menelaus (*Il.* 17.100–101), returned to the cowardly first possibility, and the expectation is that she will move directly into courageous action. What happens, however, is much like what happens to Hector in *Iliad* 22. There has already been a parallel between her momentary fantasy of taking the children to Athens and his of making a private visit to Achilles. Now, having chosen the heroic act, Medea's *thymos* is assailed by the effects of perception, the sight and touch of the children, just as Hector's is by the vision of the oncoming Achilles. In this situation she, like the Trojan, simply reverses herself, suddenly retreating where she had decided to attack. Unlike Hector, however, who relapses from a resolve to kill enemies, Medea has relapsed from a determination to kill friends (in indirect punishment of enemies), and consequently the lis-

---

47. Hector is an exception because he considers a third possible action before making his decision; on the structure of these speeches, see Burnett, "Signals," pp. 275–88.

tener's response is opposite. One is dismayed by Hector's betrayal of his own choice, whereas with Medea the spectator gasps with relief, rejoicing that the "soft words" seem after all to have won out.

Are there tragic parallels to such a change of mind? Certainly there are secondary characters who yield to external counterpersuasion (Phaedra under the Nurse's supplication, Eur. *Hipp.* 373–524; Hector influenced by Aeneas, Eur. *Rhes.* 87–148; Creon pressed by Teiresias and the Chorus, Soph. *Ant.* 1091–116), but a central tragic character as a rule proves his determination by refusing to listen to those who urge him to reverse himself. Obviously a principal deflected from the work of the *praxis* by his own internal promptings is a case apart, since he would yield only to himself. Nevertheless, among surviving tragic principals only Iphigeneia has a comparable psychic experience. Like Medea, she is given a monologue of mind-shift so that her psychic revolution can be staged (Eur. *IT* 342–91).[48] And like Medea again, she has been under the direction of a normative self that demands harshness; but now, faced with the actuality of bloodshed, she is unable to withstand an opposite impulse of pity. (Iphigeneia's reversal to pity, however, is roused not by physical stimuli but by certain memories.) Consequently, like Medea, she is left with a mere negative resolve not to do what duty asks (a resolve she only slowly begins to live up to). There is a radical difference, of course, because Iphigeneia, having reached the end of her tenure as priestess among the Taurians, will be allowed to follow her softer impulse, whereas Medea, whose service to the curse demon must still be completed, cannot effectively act upon her pity. Nevertheless the two monologues both show tragic heroines who, because of internal psychic rebellion, arrive at a state of irresolution and despair.[49]

Finally, what will be the effect upon the play as a whole, if the Monologue is read in this way? First, if Medea ends this scene not in a state of renewed resolve but in a state of helplessness, the tragedy will no longer be burdened with two proximate and identical decisions to kill. The lines at 1236–50 will have their full impact as a crisis point of resolve, instead of coming as a repetitious anticlimax.[50] Second, the chorus that immediately follows the Monologue will at last be appropriate to what has gone before. No one has been able to explain why women who have before strongly disapproved of the plan to kill the children (811–14, 816, 818) should, on hearing its reaf-

48. See ibid., pp. 294–300.

49. A phantom parallel can be sensed in the event that precedes the prologue of Eur. *IA*, when a solitary Agamemnon evidently decided that his deception of Clytemnestra was unseemly, and wrote to cancel her coming (107–109).

50. Furthermore the choral outcry that follows finally makes sense. "Why this rage? Why this slaughter?" (1265–67) cannot be effectively asked of a woman who has talked of nothing else, but it is relevant and dramatic after the resumption of a vengeance project that had apparently been abandoned.

firmation, drift away into a muted ode about the mixed pleasures of parent-hood.[51] If, by contrast, they are addressing a helpless Medea who has just abandoned her plan, their ode becomes a typically tragic response. The gifts have probably done their work, and this means that immediate pursuit, cap-ture, and stoning will follow. No escape can be expected, and thus the Medea who has given up her vengeance out of pity for her sons can now expect nothing more than to be killed with them, and shamefully at that. In this pass the chorus can only offer Medea their bitter traditional wisdom, reminding her that this is always the way, that hers is only an extension of the generic suffering that belongs to all mothers. Their argument (formally like the Hesiodic passage on marriage, *Theog.* 603–12),[52] is a commonplace pes-simistic proof that sooner or later children cause unhappiness. There is even an attempt to show that Medea's suffering could be worse: sometimes a woman brings her son safely through childhood to the bloom of youth, only to see Death take him then. As they close (1112–15), the singers join Medea and all women in a complaint against the gods for having made such pain, in this way offering the only conceivable consolation, while they also prolong and generalize this central moment of static hopelessness.

If Medea's vengeance plan suffers a reverse at the end of the Monologue, then instead of a bulldozer movement that goes from success to success, this tragedy will show a kind of peripeteia. The play will conform to the standard vengeance action by showing a moment of hesitation (like Orestes' last-minute pause when he stops and asks τί δράσω; at Aesch. *Cho.* 899; cf. *Med.* 1042), so that the audience may know that the avenger is not a pathologi-cal justice-bringer eager for blood.[53] And it will conform as well by allowing a positive and humane emotion to enter the play (as with the recognition scenes in the Orestes plays) so as to qualify its violence. The principal actor will no longer have to emit an uninterrupted blast of rage from beginning to end but will be allowed to convey the flickering existence of a contrary passion. In the early scenes Medea has seemed a mechanical monster above challenge, but now she becomes a mortal who might fail because of oppo-sition from an unplumbed part of herself. No longer a fearsome specimen of single-minded aberrance, she becomes a mixed creature in whom an audience can recognize aspects of itself, even after she has been called back into the service of those powers that make her vengeance inevitable.

51. K. Reckford suggested that the function of this chorus was to prove that "both reason and feeling lead to their own negation," but it is hard to connect this axiom either to the Monologue or to the ode; see "Medea's First Exit," *TAPA* 99 (1968) 346.

52. Cf. Thgn. 271–78, where the same sentiments are expressed from the paternal point of view, the culminating grief being not the death of the grown son but the father's rejection by him.

53. Cf. Eur. *El.* 959–70, where a brief debate is held between Electra and Orestes, repre-senting vengeance and pity.

Index of Classical Authors and Titles and Biblical Citations

Line numbers of texts cited are given in bold.

General Index

Including Renaissance and modern authors and titles.
Line numbers of texts cited are given in italics.

Achilles, 65, 204n.66; arms of, 80n.53,
95–96; ghost of, 158n.67, 159–60,
163n.85; mistreatment of Hector's
corpse, 34n.5; shield of, 245; *thymos* of,
280n.29
Acrobatic dances, 91n.85
Adultery, 55n.69, 122; blinding as punishment, 169; as source of pollution,
122n.12
Aedon, 178n.5, 179n.7
Aegeus, 205, 207, 209; as Medea's husband,
224n.130
Aegisthus:
in Aesch. *Cho.*, 111–12
in Eur. *El.*, 228n.11; corpse of, 242n.62;
depravity of, 237; murder of, 229,
230, 235–36, 238; pollution of, 233;
sacrifice of, 233–35
in Soph. *El.*, 125, 132, 141; corpse of,
134–35
Agamemnon: in early Orestes tales, 102,
107,108
in Eur. *El.*, 245
in Eur. *Hec.*, 159, 160n.72, 162n.81,
164–66, 168
in Eur. *IA*, 286n.49
in Soph. *Aj.*, 94
in Soph. *El.*, 130,132,133–34, 136
Agriona, Dionysian, 187n.37

Aianteion (Salamis), 97n.98
Aidesis, 53n.62, 267
Aidos: of Telemachus, 40
in Eur. *El.*, 236n.43
in Soph. *El.*, 122, 125
Aithra, 224n.130
Ajax, 190n.52; anger of, 83, 91, 93, 96, 98;
burial of, 94, 96–98; cult of, 96, 97n.98,
98; death leap of, 91–92; deception
speech of, 88–89, 93; decision speech of,
85, 86; madness of, 8n.25, 80–81, 94,
117n.60; revenge curse of, 86, 87–93,
96, 97; revenge of, 81, 82–83, 94; suicide
of, 80, 85–87, 92–93; rent of, 81n.54;
voice of, 90
Alastor (oath demon), 164, 201, 206n.77
Alcibiades, 67n.6; parodies of, 74n.35
Alcmaeon, 103n.20
Alcmena, 145, 146, 149–50; revenge of,
151–56, 177
Alektra (Fury), 140–41
Allies, discovery of, 59
Althaia, 86n.63, 144n.12, 178n.6
Amphidromia, 240n.56
Ananke, 195n.22, 244
Andreia, of women, 125
Andromache, 143n.11, 212
Anger: of Ajax, 83, 91, 93, 96, 98; Aristotle
on, 8; of Atreus, 12–14, 17; as defective

Compositor: Braun-Brumfield
Text: 10/12 Baskerville
Display: Baskerville
Printer and binder: Braun-Brumfield